MW01199541

REFRESHMENT FOR THE SOUL

May 18 - "Two Conformities"
July 11 - "Mary Proclaims the Resurrection."

# REFRESHMENT FOR THE SOUL

---

*A Year of Daily Readings from*
*'The Heavenly Doctor'*
*Richard Sibbes*

*Compiled and Edited by*
David B. MacKinnon

THE BANNER OF TRUTH TRUST

# THE BANNER OF TRUTH TRUST

*Head Office*  |  *North America Office*
3 Murrayfield Road  |  PO Box 621
Edinburgh, EH12 6EL  |  Carlisle, PA 17013
UK  |  USA

banneroftruth.org

© The Banner of Truth Trust 2022
First published 2022

\*

ISBN:
Print: 978 1 80040 305 5
Epub: 978 1 80040 306 2
Kindle: 978 1 80040 307 9

\*

Typeset in 10.5/13.5 Adobe Garamond Pro
at the Banner of Truth Trust, Edinburgh

Printed in the USA by
Versa Press, Inc.,
East Peoria, IL

\*

For my wife,

Linda,

who inspires me to a deeper devotion to Jesus.

I love you.

And for our three children and their spouses,

Justin and Valerie,

Karen and Micah,

Michele and Brett,

and our four grandsons,

Rex, Whitley, Henry, and Elliot.

God has graciously planned that we would share life

and Jesus together,

for which we are deeply grateful.

# Introduction

Richard Sibbes (1577–1635) was born sixty years after Martin Luther nailed his *Ninety-five Theses* on the door of Castle Church in Wittenberg, Germany, and forty-three years after King Henry VIII severed England from papal dominion, establishing himself as the supreme head of the Church of England. Sibbes was alive when James VI of Scotland became King James I of England in 1603, when the Authorised Version of the Bible (King James Bible) was published in 1611, and when the Separatist Pilgrims fled England in pursuit of religious freedom and founded a colony in Plymouth, Massachusetts in 1620. Sibbes lived his entire life during the days following the English Reformation and during the growth and influence of the religious movement within the English Protestant church called Puritanism. He is considered by some to be the quintessential Puritan minister. In this historical context, Sibbes endured the upheaval and persecution of the Church of England's religious turmoil as it fluctuated between the influences and forces of those who wanted a return to Roman Catholicism, those who wanted a political and half-reformed English church, and those called Puritans who wanted a further, more completely reformed and biblical church.

Richard Sibbes was born at Tostock in Suffolk, England in 1577. His father, Paul, was a wheelwright and expected his first-born son to follow in his footsteps. He even purchased tools for his son that he might serve as an apprentice in the family trade. However, Richard, having a great interest in books and excelling in learning, went against his father's wishes and chose to follow his own desire for higher education. With the help of others, he enrolled at St John's College, Cambridge at the age of eighteen.

Sibbes was a fine student and received a Bachelor of Arts degree in 1599, a fellowship in 1601 and a Master of Arts degree in 1602. Following graduation from St John's College, his life went in a whole new direction. First, he was converted to Christ under the preaching of Paul Baynes, who succeeded William Perkins at the Church of St Andrew the Great in Cambridge. Next, Sibbes began pursuing a life of ministry. He was ordained in the Church of England in 1608 and received a Bachelor of Divinity degree in 1610.

He served as lecturer at Holy Trinity Church in Cambridge from 1610 to 1616. In 1617, he was chosen to be the preacher at Gray's Inn, one of London's most influential pulpits. There he preached to civic leaders, court lawyers, nobles, and citizens of the city. His sermons were deeply biblical, spiritually helpful, warmly pastoral, and immensely practical. He became quite popular and singularly effective in spreading and defending the gospel of Christ. In 1626, he was asked to add to his responsibilities at Gray's Inn the position of master (dean) of Katharine Hall, Cambridge. While in Cambridge, he was also asked to return to Holy Trinity Church, this time as vicar. He held all three posts until his death.

Sibbes' life was filled with preaching the word of God and influencing the church and society with the truths of God. William Haller in his book *The Rise of Puritanism* writes that Sibbes' sermons 'were among the most brilliant and popular of all the utterances of the Puritan church militant.'[1] Peter Lewis writes of Sibbes that 'his teaching was full and expository in the best Puritan tradition, his style clear and winsome, his mind broad and cultured and his piety uncompromising and practical.'[2]

Sibbes was thoroughly Puritan in his preaching and doctrine yet also remained loyal to the Church of England. In his day that was a most difficult stance to maintain. When many of his pastoral colleagues either left their church positions or were expelled for their nonconformity to the theology and prayer book of the religious and political elite of the day, Sibbes remained at his posts and sought to bring about change and reform into the Church of England from within.

Ending a very fruitful, influential, and faithful ministry, Sibbes passed away on July 5, 1635.

---

[1] William Haller, *The Rise of Puritanism* (Philadelphia: University of Pennsylvania Press, 1938), p. 152.

[2] Peter Lewis, *The Genius of Puritanism* (Haywards Heath: Carey Publications, 1979), p. 24.

Little is known of Sibbes' private life. Alexander Grosart, who wrote a biographical memoir for the first edition of *The Complete Works of Richard Sibbes* in 1862, laments the fact that contemporaries failed to record any of Sibbes' life events, details, or circumstances. Also, being unmarried, Sibbes never had children or grandchildren who might have written his story. Even the funeral sermon, which was preached by Dr William Gouge of St Ann's Church, Blackfriars, London and paid for with twenty shillings according to Sibbes' own Last Will and Testament, was not published or saved for posterity.[3] What we do know of his private life comes from public record, his autobiographical comments in his sermons, and introductions to his various works by his colleagues.

The lasting influence of Sibbes' ministry has been through his printed sermons and his books, such as *The Bruised Reed and Smoking Flax*, *The Soul's Conflict with Itself and Victory over Itself by Faith*, and *The Returning Backslider*. His body of work has been used by God generation after generation to promote the teaching and application of the Bible. Consider the following accounts of Sibbes' impact through the centuries.

Grosart records this account from the life of Richard Baxter who lived and ministered during the late seventeenth century:

> About that time (his fifteenth year) it pleased God that a poor ped-dler came to the door that had ballads and some good books, and my father bought of him Dr Sibbes' *Bruised Reed*. This also I read, and found it suited my state and seasonably sent me, which opened more the love of God to me, and gave me livelier apprehension of the mystery of redemption, and how much I was beholden to Jesus Christ.[4]

Charles Spurgeon, who ministered in London during the latter half of the nineteenth century, said of Richard Sibbes, 'Sibbes never wastes the student's time, he scatters pearls and diamonds with both hands.'[5] D.

---

[3] *The Complete Works of Richard Sibbes* (Edinburgh: Banner of Truth Trust, 2001), vol. 1, pp. xx-xxi.

[4] *Works*, vol. 1, p. xxi.

[5] *The Bruised Reed* (Edinburgh: Banner of Truth Trust, 2016), p. vii.

Martyn Lloyd-Jones, who taught and preached in the mid-twentieth century, writes of Sibbes in his book *Preaching and Preachers*:

> You will find, I think in general, that the Puritans are almost invariably helpful. I must not go into this overmuch, but there are Puritans and Puritans! John Owen on the whole is difficult to read; he was a highly intelligent man. But there were Puritan writers who were warmer and more direct and more experimental. I shall never cease to be grateful to the one called Richard Sibbes who was balm to my soul at a period in my life when I was overworked and badly overtired, and therefore subject in an unusual manner to the onslaughts of the devil. In that state and condition to read theology does not help, indeed it may be well-nigh impossible; what you need is some gentle, tender treatment for your soul. I found at that time that Richard Sibbes, who was known in London in the early seventeenth century as 'The Heavenly Doctor Sibbes' was an unfailing remedy. His books *The Bruised Reed* and *The Soul's Conflict* quieted, soothed, comforted, encouraged and healed me. I pity the preacher who does not know the appropriate remedy to apply to himself in these various phases through which his spiritual life must inevitably pass.[6]

In a series entitled, 'Reading Sibbes Aloud,' pastor and author Mark Dever read over 60 unedited Richard Sibbes' sermons to an early morning gathering from 2010 to 2019.[7]

As you can see, Sibbes' influence and impact have endured through the years. Followers of Jesus would do well to read and consider his sermons and writings today.

To quote the publisher's foreword to *The Bruised Reed*, 'There's no better introduction to the Puritans than the writings of Richard Sibbes, who is, in many ways, a typical Puritan.'[8] Dever wrote in his

---

[6] D. M. Lloyd-Jones, *Preaching and Preachers* (Zondervan Publishing House, 1978), p. 175.

[7] Sermons, 2019, http://www.capitolhillbaptist.org. Accessed on January 19, 2021.

[8] *Bruised Reed*, p. vii.

book *The Affectionate Theology of Richard Sibbes*, 'Because Sibbes' theological style and substance can be said to be typical of and unique to the period, it is unsurprising that Christopher Hill describes Sibbes as the quintessential Puritan.'[9] Stephen J. Lawson wrote in the foreword to the aforementioned book:

> Far from embodying the misguided stereotype of the dour Puritan, Sibbes was a man on fire with passion for the gospel. Whether he was standing before the common man or before the learned man of the academy, he preached it with conviction and power. An outstanding example of a preacher who married solid Reformed theology with heartfelt zeal, Sibbes sought to unfold for his hearers the whole counsel of God in order to ensure that they understood the gospel and its implications for their lives.[10]

J. I. Packer in his book, *A Quest for Godliness*, outlines eight characteristics of Puritan preaching:

1. Puritan preaching was expository in its method.
2. Puritan preaching was doctrinal in its content.
3. Puritan preaching was orderly in its arrangement.
4. Puritan preaching was popular in its style.
5. Puritan preaching was Christ-centred in its orientation.
6. Puritan preaching was experimental in its interests.
7. Puritan preaching was piercing in its applications.
8. Puritan preaching was powerful in its manner.[11]

You will find all these characteristics in the sermons of Richard Sibbes.

In the book *Meet the Puritans*, Joel Beeke and Randall Pederson summarize Puritanism in this way: 'Doctrinally, Puritanism was a kind of vigorous Calvinism; experientially, it was warm and contagious; evangelistically, it was aggressive, yet tender; ecclesiastically, it was theocentric and worshipful; politically, it aimed to be scriptural, balanced, and bound by conscience before God in the relations of king, Parliament, and

---

[9] Mark Dever, *The Affectionate Theology of Richard Sibbes* (Reformation Trust Publishing, 2018,) p. 3.

[10] *Ibid.*, p. xi.

[11] J. I. Packer, *A Quest for Godliness* (Wheaton: Crossway, 1994), pp. 284-288.

subjects.' They also give six reasons why the literature of the Puritans has kept its relevance and power and ought to be read and studied today:

1. They shape life by Scripture.
2. They marry doctrine and practice.
3. They focus on Christ.
4. They show how to handle trials.
5. They show how to live in two worlds.
6. They show us true spirituality.[12]

Again, you will find these Puritan traits powerfully and helpfully contained within the works of Richard Sibbes.

Despite this high praise of Puritan teaching, the Puritans have been disregarded and disrespected in secular and even some Christian circles, where they are largely perceived as judgmental, legalistic, austere, and prudish. Thomas Babington Macaulay, a secular historian of the 1800s, in his Essay on Milton writes a description of the Puritans (Milton among them) which brings to light what most current historians and educators refuse to acknowledge:

> We would speak first of the Puritans, the most remarkable body of men, perhaps, which the world has ever produced. ... The Puritans were men whose minds had derived a peculiar character from the daily contemplation of superior beings and eternal interests. Not content with acknowledging, in general terms, an overruling Providence, they habitually ascribed every event to the will of the Great Being, for whose power nothing was too vast, for whose inspection nothing was too minute. To know him, to serve him, to enjoy him, was with them the great end of existence. They rejected with contempt the ceremonious homage which other sects substituted for the pure worship of the soul. Instead of catching occasional glimpses of the Deity through an obscuring veil, they aspired to gaze full on his intolerable brightness, and to commune with him face to face. ...
>
> If they [the Puritans] were unacquainted with the works of philosophers and poets, they were deeply read in the oracles of

---

[12] Joel Beeke and Randall Pederson, *Meet the Puritans* (Grand Rapids: Reformation Heritage Books, 2006), pp. xviii-xxiv.

God. If their names were not found in the registers of heralds, they were recorded in the Book of Life. If their steps were not accompanied by a splendid train of menials, legions of ministering angels had charge over them. Their palaces were houses not made with hands; their diadems crowns of glory which should never fade away. … The Puritan was made up of two different men, the one all self-abasement, penitence, gratitude, passion; the other proud, calm, inflexible, sagacious. He prostrated himself in the dust before his Maker: but he set his foot on the neck of his king. …

People who saw nothing of the godly but their uncouth visages and heard nothing from them but their groans and their whining hymns, might laugh at them. But those had little reason to laugh who encountered them in the hall of debate or in the field of battle. … When all circumstances are taken into consideration, we do not hesitate to pronounce them a brave, a wise, an honest, and a useful body.[13]

George Whitefield (1714–1770), who has been described as the 'Revived Puritan,' writes this about the Puritans of the sixteenth and seventeenth centuries:

The Puritans [were] burning and shining lights. … They in a special manner wrote and preached as men having authority. Though dead, by their writings they yet speak: a peculiar unction attends them to this very hour; and for these thirty years past I have remarked, that the more true and vital religion hath revived either at home or abroad, the more the good old puritanical writings, or the authors of a like stamp who lived and died in communion of the Church of England, have been called for. … Their works still praise them in the gates; and without pretending to a spirit of prophecy, we may venture to affirm that they will live and flourish, when more modern performances of a contrary cast, notwithstanding their gaudy and tinseled trappings, will languish and die in the esteem of those whose understandings are opened to discern what comes nearest to the Scripture standard.[14]

---

[13] Thomas Babington Macaulay, *Essay on Milton* (London: Longmans, Green and Co., 1895), pp. 72-79.
[14] *Meet the Puritans*, p. xiii.

In my own experience, I have come to feel the truth of this admiration of the Puritans. While serving as a pastor for forty years, I have sought spiritual encouragement, spiritual exhortation, and biblical understanding through the works of Puritan writers. I have greatly appreciated their love and commitment to Christ and the gospel, their emphasis on the glory and attributes of God, their unvarying allegiance to the doctrines of grace, their straightforward interpretation of the Scriptures, and their willingness to express emotion and warmth of soul in their writings. Richard Sibbes has emerged as one of my favourites. His writings have been a great help to me, and I am honoured to make them available in this devotional form, not only to encourage the reader's spiritual walk in Jesus (what I consider the most important of life's pursuits) but also, to whet the appetite for the writings of Richard Sibbes, in the hope of inspiring more Christians to read his works in full.

I want to join those who have determined to continue the influence of Richard Sibbes in the lives of the people they love, like English author Izaak Walton, who in his Last Will and Testament included these two designations: 'To my son Izaak, I give Dr Sibbes' *Soul's Conflict*, and to my daughter his *Bruised Reed*, desiring them to read them so as to be well acquainted with them.' Walton wrote in his copy of *The Returning Backslider* (preserved in the Salisbury Cathedral Library):

> Of this blest man, let this just praise be given,
> Heaven was in him, before he was in heaven.[15]

Alexander Grosart affirms Walton's description of Sibbes, writing in the preface to the final volume of Sibbes' *Works*:

> In closing his onerous labours, the Editor would, in a few sentences, characterize the Works now collected and completed; and at once that epithet, which seems by universal consent to have been associated with the name of Richard Sibbes—'HEAVENLY'—recurs, it is the one distinctive adjective for him. For if there ever has been, since apostolic times, a 'heavenly' man, the meek 'Preacher'

---

[15] *Works of Richard Sibbes*, vol. I, p. xx.

of Gray's Inn was he. Emphatically, 'he was a good man, and full of the Holy Ghost and of faith' (Acts 11:24); and in accord with this, he is pre-eminently and peculiarly a 'son of consolation,' a 'comforter.' This, I should say, is the merit of these Works. The minister of the gospel and the private reader will find abundant consolations for bruised, tried, despondent, groping souls. Nor is this characteristic a small thing. It must be a growing conviction, with all who mark the 'signs of the times,' that the want of our age, in the church as in the world, is not more intellect or genius, learning or culture, but more reality of CHRISTIAN LIFE—more 'GOOD' rather than more 'great' men. Perhaps there never has been a period—speaking generally—of more intellect in intense activity, if not in mass, more learning and diffused culture, than the present; and certainly never was there an age of such thick-coming interrogation of all problems in all realms of thought and speculation. But these seem often lamentably disassociated from GOODNESS, from conscience, from spiritual integrity and truthfulness, and above all, from Christian LIFE.[16]

Grosart penned these words in 1864. Are they not even more true today?

As I have assembled these excerpts from the works of Richard Sibbes, I have updated the occasional antiquated word and have shortened sentences and paragraphs while at the same time seeking to keep Sibbes' flow and meaning. The Scripture verses at the beginning of each reading are taken from the English Standard Version of the Bible. May these daily readings from the 'Heavenly Doctor' Richard Sibbes bring spiritual refreshment to your soul. May they challenge your thinking and affections, deepen your understanding of God's word and grace, and inspire you to abide faithfully in Christ.

DAVID B. MACKINNON
Urbandale, Iowa
2022

---

[16] *Works of Richard Sibbes*, vol. 7, p. x.

# One Thing (1)

*One thing have I asked of the Lord, that will I seek after: that I may dwell in the house of the Lord all the days of my life, to gaze upon the beauty of the Lord and to inquire in his temple.*—Psa. 27:4

Why does David say, 'One thing?'

(1) It is because of the nature of God. We must have the whole bent and sway of our souls focused on him. He will have no wavering. The devil is content with half, because if we give into sin then he is sure that he has enough. But God will have the whole heart. 'My son, give me your whole heart' (Prov. 23:26); and 'You shall love the Lord with all your heart, and with all your soul' (Luke 10:27). The bent and sway of the soul must be that way. God is offended if we do not make him our main thing. He will not have us serve him and mammon (Matt. 6:24). He will not have our hearts divided.

(2) It is because of the nature of the soul, for when the soul is about many things, it can do nothing well. A stream cut into many channels runs weakly and is unfit to carry anything. When the soul is divided into many channels, to many things; when it looks after this thing and that thing, and each with expense and intention of care and endeavour, alas, where is the desire of that one thing? For the soul cannot go with the strength it should, except it minds the one thing. The soul of man is a finite thing. Except it gather its strength, as a stream that runs stronger and rises by the inclusion of many lesser rivers; so the soul cannot desire one thing as it should, except it bring all other petty streams to it, and make the main desire its one desire. The main desire must be to be saved, and by grace to have communion and fellowship with God in Christ Jesus. Unless this be the main care, the soul can produce nothing good.

*A Breathing after God, Works,* vol. 2, p. 217

# One Thing (2)

*But only one thing is necessary. Mary has chosen the good portion, and it will not be taken away from her.*—Luke 10:42

(3) David can only desire this 'one thing' by grace. For the very nature of grace is to unite all things to the main thing. The Spirit of grace sets before the eye of the soul heavenly, spiritual things in their greatness and excellency. Then the Spirit of grace, seeing there are many useful things in this world, has a uniting, knitting, subordinating power, to rank all things so they may agree to and help the main thing. Grace confines the soul to one thing. Man, after his fall, was not content with his condition, so he 'sought out many inventions' (Eccles. 7:29). When man falls prey to this, he loses his foundation. The soul is never quiet and sure until it returns to God, who is the one thing the soul truly desires. This new, single-minded heart is a promise in the covenant of grace. For God said, 'I will give you one heart' (Jer. 32:39). As soon as a man becomes a Christian, he has one heart. His heart before was divided. There was a variety of objects the heart was set upon, and God had the least piece. The flesh had a piece, and this delight and that delight had a piece. But God said, 'I will give you one heart.' That is, a heart uniting itself in desire to the best thing, and regulating all things, so that all are one. Little streams help the main stream by running into it; so grace has a subordinating power over all things in the world, so that they help the main. 'One thing have I desired' and I desire other things if they help the main thing. Grace will teach us this art.

*A Breathing After God, Works* vol. 2, pp. 217-18

# Our Thoughts and Desires Reveal Who We Are

*For out of the abundance of the heart his mouth speaks.*—Luke 6:45

Thoughts and desires are the two primitive issues of the heart. Thoughts in the mind will strike the heart. Thoughts go from the understanding to the will and affections. What we think of, that we desire. So, thoughts and desires spring from the soul; and where they are in any strength, they will stir up action in the outward man. The desires of the soul, being the inward motion, stir up outward action, until there be an attaining of the thing desired, and then there is rest. Desire to the thing desired is as action is to rest. When action comes once to rest, it is quiet. So, desire, which is the inward motion, stirs up outward action, until the thing desired be accomplished, and then the soul rests in a loving contentment and enjoyment of the thing desired.

Holy desires issue from choice. A holy and wise desire rises from a choice of a thing that is good; for desire is nothing but the pursuing and embracing of a thing. The understanding must choose the good first, before the soul can embrace it. There is nothing that characterizes and sets a stamp upon a Christian so much as desires. All other things may be counterfeit. Words and actions may be counterfeit, but the desires and affections cannot, because they are the immediate issues and productions of the soul. A man by his desires may know who he is. God is a Spirit and looks to the spirit. It is a good character of a Christian, that his desire, for the most part, is to good; the tenor and sway and bent of his desire is to good. The Spirit of God is very effectual in stirring up these desires.

Let us examine what our desires are, what our bent is, for they show the condition of the soul more than anything in the world. As springs in low places are discovered by the steams and vapours that come out of the place, so the vapouring out of our desire for good shows that there is a spring of grace in our hearts.

*A Breathing After God, Works,* vol. 2, pp. 217-20

# The Christian's Desire for God's House (1)

*Blessed is the one you choose and bring near, to dwell in your courts! We shall be satisfied with the goodness of your house, the holiness of your temple!*—Psa. 65:4

Christians have a constant desire to dwell in the house of God.

(1) The reason is, because the soul in this world is never fully satisfied with the good things of God's house until it be in heaven. This life is a life of desires and longing; the church is but engaged to Christ in this world; the marriage will be consummated in another world. Therefore, the church desires still further and further communion with Christ in his ordinances here, and forever in heaven.

(2) There are remainders of the corruption within that deaden and dull our performances and put us on to actions that grieve our spirits and the Spirit of God. We desire to dwell in the house of the Lord, because here there is corruption in us, until grace has wrought it out fully.

(3) There is more and more to be had in the house of God. We never come to be full. The soul has a wondrous capacity, being a spiritual essence. It is capable of more grace and comfort than we can have in this world. 'God gave gifts to men' (Eph. 4:11), to preach and to edify the church more and more. So long as there is need for more and more building in the believer there will be the need of the ministry. The Christian desires to 'dwell in the house of the Lord' (Psa. 27:4), for there he can and will grow.

(4) The special reason why he desires to be in God's house is because he knows God is present there, and there is no good thing lacking where God is present. It is the presence of God that makes all things sweet and comfortable. What makes heaven to be heaven? The fact that God is there? If the soul of a Christian were among angels, angelical comforts would not be desired, if God were not there. If there were all the delights in the world, the soul would not care for them, except God were present. Heaven would not be heaven without the presence of God.

*A Breathing After God, Works*, vol. 2, p. 228

# The Christian's Desire for God's House (2)

*O Lord, I love the habitation of your house and the place where your glory dwells.*—Psa. 26:8

Heaven would not be heaven without the presence of God. The presence of God in a dungeon, in a lion's den, makes it a paradise, a place of pleasure; the presence of God makes all conditions comfortable. If there be not the presence of God, the greatest comfort in the world is nothing. What makes the church longed for by holy men? God is present there. Wherever God is present in the communion of saints, they must be esteemed simply because of his presence. What makes hell to be hell? There is no presence of God there; no testimony of his presence in hell; nothing but 'utter darkness' (Matt. 8:12). What makes the life of man comfortable? There is some presence of God in everything. There is a presence of God in meat, in drink, in friends, that a man may say, 'Oh, here is a good God, here is some presence of God.' There is not the vilest reprobate in the world, but he has some testimony of God's presence. He tastes of God in somewhat or other; though he sees not God in it, yet God shows himself to him in some comfort. But when God will remove all his presence from a man, that is hell itself. What is hell but where there is no presence of God? When there is no communion with the chief good, that man is in darkness and horror, which is hell, as we see in the story of the rich man and Lazarus (Luke 16). It is the presence of God that makes things comfortable. That is heaven, to enjoy nearer and nearer communion with God.

Therefore let us labour to enjoy the presence of God in his ordinances, that we may have a heaven upon earth, that we may desire still more and more to delight in them, until we come to heaven, where all desires will be accomplished. David knowing that God was present in his temple, he said, 'Oh, that I might dwell in the house of God all the days of my life' (Psa. 27:4).

*A Breathing After God, Works*, vol. 2, pp. 228-29

# What the Soul Was Made For

*The kingdom of heaven is like a merchant in search of fine pearls, who, on finding one pearl of great value, went and sold all that he had and bought it.*—Matt. 13:45, 46

The apostle Paul was an excellent man, and had excellent privileges to glory in. Oh but, said he, 'I account all dung and dross in comparison of the excellent knowledge of Christ' (Phil. 3:8). Our blessed Saviour, who was the most able of all to judge, he would have all 'sold for the pearl.' He would have us sell all to be a part of the kingdom of heaven. When Martha and Mary entertained Jesus, Mary sat at his feet to hear him expound the truth of God; Christ said, 'one thing is necessary,' and 'she chose the better part' (Luke 10:42). 'One thing have I desired,' said David (Psa. 27:4). All things in comparison to that are not necessary; they may well be set aside.

From this we learn what our souls were made for. What more could our souls be made for than to dwell in the meditation of the beauty of God. What are our souls made for but for excellent things? What is excellent but that which is about the truth of God in the gospel? Is the soul made to study debates and attacks between man and man in our own personal vocations? Is the soul made to get a little wealth, that we will leave perhaps to an unthrifty generation after? Are our souls, which are the most excellent things under heaven; they are the price of the blood of the Son of God, and in his judgment the world is not worth a soul—are they for these things? No! They are for union and communion with God through the truth of the gospel, to grow in nearer communion with God by his Spirit, to have more knowledge and affection, more love and joy and delight in the best things daily. Our souls are for these things that will make us gracious here, and glorious forever after in heaven. It is a great disordering, when we study and care only for earthly things, and have slight concern of those things that are incomparably the best things, in the judgment of God and of Christ himself, and of all good men.

*A Breathing After God, Works*, vol. 2, pp. 245-47

# God Makes the Heart Tender

*Blessed is the one who fears the Lord always, but whoever hardens his heart will fall into calamity.*—Prov. 28:14

Is there anything in man that can cause God to do him good? No. Where God intends to do any good, he first works in the heart a gracious disposition: after which he looks upon his own work as upon a lovely object, and so does give them other blessings. Now in a tender heart these three properties concur: 1. It is sensible. 2. It is pliable. 3. It is yielding.

(1) A tender heart is always a sensible heart. It has life, and therefore sense. Some senses are not altogether necessary for the being of a living creature, as hearing and seeing; but sensibleness is needful to the being of every living creature. It is a sign of life in a Christian when he is sensible of dangers. God has planted such affections in man, as may preserve the life of man, as fear and love. Fear is that which makes a man avoid many dangers. God has given us fear to cause us to make our peace with him.

(2 & 3) A tender heart is pliable and yielding. Now that is said to be yielding and pliable, which yields to the touch of anything that is put to it, as wax is yielding and pliable to the disposition of him that works it. In a tender heart there is no resistance, but it yields presently to every truth, and has a fitness to receive any impression. A tender heart, so soon as the word is spoken, yields to it. It quakes at warnings, obeys precepts, melts at promises, and the promises sweeten the heart. But hardness of heart is quite opposite. It will not yield to the touch. Such a heart may be broken in pieces, but it will not receive any impression. A hard heart is like a stone to God or goodness. It is not yielding but resists and repels all that is good. You may break it in pieces, but it is unframeable for any service. On the contrary, a melting and tender heart is sensible, yielding, and fit for any service both to God and man.

*Josiah's Reformation*, pp. 6-10 [5-8]

# Maintaining a Tender Heart (1)

*Finally, all of you, have unity of mind, sympathy, brotherly love, a tender heart, and a humble mind.*—1 Pet. 3:8

How a tender heart may be preserved and maintained.

(1) Be under the means whereby God's Spirit will work; for it is he by his Spirit that works upon the heart and does preserve tenderness in us; and he will work only by his own means. All the devices in the world will not work upon the heart. Let us hear what God's word says of our state by nature, of the wrath and justice of God, and of the judgment that will shortly come upon all the world.

(2) Present before yourselves the miserable and forlorn state of the church of God abroad. It was this that broke Nehemiah's heart. When he heard that the Jews were in great affliction and reproach, that the wall of the city was broken down, and the gates burnt with fire, he sat down and wept, and mourned certain days, fasted and prayed before the God of heaven (Neh. 1:4). This also made Moses' heart to melt when he looked on his brethren's affliction in Egypt. We might keep our hearts tender if we did but set before our eyes the pitiful state of God's church abroad, and that we may come to be in such a state ourselves before long.

(3) Labour for an evangelical faith. We must believe that all the warnings of God's vengeance against the wicked will come to pass. Faith does make these things present before our eyes; for it is the nature of faith to set things absent as present before us. What makes the sinner tremble and be cast down, but when he sees that he is about to die and sees death look him in the face? So, faith setting the day of judgment before our eyes, will make us to tremble. Paul so often urged Timothy by the coming of the Lord Jesus to judgment (2 Tim. 4:1). If we had an evangelical faith to believe the goodness of God, pardon from him, and everlasting life, this would preserve tenderness of heart.

(4) Good company will preserve tenderness of heart, be careful to associate yourself with those that are tender-hearted.

*Josiah's Reformation*, pp. 16-18 [12-14]

# Maintaining a Tender Heart (2)

*No one can serve two masters, for either he will hate the one and love the other, or he will be devoted to the one and despise the other. You cannot serve God and money.*—Matt. 6:24

(5) Take heed of the least sin against conscience. Sins that are committed against conscience darken the understanding, deaden the affection, and take away life; so that one has not the least strength to withstand the least temptation. For the heart at first being tender, will endure nothing, but the least sin will trouble it. As water, when it begins to freeze, will not endure anything, not so much as the weight of a pin upon it, but after a while will bear the weight of a cart; even so at the beginning, the heart being tender, trembles at the least sin; but when it once gives way to sins against conscience, it becomes so frozen, so hard, that it can endure any sin.

(6) Take heed of spiritual drunkenness; that is, that you be not drunk with setting your love too much upon outward things. The immoderate use of any earthly thing takes away spiritual sense; for the more sensible the soul is of outward things, the less it is of spiritual. When the heart is filled with the pleasures of this life, it is not sensible of any judgment that hangs over the head. As in the old world, 'they ate and drank, they married and gave in marriage, they bought and sold, while the flood came upon them and swept all away' (Matt. 24:38, 39). When a man sets his love upon the creature, the very strength of his soul is lost. In the Scripture, God joins prayer and fasting both together (Matt. 17:21); that when he would have our hearts raised up to heaven, we should have all use of earthly things taken away. Talk of religion to a carnal man, whose senses are lost with love of earthly things, he has no ear for that; his sense is quite lost, he has no relish or savour of anything that is good. Therefore, we are bidden to take heed that our hearts be not overcome with the cares of this life, for these will make a man to be insensible of spiritual things (Luke 21:34).

*Josiah's Reformation*, pp. 18-20 [14-16]

# Maintaining a Tender Heart (3)

*But exhort one another every day, as long as it is called 'today,' that none of you may be hardened by the deceitfulness of sin.*— Heb. 3:13

(7) Take heed of hypocrisy; for it causes swelling, and pride makes the heart to condemn others that be not like unto us. They bless themselves that they live thus and thus, they think themselves better than any other; and if they hear the minister reprove them for sin, they will shift it off, and say, 'Oh, this belongs not to me, but to a carnal man, and to a wicked person.' The Scribes and Pharisees, who were vile hypocrites, were the cause of all mischief, and more hard-hearted than Pilate, a heathen man; for he would have delivered Christ, but they would not (Luke 23:14). Therefore, if thou wilt have tenderness of heart, take heed of hypocrisy.

(8) Take heed of great sins, which will harden the heart; for little sins do many times not deaden the heart, but stir up the conscience; but great sins do stun and dull a man; as a prick of a pin will make a man to start, but a heavy blow makes a man dead for the present. Therefore, take heed of great sins. So it was with David. He sinned in numbering the people, and for this his heart smote him; but when he came to the great and devouring sin of Uriah and Bathsheba, this was a great blow that struck him and laid him for dead, till Nathan came and revived him (2 Sam. 12:1). For when men fall into great sins, their hearts are so hardened, that they go on from sin to sin. The eye being a tender part, and easily hurt, how watchful is man by nature over it, that it be not hurt. So, the heart, being a tender thing, let us preserve it by all watchfulness to keep blows from off it. It is a terrible thing to keep a wound of some great sin upon the conscience, for it makes a way for a new breach; because when the conscience once begins to be hardened with some great sin, then there is no stop, but we run on to commit sin with all greediness.

*Josiah's Reformation*, pp. 20-22 [16-17]

# Maintaining a Tender Heart (4)

*But watch yourselves lest your hearts be weighed down with dissipation
and drunkenness and cares of this life, and that day come upon you
suddenly like a trap.*—Luke 21:34

(9) Lastly, consider the miserable state of hardness of heart. Such a
one that has a hard heart is next to hell itself, to the state of a damned
spirit, a most terrible state. A hard heart is neither melted with promises
nor broken with warnings. He has no pity for men or love to God. He
forgets all judgment for things past and looks for none to come. When
the soul is in this case, it is fit for nothing but for sin and the devil,
whereas a tender-hearted man is fit for all good. Let God threaten, he
trembles and quakes; let God promise, his heart melts and rejoices; let
God command, he will perform all. But when a man's heart is hardened
by hypocrisy, covetousness, or custom in sin, he has no pity, no compassion. Let God command, threaten, or promise, yet the heart is never a bit
moved. This is a terrible state of soul.

Let those that are young labour to keep tenderness of heart; before
the heart be pestered with the cares of the world. God delights much in
the prayers of the young, because they come not from so polluted a soul,
hardened with the practices of this world. Let the young repent in the
time of their sins and let them not put it off unto their old days. In our
youth let us acquaint ourselves with those that are good; as it is says in
Hebrews 3:13, 'Let us provoke one another daily, while it is called today,
lest any of you be hardened through the deceitfulness of sin.' Let us use
all means to keep our hearts tender. Oh, it is a blessed state! We are fit
to live when our hearts are tender, fit to die, fit to receive anything from
God, fit for duties of honesty to men, and fit for any service to God.
But when we have lost sense and feeling, it must be the almighty power
of God that must recover us again. Therefore, labour to preserve and
maintain a tender, soft, and melting heart.

*Josiah's Reformation*, pp. 22-24 [17-18]

# Test to See if Your Heart is Tender

*But this is the one to whom I will look: he who is humble and contrite in spirit and trembles at my word.*—Isa. 66:2b

We may test our tenderness of heart these four ways:

(1) As it is tender from God, so it is tender for God; for the three persons of the Trinity. He that has a tender heart cannot endure to dishonour God himself, or to hear others dishonour him. He cannot endure to hear God's name blasphemed. So again, a man has a tender heart when he yields to the motions of the Holy Spirit. When the Spirit moves and he yields. But a hard heart beats back all, and as a stone to the hammer, will not yield to any motion of God's Spirit.

(2) A tender heart is sensible in regard to the word of God. It will tremble when it hears of the terrors of the Lord at the day of judgment, as Paul did, 'Now knowing the terrors of the Lord, we persuade men' (2 Cor. 5:11). The apostle Peter would have us make this use of it: 'Since all these things are thus to be dissolved, what sort of people ought you to be in lives of holiness and godliness?' (2 Pet. 3:11). How can the heart but melt at God's promises, for they are the sweetest things that can be? A tender heart will be pliable to any direction from the word.

(3) By applying it to the works of God; for a tender heart quakes when it sees the judgment of God upon others. So again, a tender heart rejoices at the mercy of God, for it sees that mercy proceeds from the love of God.

(4) A man may know his heart to be tender in regard to the state of others. If they be wicked, he has a tender heart for them; as David said, 'Mine eyes gush out with rivers of water, because men keep not your law' (Psa. 119:136). As Paul said in Philippians 3:18, 'There are many that walk as enemies to the cross, of whom I have told you before, and now tell you weeping.' By these marks we may know whether we have tender hearts.

*Josiah's Reformation*, pp. 30-33 [23-25]

# How to Recover a Tender Heart

*But exhort one another every day, as long as it is called 'today,' that none of you may be hardened by the deceitfulness of sin.*—Heb. 3:13

How will men recover themselves when their hearts are subject to hardness, deadness, and insensibleness?

(1) As when things are cold, we bring them to the fire to heat and melt, so we bring our cold hearts to the fire of the love of Christ. Consider our sin is against Christ, and Christ's love towards us; dwell upon this meditation. Think what great love Christ has showed to us, and how little we have deserved, and this will make our hearts to melt, and be as pliable as wax before the sun.

(2) If you would have a tender and melting heart, then use the means; be always under the sunshine of the gospel; and help one another. Physicians love not to give medicine to themselves. So, a man is not always fit to help himself when he is not right; but good company is fit to do it. 'Did not our hearts burn within us while he talked with us?' said the two disciples, holding communion with each other at Emmaus (Luke 24:32). Christ says, 'Where two or three are met together in his name, he is in the midst of them' (Matt. 18:20). Where two hold communion, there Christ will make a third. David could not recover himself but needed Nathan to help him (2 Sam. 12:7). Therefore, if we would recover ourselves from hard and insensible hearts, let us use the help of one another.

(3) We must with boldness and reverence challenge the covenant of grace; for this is the covenant that God has made with us, to give us tender hearts, hearts of flesh, as Ezekiel 11:19 says, 'I will give them one heart, and put a new spirit within them; I will take away the stony hearts out of their bodies, and I will give them a heart of flesh.' Now seeing this is a covenant God has made let us challenge him with his promise and go to him by prayer. Entreat him to give you a fleshly heart; go to him, wait his time, for that is the best time. These are the means to bring tenderness of heart.

*Josiah's Reformation*, pp. 35-37 [27-28]

# Benefits of a Tender Heart

*I dwell in the high and holy place, and also with him who is of a contrite and lowly spirit, to revive the spirit of the lowly, and to revive the heart of the contrite.*—Isa. 57:15b

(1) God has promised to dwell in a tender heart. Isaiah 57:15 says, 'For thus says he that is high and excellent, he that inhabits eternity, whose name is the Holy One: I will dwell in the high and holy place, and with him also that is of a contrite and humble spirit, to revive the spirit of the humble, and to give life to them that are of a contrite heart.' Now God having promised to dwell where there is a soft heart; can God come into a heart without a blessing? When the heart therefore is pliable and tender, there is an immediate communion between the soul and God; and can that heart be miserable that has communion with God? Surely no.

(2) Consider that a man is fit for that end for which he was made when he has a tender heart. What are we redeemed for, but that we should serve God? And who is fit to be put in the service of God but he that has a tender heart for God?

(3) Consider that a tender heart is fit for any blessedness. It is capable of any beatitude. A tender heart will make a man to hear the word, to read, to show mercies to others, and therefore is blessed.

(4) Consider the wretched state of a heart that is not tender and will not yield. What a fearful thing was it to see what strange things fell out at Christ's death, what darkness there was, what thunders and lightnings. The veil of the temple rent, the sun was turned into darkness, the graves opened, and the dead did rise, yet notwithstanding none of these would make the hypocritical Pharisees to tremble, but they mocked at it, although it made a very heathen man to confess it the work of God (Matt. 27:54). What fearful things may a man come to if he gives way to hardness of heart! Therefore, let everyone be persuaded to labour for a tender and yielding heart here, else we shall have it hereafter against our wills, when it will do us no good.

*Josiah's Reformation*, pp. 37-40 [28-31]

# Kings Must Humble Themselves before God

*For there is no authority except from God, and those that exist have been instituted by God.*— Rom. 13:1b

It is not unbefitting kings to humble themselves before God, seeing they have to deal with him who is a 'consuming fire' (Heb. 12:29), before whom the very angels cover their faces. I say it is no shame for the greatest monarch of the earth to abase himself when he has to do with God; yea, kings, of all other persons, ought most to humble themselves, to show their thankfulness to God, who has raised them from their brethren to be heads of his people. And considering the endowments which kings usually have, they are bound to humble themselves, as also in regard of the authority and power which God has put into their hands, saying, 'By me kings reign' (Prov. 8:15). But usually we see, from the beginning of the world, that kings forget God. Where there is not grace above nature, there kings will not stoop to God. Only so far as it agrees with their pleasure and will, so far shall God be served, and no farther.

As that ointment poured upon Aaron's head fell from his head to the skirts, and so spread itself to the rest of the parts, even to his feet (Psa. 133:2), so a good example in a king descends down to the lowest subjects, as the rain from the mountains into the valleys. Therefore, a king should first begin to humble himself. Kings are called fathers to their subjects, because they should bear a loving and holy affection to their people, that when anything troubles the subjects, they should be affected with it. The welfare of their subjects should be their glory.

It is no benefit for a man to be humbled by God, as Pharaoh was; for God can humble and pull down the proudest. God by this gets himself glory. But here is the glory of a Christian, that he has grace from God to humble himself. Many are humbled that are not humble; many are cast down that have proud hearts still, as Pharaoh had.

*Josiah's Reformation*, pp. 43-46 [34-36]

# How to Humble Ourselves (1)

*Whoever exalts himself will be humbled, and whoever humbles himself will be exalted.*— Matt. 23:12

How may we come to humble ourselves as we should?

(1) Get poor spirits, spirits that see the want in ourselves; the emptiness of all earthly things without God's favour; the insufficiency of ourselves at the day of judgment. Let us consider our origin. From where do we come? From the earth, from nothing. Where do we go? To the earth, to nothing. And in respect of spiritual things, we have nothing. We are not able to do anything of ourselves, not so much as to think a good thought. Likewise, consider the guilt of our sins. What do we deserve? Hell and damnation, to have our portion in that 'lake that burns with fire and brimstone.' Let us have before our eyes the picture of our sinful nature: how we are drawn away by every object; how ready to be proud of anything; how unable to resist the least sin; how ready to be cast down under every affliction; that we have no strength of ourselves to perform any good; in a word, how that we carry a nature about us indisposed to good, and prone to all evil. This consideration humbled Paul, and made him to cry out, 'O miserable man that I am, who shall deliver me from this body of death?' (Rom. 7:24). By this means we come to be poor in spirit.

(2) If we would have humble spirits, let us bring ourselves into the presence of God. Consider his attributes, his works of justice in the world and upon ourselves. Compare his wisdom, holiness, power, and strength, with our own. Job, when he brought himself into God's presence, said, 'I abhor myself, and repent in dust and ashes' (Job 42:6). 'I am not worthy,' says John the Baptist (John 1:27). So Paul: 'I am not worthy to be called an apostle' (1 Cor. 15:9). So the centurion: 'I am not worthy thou should come into my house' (Matt. 8:8). Let us come into the presence of God, under the means of his word, and then we will see our own vileness, which will work humiliation.

*Josiah's Reformation*, pp. 51-54 [41-43]

# How to Humble Ourselves (2)

*Because your heart was penitent, and you humbled yourself before the Lord, when you heard how I spoke against this place and against its inhabitants, that they should become a desolation and a curse, and you have torn your clothes and wept before me, I also have heard you, declares the Lord.*—2 Kings 22:19

(3) That we may humble ourselves, let us be content to hear of our sins and baseness by others. Let us be content that others should acquaint us with anything that may humble us. Proud men are the devil's pipes, and flatterers the musicians to blow these pipes. Though men have nothing of their own, yet they love to give heed to flatterers. Whereas a true, wise man, will be content to hear of anything that may humble him before God.

(4) That we may humble ourselves, look to the time to come, what we shall be ere long, earth and dust; and at the day of judgment we must be stripped of all. What should puff us up in this world? All our self-glory shall end in shame, all our magnificence in confusion, all our riches in poverty.

(5) If we would humble ourselves, let us set before us the example of our blessed Saviour. He left heaven, took our nature, and humbled himself to the death of the cross, yea, suffered himself to be killed as a traitor (Phil. 2:5-8); and all this to satisfy the wrath of God for us that he might be a pattern for us to be like-minded. Let us be transformed into the likeness of him; yea, the more we think of him, the more we will be humbled. A heart that believes in Christ will be humbled like Christ. Is it possible, if a man consider he is to be saved by an abased and humble Saviour, that was pliable to every base service, that had not a house to hide himself; I say, is it possible that he which considers of this, should ever be willingly or wilfully proud? Do we hope to be saved by Christ, and will we not be like him? Therefore, let us take counsel of Christ: 'Learn of me, for I am humble and meek; and you shall find rest to your souls' (Matt. 11:29).

*Josiah's Reformation*, pp. 54-58 [43-46]

# How to Humble Ourselves (3)

*Whoever humbles himself like this child is the greatest in the kingdom of heaven.*—Matt. 18:4

(6) That we may humble ourselves, let us work upon our own souls by reasoning, discoursing, and speaking to our own hearts. For the soul has a faculty to work upon itself. So, discourse thus: If a prince should but frown upon me when I have offended his law, in what case should I be! Yet, when the great God of heaven threatens, what an atheistic unbelieving heart have I, that can be moved at the warnings of a mortal man, that is but dust and ashes, and yet cannot be moved with the warnings of the great God! Consider also, if a man had been so kind and bountiful to me, if I should reward his kindness with unkindness, I should have been ashamed, and covered my face with shame; and yet how unkind have I been unto God, who has been so kind to me, and yet I never a whit ashamed! If a friend should have come to me, and I have given him no hospitality, what a shame were this! But yet how often has the Holy Spirit knocked at the door of my heart, and suggested many holy motions into me of mortification, repentance, and newness of life, yet notwithstanding I have given him the repulse, opposed the outward means of grace, and have thought myself unworthy of it; what a shame is this! Thus, if we compare our interest in earthly things with our interest in heavenly, this will be a means to work upon our hearts, inwardly to humble ourselves. Let us labour to work our hearts to humility, into true sorrow, shame, true fear, that so we may have God to pity and consider us, who only does regard a humble soul.

There is an order, method, and agreement in these actions. We must examine ourselves strictly, and then bring ourselves before God, judge and condemn ourselves; for humiliation is a kind of execution.

*Josiah's Reformation*, pp. 58-60 [46-47]

# Proneness to Pride

*As it is, you boast in your arrogance. All such boasting is evil.*—James
4:16

It is a strange thing that the devil should raise men to be proud of
that which is not of themselves, but of things they have borrowed or
have been given; as for men to be proud of themselves in regard to their
parents. There are many who think the better of themselves for their
apparel, when they are clothed with nothing they have made themselves.
By this the devil has besotted our nature, to make us glory in that which
should humble us, and to think the better of ourselves, for that which
is none of our own. Nay, many in the church of God are so far from
humbling themselves that they are puffed up with a base empty pride,
even before God. Therefore, let us take notice of our startling proneness
to have a conceit of ourselves for if a man has a new fashion, or some
new thing, which nobody else knows besides himself, how astonishingly
conceited he is in himself.

Let us take notice, I say, of our proneness to this sin of pride; for the
best are prone to it. Consider it an extremely hateful sin, a sin of sins,
that God most hates. It was this sin which made him thrust Adam out
of paradise. It was this sin which made him thrust the evil angels out of
heaven, who shall never come there again. Yea, it is a sin that God cures
with other sins, so far he hates it; as Paul, being subject to be proud
through the abundance of revelations, was cured of it by a prick in the
flesh: being exercised with some dangerous, noisome, and strange cure.
Indeed, it is profitable for some men to fall, that so by their humiliation
for infirmities, they may be cured of this great sacrilegious sin. And why
it is called a sacrilegious sin? Because it robs God of his glory. For God
has said, 'My glory I will not give to another' (Isa. 42:8).

*Josiah's Reformation*, pp. 55-56 [43-44]

# Humility

*God opposes the proud but gives grace to the humble.*—James 4:6

A humble heart is a grace itself, and a vessel of grace. It does better the soul and make it holy, for the soul is never fitter for God than when it is humbled. It is a fundamental grace that gives strength to all other graces. So, much humility, much grace. Humility empties the heart for God to fill it. When the heart is made low, there is a spiritual emptiness, and what fills this up but the Spirit of God? In that measure we empty ourselves, in that measure we are filled with the fullness of God. God has but two heavens to dwell in, the heaven of heavens, and the heart of a humble man. The proud swelling heart, that is full of ambition, high conceits, and self-dependence, will not endure to have God enter; but he dwells largely and easily in the heart of a humble man. If we will dwell in heaven hereafter, let us humble ourselves now.

A humble soul is a secure and safe soul; for a man that is not high, but of a low stature, needs not to fear falling. A humble soul is also safe in regard of outward troubles; for when we have humbled ourselves, God ceases to afflict it. Will the ploughman plough when he has broken up the ground enough? (Isa. 28:28) Such a one may say to God, 'Lord, I have humbled and judged myself, therefore do not judge me; I am ready to do whatsoever you will.' But if we do not do this ourselves, God will take us in hand; for God will have but one God. Is it not better for us to humble ourselves than for God to give us up to the merciless rage and fury of men, for them to humble us, or to fall into the hands of God, who is a 'consuming fire'? If we will judge ourselves, the apostle promises, we shall not be judged of the Lord (1 Cor. 11:31). Wherefore upon any occasion be humble, let us prepare ourselves to meet the Lord our God.

*Josiah's Reformation*, pp. 61-65 [48-51]

# True versus False Humility (1)

*Clothe yourselves, all of you, with humility toward one another, for 'God opposes the proud but gives grace to the humble.'*—1 Pet. 5:5b

How may we know holy from hypocritical humility?

(1) Holy humility is voluntary. But, on the contrary, the humility of other men is against their will and by force it is extorted from them. God will break, crush, and deal harshly with them, which they grieve and murmur at. But the children of God have the Spirit of God, which is a free Spirit, that works upon their hearts, and hereby they willingly humble themselves, whereas the wicked, wanting the Spirit of God, cannot humble themselves willingly, but are cast down against their wills. God can pluck down the proudest.

(2) True humility is ever joined with reformation. As Micah 6:8 says, 'He has showed you, O man, what he does require of you, to humble yourself, and walk with your God.' Now the humiliation of wicked men is never joined with reformation for there is no walking with God in them.

(3) Sin must appear bitter to the soul or else we will never be truly humbled for it. There is in every renewed soul an inner hatred and loathing of evil, which manifests the soundness both of true humiliation and reformation. This shows itself in a serious purpose and resolution not to offend God in the least kind. Also, in a constant endeavour to avoid the occasions and allurements of sin. Job made a covenant with his eyes, that 'he would not look upon a maid' (Job 31:1). A true Christian will not hide his sins, but lay them open, before God. We will hate sin universally; not one sin, but every kind of sin, and that most of all which most rules in us, and which is most prevalent in our own hearts. He that truly hates sin will not think much to be admonished and reproved when he errs. On the contrary, can we say that men hate not sin, which, when they are reproved for it, labour to defend it or excuse it, counting their pride but comeliness, their miserable covetousness but thirst, and their drunkenness as only good fellowship?

*Josiah's Reformation*, pp. 65-71 [51-55]

# True versus False Humility (2)

*He has told you, O man, what is good; and what does the Lord require of you but to do justice, and to love kindness, and to walk humbly with your God?*—Mic. 6:8

(4) True humility proceeds from faith and is in the faithful not only when judgment is upon them, but before the judgment comes. True humility quakes at the threats, as the very frowns of a father will distress a dutiful child. Carnal people are like men that, hearing thunderclaps afar off, are never a whit moved; but when it is present over their heads, then they tremble. So, hypocrites care not for judgments that are far off. It is of no benefit for a man to be humbled when the judgment is upon him, for so Pharaoh was, who yet, when the judgment was off, then he goes to his old bias again. The carnal say, 'If any judgment come upon me, then I will repent, and cry to God for mercy; and why should I deny myself of my pleasures of sin before?' Oh, this is but a forced humiliation, not from love to God, but love to self. This is but Ahab's and Pharaoh's humiliation. It is not out of any love to God, but merely forced. It is too late to do it when God has seized upon us for judgment.

(5) True humility is joined with hope. The devils do chafe, vex, and fret themselves, in regard of their desperate estate, because they have no hope. If there be no hope, it is impossible there should be true and sound humiliation; but true humiliation does carry us to God. That what we have taken out of ourselves by humiliation, we may recover it in God. Humility is such a grace, that though it makes us nothing in ourselves, yet does it carry us to God, who is all in all. Humility works between God and us, and makes the heart leave itself, to plant and pitch itself upon God, and looks for comfort and assurance from him. There is nothing more profitable in the world than humility, because, though it seems to have nothing, yet it carries the soul to him who fills all in all.

*Josiah's Reformation*, pp. 73-75 [57-59]

# True versus False Humility (3)

*Before destruction a man's heart is haughty, but humility comes before honour.*—Prov. 18:12

(6) In false humility the hypocrites are sorrowful for the judgment, that is upon them; but not for that which is the cause of the judgment, which is sin; but the child of God, he is humbled for sin, which is the cause of all judgments. As good Josiah, when he heard read out of Deuteronomy the curses threatened for sin, and comparing the sins of his people with the sins against which the curses were threatened, he humbled himself for his sin and the sins of his people. Whereas the wicked, they humble themselves only because of the smart and trouble which they do endure.

(7) True humiliation is a thorough humiliation. It is twice repeated in 2 Chronicles 34:27, 'you did humble yourself before God when you heard the words against this place and against the inhabitants thereof and humbled yourself before me.' It was a thorough humiliation. The children of God thoroughly humble themselves, but the hypocrite, when he does humble himself, it is not thoroughly. They count it a light matter. As soon as the judgment is off, they have forgotten their humiliation, as Pharaoh did. Many will breathe a few sighs and hang down the head like a bulrush for a time; but it is, like Ephraim's morning dew, quickly gone. It is but a mere offer of humiliation. Whereas the children of God, when they begin, they never cease working upon their own hearts with meditation, until they have brought their heart to a blessed temper, as we see in David, Ezra, Hezekiah, and Daniel, how they did humble themselves. But why do God's children take pains in humbling themselves? Partly because it must be done, else God will not accept it; and partly because there is a great deal of hardness and pride in the best. If a man be once thoroughly and truly humbled, he shall soon have comfort.

By these seven marks we may know a true humility from a counterfeit humility.

*Josiah's Reformation*, pp. 75-77 [56-60]

## Both Outward Devotion and Inward Affection

*Well did Isaiah prophesy of you hypocrites, as it is written, 'This people honours me with their lips, but their heart is far from me.'*—Mark 7:6

Tears and mourning for sin, when it comes from inward grief, is a temper well befitting any man. It is not an unmanly or base thing. When one has to deal with God, he must forget his state and take the best way to meet with God. This is evident by many instances, for David, though a man of war, yet when he had to deal with God, he watered his couch with his tears (Psa. 6:6); Hezekiah, though a great king, yet he humbled himself (Isa. 58:1). Our blessed Saviour himself did it 'with strong cries and tears' (Heb. 5:7) when he had to deal with God. When we have to deal with God, then all abasement is the mere minimum. 'I will be yet more undignified than this, and I will be humiliated in my own eyes,' said David (2 Sam. 6:22). Let us say when we have to deal with God; I will be yet more undignified, and so cast ourselves down before the Lord. All expression of devotion is the minimum, be it without hypocrisy.

A warning concerning outward actions alone; for most have thought wrongly of devotion and humiliation. They think that devotion is only in outward actions; as in a little hearing, or reading, or praying. Whereas in truth these outward acts do only make up the body of devotion, which, without the soul, namely, the inward religious affection, is no better than a dead carrion. Our outward expression must come from the apprehension of the goodness, mercy, and justice of God, before whom the very angels veil their faces. It is not outward devotion that will serve the turn; if I go pray, and kneel, and express all outward carriage, in the meantime neglecting to stir up the soul to worship God; I will be judged at the last day. Therefore, let all holy actions come from within first, and then to the outward man. Let us work upon our hearts a consideration of the goodness, justice, majesty, and mercy of God, and then let there be an expression in body.

*Josiah's Reformation*, pp. 94-97 [73-75]

# Weeping for the Church

*Therefore be alert, remembering that for three years I did not cease night
or day to admonish every one with tears.*—Acts 20:31

The best way to weep is to enter into the house of mourning and
set before our eyes the afflictions of others. The very sight of misery is a
means to make the soul weep. And let us be willing to hear that which we
cannot see; as Nehemiah was content to hear, nay, to inquire, concerning
God's people abroad; and when he heard that it was not well with them it
made him weep. Every man will cry, 'What news?' But where is the man,
when he hears of the news beyond the seas, will send up sighs to God in
prayer, that he would take pity upon his church? It is a good way to use
our senses, to help our souls to grieve.

Therefore, let us shame ourselves for our own deadness, dryness, and
spiritual barrenness this way, that we can yield no sighs, no tears for God,
for his church and his glory. Let us reason with our souls, 'If I should lose
my wife, or child, or my estate, this wayward heart of mine would weep
and be grieved; but now there is greater cause for mourning for myself
and the church of God, and yet I cannot grieve.' Augustine said he could
weep for her who killed herself out of love to him, but he could not
weep for his own want of love to God. We have many who will weep for
the loss of friends, wealth, and such like things, but let them lose God's
favour, be in such a state there is but one step between them and hell,
they are never grieved nor moved at all. Therefore, seeing they do not
weep for themselves, let us weep for them. Can we weep when we see a
man hurt in his body, and ought we not much more for the danger of his
soul? Therefore, let us work this sorrow upon our hearts.

*Josiah's Reformation*, pp. 106-08 [82-84]

# Weeping and Rejoicing Mixed (1)

*In that day the Lord God of hosts called for weeping and mourning, ...*
*and joy and gladness.*—Isa. 22:12, 13

We are told to weep and mourn always and to rejoice and be thankful always, how can these agree? To this I answer that the state of a Christian in this life is a mixed state. The outward state and the inward disposition of the soul are mixed. As we have always cause of mourning and rejoicing both from that in us and from without us, therefore a Christian ought to rejoice always and in some measure to mourn always. For example, a Christian has cause of mourning within himself when he looks upon his sinful nature and the sins which he does daily commit, at the same time, there is cause of joy when he considers that God has pardoned his sins in Christ. It is what Paul did in Romans 7 when he looked upon himself and his own vileness, he cried out, 'O wretched man that I am, who shall deliver me from this body of death!' yet at the same time he rejoiced and blessed God; 'I thank God through Jesus Christ my Lord, who has freed me from the law of sin and of death.' We have always from within ourselves both cause of joy and mourning. So from without.

You see the rare mixture of joy and sorrow in a Christian, whereby he is made capable of this great privilege, as neither to be swallowed up in grief because his sorrow proceeds from a heart where there is cause of joy, nor to lose himself in excessive joy because he always sees in himself cause of sorrow. Now, as it is seen in other mixtures that there is not at all times an equal quantity or portion of each particular thing to be mingled, so is it in this mixture of joy and sorrow for ourselves. Sometimes joy must abound with the causes of it, and sometimes sorrow when its causes do super-abound. We will know when to joy most, and when to weep most by God's call and by the Spirit of discretion within us, which will guide us.

*Josiah's Reformation*, pp. 109-12 [85-86]

# Weeping and Rejoicing Mixed (2)

*For his anger is but for a moment, and his favour is for a lifetime. Weeping may tarry for the night, but joy comes with the morning.*—Psa. 30:5

How will we know when to cease and leave off mourning? The soul has many things to do and it cannot always mourn nor always rejoice. We have mourned enough, when we have overcome our hearts, and brought them to a temper of mourning, and have complained before God, spread the ill of the times before him, and entreated pity from him, having poured out ourselves in prayer. When we have this done, then we have discharged our duty in mourning and must then look upon causes of rejoicing and thanksgiving. Looking upon God's blessing upon us both in kingdom, state, and our own particular persons, we may be excited to thankfulness

We have cause of thankfulness when we consider that many churches in other places are invaded by enemies, oppressed with cruelty, and deprived of liberty, while yet we enjoy the liberty and free passage of the gospel, being freed from the destruction of war and pestilence, which devours so many that it makes the land to mourn. He continues to give us liberty to hear the word and gives us many blessings which others have not. We have cause to bless God for freeing us from that terrible judgment of all judgments—which makes both church and common-wealth to mourn—because he does not suffer us to fall into the hands of man, but takes us into his own hand to correct. It is God's infinite mercy that he does not humble us by our enemies. Therefore, let us mourn, seeing we have cause, for ourselves and the states of others; but yet let us be thankful, for if we would be more thankful for God's benefits, we should have them longer continued. For, as prayer begs blessings, so thanksgiving continues them. As the best way to obtain good things is prayer and mourning, so the best way to preserve them is thanksgiving and rejoicing. We have plainly seen that Christians should not always be dumpish and look sourly, instead they must as well rejoice and be thankful, as mourn and weep.

*Josiah's Reformation*, pp. 112-14 [87-88]

# God Hears Our Prayers—His Part

*But truly God has listened; he has attended to the voice of my prayer.*
—Psa. 66:19

How do we know God hears the groans of his children? David said, 'My groaning is not hidden from you' (Psa. 38:9). Also, 'He will fulfil the desire of them that fear him; he will also hear their cry, and will save them (Psa. 145:19). This must be so:

(1) Because he is gracious and merciful; he is a God who hears prayers.

(2) Because of the relations which in his love he has taken upon himself, to be a Father. So that when a man will, by the Spirit of adoption, call God 'Father,' he cannot choose but hear. Even as a child, when he speaks to his father, and calls him by this name, he cannot but hear.

(3) Because of his nature and love, which is above the love of an earthly father. Though a mother should forget, and not hear her child, yet the Lord will hear us. This is his promise, 'Call upon me in the day of trouble, and I will hear you, and you shall glorify me' (Psa. 50:15).

(4) Because God cannot ignore our prayers, because they are the motions of his own Spirit. Oh, but they are broken prayers. It is true; but the Spirit understands them and makes intercession for us, with sighs and groans that cannot be expressed; and none can understand them but the Spirit (Rom. 8:26).

(5) God cannot but hear our prayers because they are offered up in the name of a mediator. They are perfumed with the incense and sacrifice of his Son.

(6) Because our prayers are made according to his will. When we pray for ourselves, and for the church of God, it is according to God's will. So then, if we consider these respects, God cannot but hear our prayers.

*Josiah's Reformation*, pp. 121-23 [94-95]

# When It Seems God Doesn't Hear

*For the eyes of the Lord are on the righteous, and his ears are open to their prayer. But the face of the Lord is against those who do evil.—*
1 Pet. 3:12

Some will object, God does not hear me: I have prayed a long while, and yet he has not given me an answer.

(1) God does always hear, though he seems not to hear sometimes, to increase our importunity. Christ heard the woman of Canaan at first; yet, to increase her importunity, he gave her the repulse and denial, and with the same, inward strength to wrestle with him.

(2) God seems not to hear, because he delights in the music of his children's prayers. Oh, how he loves to hear the voice of his children! As a father to hear the language of his child, though it may be none of the best; so, it is sweet music in God's ears to hear the prayers of his children. He will have prayers to be cries. In deferring he increases our strength, as in Jacob's wrestling, that we might cry after him and wrestle with him.

(3) Sometimes, he will not hear us, because, it may be, there is some secret Achan in the camp, or some Jonah in the ship; some sin, I mean, in the heart unrepented of. For in this case we may come before God again and again, but he will not hear us. This is the reason why God hears not many Christians, because they have not made a thorough inquisition into their own state, found out their sins, and humbled themselves for it.

*Josiah's Reformation*, pp. 123-24 [95-96]

# The Privilege of Prayer

*Because he inclined his ear to me, therefore I will call on him as long as I live.*—Psa. 116:2

If this be so, that God does hear us, let us be plentiful in prayers, and lay up a great store of them in the bosom of God, for this is what will do us the most good. He hears everyone in due time. We do never lose a sigh, a tear, or anything that is good, which proceeds from his own Spirit, but he will answer abundantly in his own time. For he that gives a desire, and prepares our heart to pray, and gives us a Mediator by whom to offer them up, will doubtless accept of them in his own Son, and will answer them. The time will come when he will accept of nothing else, and we will have no other thing to offer up. What a comfort will it then be, that we have in former times, and can now call upon God! The day is coming when goods will do us no good, but prayer will. What a comfort then is it to a Christian, that he has a God to go to, that hears his prayers! Let all the world join together against a Christian, take away all things else and cast him into a dungeon, yet they cannot take away his God from him. What a happiness it is to pray! We can never be miserable so long as we have the Spirit of prayer. Though we were in a dungeon with Jeremiah, or in the whale's belly with Jonah, yea, though in hell, yet there we might have cause of comfort.

Seeing, then, God hears our prayers, let us think of this glorious privilege, that we have liberty to go to the throne of grace in all our wants. The whole world is not worth this one privilege.

*Josiah's Reformation*, pp. 124-26 [96-97]

# God Hears Our Prayers—Our Part

*And this is the confidence that we have toward him, that if we ask any-*
*thing according to his will he hears us.*—1 John 5:14

How should we pray so that God will hear?

(1) If we want God to hear us, then let us hear him. For 'he that turns away his ears from hearing the law, even his prayers shall be abominable' (Prov. 28:9). Is it not good reason for God not to hear us, when we will not hear him? 'Because I have called, and you have refused; when you are in misery, and will out of self-love cry to me to be delivered, then I will refuse to hear you' (Prov. 1:24, 25). Let all profane persons, that will not hear God, know a time will come, that though they cry and roar, yet he will not hear them.

(2) If we will have God hear our prayers, they must proceed from a broken heart. Prayers are the sacrifice of a broken spirit. David pleads with God, 'The sacrifices of God are a broken and contrite spirit' (Psa. 51:17). Bernard of Clairvaux said, 'I have led a life unbefitting me; but yet my comfort is, that a broken heart and a contrite spirit, Lord, you will not despise.' God will hear the prayers and tears of relenting hearts.

(3) To strengthen our prayers, we must add to them the wings of love, faith, hope, and earnestness. Oh! the prayers that have tears with them cannot go without a blessing.

(4) If we would have God to hear us, let us have a resolution and purpose of reformation. To this purpose David said, 'If I regard wicked-ness in my heart, God will not hear my prayer' (Psa. 66:18). If we come with a traitorous mind to God, with our sins in our arms, we must look for no acceptance from him. When a man comes to a king to put a petition to him, and comes with a dagger in his hand to stab him, will the king accept of this man's petition? Do we think that God will hear our prayers when we bring a dagger in our hand, to stab him with our sins? If we will not leave our sin, we shall never go away with a blessing.

*Josiah's Reformation*, pp. 126-28 [98-99]

# Death Is a Gathering (1)

*Behold, I will gather you to your fathers, and you shall be gathered to your grave in peace.*—2 Chron. 34:28a

It is a very sweet word, that death is nothing but a gathering. It presupposes that God's children are all scattered in this world amongst wicked men, in a forlorn place, as pilgrims in a strange land. It is a comfort to be gathered. From where will we be gathered? We shall be gathered from a wicked, confused world. To whom will we go? To our Father. At death, the changes for God's children are for the better. Death to them is but a gathering. This gathering shows the preciousness of the thing gathered; for God does not gather things of no value. Every Christian is dearly bought, with the blood of Christ. As men gather jewels before fire comes into their houses; or as farmers will be sure to gather their corn before they let the beasts come into the field; so says God, I will be sure to gather you. We are all by nature lost in Adam, and scattered from God, therefore we must be gathered again in Christ, for he is the head of all union that is good. Christ speaks to Jerusalem, 'How often would I have gathered you together, as a hen gathers her chickens under her wings, but you would not' (Matt. 23:37). Christ would have gathered them unto himself, by his word, but they refused. All the gathering of a Christian in this life is a gathering to Christ by faith, and to the communion of saints by love (1 Thess. 4:17). After this there comes by death a gathering to Christ in glory. For the soul goes forever to be with the Lord. Then comes a higher degree of gathering at the day of judgment, when there shall be a great meeting of all saints, and the soul and body shall be reunited together, to remain forever with the Lord. Let us then think of this, that whatsoever befalls us in the world, we will surely be gathered, for death is but a gathering. A gathering to a better place, to heaven, where we will be forever praising the Lord, never offending him, loving and pleasing one another.

*Josiah's Reformation*, pp. 137-40 [105-07]

# Death Is a Gathering (2)

*And these will go away into eternal punishment, but the righteous into eternal life.*—Matt. 25:46

This is a comfort to us in the departure of our believing friends, to render their souls up with comfort into the hands of God. We know they are not lost but sent before us. Why should we inappropriately grieve? They are gathered in quietness and rest to their fathers. This should also make us render our souls to God, as into the hands of a faithful Creator and Redeemer. From where do we go? From a sinful world and place of tears, to a place of happiness above expression. Why should we be afraid of death? It is but a gathering to our fathers. What a comfort it is to us in this world, that we will go to a place where all is good, where we will be perfectly renewed, made in the image of God, and will have nothing defaced?

The wicked shall be gathered together, but a woeful gathering it is. They shall be gathered like a bundle of tares, to be thrown into hell, there forever to burn. They are dross and chaff, never gathered to Christ by faith, nor to the body of the church by love, which the wind scatters here and will forever be scattered hereafter (Psa. 1:4). They are as Cain, vagabonds in regard of the life of grace here; and will be forever scattered from the life of glory hereafter. They shall be gathered to those whom they delighted in, and kept company with, while they were in this world. They loved to keep company with the wicked here, therefore they will be gathered to them in hell hereafter. This is sure, you will live in heaven or hell afterwards, with those whom you lived with here. If you live only delighted in evil company now, then you will be gathered to them in hell and destruction hereafter. It is a comfortable evidence to those that delight in good company, that they will be with them in heaven for ever. 'Hereby we know that we are translated from death to life, because we love the brethren' (1 John 3:14).

*Josiah's Reformation*, pp. 137-40 [107-08]

# The Righteous Preserve their Nation

*Righteousness exalts a nation, but sin is a reproach to any people.*—
Prov. 14:34

The lives of God's children do keep back judgment and evil from the place where they live, and their death is a forerunner of judgment. The reasons:

(1) Because gracious men do make the times and the places good where they live. It is a world of good that is done by their example and help.

(2) The gracious keep back ill because they bind God by their prayers. They force, as it were, a necessity upon God, that he must let the world alone. As the angel said to Lot in Sodom, 'I can do nothing until you are gone' (Gen. 19:22). They stand in the gap and keep God from pouring down the vials of his wrath. But when they are gone, there is nothing to hinder or stop the current of divine justice. When God's jewels are gathered to himself, then woe to the wicked world, for then God will break forth in wrath upon them. Woe to the old world when Noah goes into the ark, for then follows the flood. Woe to Sodom when Lot goes out of it, for then it is sure to be burned.

This should teach us to make much of such men as truly fear God. They carry the blessing of God with them wherever they go. As Laban's house was blessed for Jacob's sake (Gen. 30:27), and Potiphar's for Joseph's sake (Gen. 39:23), so the wicked are spared and fare the better for the saints who live among them. But what is the common course of wicked men? To hate such with a deadly hatred above all others because their lives and speeches do discover the wickedness of theirs, and because they tell them the truth, and reprove them. They labour to root out all the good men. Surely it will be a thousand times worse with them than it is.

This should also teach us to pray to God to bless those that are good. Is it not good for us to uphold those pillars whereby we stand?

Well may we lament the death of those that are good and bewail their loss.

*Josiah's Reformation*, pp. 155-59 [119-21]

# God's Righteous Judgment

*The Rock, his work is perfect, for all his ways are justice. A God of faithfulness and without iniquity, just and upright is he.*— Deut. 32:4

The evils which we suffer are from the meritorious evil of sin. It is sin that makes God to bring evil upon the creature. We must know that the evil of punishment is the good of justice, because it does good to them that are punished, either to cause them to return, or if they will not, to show the glory of his justice in condemning them.

In all our afflictions we are to go to heaven and make our peace with God, and not go to secondary causes. For all evil of punishment comes from him. Let us make our peace with God by repentance and new obedience; and then he will overrule all secondary causes so as to help us. Go not to the jailer, or to the executioner, but go to the judge. Let us make our peace in heaven first, and then there will be soon a command for our ease. Let us learn this lesson, and not fret against the instrument God uses to correct us. Job said, 'It is God that gives, and God that takes away' (Job 1:21). But it was the Chaldeans that took it away. Yes, but God gave them leave. Let us carry ourselves patiently in all troubles, submitting ourselves under the mighty hand of God, from whom we have all evil of punishment.

Here we have another mystery of divine providence. For it may be objected: will God bring evil upon his own church and people and that by idolaters? Where is divine justice now? Hold your peace. He knows what is best for us – better than we ourselves. We must not call God to our bar, for we shall all appear before his. God uses servants and slaves to correct his sons; worse men than his people to correct his people. Let us not call into question God's providence when he punishes his people. It is the will of God so to dispose, and the will of God is the height of justice. Let us make our peace with him, and not demand to know why he does what he does.

*Josiah's Reformation*, pp. 161-64 [123-25]

# The Importance of Knowing God Loves Me (1)

*No, in all these things we are more than conquerors through him who loved us. For I am sure that neither death nor life, nor angels nor rulers, nor things present nor things to come, nor powers, nor height nor depth, nor anything else in all creation, will be able to separate us from the love of God in Christ Jesus our Lord.*— Rom. 8:37-39

We cannot be thankful to God until we know that he loves us in Christ. Who can be thankful to someone he doesn't know? It is a duty to joy in the Lord as our portion, but we must be certain of his love first. What joy and cheerfulness can come without the love of God shining upon us and enlarging our hearts to joy? As the shining of the sun in the springtime enlarges the spirit of the birds to sing, so proportionately the understanding of the sweet love of God in Christ enlarges the spirit of a man and makes him full of joy and thanksgiving. He breaks forth into joy, so that his whole life is a matter of joy and thanksgiving.

In suffering any cross, any opposition, who will endure to lose his temporal goods, his life and liberty, to be restrained in anyway, who doesn't know that God loves them? What sets us to suffer anything for God? Knowing that he loves us. What makes a man willing to die and yield up his soul to God? Knowing that he yields his soul to a Father who loves him and will save his soul. Can a man be willing to leave his home here on earth, when he doesn't know whether he is going to a better one? Can a man commend his soul to one that he doesn't know to be his friend? No! Oh, to be like Simeon, 'Lord, let your servant depart in peace, for mine eyes have seen your salvation' (Luke 2:29). Does not all joy and comfort come from the love of God in Christ? We can neither have grace, nor joy, nor suffer anything with thankfulness, nor end our days with joy and comfort, until we are assured that we are in the covenant of grace and know that God loves us.

*The Matchless Love and Inbeing, Works, vol. 6, p. 388*

# The Importance of Knowing God Loves Me (2)

*In this the love of God was made manifest among us, that God sent his only Son into the world, so that we might live through him.—*
1 John 4:9

It is clear to anybody who knows anything in religion that we ought to labour to know God's love for us. Avoid any who teach that we ought to doubt God's love for us. Are we not prone enough to distrust the love of God, that we must be taught it? Is not Satan malicious enough, that we must arm his malice with the false doctrine that we ought to doubt God's love for us? Satan is the master of doubts. What does he aim at by the sins he tempts us to but to shake our assurance of God's love? This is to overthrow the intention of Christ's prayer in John 17. What does he pray for? That God would show them his love, 'that the world may know that you sent me and loved them even as you loved me' (John 17:23).

What is faith, which is the work of the gospel and grace of the new covenant, but the apprehension of the love of God in Christ? We who are Christians may attain to it because we have the Spirit of God, who 'searches the deep things of God' (1 Cor. 2:10). Our spirit knows what is in us, and God's Spirit knows what is in God, and we have the Spirit of God to show us the things of God, and all the benefits and fruits of his love. A Christian in the covenant of grace knows that God loves him. There is no truth in the world so illustrious, so gloriously and apparently true, as this. Would you have a better pledge of his love than Jesus Christ, the Son of his love, to be given for us, the dearest thing that God has? He would not have us doubt his love who has given such an invaluable thing as his own Son to assure us of it.

*The Matchless Love and Inbeing, Works,* vol. 6, pp. 388-89

# Abundance Is Not an Accurate Sign of God's Love

*But Abraham said, 'Child, remember that you in your lifetime received
your good things, and Lazarus in like manner bad things; but now he
is comforted here, and you are in anguish.'* — Luke 16:25

We must help unbelievers realize that they misread the abundant
common blessings of this life as a sign that God must love them. For
example, some think their case is good because God has given them
outward blessings, and accompanies those blessings with patience and
long-suffering. Because God has given them abilities, gifts, place, and
reputation, they begin to reason, 'Certainly God must love me.' But if
someone would examine their lives, they would find that there is no
evidence of God's special love to them at all. Such must be convinced,
that they dare not measure God's love by these outward things. That
which is common to everyone cannot be a sign of God's love. Abraham
gave Ishmael many temporary things but to Isaac he gave the inheritance
(Gen. 25:5, 6). Esau had his portion in the things of this life, but Jacob
went away with the blessing. God fills their bellies with abundance of
outward things, whose hearts he never fills with his love (Luke 16:25).
Further, God's patience in enduring me in such a state as I am in, is also
no argument. God is patient with them to lead them to repentance, yet
they do not make a right use of God's patience. God, after his patience,
is justified in his vengeance and judgment. What about an abundance of
good circumstances and giftedness? Didn't Judas have excellent circumstances? Judas was an apostle. As for giftedness, Ahithophel and Saul had
great gifts of leadership. All these are no evidence of the love of God.

If their consciences are prompted to see that they are laid open
to the wrath of God, then Satan soothes their consciences and makes
them reason, 'As for such a wretch as I, there is no hope; I might as well
continue on in my sinful course, and enjoy abundance in this world,
than to be without heaven and the comforts of this life, too.' Satan keeps
them in darkness, because they think there is no hope of another course,
and that it is impossible they could be made right with God.

*The Matchless Love and Inbeing, Works,* vol. 6, p. 390

# Run to God

*All that the Father gives me will come to me, and whoever comes to me
I will never cast out.*—John 6:37

As for unbelievers, we must know that God shuts out no one but those who shut themselves out, those who think the things of the gospel are too good to be true, and therefore will enjoy their pleasures, and continue in sin and pacify their consciences. But if their hearts are awakened, if they go to God and cast themselves upon his mercy—whosoever is weary, whosoever is thirsty, whosoever is heavy laden—God will show mercy if he comes in and accepts the proclamation of pardon (Ezek. 18:22). If he comes in and will not continue in his rebellion, but casts himself upon God's mercy, and resigns and yields himself to God and to Christ's government, to be ruled by him, he will find mercy. Let the devil keep no one in bondage, in the dungeon of ignorance and unbelief, for the end of the gospel is to bring in anyone who will come.

As for believers, never be discouraged from going to God, humbled as we ought to be. There is place for humiliation, but there is no place for discouragement or calling God's love into question. A son under anger is still a son; and though Satan presents to him an angry God because of his sin, yet he ought to lay hold of the rich mercies of God in Christ. What else should he do? Will he run away from God? No! A son runs to him. A child, when he has offended his father, does not run away from him; but, knowing that his father is merciful and loving, he goes and studies to appease his father, casts himself upon his favour and mercy, and endures his correction. However, Satan, when he has gotten us to sin, says, 'Now you might as well run on, for God follows you with judgments. You have offended God, and there is no hope for you.' Satan, by this means, keeps us without comfort, and God without service. Oh, instead come in and repent. Never call in question God's love for you.

*The Matchless Love and Inbeing, Works*, vol. 6, pp. 391-92

# Christian Unity

*That they may all be one, just as you, Father, are in me, and I in you,*
*that they also may be in us, so that the world may believe that you*
*have sent me.*—John 17:21

Christ is in all believers, as the vine is in the branches and as the head is in the members. Here is a notable bond of union between Christians; Christ by his Spirit is in them all. Christ is one in them all, not divided; his Spirit is the same spirit in them all. It would be an excellent thing if all the people of the world had the same mind of Christ, the same faith, the same aims, the same affection to good things, all as one person. How strong they would be against any opposition from Satan and how peaceful it would be between them if they all had one heart, one affection, one aim! This should be the experience of all Christians. It is the end of Christ's prayer in John 17, that we would be one in him, and in the Father, and with each other (John 17:21). We must take heed that we do not think this phrase to be a shallow phrase, as if it is in common life. We say of two friends, that there is one soul between the two of them, because they love each other; we make it nothing but a matter of affection. No; Jesus said, 'I in them' and 'I have made known to them your name and will continue to make it known' (John 17:26). It argues more than union in affection. It is a wonderful working and operative power when Christ is said to be in us. As the vine transfuses juice and life to the branch to make it fruitful, so must we understand the depth and comfort of the phrase, Christ in you.

Christ in you, also directs us how to look on other Christians as the temples and houses where Christ dwells. If Christ consents to dwell in a person, will that person not dwell in our love? We will all be together in heaven, and will we not love each other here? For Christ has two heavens; the heaven where he is, and the heart of a believing Christian. Oh, how truly, deeply, and affectionately we should value and love one another!

*The Matchless Love and Inbeing, Works,* vol. 6, pp. 402, 408

# Christ In Us (1)

*When Herod the king heard this, he was troubled, and all Jerusalem with him.*—Matt. 2:3

How can we know that Christ is in us?

(1) If Christ is in us by his Spirit, he will work great matters in us and there will be tumults in the soul. For when Christ comes to us, he finds all in rebellion and in opposition. As soon as Christ was born into the world, Herod was mightily troubled and all Jerusalem with him (Matt. 2:3). Herod thought one was born that would depose him, and therefore he was jealous, much troubled, and laboured to kill him if he could. So it is when Christ is born in the soul, there are tumults. Those lusts that held sway before, those desires, down they go, they plead allowance, and are loath to yield. Natural desires, that have been from before, are loath to yield to Christ, a newcomer. He is as a new conqueror that comes with new laws, fundamentally new. He overturns all the laws of lust and of the flesh. He comes in with strength. In conversion, where Christ is born, there is first a strife, the soul does not quickly yield to him. There are some now in the bosom of the church, that had no violent conversion from a wicked state to a good. But from a less degree to a greater, they grow more and more. They were brought up in the Spirit of Christ from the beginning. They are not much troubled with such inward oppositions.

(2) Where Christ is, he will drive out all that is contrary. As when he entered into the temple, he drove out the money changers, and whipped out the corrupt persons there (Matt. 21:12), so, as soon as he comes into the soul by his Spirit, out go those lusts, those desires that were there before, worldliness, profaneness, fury, and rage, those things the soul was consumed with before, that possessed the habitation that God should dwell in. When Christ comes in, he scourges out all. Where these therefore are in any force, there certainly Christ is not.

*The Matchless Love and Inbeing, Works,* vol. 6, p. 403

# Christ In Us (2)

*After this he went out and saw a tax collector named Levi, sitting at the tax booth. And he said to him, 'Follow me.'*—Luke 5:27

(3) Where Christ is, he rules; for he takes the keys of the house and governs all. Where he is in the heart and affections—there he rules; and where he takes not his lodging in the affections and in the heart, in the joy, desire, and delight, he is not at all. To have him in the brain to talk, and in the tongue to discourse, and yet to keep the heart filled with worldly lusts, shows that Christ does not reside there. By heart, I mean, especially, the will and the affections. He draws the will to cleave to him, to choose him for the best good.

(4) Where Christ is in the heart by faith, and he takes up the affections, there is a low esteem of all the excellencies of this world. Moses did but see from afar the excellency that came by Christ, and he accounted all the pleasures of this world to be nothing (Heb. 11:27). Paul accounted all but dung and dross (Phil. 3:8); having in his heart and soul an admiration of the all-sufficiency and excellency of Christ. As soon as Christ came into his house, Zacchaeus grew generous, 'Half my goods I give to the poor' (Luke 19:8). Before he loved extortion and low courses, but now down they go, he will be an oppressor no longer. However busy the disciples were before, once Christ opened their eyes to see the excellency that was in him, away goes all their previous undertakings, that they might follow Christ. It is impossible for the heart that entertains our blessed Saviour to have an over-abundant admiration for any earthly excellency. For it is the nature of the soul, upon the discovery of better things, to let the estimation of other things of less value fall away. Children, when they come to be adults, outgrow their childish toys. So it is with a man who is converted. When Christ enters and opens the understanding and enlarges the heart to see and admire better things, immediately that heart begins to care nothing for this world in comparison.

*The Matchless Love and Inbeing, Works, vol. 6, pp. 403-04*

# Christ In Us (3)

*And we all, with unveiled face, beholding the glory of the Lord, are being transformed into the same image from one degree of glory to another. For this comes from the Lord who is the Spirit.*—2 Cor. 3:18

(5) If Christ is in us, he transforms us to his own likeness; where he rules by the Spirit, he changes his people (2 Cor. 3:18). Christ renews and changes his spouse, the church. He is such a head as quickens his members; such a vine as puts life in the branches. You may know by this altering, changing, transforming power, whether he is in you or not. He alters and changes us to his own likeness. We should have the same disposition, the same mind, and the same will as him; for he will alter us to himself, that he may take the more delight in us. We will judge of things as he judges them. There will be a delight to do our Father's will, as it was his meat and drink to do his Father's will (John 4:34). We will have a spirit of obedience, as Christ had, to look to our Father's glory and to his commands in all things. We will have compassion and melting hearts to the misery of others, as he had deep yearning in seeing sheep without a shepherd. We will have humble and meek hearts, as he had. 'Come, learn of me, for I am humble and meek' (Matt. 11:29). For where he dwells and takes up his throne, he alters and changes the disposition in all things to be like himself. For when he comes to the soul, he takes up the eyes, the ears, the understanding, and the affections. Even as we shut up the doors and windows against all that is threatening to us, so the Spirit of Christ, where he is, shuts the door of the senses both to Satan and all his suggestions, and whatever else might hurt us.

*The Matchless Love and Inbeing, Works, vol. 6, pp. 404-05*

# Christ In Us (4)

*Therefore put away all filthiness and rampant wickedness and receive with meekness the implanted word, which is able to save your souls.—*
James 1:21

(6) Where he enters, he possesses the whole inward and outward man. He rules the eyes, the ears, the hands; he renews all, so that our delights are made clean unlike they were before. There is such a power in his truth, that, like a branch engrafted, it changes us into itself. Where Christ dwells, he has as much power as his word. His word is like leaven, which alters the whole lump to be like itself. For the word engrafted makes the soul that believes it heavenly like itself (James 1:21). How is this? Because Christ comes with his word, and leavens, alters, changes, and turns the soul.

(7) You may know who dwells within a house by those who come in and out of it. Would you know who dwells in the soul? See what comes from within: filthy thoughts, blasphemous words, oaths, rotten discourse, eyes full of adultery, ears open to receive that which may taint the soul. Does Christ dwell there? No! Where nothing but filth comes out, the devil dwells there. These two are direct opposites; there is no third; either Christ or the devil dwells in us. When nothing comes out of a man but scorning of goodness, and that which is rotten and offensive—the devil is there. Is Christ in the heart that lets open all the senses to all that is evil, that drinks in corruption, hears all kinds of things that may cherish corruption, and sees all that may puff up the flesh? Is Christ fed with filthy discourse and seen with filthy spectacles? Oh no! Surely the spirit that is fed by these things is the devil. From the heart where Christ is there often proceeds prayer, sighs, and groans to God, and fruitful discourses to others; and all the senses and passages of the body are open to good things. He has desires to see that which is good, which may edify. He desires to speak, and to have others to speak, that which may feed the soul.

*The Matchless Love and Inbeing, Works*, vol. 6, p. 405

# Christ In Us (5)

*Examine yourselves to see whether you are in the faith; test yourselves.
Can't you see for yourselves that Jesus Christ is in you—unless you
actually fail the test?*—2 Cor. 13:5

(8) Where the Spirit is, there is often prayer, as Christ often prayed.
There is also a perpetual endeavour of doing good, as his Spirit in him
stirred him to go from place to place to do good. Where his Spirit is,
there is holiness. If we consider what a sweet guest Christ is, where he
is there is all beauty, work, comfort, strength, and all. Where he is, he is
forever. He never forsakes his lodging; he never forsakes his house and
temple. He had two temples built with stone, one by Solomon and the
other after the captivity. Both lie now in the rubbish and are demolished.
But his spiritual temples he never leaves; for whose souls he now dwells
in, he will take them by the Spirit and carry them to heaven, to be where
he is.

I beseech you, therefore, test yourself. Examine what spirit is in you.
If we find the Spirit of Christ to be in us, what a comfortable state that
is! He is the best guest that ever we could entertain in this world, for he
does to the soul what the soul does to the body. What does the soul to
the body? From where has the body the beauty that it has? From where
does all that is excellent, good, and useful come? From the soul—the
reasonable, understanding soul. For as soon as the soul is out of the body,
the body is an ugly, deformed thing, a dead creature. Now, as the soul is
to the body, so is Christ to the soul. For he gives beauty and loveliness
to it. He transforms it to his own likeness and image, that it may be the
object of God's love; that he may love us, not only because we are in his
Son, but because his Son's image is in us. We have not only beauty from
Christ dwelling in us, but where he is, he works and stirs us to all holy
and heavenly duties. If Christ be in us, we may comfort ourselves.

*The Matchless Love and Inbeing, Works,* vol. 6, p. 406

# Christ the Servant: the Mediator

*Behold, my servant whom I have chosen, my beloved with whom my soul is well pleased. I will put my Spirit upon him.*—Matt. 12:18

God calls Christ here his servant. Christ was God's servant in the greatest piece of service that ever was, a choice servant who did and suffered all by commission from the Father. In this we may see the sweet love of God to us, in that he counts the work of our salvation by Christ his greatest service, and in that he put his only beloved Son to that service. He might well prefix it with 'Behold' to raise up our thoughts to the highest pitch of attention and admiration. In time of temptation, apprehensive consciences look so much to the present trouble that they need to be roused up to behold him in whom they may find rest. In temptations it is safest to behold nothing but Christ the true brazen serpent, 'the true Lamb of God that takes away the sin of the world' (John 1:29). This saving object has a special influence of comfort to the soul, especially if we look not only on Christ, but upon the Father's authority and his love for us in Christ. For in all that Christ did and suffered as Mediator, we must see God in him reconciling the world unto himself (2 Cor. 5:19). What a support to our faith is this, that God the Father, the party offended by our sins, is so well pleased with the work of redemption! And what a comfort is this, that seeing God's love rests on Christ, as well pleased in him, we may gather that he is as well pleased with us, if we be in Christ! Let us, therefore, embrace Christ, and in him God's love, and build our faith safely on such a Saviour that is furnished with so high a commission. See here, for our comfort, a sweet agreement of all three persons: The Father gives a commission to Christ; the Spirit furnishes and sanctifies it, and Christ himself executes the office of a Mediator. Our redemption is founded upon the joint agreement of all three persons of the Trinity.

*The Bruised Reed*, pp. 1-2

# The Bruised Reed and the Smoking Flax (1)

*Behold my servant, whom I uphold, my chosen, in whom my soul delights; I have put my Spirit upon him; he will bring forth justice to the nations. He will not cry aloud or lift up his voice or make it heard in the street; a bruised reed he will not break, and a faintly burning wick he will not quench; he will faithfully bring forth justice.*—Isa. 42:1-3

The bruised reed is a man who for the most part is in some misery, as those were who came to Christ for help, and by misery he is brought to see sin as the cause of it. He is sensible of sin and misery and seeing no help in himself, is carried with restless desire to get supply from another, with some hope, which raises him out of himself to Christ. This spark of hope being opposed by doubts and fears rising from corruption makes him as smoking flax; so that both these together, a bruised reed and smoking flax, make up the state of a poor distressed man.

This bruising is required before conversion so that the Spirit may make way for himself into the heart by levelling all proud, high thoughts, and that we may understand ourselves to be what indeed we are by nature. We love to wander from ourselves and to be strangers at home, until God bruises us by one cross or other, and then we 'begin to think' and come home to ourselves with the prodigal (Luke 15:17). It is a very hard thing to bring a dull and an evasive heart to cry with feeling for mercy. This bruising also makes us set a high price upon Christ. Then the gospel becomes the gospel; then the fig leaves of morality will do us no good. This dealing of God establishes us more in his ways, having had knocks and bruises in our own ways. Often the cause of relapses and apostasy is because men never smarted for sin at the first; they were not long enough under the lash of the law. This work of the Spirit in bringing down high thoughts (2 Cor. 10:5) is necessary before conversion. After conversion we need bruising so that reeds may know themselves to be reeds, and not oaks. Even reeds need bruising, by reason of the remainder of pride in our nature, and to let us see that we live by mercy.

*The Bruised Reed*, pp. 3-5

# The Bruised Reed and the Smoking Flax (2)

*This was to fulfil what was spoken by the prophet Isaiah: 'Behold, my servant whom I have chosen, my beloved with whom my soul is well pleased. I will put my Spirit upon him, and he will proclaim justice to the Gentiles. He will not quarrel or cry aloud, nor will anyone hear his voice in the streets; a bruised reed he will not break, and a smouldering wick he will not quench, until he brings justice to victory; and in his name the Gentiles will hope.'*—Matt. 12:17-20

Such bruising may help weaker Christians not to be too much discouraged, when they see stronger ones shaken and bruised. Peter was bruised when he wept bitterly (Matt. 26:75). This reed, until he met with this bruise, had more wind in him than substance when he said, 'Though all forsake you, I will not' (Matt. 26:33). The people of God cannot be without these examples. The heroic deeds of those great worthies do not comfort the church so much as their falls and bruises do. David was bruised until he came to a free confession, without guile of spirit (Psa. 32:3-5); his sorrows did rise in his feeling unto the extreme pain of breaking his bones (Psa. 51:8). Hezekiah complains that God had 'broken his bones' as a lion (Isa. 38:13). The chosen vessel Paul needed the messenger of Satan to buffet him lest he should be lifted up above measure (2 Cor. 12:7). We learn that we must not pass too harsh a judgment upon ourselves or others when God buffets us with bruising upon bruising. There must be a conformity to our head, Christ, who 'was bruised for us' (Isa. 53:5) that we may know how much we are bound to him. Ungodly spirits, ignorant of God's ways in bringing his children to heaven, censure broken-hearted Christians as miserable persons. Whereas God is doing a gracious, good work with them. It is no easy matter to bring a man from nature to grace, and from grace to glory, so unyielding and intractable are our hearts.

*The Bruised Reed*, pp. 5-6

# The Bruised Reed and the Smoking Flax (3)

*A bruised reed he will not break, and a faintly burning wick he will not quench; he will faithfully bring forth justice.*—Isa. 42:3

In pursuing his calling, Christ will not break the bruised reed, nor quench the smoking flax, in which more is meant than spoken, for he will not only not break nor quench, but he will cherish those with whom he so deals. Physicians, though they put their patients to much pain, will not destroy nature, but raise it up by degrees. A mother who has a sick and self-willed child will not therefore cast it away. Consider the comfortable relationships he has taken upon himself of husband, shepherd, and brother, which he will discharge to the utmost. Will others by his grace fulfil what he calls them to, and not he who, out of his love, has taken upon himself these relationships? Consider his very name Jesus, a Saviour, given him by God himself. Consider his office answerable to his name, which is that he should 'bind up the broken hearted' (Isa. 61:1).

As a prophet, he came with blessing in his mouth, 'Blessed are the poor in spirit' (Matt. 5:3), and invited those to come to him whose hearts suggested most exceptions against themselves, "Come unto me, all ye that labour and are heavy laden' (Matt. 11:28). How did his heart yearn when he saw the people 'as sheep having no shepherd' (Matt. 9:36)! He never turned any back again that came to him, though some went away of themselves. He shed tears for those that shed his blood, and now he makes intercession in heaven for weak Christians. He is a meek king; he will admit mourners into his presence. As he has beams of majesty, so he has a heart of mercy and compassion. Why was he tempted, but that he might 'succour them that are tempted' (Heb. 2:18)? What mercy may we not expect from so gracious a Mediator (1 Tim. 2:5) who took our nature upon him that he might be gracious? He is a physician good at all diseases, especially at the binding up of a broken heart. He died that he might heal our souls with a bandage of his own blood, and by that death save us.

*The Bruised Reed*, pp. 7-8 [7-9]

# The Bruised Reed and the Smoking Flax (4)

*A bruised reed he will not break, and a smouldering wick he will not quench.*—Matt. 12:20

He will not show his strength against those who prostrate themselves before him.

(1) What should we learn from this, but to 'come boldly to the throne of grace' (Heb. 4:16)? Will our sins discourage us when he appears there only for sinners? Be of good comfort, he calls you. Conceal not your wounds, open all before him and take not Satan's counsel. Go to Christ, although trembling, as the poor woman who said, 'If I may but touch his garment' (Matt. 9:21). Never fear to go to God, since we have such a Mediator with him, who is not only our friend but our brother and husband. Well might the angel proclaim from heaven, 'Behold, I bring you good tidings of great joy' (Luke 2:10). His presence makes any condition comfortable. 'Be not afraid,' he said to his disciples, when they were afraid, as if they had seen a ghost, 'It is I' (Matt. 14:27), as if there were no cause of fear where he was present.

(2) Let this support us when we feel ourselves bruised. Christ's way is first to wound, then to heal. No sound, whole soul will ever enter into heaven. Think when in temptation, Christ was tempted for me; according to my trials will be my graces and comforts. If Christ be so merciful as not to break me, I will not break myself by despair, nor yield myself over to the roaring lion, Satan, to break me in pieces.

(3) See the contrary disposition of Christ on the one hand and Satan and his instruments on the other. Satan sets upon us when we are weakest, as Simeon and Levi upon the Shechemites, 'when they were sore' (Gen. 34:25). But Christ will make up in us all the breaches which sin and Satan have made. He 'binds up the broken hearted' (Isa. 61:1). As a mother is tenderest to the most diseased and weakest child, so does Christ most mercifully incline to the weakest. The consciousness of the church's weakness makes her willing to lean on her beloved, and to hide herself under his wing.

*The Bruised Reed*, pp. 9-10

# God Knows Our Frame

*I will seek the lost, and I will bring back the strayed, and I will bind up
the injured, and I will strengthen the weak.*—Ezek. 34:16

The Lord knows our frame; he remembers that we are but dust (Psa.
103:14), that our strength is not the strength of steel. This is a branch of
his faithfulness to us as his creatures, thus he is called 'a faithful Creator'
(1 Pet. 4:19). 'God is faithful, who will not suffer you to be tempted above
that you are able' (1 Cor. 10:13). There were certain commandments
which the Jews called the hedges of the law. So as to fence men off from
cruelty, God commanded that they should not 'boil a kid in his mother's
milk' (Exod. 23:19), nor 'muzzle the mouth of the ox' (Deut. 25:4). Does
God take care of beasts, and not his more noble creatures?

Our encouragement to a thorough work of bruising, and patience
under God's bruising of us, let all know that none are fitter for comfort
than those who think themselves furthest off. Men, for the most part,
are not lost enough in their own feeling for a Saviour. A holy despair in
us is the ground of true hope. In the God of the fatherless find mercy
(Hos. 14:3); the God who dwells in the highest heaven dwells likewise
in the lowest soul (Isa. 57:15). Christ's sheep are weak sheep and lacking
in something or other; he therefore applies himself to the necessities of
every sheep. He seeks that which was lost and binds up that which was
broken, and strengthens the weak (Ezek. 34:16). His tenderest care is over
the weakest. The lambs he carries in his bosom (Isa. 40:11). He says to
Peter, 'Feed my lambs' (John 21:15). He was most familiar and open to
troubled souls. How careful he was that Peter and the rest of the apostles
should not be too much dejected after his resurrection! 'Go your way,
tell his disciples and Peter' (Mark 16:7). Christ knew that guilt of their
unkindness in leaving of him had dejected their spirits. How gently he
endured the unbelief of Thomas and stooped so far unto his weakness, as
to suffer him to thrust his hand into his side.

*The Bruised Reed*, pp. 11-15 [14-15]

# Little at First (1)

*Like newborn infants, long for the pure spiritual milk, that by it you may grow up into salvation.*—1 Pet. 2:2

There are several ages in Christians, some babes, some young men. Faith may be as 'a grain of mustard seed' (Matt. 17:20). Nothing so little as grace at first, and nothing more glorious afterward. Things of greatest perfection are longest in coming to their growth. Man, the most perfect creature, comes to perfection little by little; worthless things, as mushrooms and the like, like Jonah's gourd, soon spring up, and soon vanish. A new creature in Christ is the most excellent creature in all the world; therefore, it grows up by degrees.

We see in nature that a mighty oak rises from an acorn. It is with a Christian as it was with Christ, who sprang out of the dead stock of Jesse, out of David's family (Isa. 11:1; 53:2), when it was at the lowest, but he grew up higher than the heavens. It is not with the trees of righteousness as it was with the trees of paradise, which were created all perfect at the first. The seeds of all the creatures in the present frame of the world were hid in the chaos, in that confused mass at the first, out of which God commanded all creatures to arise. In the small seeds of plants lie hidden both bulk and branches, bud and fruit. In a few principles lie hidden all comfortable conclusions of holy truth. All these glorious fireworks of zeal and holiness in the saints had their beginning from a few sparks.

Let us not therefore be discouraged at the small beginnings of grace but look on ourselves as elected to be 'holy and without blame' (Eph. 1:4). Let us look on our imperfect beginning only to enforce further striving to perfection, and to keep us in a low opinion of ourselves. Christ values us by what we will be, and by what we are elected to. We call a little plant a tree because it is growing up to be so. 'Who has despised the day of small things?' (Zech. 4:10). Christ would not have us despise little things.

*The Bruised Reed*, pp. 16-17 [17-18]

# Little at First (2)

*But grow in the grace and knowledge of our Lord and Saviour Jesus Christ. To him be the glory both now and to the day of eternity. Amen.*—2 Pet. 3:18

Christ would not have us despise little things. The glorious angels disdain not attendance on little ones. It is Christ that raises the worth of little and wretched places and persons. Bethlehem was the least (Mic. 5:2; Matt. 2:6), and yet not the least; the least in itself, not the least in respect that Christ was born there. The second temple (Hag. 2:9) came short of the outward magnificence of the former; yet it was more glorious than the first because Christ came into it. A pearl, though little, yet is of much esteem. Nothing in the world is of so good use as the least grain of grace.

But grace is not only little but mingled with corruption. So, we see that grace does not do away with corruption all at once, but some is left for believers to fight with. The purest actions of the purest men need Christ to perfume them; and this is his office. The reason for this mixture is that we carry about us a double principle: grace and nature. The end of it is to preserve us from those two dangerous rocks which our natures are prone to dash upon—security and pride—and to force us to pitch our rest on justification, not sanctification, which, besides imperfection, has some stains. Our spiritual fire is like our ordinary fire here below, that is, mixed. Fire is most pure in its own element above; so will all our graces be when we are where we would be, in heaven, which is our proper element. From this mixture arises the fact that the people of God have so different judgments of themselves, looking sometimes at the work of grace, sometimes at the remainder of corruption, and when they look upon that, then they think they have no grace. Though they love Christ in his ordinances and his children, yet they dare not claim so near acquaintance as to be his. Even as a candle sometimes shows its light, and sometimes the show of light is lost; so sometimes they are well persuaded of themselves, sometimes at a loss.

*The Bruised Reed*, pp. 17-19 [18-21]

# Sometimes Tender, Sometimes Tough (1)

*Have mercy on those who doubt.*—Jude 22

See the opposite dispositions in the holy nature of Christ and the impure nature of man. Man, for a little smoke will quench the light. Christ ever cherishes even the least beginnings. How he bore with the many imperfections of his poor disciples! If he did sharply check them, it was in love, that they might shine the brighter. Can we have a better pattern to follow than this from him by whom we hope to be saved? 'We, then, that are strong ought to bear the infirmities of the weak' (Rom. 15:1). 'I am made all things to all men, that I might by all means save some' (1 Cor. 9:22). Oh, that this gaining and winning disposition were more in many! Many, so far as in us lies, are lost for want of encouragement. How careful was our blessed Saviour of little ones, that they might not be offended! How careful not to put new wine into old vessels (Matt. 9:17), not to alienate new beginners with the austerities of religion (as some do indiscreetly). It is not the best way, to assail young beginners with minor matters, but to show them a more excellent way and train them in fundamental points. It is not amiss to conceal their defects, to excuse some failings, to commend their performances, to encourage their progress, to remove all difficulties out of their way, to help them in every way to bear the yoke of religion with greater ease, to bring them to love God and his service, lest they acquire a distaste for it before they truly know it. For the most part we see that Christ plants in young beginners a love which we call their 'first love' (Rev. 2:4), to carry them through their profession with more delight, and does not expose them to crosses before they have gathered strength. Mercy to others should move us to deny ourselves in our liberties oftentimes, in case of offending weak ones. It would be a good contest among Christians, one to labour to give no offence, and the other to labour to take none. The best men are severe to themselves, tender toward others.

*The Bruised Reed*, pp. 21-23 [24-26]

# Sometimes Tender, Sometimes Tough (2)

*Save others by snatching them out of the fire.*—Jude 23a

On the other hand, people should not tire and wear out the patience of others; nor should the weaker so far demand moderation from others as to rely upon their indulgence and so to rest in their own infirmities, with danger to their own souls and scandal to the church.

When blindness and boldness, ignorance and arrogance, weakness and wilfulness, meet together in men, it renders them odious to God, burdensome in society, disturbers of better purposes, intractable and incapable of better direction, and miserable in the outcome. Christ shows his gracious power by patiently letting men come to understand themselves in order to breed humility. He does it as a preservative against discouragements from weakness and to bring men closer to grace. Christ refuses none for weakness of parts, that none should be discouraged, but accepts none for greatness, that none should be lifted up with that which is of so little reckoning with God. The scope of true love is to make the person better, which concealment can hinder. With some a spirit of meekness prevails most, but with some a rod. Some must be 'pulled out of the fire' (Jude 23) with violence, and they will bless God for it in the day of his visitation. We see that our Saviour multiplies woe upon woe when he has to deal with hard-hearted hypocrites (Matt. 23:13), for hypocrites need stronger conviction than gross sinners, because their will is bad, and therefore usually their conversion is violent. A hard knot must have an answerable wedge. A sharp reproof sometimes is a precious pearl and a sweet balm. The wounds of secure sinners will not be healed with sweet words. The Holy Spirit came as well in fiery tongues as in the likeness of a dove, and the same Holy Spirit offers a spirit of prudence and discretion which is the salt to season all our words and actions. Such wisdom will teach us 'to speak a word in season' (Isa. 50:4), both to the weary, and likewise to the secure soul.

*The Bruised Reed*, pp. 23-24 [26-28]

## Avoiding Unnecessary Rules

*They tie up heavy burdens, hard to bear, and lay them on people's shoulders, but they themselves are not willing to move them with their finger.*—Matt. 23:4

We need to take heed therefore how we deal with young believers. Let us be careful not to pitch matters too high, making things necessary evidences of grace which do not equal the experience of many a good Christian, and laying salvation and damnation upon things that are not fit to bear so great a weight. In this way men are needlessly cast down and may not soon be raised again by themselves or others. The ambassadors of so gentle a Saviour should not be overbearing, setting up themselves in the hearts of people where Christ alone should sit as in his own temple. Paul was so careful in the cases of conscience not to lay a snare upon a weak conscience.

Christ chose those to preach mercy who had felt the most mercy, as Peter and Paul, that they might be examples of what they taught. Paul became all things to all men (1 Cor. 9:22), stooping to them for their good. Christ came down from heaven and emptied himself of majesty in tender love to souls. Will we not come down from our high conceits to do any poor soul good? Will man be proud after God has been humble?

*The Bruised Reed*, pp. 26-27 [29-30]

# The Weaker Brother

*So by your knowledge this weak person is destroyed, the brother for whom Christ died.*—1 Cor. 8:11

In our common relationships with other believers: we are debtors to the weak in many things.

(1) Let us be watchful in the use of our liberty, and labour to be inoffensive in our behaviour. There is a commanding force in an example. Looseness of life is cruelty to us and to the souls of others.

(2) Let men take heed of taking up Satan's office, in misrepresenting the good actions of others, as he did in Job's case; 'Does Job fear God for naught?' (Job 1:9). The devil gets more by such discouragements and reproaches that are cast upon believers than by fire and faggot. These, as unseasonable frosts, nip all gracious inclinations in the bud. A Christian is a hallowed and a sacred thing, Christ's temple; and he that destroys his temple, him will Christ destroy (1 Cor. 3:17).

(3) Take heed, there is among Christians a bold censuring of others, while not considering their situations. Some will unchurch and unbrother in a passion. But ill humours do not alter true relations. We should not smite one another by hasty censures, especially in things of a secondary nature. Some things are as the mind of him that does them or does them not; for both may be unto the Lord. Christ, for the good motivations he sees in us, overlooks any ill in them, so far as not to lay it to our charge. Men must not be too curious in prying into the weaknesses of others. We should labour rather to see what they have that is for eternity, than the weakness which the Spirit of God will in time consume. Some think it is strength to not bear with the faults of the weaker Christian, but the truth is that the strongest are those readiest to bear with the infirmities of the weak. Where most holiness is, there is most moderation. We see in Christ a marvellous temper of absolute holiness, with great moderation. What would have become of our salvation, if he had stood his ground, and not stooped so low to us?

*The Bruised Reed*, pp. 31-33 [35-36]

## Extend Grace to One Another

*Brothers, if anyone is caught in any transgression, you who are spiritual should restore him in a spirit of gentleness. Keep watch on yourself, lest you too be tempted. Bear one another's burdens, and so fulfil the law of Christ.*—Gal. 6:1, 2

The Holy Spirit is content to dwell in smoky, offensive souls (Isa. 42:1-3). Oh, that that Spirit would breathe into our spirits the same merciful disposition! We endure the bitterness of wormwood, and other distasteful plants and herbs, only because we have some experience of some wholesome quality in them; and why should we reject men of useful parts and graces, only for some harshness of disposition, which, as it is offensive to us, so it grieves themselves?

Grace, while we live here, is in souls which, because they are imperfectly renewed, dwell in bodies subjected to several impulses, and these will incline the soul sometimes to excess in one passion, sometimes in excess in another. Martin Bucer was a deep and moderate pastor. After long experience he resolved to refuse none in whom he saw *aliquid Christi*, something of Christ. The best Christians in this state of imperfection are like gold that is a little too light, which needs some grains of allowance to make it pass. You must grant the best their allowance. We must supply out of our love and mercy that which we see wanting in them. The church of Christ is a common hospital, wherein all are in the same measure sick of some spiritual disease or other, so all have occasion to exercise the spirit of wisdom and meekness.

So that we may do this better, let us put on the Spirit of Christ. And we should think what affection Christ would carry. That great physician, as he had a quick eye and a healing tongue, so had he a gentle hand, and a tender heart.

*The Bruised Reed*, pp. 33-34 [36-37]

# The Covenant of Grace

*Behold my servant, whom I uphold, my chosen, in whom my soul delights; I have put my Spirit upon him; he will bring forth justice to the nations. He will not cry aloud or lift up his voice or make it heard in the street; a bruised reed he will not break, and a faintly burning wick he will not quench; he will faithfully bring forth justice.—Isa. 42:1-3*

We must acknowledge that in the covenant of grace God requires the truth of grace, not any certain measure. A spark of fire is fire, as well as the whole element. Therefore, we must look to grace in the spark as well as in the flame. All have not the same strength, though they have the same precious faith (2 Pet. 1:1), whereby they lay hold of, and put on, the perfect righteousness of Christ. A weak hand may receive a rich jewel. A few grapes will show that the plant is a vine, and not a thorn. It is one thing to be deficient in grace, and another thing to lack grace altogether. God knows we have nothing in ourselves, therefore, in the covenant of grace he requires no more than he gives, but gives what he requires, and accepts what he gives: 'If she be not able to bring a lamb, then she shall bring two turtle doves' (Lev. 12:8). What is the gospel itself but a merciful moderation, in which Christ's obedience is counted as ours, and our sins laid upon him, wherein God, from being a judge, becomes our Father, pardoning our sins and accepting our obedience, though feeble and blemished? We are now brought to heaven under the covenant of grace by a new love and mercy.

It will prove a special help to know distinctly the difference between the covenant of works and the covenant of grace, between Moses and Christ. Moses, without any mercy, breaks all reeds, and quenches all smoking flax. For the law requires personal, perpetual, and perfect obedience from the heart, and that under a most terrible curse, but gives no strength. It is a severe taskmaster, like Pharaoh's, requiring the whole number of bricks and yet giving no straw. Christ comes with blessing after blessing, even upon those whom Moses cursed, and with healing balm for the wounds which Moses had made.

*The Bruised Reed*, pp. 36-37 [40-41]

# The Light of God Compared to Fire (1)

*Your word is a lamp to my feet and a light to my path.*— Psa. 119:105

The presence of the heavenly fire:

(1) If there be any holy fire in us, it is kindled from heaven by the Father of lights, who 'commanded the light to shine out of darkness' (2 Cor. 4:6). The light in us and the light in the word spring the one from the other and both from the one Holy Spirit. In every converted man, God puts a light into the eye of his soul proportionable to the light of truths revealed to him.

(2) The least divine light has heat with it in some measure. Light in the understanding produces heat of love in the affections. In the measure that the sanctified understanding sees a thing to be true or good, in that measure the will embraces it. A little spiritual light is of strength enough to answer strong objections of flesh and blood, and to see beyond all earthly allurements and opposing hindrances, presenting them as far inferior to those heavenly objects it beholds. All light that is not spiritual, because it lacks the strength of sanctifying grace, yields to every little temptation. This is the reason why Christians that have light that is little for quantity, but heavenly for quality, persevere, when men of larger intellects sink.

(3) Where this heavenly light is kindled, it directs in the right way. For it is given for that use, to show us the best way, and to guide us in our passages of life. We must, therefore, walk by his light, not the blaze of our own fire. God must light our candle (Psa. 18:28) or else we will abide in darkness. Those sparks that are not kindled from heaven are not strong enough to keep us from lying in sorrow, though they make a greater blaze than the light from above, as madmen do greater things than sober men, but by a false strength. 'The light of the wicked shall be put out' (Job 18:5). The light which some men have is like lightning which, after a sudden flash, leaves them more in darkness. A little holy light will enable us to keep Christ's word, and not deny his name.

*The Bruised Reed*, pp. 38-40 [42-44]

# The Light of God Compared to Fire (2)

*For God, who said, 'Let light shine out of darkness,' has shone in our hearts to give the light of the knowledge of the glory of God in the face of Jesus Christ.*—2 Cor. 4:6

(4) Where this fire is, it will show a difference between such things as gold and dross. It will sever between flesh and spirit, and show that this is of nature, this of grace. All is not ill in a bad action, or good in a good action. There is gold in ore, which God and his Spirit in us can distinguish. This light makes us humble upon clearer sight of God's purity and our own uncleanness and makes us able to discern the work of the Spirit in another.

(5) So far as a man is spiritual, so far is light delightful to him. He is willing to see anything amiss that he may reform, and any further service discovered that he may perform. If he goes against light discovered, he will soon be reclaimed, because light has a friendly party within him. At a little sight of his error, he is soon open to counsel, as David was in his intention to kill Nabal; and he blessed God afterwards, when he was stopped (1 Sam. 25:32). In the case of a carnal man, the light breaks in on him, but he labours to block its entrance. He has no delight in coming to the light. It is impossible, before the Spirit of grace has subdued the heart, that it should not sin against the light, either by resisting it, keeping it prisoner under base lusts, or perverting it by making it an agent for the flesh; thus abusing that little measure of light men have so as to keep out a greater, higher, and more heavenly light. We see that light often enrages men. Those that plead and plot for liberties for the flesh show themselves strangers from the life of God. Feeling this inner strife, gracious men often complain that they have no grace. But they contradict themselves in their complaints, as if a man that sees should complain he cannot see; whereas the very complaint, springing from a displeasure against sin, shows that there is something in him opposite to sin. Can a dead man complain?

*The Bruised Reed*, pp. 40-42 [44-46]

# The Light of God Compared to Fire (3)

*For it is you who light my lamp; the Lord my God lightens my dark-ness.*—Psa. 18:28

(6) Fire, where it is present, is in some degree active. The least measure of grace works, as springing from the Spirit of God, who is compared to fire. Even in sins, when there seems nothing active but corruption, there is a contrary principle, which breaks the force of sin, so that it is not boundlessly sinful (Rom. 7:13).

(7) Fire makes metals pliable and malleable. So, grace, where it is given, makes the heart pliable and ready to receive all good impressions.

(8) Fire, as much as it can, sets everything on fire. Grace makes a gracious use even of natural and morally right things. What another man does only in a moral way, a gracious man will do in a godly way. Whether he eats or drinks or whatever he does, he does all to the glory of God (1 Cor. 10:31).

(9) Sparks by nature fly upwards. So, the Spirit of grace carries the soul heavenward and sets before us holy and heavenly aims. Where the aim and bent of the soul is towards God, there is grace, though opposed. The least measure of it is seen in holy desires, springing from faith and love, for we cannot desire anything which we do not believe first. These desires must be directed to spiritual things, such as to believe, to love God, not because of a particular emergency, in that one thinks one might escape some danger if one had grace, but as a loving heart is carried to the thing loved for the sake of some excellency in it. These desires also must be accompanied with grief when the desire is hindered, so as to stir us up to pray: 'Oh, that my ways were directed that I might keep thy statutes!' (Psa. 119:5).

(10) Fire, if it has any matter to feed on, enlarges itself and mounts higher and higher, and the higher it rises, the purer is the flame. So where true grace is, it grows in measure and purity. The Holy Spirit cleanses us by degrees to be suitable to so holy a Head.

*The Bruised Reed*, pp. 42-44 [46-48]

# Temptation (1)

*But I see in my members another law waging war against the law of my mind and making me captive to the law of sin that dwells in my members.*—Rom. 7:23

(1) Some think they have no faith at all because they have no full assurance. The best actions will smell of the smoke; so, all our actions will savour something of the old man.

(2) In weakness of body some think grace dies because their performances are feeble. But they do not consider that God regards the hidden sighs of those that lack abilities to express them outwardly.

(3) Some again are haunted with hideous imaginations, and with vile and unworthy thoughts, which disquiet and molest their peace. Will every sin and blasphemy of man be forgiven, and not these blasphemous thoughts, when Christ himself was molested in this same way? But there is a difference between Christ and us in this case. Because Satan had nothing of his own in Christ his suggestions left no impression at all in his holy nature and were presently quenched. But when Satan comes to us, he finds something of his own in us. There is the same enmity in our nature to God and goodness, in some degree, that is in Satan himself. Therefore, his temptations fasten some taint upon us. These thoughts, if the soul dwell on them so long as to draw by them any sinful delight, then they leave a heavier guilt upon the soul, hinder our sweet communion with God, and put a contrary relish into the soul, disposing it to greater sins. All scandalous actions are only thoughts at the first. These ill thoughts force the soul to all spiritual exercises, to watchfulness and a nearer walking with God. They reveal to us a necessity of daily purging and pardoning grace, and of seeking to be found in Christ, and so bring the best often upon their knees. Our chief comfort is that our blessed Saviour, as he bade Satan depart from him (Matt. 4:10), so he will command him to be gone from us, when it will be good for us. Christ can and will likewise, in his own time, rebuke the rebellious and extravagant stirrings of our hearts and bring all the thoughts of the inner man into subjection to himself.

*The Bruised Reed*, pp. 45-49 [49-53]

# Temptation (2)

*But I say, walk by the Spirit, and you will not gratify the desires of the flesh. For the desires of the flesh are against the Spirit, and the desires of the Spirit are against the flesh, for these are opposed to each other, to keep you from doing the things you want to do.*—Gal. 5:16, 17

(4) Some think, when they become more troubled with the smoke of corruption than they were before, therefore they are worse than they were. It is true that corruptions appear now more than before, but they are less.

For, first, the more sin is seen, the more it is hated, and therefore it is less. Dust particles are in a room before the sun shines, but they only appear then.

Secondly, the nearer contraries are one to another, the sharper is the conflict between them. Now, of all enemies the spirit and the flesh are nearest one to another, being both in the soul of a regenerate man, in the faculties of the soul, and in every action that springs from those faculties, and therefore it is no marvel that the soul, the seat of this battle, thus divided within itself, is as smoking flax.

Thirdly, the more grace, the more spiritual life, and the more spiritual life, the more antipathy to the contrary. Therefore, none are so aware of corruption as those whose souls are most alive.

Fourthly, when men give themselves up to self-indulgence, their corruptions do not trouble them, as not being bound, and tied up; but when once grace suppresses their extravagant and licentious excesses, then the flesh boils, as disdaining to be confined. Yet they are better now than they were before. That matter which yields smoke was in the torch before it was lighted, but it is not offensive until the torch begins to burn. Let such know that if the smoke be once offensive to them, it is a sign that there is light. It is better to enjoy the benefit of light, though with smoke, than to be altogether in the dark. Nor is smoke so offensive to us as light is pleasant to us, since it yields an evidence of the truth of grace in the heart. Therefore, though it is cumbersome in the conflict, yet it is comfortable as evidence.

*The Bruised Reed*, pp. 49-50 [53-54]

# The Source of Discouragements

*Do not be frightened, and do not be dismayed, for the Lord your God is
with you wherever you go.*—Josh. 1:9

Where do discouragements come from?

(1) Not from the Father, for he has bound himself by covenant to
pity us as a father pities his children (Psa. 103:13) and to accept as a father
our weak endeavours. What is wanting in the strength of duty, he gives
us leave to take up in his gracious supply. In this way we will honour that
grace in which he delights as much as in perfect obedience.

(2) Not from Christ, for he by office will not quench the smoking
flax (Isa. 42:3). We see how Christ bestows the best fruits of his love on
persons who are poor in condition, weak in abilities, and offensive for
infirmities. This he does, first, because it pleases him to confound the
pride of the flesh, which usually measures God's love by some outward
excellency; and secondly, in this way he delights to show the freedom
of his grace and confirm his royal prerogative that 'he that glories' must
'glory in the Lord' (1 Cor. 1:31). In Hebrews 11, among that cloud of
witnesses, we see Rahab, Gideon and Samson ranked with Abraham, the
father of the faithful (Heb. 11:31, 32). Our blessed Saviour glorified his
Father by revealing the mystery of the gospel to simple men, neglecting
those that carried the chief reputation of wisdom in the world (Matt.
11:25, 26). Augustine speaks of a simple man in his time, destitute almost
altogether of the use of reason, who, although he was most patient of all
injuries done to himself, yet from a reverence of religion he would not
endure any injury done to the name of Christ. This shows that none have
abilities so meagre as to be beneath the gracious regard of Christ.

(3) Not from the Holy Spirit. He helps our infirmities and by office
is a comforter (John 14:16). If he convicts of sin, and so humbles us, it is
that he may make way for his work of comforting us.

Discouragements, then, must come from ourselves and from Satan,
who labours to fasten on us a loathing of duty.

*The Bruised Reed*, pp. 56-57 [62-63]

# Responding to Christ's Kindness

*I appeal to you therefore, brothers, by the mercies of God, to present your bodies as a living sacrifice, holy and acceptable to God, which is your spiritual worship.*—Rom. 12:1

Let us think to ourselves: when he is so kind to us, will we be cruel against him in his name, in his truth, and in his children? It cannot but cut the heart of those that have felt this love of Christ to hear him wounded who is the life of their lives and the soul of their souls. This makes those who have felt mercy weep over Christ whom they have pierced with their sins. The apostle could not find a more heartbreaking argument to enforce a sacrifice of ourselves to God than to appeal to us 'by the mercies of God' in Christ (Rom. 12:1).

This mercy of Christ should also move us to commiserate the state of the poor church, torn by enemies without, and rending itself by divisions at home. What a joyful spectacle is this to Satan and his faction, to see those that are separated from the world fall in pieces among themselves! Our discord is our enemy's melody. So far as men are not of one mind, they will hardly be of one heart, except where grace and the peace of God bear great rule in the heart (Col. 3:15). Open show of difference is only good when it is necessary, although some, from a desire to be somebody, turn into byways and yield to a spirit of contrariness in themselves. If it be wisdom, it is wisdom from beneath: for the wisdom from above, as it is pure, so it is peaceable (James 3:17). Our blessed Saviour, when he was to leave the world, what did he press upon his disciples more than peace and love? In his last prayer, with what earnestness did he beg of his Father that 'they all may be one' as he and the Father were one (John 17:21).

Further, what spirit will we think them to be of who take advantage of the infirmities of men's spirits to relieve them with false peace for their own worldly ends? A wounded spirit will part with anything. Spiritual tyranny is the greatest tyranny, especially when it is where most mercy should be shown.

*The Bruised Reed*, pp. 73-78 [81-84]

# Victory in Spiritual Battles

*For we do not wrestle against flesh and blood, but against the rulers, against the authorities, against the cosmic powers over this present darkness, against the spiritual forces of evil in the heavenly places.—* Eph. 6:12

(1) God's children usually, in their troubles, overcome by suffering. Here lambs overcome lions, and doves overcome eagles, by suffering. That they may be conformable to Christ, who conquered most when he suffered most.

(2) God's victory is by degrees. They are too hasty spirited that would conquer as soon as they strike the first stroke. The Israelites were sure of their victory in their journey to Canaan, yet they still had to fight it out.

(3) God often works by contraries: when he means to give victory, he will allow us to be foiled at first; when he means to comfort, he will terrify first; when he means to justify, he will condemn us first; when he means to make us glorious, he will abase us first. Even when the believer is conquered by some sins, he gets victory over others more dangerous, such as spiritual pride and security in self.

(4) Christ's work, both in the church and the hearts of Christians, often goes backward so that it may better go forward. A seed rots in the ground in the winter time, but after comes up better. So, we learn to stand by falls, and get strength by weakness discovered. Let us labour to exercise our faith. When we are foiled, let us believe we will overcome; when we have fallen, let us believe we will rise again. Jacob, after he received a blow, yet would not give over wrestling (Gen. 32:25) till he had obtained the blessing. So, let us never give up, but, in our thoughts, knit the beginning, progress, and end together, and then we will see ourselves in heaven out of the reach of all enemies. Weakness with watchfulness will stand when strength with too much confidence fails. Weakness also is the fittest seat and subject for God to perfect his strength in; for consciousness of our infirmities drives us out of ourselves to him in whom our strength lies.

*The Bruised Reed*, pp. 94-96 [106-08]

# His Power Not Ours

*I can do all things through him who strengthens me.*—Phil. 4:13

It is dangerous to look for that from ourselves which we must have from Christ. We are but subordinate agents, moving as we are moved, and working as we are first wrought upon, free in so far as we are freed, no wiser nor stronger than he makes us to be. It is his Spirit who actuates and enlivens, and applies that knowledge and strength we have, or else it fails and lies useless in us. Dependent spirits are the wisest and the ablest. Nothing is stronger than humility, which goes out of itself; nothing is weaker than pride, which rests on its own foundation. We naturally aspire to a kind of divinity in our own strength; but Christ says, 'Without me you,' the apostles, who were in a state of grace, 'can do nothing' (John 15:5). He does not say, you can do a little, but nothing. Of ourselves, how easily are we overcome! How weak we are to resist! We shake at the very noise and thought of poverty, disgrace, or losses. We have no power over our eyes, tongues, thoughts, or affections, but let sin pass in and out. Therefore in all, especially difficult encounters, let us lift up our hearts to Christ, who has Spirit enough for us all, in all our troubles, and say with good Jehoshaphat, 'We are powerless ... neither do we know what to do: but our eyes are upon you' (2 Chron. 20:12). 'The battle we fight is yours, and the strength whereby we fight must be yours. If you go not out with us, we are sure to fall.' Satan knows that nothing can prevail against Christ, or those that rely upon his power. His study is how to keep us in ourselves. But we must carry this always in our minds, that that which is begun in self-confidence ends in shame. We know where to obtain power, and to whom to return the praise. It is our happiness that it is so safely hid in Christ, in one so near to God and us.

*The Bruised Reed*, pp. 114-17 [128-31]

# Courage Until the End (1)

*I tell you, you are Peter, and on this rock I will build my church, and the gates of hell shall not prevail against it.*—Matt. 16:18

If we look to the present state of the church of Christ, it is as Daniel in the midst of lions, as a lily among thorns, as a ship not only tossed but almost covered with waves. How strong a conspiracy is against it! The spirit of antichrist is now lifted up and marches furiously. Things seem to hang on a small and invisible thread. But our comfort is that Christ lives and reigns and stands on Mount Zion in defence of those who stand for him (Rev. 14:1). At this very time, the delivery of his church and the ruin of his enemies are in progress. We see nothing in motion till Christ has done his work, and then we will see that the Lord reigns. Christ and his church, when they are at the lowest, are nearest rising. His enemies, at the highest, are nearest their downfall. The Jews are not yet come in under Christ's banner. The 'fulness of the Gentiles' has not yet come in (Rom. 11:25), but Christ, who has the uttermost parts of the earth given to him for his possession (Psa. 2:8), will gather all the sheep his Father has given him into one fold, that there may be one sheepfold and one shepherd (John 10:16). The faithful Jews rejoiced to think of the calling of the Gentiles and why should we not rejoice to think of the calling of the Jews? No creature can hinder the course of the sun, nor stop the influence of heaven, nor hinder the blowing of the wind, much less hinder the prevailing power of divine truth, until Christ has brought all under one head, and then he will present all to his Father, and say: 'These are those you have given to me; these are those that have taken me for their Lord and King, that have suffered with me. My will is that they may be where I am and reign with me.' And then he will deliver up the kingdom to his Father, and put down all other rule, authority, and power (1 Cor. 15:24).

*The Bruised Reed*, pp. 125-27 [140-42]

# Courage Until the End (2)

*This gospel of the kingdom will be proclaimed throughout the whole world as a testimony to all nations, and then the end will come.—* Matt. 24:14

Let us then bring our hearts to holy resolutions, and set ourselves upon that which is good, and against that which is ill, in ourselves or others, according to our callings, with this encouragement, that Christ's grace and power will go along with us. What would have become of that great work of reformation of religion in the latter spring of the gospel if men had not been armed with invincible courage to overcome all hindrances, with this faith, that the cause was Christ's, and that he would not fail to help his own cause? Martin Luther confessed that he often acted inconsiderately and was moved by various passions. But when he acknowledged this, God did not condemn him for his errors, but the cause being God's, and his aims being holy, to promote the truth, and being a mighty man in prayer, and strong in faith, God by him kindled that fire which all the world will never be able to quench. According to our faith, so is our encouragement to all duties. Believe it, therefore, that though the church is often as smoking flax, yet it will prevail. Let us wait a while, 'stand still, and see the salvation of the Lord' (Exod. 14:13). May the Lord reveal himself more and more to us in the face of his Son Jesus Christ and magnify the power of his grace. May he persuade us that, since he has taken us into the covenant of grace, he will not cast us off. And because Satan labours to obscure the glory of God's mercy and hinder our comfort by discouragements, the Lord adds this to the rest of his mercies: that since he is so gracious to those that yield to his rule, we may make the right use of this grace, and not lose any portion of comfort that is laid up for us in Christ. May he grant that the prevailing power of his Spirit in us should be an evidence of the truth of grace begun, and a pledge of final victory, at that time when he will be all in all, in all his, for all eternity. Amen.

*The Bruised Reed*, pp. 127-28 [142-43]

# Our Hearts—God's Temple

*Or do you not know that your body is a temple of the Holy Spirit within you, whom you have from God? You are not your own.*—1 Cor. 6:19

The heart of true Christians is God's private closet. And as in every house or building, there are some open places and some private closets, so is it here. God has his private chamber, and his retiring-place, which is the heart of every true Christian. He counts it not sufficient to dwell in his house at large, but he will dwell in the best part of it, the heart, and the affections. Therefore, 'he knocks at the doors of our hearts for entrance' (Rev. 3:20), and his best children are glad he will reside in them. They set him up in the highest place of their souls and set a crown upon him; their desire is that God may govern and rule their whole life; they have no idol above God in their hearts.

Oh, what comfort arises to a Christian soul from the due meditation of this point. If we are God's house, then God will be our house; 'You are our habitation,' said Moses, 'from generation to generation' (Psa. 90:1). Wherever we shuffle in the world, now here and now there, yet in God we always have a home. He is ours, and we are his. What a comfort this is that we are God's house.

This should instruct us to labour that God may dwell largely and comfortably in us, to deliver up all to this keeper of our house and allow him to rule and reign in us. O beloved, it must concern us to cleanse and purify our hearts, so that we may entertain Christ and he may delight to abide and dwell with us. You know how terribly he took it when his house was made a den of thieves (Luke 19:46), and will he not take it much worse that our hearts should be made the very containers and cages of all manner of uncleanness? Our hearts should be as the holy of holies. Paul exhorts us 'to abstain from all filthiness both of flesh and spirit' (2 Cor. 7:1), for this cause 'that God may dwell amongst us' (2 Cor. 6:16); for, 'what communion has light with darkness?' (2 Cor. 6:14).

*The Church's Visitation, Works,* vol. 1, pp. 374-75

# Sin in God's People

*For it is time for judgment to begin at the household of God; and if it
begins with us, what will be the outcome for those who do not obey
the gospel of God?*— 1 Pet. 4:17

Why does God chiefly afflict his own people more than others?

(1) Because they are his own family and are called by his name
(Num. 6:27). Now the disorders of the family lead to the disgrace of the
leader of it. The sins of the church touch God more nearly than others,
and therefore 'judgments must begin at the sanctuary first' (Ezek. 5:5-7).
Beloved, the gospel suffers much because of the sins of those who profess
to be its followers. What says the world? These be your professors? Look
at the way they live! What little conscience they have of their sins! Little
do men know how much religion is vilified and the ways of God spoken
evil of because of the sinful lifestyles of those who profess to be followers
of the gospel. It is as if there were no force in the grace and favour of
God to make us love and obey him in all things. As if religion consisted
in word only, and not in power. What a scandal this is to the cause of
Christ! It is no marvel God begins with them first. A man may see and
pass by dirt in his yard, but he will not allow it in his dining chamber nor
endure it in his parlour.

(2) Because the sins of the godly are more heinous than others. They
are committed against more light and against more benefits and favours.
What! to make 'the temple of God a den of thieves' to defile their bodies
and souls, who are bought with the precious blood of Jesus Christ—is
this a small matter? Their sins are idolatry; for they are not only the
house of God, but the spouse of God. Now, for a spouse to be false and
adulterous, this is greater than fornication, because the bond is nearer;
so the nearer any come to God in profession, the higher is the aggrava-
tion of their sin, and as their sin grows, so must their punishment grow
answerable and proportionable. They that know God's will most of all
others, must look for most stripes if they do it not (Luke 12:47, 48).

*The Church's Visitation, Works*, vol. 1, pp. 377-78

# Signs of God's Impending Judgment (1)

*You only have I known of all the families of the earth; therefore I will punish you for all your iniquities.*—Amos 3:2

What are the signs that judgment is to fall upon the people of God?

(Sign 1) 'This and that have I done,' said the Lord, 'and yet you have not returned to me' (Amos 4:6, 7). There are declines before the ruin of a house. Lesser judgments make way for greater. Where less afflictions prevail not, there cannot but be an expectation of greater.

(Sign 2) Usually before some great calamity God takes away worthy men, 'the counsellor, and the captain, and the man of war' (Isa. 3:2, 3). This is a fearful warning that God threatens some future destruction, for they are the pillars of the church and the strength of the nation. They are those that make the times and places good wherein they live; for they keep away evil and do good by their example and by their prayers. A good man is a common good. The city thrives the better for a righteous man (Prov. 11:10, 11; Eccles. 9:15). Therefore, we have cause to rejoice in them and it is a sign of pending judgment when such are removed.

(Sign 3) God usually visits a people when some horrible sins reign among them. Sins such as atheism. Beloved, God stands upon his prerogative then, when he is scarce known in the world; when they say, 'Where is God? God sees us not.' Also, when idolatry prevails. This is a breach of covenant with God. Also, when divisions grow among people. Union is a preserver. Where there is dissension of judgment there will soon be dissension of affections. For the most part, ecclesiastical dissensions end in civil dissension. Before the destruction of Jerusalem, what a world of schisms and divisions were amongst the Jews. It was the ruin of the ten tribes at length, the rent that Jeroboam caused in religion. It is a fearful sign of some great judgment to fall upon a church when dissensions are not stopped. They may be easily stopped at first, as waters in the beginning; but when they are once gotten into the very vital parts of the church and commonwealth, we may see the mischief, but it is remedied with difficulty.

*The Church's Visitation, Works,* vol. 1, p. 379

# Signs of God's Impending Judgment (2)

*Every branch in me that does not bear fruit he takes away, and every branch that does bear fruit he prunes, that it may bear more fruit.—* John 15:2

(Sign 4) When sin grows ripe, and abounds in a land or nation, at such time as this a man may know there is some fearful judgment approaching. But when is sin ripe? When it is impudent; when men grow bold in sin, making it their whole course and trade of life. When men's wicked courses are their common lifestyle, and they don't even know how to do otherwise. When sin grows common and spreads far. It is an ill plea to say, 'Others do as I do.' The more sin, the more danger. When men are secure in their sinning, it is as if they are daring the God of heaven to do his worst. The old world was very secure in their sinning. They mocked at holy Noah when he made the ark, as if he was a doting old man. Notwithstanding, he foretold them of the wrath to come. Our Saviour said, 'Before the end of the world it will be as in the days of Noah' (Matt. 24:38). If we have the same course and security in sinning, we must look for the same judgments. Compare times with times. If the times now are like the former times, when God judged them, we may well expect the same fearful judgments to fall upon us.

(Sign 5) Unfruitfulness threatens a judgment upon a people. God expects and looks for fruitfulness. The fig tree in the gospel had some respite given it by reason of the prayers of the vinedresser; but afterward, when it brought forth no fruit, it was cut down and cast into the fire. Beloved, who among us would endure a barren tree in his garden? That which is not fit for fruit is most fit for fire. We can endure a barren tree in the wilderness, but not in our orchards. When God, the great husbandman in his church, sees that upon so great and continual cost bestowed upon us, we remain yet unfruitful, he will not allow us long to burden the ground of his church.

*The Church's Visitation, Works,* vol. 1, pp. 379-80

# Signs of God's Impending Judgment (3)

*But I have this against you, that you have abandoned the love you had*
*at first. Remember therefore from where you have fallen; repent and*
*do the works you did at first. If not, I will come to you and remove*
*your lampstand from its place, unless you repent.*—Rev. 2:4, 5

(Sign 6) Again, decay in our first love is a sign of approaching judgment. God threatened the church of Ephesus to remove his candlestick from among them, for their decay in their first love (Rev. 2:4). God cannot endure his glorious gospel to be slighted, as not deserving the richest strain of our love. The Lord takes it better where there is but little strength and a striving to be better, than when there is great means of grace and knowledge, and no growth answerable, but rather a declining in goodness. The Lord is much displeased when Christians are not as zealous as they should be; when there is not that sweet communion of saints among them, to strengthen and encourage one another in the ways of holiness as there might be; when there is not a beauty in their profession to allure and draw others to a love and liking of the best things; when there is not a care to avoid all scandals that may weaken the respect of good things, and bring an evil report on the ways of God; when they labour not with their whole hearts to serve the Lord in a cheerful manner. These are certain signs of ensuing danger.

I beseech you, let us look about us whether these be not the times in which we live, that judgment must begin with the house of God (1 Pet. 4:17). The Lord complains in Jeremiah that the turtle dove and other silly creatures knew the time of their standing and removing, but his people did not know his judgments (Jer. 8:7). Do the creatures know their times and seasons, and will Christ complain that we know not the day of our visitation? What a shame this is! I beseech you, let us know and consider our times. If we have a time of sinning, God will have a time of punishing.

*The Church's Visitation, Works,* vol. 1, pp. 380-81

# Preventing God's Judgment on Our Nation (1)

*And the people of Nineveh believed God. They called for a fast and put on sackcloth, from the greatest of them to the least of them. The word reached the king of Nineveh, and he arose from his throne, removed his robe, covered himself with sackcloth, and sat in ashes.*—Jon. 3:5, 6

What course should we take to prevent the judgment of God, and keep it from us?

(1) Labour to meet God by speedy repentance before any decree comes forth against us. There is yet hope; for as we have many things to fear, so we have many things to encourage us to go to God for comfort. We have yet time to seek the Lord. Let us not delay until the very time of judgment comes upon us. Assure yourself of this, you can have no more comfort in troubles and afflictions when they do come, than you have care to prevent them before they come. Get into Christ now, be provided now with a sound profession of religion, and that will be as an ark to shelter us in the evil day. What we know let us do, and then we shall be built on a rock, that if waves or anything come, we shall not be stirred (Matt. 7:24, 25).

(2) Examine upon what ground you profess religion, whether it will hold water or not, and whether you will stand when evil times come. It concerns us all, to seriously consider and narrowly search upon what grounds we venture our lives and souls. If men would search and plough up their own hearts, they would not need the ploughing of God's enemies. The people of God complained that the enemies had made long furrows on their backs, but if they had ploughed themselves, they would have saved the enemies that labour (Psa. 129:3).

(3) Before any judgment comes, let us store up the fruit of a holy life; every day be doing something; do that now, which may comfort you then. When the 'night is come, we cannot work' (John 9:4). Let us look about us and do what good we can 'while we have time' (1 Cor. 7:29). The time will come before long that you will wish, 'O that I had that opportunity and advantage of doing good as I have had!' But then it will be too late.

*The Church's Visitation, Works*, vol. 1, pp. 381-82

# Preventing God's Judgment on Our Nation (2)

*When Mordecai learned all that had been done, Mordecai tore his clothes and put on sackcloth and ashes, and went out into the midst of the city, and he cried out with a loud and bitter cry.*—Esth. 4:1

(4) If we would have God to shield us and be a hiding-place in the worst times, let us mourn for our own sins and the sins of the times in which we live. Let us keep ourselves unspotted by the sins of the world; let us not make the times worse by us, but better. Let us not only mourn for the sins of the times, but labour also to repress them all we can, and stand in the gap, endeavouring by our prayers and tears to stop God's judgments.

(5) We should esteem the treasure of the gospel at a higher rate than ever we have done. We see how it is slighted by most of the world; how they shake the blessed truths of God and call them into question. It is fitting for us to store up all the sanctified knowledge we can, and to take heed we yield not to any that would either weaken our judgment in religion, or our affections to the best things. We should, everyone in his place, labour to stop dissensions in this kind, and knit our hearts together as one man in unity and concord. Unity makes strong, but division weakens any people. Even Satan's kingdom (Matt. 12:25, 26), divided against itself, cannot stand.

What is the glory of England? Take away the gospel, and what have we that other nations have not better than ourselves? Alas, if we labour not to maintain truth, we may say with Eli's daughter, 'The glory of God has departed from us' (1 Sam. 4:21). I beseech you, let us highly esteem the gospel, while we do enjoy it. If we allow that to be shaken in any way, our peace and prosperity will leave us, and judgment upon judgment will come upon us. If we will not regard the truth of God, which he esteems most, he will take away outward prosperity, which we esteem most.

*The Church's Visitation, Works,* vol. 1, pp. 382-83

# The Ugliness of Sin (1)

*But your iniquities have made a separation between you and your God, and your sins have hidden his face from you so that he does not hear.*—Isa. 59:2

How to discern the ugliness of sin. In what way are we to look upon the ugly thing, sin, to make it uglier to us? Beloved, if we would think right about sin, let us see it in the casting of Adam out of paradise (Gen. 3:23, 24), and us in him. See it in the destruction of the old world, and the Jews carried to captivity, and in the general destruction of Jerusalem. But if you would indeed see the most ugly colours of sin, then see it in Christ upon the cross, see how bitter a thing it was to his righteous soul, sending forth strong cries to his Father, 'My God, my God, why have you forsaken me?' (Mark 15:34). If sin but imputed to Christ as our surety, so affected him who was the God-man, and lay so heavy upon his soul, what will it do to those that are not in Christ? See sin therefore chiefly in the death of Christ. How odious it is to God, that it could be purged in no other way than by the death of his beloved Son. Sin is another matter than we take it to be. We must consider the attributes of God, his anger against sin because of his justice and holiness. Beloved, men forget this. So odious is sin to the holy nature of God, that he left his Son while he struggled with his wrath for it; and so odious was sin to the holy nature of Christ, that he became a sacrifice for the same. So odious are the remainders of sin in the hearts of the saints, that all that belong to God have the Spirit of Christ, who works as fire to consume and waste the old Adam little by little out of them. No unclean thing may enter heaven (Rev. 21:27). Those that are not in Christ by faith, that have not a shelter in him, must suffer for their transgressions eternally, 'Depart, you cursed, into everlasting fire' (Matt. 25:41); so holy is God that he can have no society and fellowship with sinners.

*Christ's Sufferings for Man's Sin, Works*, vol. 1, pp. 358-59

## The Ugliness of Sin (2)

*There are six things that the Lord hates, seven that are an abomination
to him: haughty eyes, a lying tongue, and hands that shed innocent
blood, a heart that devises wicked plans, feet that make haste to run
to evil, a false witness who breathes out lies, and one who sows discord
among brothers.*—Prov. 6:16-19

Do you wonder why God hates sin so much and that men regard
it so little? This is done not only by the lewd sort of the world, but
by common dead-hearted persons, who regard not spiritual sins at all,
especially hatred, malice, and pride. Certainly, you would not wonder
that God hates sin, if you did but consider how sin hates God? What
is sin but a setting of itself on God's throne, a setting the devil in God's
place? For when we sin, we leave God, and set up the thing, and by
consequence Satan, who brings the temptation to us; setting it in our
hearts before God. Beloved, God is very jealous, and cannot endure that
filthy thing sin, to be in his place. Sin is such a thing as desires to take
away God himself. Ask a sinner when he is about to sin, 'Could you not
wish that there were no God at all, that there was no eye of heaven to
take vengeance on you?' 'Oh yes, with all my heart,' would be the reply.
Can you then wonder that God hates sin so, when it hates him so, as to
wish that there was no God? Oh marvel not at it, but have such thoughts
of sin as God had when he gave his Son to die for it, and such as Christ
had, when in the sense of his Father's anger cried, 'My God, my God,
why have you forsaken me?' (Mark 15:34).

The deeper our thoughts are of the odiousness of sin, the deeper our
comfort and joy in Christ will be afterward. Therefore, I beseech you to
work your hearts to a serious consideration of what sin you cherish and
will not repent of, and for which you leave God and heaven to embrace.
Think of it as God does, who as a judge will one day call us to a strict
account for the same.

*Christ's Sufferings for Man's Sin, Works,* vol. 1, p. 359

# Far but Near

*And about the ninth hour Jesus cried out with a loud voice, saying, 'Eli, Eli, lema sabachthani?' that is, 'My God, my God, why have you forsaken me?'*—Mark 15:34

Christ knew that God is nearest in support when he is furthest off in feeling. Often, where he is nearest the inward man, to strengthen it with his love, he is furthest off in comfort to outward sense. To whom was God nearer than Christ in support and grace and yet to whom was he further off in outward sense when Christ was on the cross? Christ had the secret sense of God, knowing that he was his Father, but he did not have the sensible sense of God's love.

This should teach us in any trouble to set faith to work and feed faith with the consideration of God's unchangeable nature, and the unchangeableness of his promises, which endure forever. We change, but God's promises change not, and God changes not. 'The word of the Lord endures forever' (1 Pet. 1:25). God deals with his people in a hidden manner; he supports with secret, though not always with sensible comfort, and will be nearest when he seems to be furthest from his children. Present to your soul the nature of God, his custom and manner of dealing, so that you might apprehend his favour in the midst of wrath, and his glory in the midst of shame. We will see life in death; we will see through the thickest clouds that are between God and us. For as God shines secretly in the heart through all temptations and troubles, so should there be a spirit of faith that goes back to him. Christ had a great burden upon him, the sins of the whole world; yet he breaks through all and could know, 'I am now sin, I bear the guilt of the whole world, yet I am his son, and God is my God still, notwithstanding all this weight of sin upon me.' Will we not say, 'My God,' in any affliction or trouble that befalls us? In the sense of sin, which is the bitterest of all, and in the sense of God's anger, in losses and crosses, in our families, etc., let us break through those clouds, and still say, 'My God.'

*Christ's Sufferings for Man's Sin, Works, vol. 1, pp. 365-66*

# Christ's Dying Words of Comfort

*Let not your hearts be troubled. Believe in God; believe also in me.—*
John 14:1

'Let not your hearts be troubled.' Hear the dying words of our Saviour to his disciples.

Comforts must be founded on strong reasons. He stays our spirits by reasons stronger than the trouble. For what is comfort but that which establishes and upholds the soul against the evil that is feared or felt, from a greater strength which overmasters the evil? Christ's comforts are of a higher nature than any trouble. He had told them, that he should leave them; the best of them all, even Peter, should deny him, and that all the rest should leave him. From these they might gather that the approaching trouble should be great. Our Saviour saw into their hearts, and in their looks he saw a spirit of discouragement seizing on them. Christ discerning this dejection of their spirits, he raises them by this, 'Let not your hearts be troubled.' The heavenly Physician of our souls applies the remedy when it is the fittest season.

If they had not been at all affected with the absence of Christ, it would have been a sin, and no less a stupidity; yet it was their sin to be over much troubled. How do we know that our hearts are more troubled than they should be? In a word, a trouble is sinful when it hinders us in duties to God or to others; or from duty, that is, when the soul is disturbed by it, and, like an instrument out of tune, made fit for nothing. When we find this in our trouble, we may know it is not as it should be. Naturally, affections should be helps to duty, they are the winds that carry the soul on. So that a man without affections is like the Dead Sea, that moves not at all. But they must be raised up and laid down at the command of a spiritual understanding. When they be raised up of themselves, by shallow and false conceits and opinions, they be irregular. When they be raised up by a right judgment of things, and laid down again when they ought to be, then they are right and orderly.

Sibbes's Last Two Sermons: First Sermon, *Works*, vol. 7, pp. 339-41

# The Wrong of Excessive Sorrow

*But take heart; I have overcome the world.*—John 16:33b

Reasons we should not yield to excessive sorrow in trouble.

(1) We wrong our own selves when we give way to grief and sorrow that is immoderate and inordinate. The soul is put out of joint by it. We make actions difficult for us. Joy and comfort are oil to the soul. Nehemiah said, 'The joy of the Lord is your strength' (Neh. 8:10). When we give way to excessive fear and grief it weakens the soul. It causes a cloud betwixt God's love and us. Joy enlarges the soul, but inordinate grief shrinks it.

(2) By over-much sorrow and grief, what a great deal of dishonour do we to God. Often, with over-much fear and sorrow, there is joined murmuring and discontent, and a spirit unsubdued to God. There is a wronging of his care in providence and of his graciousness in his promises. There is a grieving of his good Spirit; a questioning of his government, as if he did not dispose of things as he should. It argues a great deal of pride to be sad and dejected as if such worthy and excellent persons as we should be so afflicted. Whereas if we balance our grounds of comfort, being Christians, as we should do, they will appear incomparably above the grounds of our discouragements.

(3) Though we should be troubled for sin, yet to be overmuch troubled for sin is a dishonour to Christ, and to the love of God in Christ; for it is as if we had not in him a sufficient remedy for that great malady. It is sinful when grief for sin makes us forget the mercies of God in Christ; to forget the healing virtue of him our brazen serpent. Overmuch sadness, even though it be for sin, is hurtful and disgraceful. Joshua was much cast down when he saw it went not well with Israel; but God said, 'Get up, Joshua, what are you doing lying here?' Up and do your duty! There is an Achan in the camp. So, when things go not well, let not your thoughts be conversant about the matters of trouble, so much as about your duty.

Sibbes's Last Two Sermons: First Sermon, *Works*, vol. 7, pp. 341-43

# Steps to Bring Comfort to our Hearts (1)

*Blessed are those who mourn, for they shall be comforted.*—Matt. 5:4

Ways we labour to comfort our hearts.

(1) There must be a search into the heart for the grounds of our trouble. Oftentimes Christians are troubled, but they cannot tell from where. They must search the heart honestly to get to the bottom of it and see if there be not some Achan in the camp, some sin in the heart. Search your hearts thoroughly; what sin lies there unrepented of, and for which you have not been humbled.

(2) When you have found out your sin, give it vent by confession of it to God, and in some cases to others.

(3) When we have done so, consider what promises and comforts, in the word of God that are fitted to that condition. For we can be in no condition but there are comforts for it and promises fitted to yield comfort. We ought to be skilful and well seen in the word of God, that we may store up comforts beforehand. Those comforts do not, for the most part, hold out in the day of adversity, which were not procured in the day of prosperity. It is not wisdom to learn religion when we should need it. Let us be good cultivators for our souls, by storing up comforts out of the word of God. There are some promises of a more general use, fitted for all sorts of grievances. How many promises and comforts are there in that one promise, 'All things shall work together for the good, to them that love God' (Rom. 8:28). Those things that are worst shall work together. As in a clock the wheels go several ways, but all join to make the clock strike. So in the carriage and ordering of things, one passage crosses another, but in the issue we shall be able to say, I found God turning all things for my good; and I could not have been without such a cross, such an affliction. God's promises, well digested, will arm the soul with confidence, that it shall be able to put to any trouble that can arise from Satan or our own hearts.

*Sibbes's Last Two Sermons: First Sermon, *Works*, vol. 7, pp. 343-45*

# Steps to Bring Comfort to our Hearts (2)

*Blessed be the God and Father of our Lord Jesus Christ, the Father of mercies and God of all comfort, who comforts us in all our affliction, so that we may be able to comfort those who are in any affliction, with the comfort with which we ourselves are comforted by God.—* 2 Cor. 1:3, 4

(4) When we have these promises, let us labour to thoroughly understand them and our comfort in them. Next, to believe the truth of them, which are as true as God, who is truth itself. Then to love them, and digest them in our affections, and so make them our own, and then to walk in the strength and comfort of them.

(5) Labour likewise to have them fresh in memory. It is a great defect of Christians, that they forget their consolation, as it is in the Hebrews 12:5, 'Have you forgotten the exhortation that addresses you as sons?' Though we know many things, yet we have the benefit of our comfort from no more than we remember.

(6) But, above all, if we will keep our hearts from trouble, let us labour to keep unspotted consciences. Innocence and diligence are marvellous preservers of comfort. And, therefore, if the conscience be spotted and unclean, wash it in the blood of Christ, which is first purging, and then purifying. It first purges the soul, being set at work to search our sins, and confess them, which makes us see our need of Christ, who died to satisfy divine justice. Then, God sprinkles our heart with his blood, which was shed for all penitent sinners; by which, when the heart is purged, the conscience will be soon satisfied also, by Christ's blood. And when it is purged and purified, then keep it clean; for a foul soul is always a troubled soul; and though it may be quiet, yet it is sure to break out afterwards.

# Steps to Bring Comfort to our Hearts (3)

*Remember your word to your servant, in which you have made me hope.*
*This is my comfort in my affliction, that your promise gives me life.*
*The insolent utterly deride me, but I do not turn away from your law.*
*When I think of your rules from of old, I take comfort, O Lord.*—Psa.
119:49-52

(7) And because there can be no more comfort than there is care of duty, therefore, together with innocence, let us be careful of all duties in all our several relations. Let us consider in what relations we stand, and what duties we owe, and be careful to satisfy them all. Neglect of duty is a debt, and debts are troublesome. When the soul reflects upon the omission of a necessary duty; I owe such a duty to such a person; I should have done such a thing, in such a relation, but I have omitted it, it is a disquieting thing, and that upon good grounds. If you have been negligent, there must be a setting upon the duty, with fresh endeavour to make amends for former negligence; or else the soul will have no comfort, nor will God suffer it to admit of comfort.

(8) But above all, that we may receive comfort, let us labour for a spirit of faith. Surely there is nothing that can stay the soul more, especially when it is deeply humbled, than to consider God in the second person incarnate, and abased and crucified, and made a curse and sin for us; to see the great God of heaven and earth, whose excellencies we cannot comprehend, to take our nature, and in our nature to suffer for us those things which he did endure. This will establish the soul indeed. Can the soul think that this was done for any small or to little purpose? Or can there be any grief or sin that should hinder comfort, or persuasion of the possibility of pardon, when the great God became man on purpose to die for sin? We may set this against all discouragements whatsoever.

Sibbes's Last Two Sermons: First Sermon, *Works*, vol. 7, pp. 345-46

# When We Feel Our Faith Is Weak (1)

*Now faith is the assurance of things hoped for, the conviction of things not seen.*—Heb. 11:1

My faith is weak!

(1) The office of faith is to knit us to Christ, and the weakest faith will do that, as well as the strongest. Faith is to bring us to Christ; and then to look to him for all perfections and for your title to heaven, and not to faith. True faith is faith even in the least degree of it. The arguments will not hold, if we have not much faith, we have no faith; or if we have no feeling, we have no faith.

(2) But this is not sufficient to satisfy the soul. The very cleaving to Christ is indeed a sufficient ground of comfort, yet to obtain actual comfort, there must be a knowledge that we do cleave to Christ and believe. It must appear to ourselves that we do believe before we can have comfort, though we may be true Christians, and go to heaven without it. Therefore, let us labour 'to make our calling and election sure' (2 Pet. 1:10), that is, in ourselves, and in our own apprehension. You see the advice of the apostle, 'Give all diligence.' It is not got without diligence, nor without all diligence, to make our calling and election sure. To that end 'add grace to grace' (2 Pet. 1:5). It is the growing Christian that is the assured Christian.

(3) And when we have attained any evidence of true faith, labour to keep that evidence clear. Let it not be spotted or defiled by any sinful acts. Some have much good evidence that are so blurred with negligence, and daily errors, that when they reflect upon themselves, they conclude, 'Can such a wretch as I, that have no more watchfulness over my heart, have any faith at all?' Though they may be in a good state for the main, yet they will not know it; and all because they are not careful to keep their evidence, which we should preserve clear and bright. That it might be seen and read upon all occasions, and may witness with us, and that the Spirit and the word may join their witness with our consciences.

Sibbes's Last Two Sermons: Second Sermon, *Works*, vol. 7, pp. 352-53

# When We Feel Our Faith Is Weak (2)

*And without faith it is impossible to please him, for whoever would draw near to God must believe that he exists and that he rewards those who seek him.*—Heb. 11:6

(4) Let us make conscience not to yield to any base doubts, fears, objections of Satan, and our own hearts. When we find any work of grace, deny not the work of God, lest we grieve the Spirit of God. Some melancholy Christians, though every man may see the work of God in them, yet yield so slavishly to the misgivings of their hearts that they conclude they have no faith. What dishonour this is to God and his Spirit. This is a great bondage which Satan brings the soul into. In such cases hearken not to what fear says, or Satan says, or what the world says, but hearken to what truth itself says.

(5) When we have found any work of grace, and see that our faith is true, we ought to comfort ourselves, and to maintain our comfort by all means. Every grace is but faith exercised. If any grace be found, as love to the brethren, hope of life everlasting, or the like, there is faith. For the root and branches be together, though the root is not always discerned. For when a man is in Christ, and by Christ an heir of heaven, and a child of God, what in the world can befall him, that should deject overmuch, and cast him down? Has he not all in God, and in Christ, and in the promise? Christians have two sides, one to heaven-ward and God-ward that is full of glory, certain and immoveable. Another towards the world that is oftentimes full of disgrace, and dejection, that is moveable; sometimes better, sometimes worse. Let us look to grace and to the comforts that belong to that grace, to the promises, the best side; and not to be carried away with the darkness of the other. We must not be so malignant as to look all upon one side of a Christian, and that the worser part. If we be Christians, let us live by faith, look to the best side; look upwards and forwards to that which is eternal.

Sibbes's Last Two Sermons: Second Sermon, *Works*, vol. 7, pp. 353-54

# When We Feel Our Faith Is Weak (3)

*The apostles said to the Lord, 'Increase our faith!'*—Luke 17:5

(6) Keep the graces of the Spirit, that emerge from a true faith, in continual exercise. For grace exercised, brings certain comfort. Sincerity alone will not comfort a man, unless it grows up to fruitfulness. Fruitfulness which springs from the exercise of grace, has a sweet reflection upon the soul. The heathen men, Socrates and the best of them, so far as they exercised the natural goodness that was in them, their consciences reflected peace; so far as they were good, and did good, they had peace, much more peace than bad men had. God gave even them some rewards upon discharge of their duties. He will not be beholden to any man that exercises any degree of goodness. How much more will a child of God enjoy it when he exercises his graces in any temptation. When he overcomes any unclean, earthly, vainglorious, vindictive, or any other base lust, he will find peace of conscience. The more he grows in strength and resolution, the more he grows in inward peace. Righteousness and peace go together, not only the righteousness of Christ and our reconciliation before God, but also the righteousness of a holy life and peace in our own consciences. The righteousness of Christ entitles us to heaven; and the righteousness of a holy life shows our title to comfort. They that would have inward peace, let them labour to be gracious; and that not only in the inward frame of the heart, but in the exercise of grace upon all occasions. 'For they that walk according to this rule,' that is, of the new creature, 'peace be to them' (Gal. 6:16). What a blessed condition will we be in, to be in Christ, and to know that we are so! Whatever way he looks, he finds matter of comfort. If he looks backward, to the government of the Spirit that has ruled him in the former part of his life. If he looks forward, he sees a place prepared for him in heaven and there he sees himself already in Christ.

Sibbes's Last Two Sermons: Second Sermon, *Works*, vol. 7, pp. 354-55

# Christ and the Holy Spirit

*And John bore witness: 'I saw the Spirit descend from heaven like a dove, and it remained on him.'*—John 1:32

Christ has the Spirit in himself in a more eminent and excellent manner than all others; and it must be so for these reasons:

(1) From the near union between the human nature and the divine. There is more Spirit in Christ than in all creatures put together; more than in all the angels, and all men, because the divine nature is nearer to Christ than it is to the angels or to any creature.

(2) Christ has the Spirit without measure, intensively and extensively. He has all graces in all degrees. All others have it in their measure and proportion.

(3) The Spirit rests upon Christ without variation. In men the Spirit ebbs and flows. But the Spirit rests on Christ eternally in full measure; as it says, 'The Spirit of the Lord will rest upon him, the Spirit of wisdom and understanding, the Spirit of counsel and might' (Isa. 11:2).

(4) By reason of his offices in the church. He is head, husband, king, priest, and prophet. The head is made the seat of the more noble faculties, as of seeing, hearing, understanding, judging, and is furnished accordingly with greater capacity for ruling and governing the whole body. So Christ is the Head of the church, and the government of all the world is laid upon him. Therefore, he must have the Spirit in greatest abundance. His fullness of the Spirit is as the fullness of the fountain; ours is but as the fullness of the cistern. We have nothing but what we have received.

(5) He is to be the pattern, and we are to follow him. We are 'predestinated to be conformed to him' (Rom. 8:29) and to grow up to that fullness which is in him. And in this respect, he has the Spirit and all the graces in greater abundance, that he might exceed all, even Christians of greatest growth and perfection. Even Paul himself, who was a leader to others, yet was a follower of Christ. 'Be you followers of me, as I am of Christ' (1 Cor. 11:1).

*Glorious Freedom*, pp. 6-9 [10-12]

# Christ Is the Heart and Power of the Scriptures (1)

*You search the Scriptures because you think that in them you have eternal life; and it is they that bear witness about me.*—John 5:39

The scope of the whole Scriptures is Christ.

What are all the Scriptures without Christ? The law is a dead letter; and indeed, so is the gospel without Christ. He is that Spirit which gives life to all the Scriptures. Moses without Christ is but a shadow without a body, or a body without a soul. Take away Christ, what was the brazen serpent? What was the ark? What were the sacrifices? What is all? Is not Christ all in all in these? The kings and priests and prophets, they were types of Christ; all the promises were made and fulfilled in Christ. The ceremonial law aimed at Christ; the moral law is to drive us to Christ. Christ is the Spirit of all. And the Scripture without Christ is but a mere dead thing; it is but a shell without a kernel.

Christ is the also the Spirit of the Scriptures, of all truths, of all ordinances. We can therefore reconcile the Scriptures with one another when they seem to contradict. The law is said to be a dead letter, a 'ministration of condemnation' (2 Cor. 3:6, 9), but in Psalm 19:7 it says, 'The law of the Lord is perfect, converting the soul.' These texts are reconciled in this way: the law is said to be dead, and it is so without Christ, without the Spirit who gives life; and the gospel, too, is 'a savour of death' (2 Cor. 2:16). But the law is 'perfect' and able 'to convert the soul' when the Spirit goes along with it.

We can also understand why we obtain more comfort at one time than another from an ordinance, and why it benefits one person and not another. This is from the presence or absence of Christ. Why does the reading or hearing of the same thing affect one, and not another at all? The substance of the thing is the same, but the Spirit is not the same. The Spirit goes with the one, and not with the other. The efficacy and fruit of any ordinance depends upon Christ's being present in it, who is that Spirit that quickens.

*Glorious Freedom*, pp. 9-10, 15-16 [13, 19-20]

# Christ Is the Heart and Power of the Scriptures (2)

*And beginning with Moses and all the Prophets, he interpreted to them*
*in all the Scriptures the things concerning himself.*—Luke 24:27

The most powerful means that ever was ordained for our good will be dead and heartless if Christ is not there by his Spirit to put life into it. The Scriptures profit nothing, preaching profits nothing, the ordinances profit nothing; none of these will be spiritual food indeed unless the Spirit of Christ quickens them.

We should therefore desire that Christ would join his Spirit to all the ordinances of God and make them effectual. We ought to come to the ordinances in a dependence upon Christ for a blessing upon them, and for his presence in them, who is the life and scope of all; and then we would not find such dullness and deadness in them. Take those that conform themselves in some fashion to religion, they will hear a sermon now and then, look at a book, and perhaps pray morning and evening, but never look up to the living and quickening Spirit, Jesus Christ. All they do is dead and loathsome, like salt that has no savour. The Lord loathes such sacrifices as he did Cain's; and so he does all our flat and lifeless services.

What need there is to sanctify all we take in hand by prayer! When we go to hear a sermon, when we take up the Bible to read a chapter, alone or in our families, we should lift up our eyes and hearts and voices to heaven; we should say to Christ, 'Lord, by your Spirit be present with us; without you your word is dead, our hearts are dead, and will harden under the means, and darken in the light, and we will fall under heavy condemnation, if you leave us.'

*Glorious Freedom*, pp. 16-17 [20-21]

93

# Go to Christ, the Giver of the Spirit

*Nevertheless, I tell you the truth: it is to your advantage that I go away, for if I do not go away, the Helper will not come to you. But if I go, I will send him to you.*—John 16:7

It is a point of much comfort, that there is such abundance of Spirit in Christ, that we have a fullness from which to receive. Is it not a comfort for Christians to know that Christ has the Spirit to give, the Spirit of wisdom in all difficulties, the Spirit of truth to keep us from all errors, the Spirit of strength for all services, the Spirit of comfort for all afflictions? Our Lord Jesus has abundance of Spirit in him, and for us.

Therefore, when we want any grace, or gift of the Spirit, we should go to Christ; for God does all by Christ and Christ does all by the Spirit. Desire Christ that he would grant his Spirit to rule us, counsel us, comfort us, and strengthen us. In our emptiness, as indeed we are empty creatures of ourselves, let us go to Christ for the Spirit. The reason why Christians are so dead and so dull and so dark in their spirits is that they do not first consider themselves, and then go to Christ. We should all, in all necessities whatever, make use of this our great high treasurer, the great high steward of heaven and earth, the second person in heaven. Our comfort is now that our strength and comfort lie hidden in Christ, who as man, is near to us, and as God is near to God. He is between the Father and us; he is near the Father as being of the same nature with him; he is near us as being of the same nature with us. So being a mediator in office, and being so fit for a mediator in nature, what a comfort is this.

Indeed, there is no coming to God, no interaction between God and us directly, but only through the God-man. In Christ we go to God, in our flesh, in our nature; and in Christ, and from Christ, and by Christ, we have all grace and comfort. Therefore, we should go to Christ in every way.

*Glorious Freedom*, pp. 18-19 [21-23]

# Evidence of the Holy Spirit's Presence (1)

*And in the last days it shall be, God declares, that I will pour out my*
*Spirit on all flesh, and your sons and your daughters shall prophesy,*
*and your young men shall see visions, and your old men shall dream*
*dreams; even on my male servants and female servants in those days I*
*will pour out my Spirit, and they shall prophesy.*—Acts 2:17, 18

How can we know whether or not we have the Spirit of Christ?

(1) By the activity of the Spirit. The Spirit is a vigorous working being, and therefore all three persons of the Trinity take upon themselves the name of Spirit, but the Holy Spirit especially, because he is the spiritual vigour. The Spirit is an operative entity. God, who is nothing but a pure act, is said to be a spirit. Those that have the Spirit are full of activity and energy. Will the spirits of bodies be vigorous, and will not the Holy Spirit be vigorous, who is a substantial vigour? Therefore, if a man has the Spirit of God in him, the Spirit will be working in him and very operative.

The Spirit is compared to fire in several respects: Fire is of a working nature. It is the instrument of nature. If we did not have fire, what could we work? All materials and all things are worked by fire, especially metals; they are framed and made malleable by fire. The Holy Spirit, too, works to soften the heart, and makes us malleable; he makes us fit for the impression of all good. Fire makes dark bodies light like itself. Iron is a dark body, but if the fire penetrates it, it makes it light. We are dark creatures of ourselves: if we have the Spirit he makes us light. Fire makes us cheerful and it ascends upwards. If a man has the Spirit of God, his way of life will be upward and heavenly; his mind is on the things of God, and he does not grovel here below. So in different ways the Holy Spirit is compared to fire, and has certain effects in us. In some sort we find our understandings enlightened, and ourselves quickened, and carried up to the above nature, in holy and heavenly actions; and that is a good sign that we that have the Spirit of Christ.

*Glorious Freedom*, pp. 21-22 [25-26]

# Evidence of the Holy Spirit's Presence (2)

*May the God of hope fill you with all joy and peace in believing, so that by the power of the Holy Spirit you may abound in hope.*—Rom. 15:13

(2) By the conviction given by the Spirit. The Spirit of Christ convinces (John 14:8). That is, he brings a clear, evident conviction that the truth of God is the truth of God. It is not doubtful. Therefore, when a man staggers in the truth, whether he should do this and that, it is a sign he does not have the Spirit, or that he has him in a very small measure, because as light the Spirit is convincing. A man does not doubt what he sees at noonday. So what he sees by the Spirit he is convinced of. When a man doubts and wavers, whether he should take a good course or a bad, it is a sign he is carnal, and does not have the Spirit of God; for the Spirit would convince him. You must take this course if you are saved. When the Spirit says something to convince, that says more for a thing than anything can say against it.

Now when a man has the Spirit of God, he can say more for God and for good things and good ways, than all the devils in hell by discouragement can say against them. When a man cannot say anything for God, and for good causes to purpose, he does not have the Spirit of God. The Spirit of God would so convince him, that he would answer all cavils and objections. The argument for this is wondrously full, and I have given you but a taste, to know whether or not the Spirit of Christ be in you.

(3) By the Spirit's transforming us. In a word, Christ is that Spirit, and has infused the Holy Spirit into us, the Spirit will make us like Christ; the Spirit will transform us into Christ's likeness, making us holy and humble and obedient as Christ was on earth, even to death. That you may know you have the Spirit of God, consider these directions.

*Glorious Freedom*, pp. 22-23 [26-27]

# Study Christ if You Want the Spirit

*But when the Helper comes, whom I will send to you from the Father, the Spirit of truth, who proceeds from the Father, he will bear witness about me.*—John 15:26

If we will have the Holy Spirit, study the gospel of Christ. Why, before Christ, was there was so little of the Spirit? Because there was but little measure of the knowledge of Christ. The more Christ is revealed, the more the Spirit is given. The more the free grace and love of God in Christ alone are made known to the church, the more Spirit there is. The reverse is also true, the more Spirit then the more knowledge of Christ; for there is a reciprocal connection between these two.

Why was there little of the Spirit in the clever and able schoolmen of popery? They savoured not the gospel. They were wondrously bright, but they savoured not the matters of grace, and of Christ. The gospel was revealed to them, but they attributed salvation to human merits, to the pope, and so on. They did not know Christ; they lacked the Spirit of Christ; and so they did not teach Christ as they should. Those were dark times because Christ was veiled in idle ceremonies. Christ was hidden and wrapped in idle traditions and ceremonies of men; and that was the reason that God's truth was obscured.

When Christ, and all good things by Christ, and by Christ only, are revealed, the veil is taken off. Now the past hundred years, in the time of reformation, there has been more Spirit, more light and more comfort. Christians have lived and died more comfortably. Why? Because Christ has been more known. And as it is with the church, so it is with individual Christians: the more they study Christ, and all the comfort in him alone to be had—'wisdom, righteousness, sanctification, and redemption' (1 Cor. 1:30)—the more they grow up in the knowledge of Christ, the more they grow spiritually. And the more spiritually they grow, the more they grow in the knowledge of Christ. Therefore, if we want to have the Spirit, let us come near to Christ, and labour to know him more, who is the fountain of all that is spiritual.

*Glorious Freedom*, pp. 23-25 [27-29]

# Spiritual Liberty (1)

*And when he comes, he will convict the world concerning sin and right-*
*eousness and judgment.*—John 16:8

The Spirit of God sets us at liberty, in the whole course of salvation, from the beginning to the end, when he calls us, justifies us, sanctifies us, and fully glorifies us.

(1) The Spirit of God calls us powerfully and effectually. Living in the church does not set us at liberty unless the Spirit stirs us up to answer a divine call. 'For many are called but few are chosen' (Matt. 22:14). In the church there are hypocrites as well as sound Christians. A man may have all the outward privileges, and still be a spiritual slave in the very heart of the church.

The beginning of spiritual liberty is when the Spirit of God stirs up the heart to answer God's call to salvation. When we are exhorted to believe and repent, the Spirit gives power to respond to God, 'Lord, I believe; help my unbelief' (Mark 9:24). When the Spirit of God in the ordinance says, 'Seek my face,' the soul replies, 'your face, Lord, will I seek' (Psa. 27:8). Now this answer of the soul, by the power of the Spirit subduing our corruptions, goes together with the obedience of the inward man. For man answers the call, not only by the speech of the heart, 'Lord, I do it'; but he indeed does it. When by the power of the Spirit we come out of the world and out of our corruptions, and walk more freely in the ways of God, we are set at spiritual liberty. Now it is the Spirit who does all this. For if it were not the Spirit that persuaded the soul when the minister speaks, alas! all ministerial persuasions are to no purpose. It is enough for the soul to be convinced of his misery and bondage, of what he is by nature; for let him be convinced of that once, and all the rest of the links of the golden chain of salvation will follow. The first work of the Spirit in spiritual liberty is to convince us of sin and misery; and then to work an answer of the soul and an obedience of the whole man.

*Glorious Freedom*, pp. 32-33 [36-38]

# Spiritual Liberty (2)

*He saved us, not because of works done by us in righteousness, but according to his own mercy, by the washing of regeneration and renewal of the Holy Spirit.*—Titus 3:5

(2) The Spirit of God justifies us. In justification the Spirit liberates our conscience from sin and the curse of sin. But you will say, the liberty of justification is wrought by Christ; we are justified by the obedience of Christ; and the righteousness of Christ is imputed to us. It is true Christ is our righteousness. But what is that to us unless we have something to put it on? For his riches to be ours, and our debt to be his, there must first be a union. Now this union is wrought by the Spirit. From this union there comes a change; his righteousness is mine, as if I had obeyed and done it myself; and my debts and sins are his. This is by the Spirit because the union between Christ and me is by the Spirit. For whatever Christ has done, it is nothing to me until there be a union.

And likewise, freedom is by the Spirit, because the Spirit of God works faith in me, not only to unite and knit me to Christ, but to persuade me that Christ is mine, that all his is mine, and that my debts are his. The Spirit is light, and he not only tells me that Christ is mine when I believe, but he assures me that I do believe. For the Spirit is given me to know the things that I have in Christ. For the soul always thinks God is holiness itself, and I am a mass of sin, full of terrors and fears and jealousies. What reason have I to think that God will be so favourable to such a wretch, to such a lump of sin as I am, were it not that God the Son has satisfied God the Father? God has satisfied God; and the Spirit assures my conscience. God must establish the heart in a gracious liberty of justification, as well as in the fact that God the Son has wrought it. We see then, how the Spirit sets us at liberty in the great matter of justification.

*Glorious Freedom*, pp. 33-36 [38-40]

# Spiritual Liberty (3)

*According to the foreknowledge of God the Father, in the sanctification of the Spirit, for obedience to Jesus Christ and for sprinkling with his blood: May grace and peace be multiplied to you.*—1 Pet. 1:2

(3) The Spirit of God sanctifies us. In sanctification we are liberated from the slavery to sin. The same Spirit that assures me of the pardon of my sin sanctifies my nature. The Spirit of sanctification breaks the ruling power of sin. Before then the whole life is nothing but continually sinning and offending God. But now there is a gracious liberty of disposition, a largeness of heart which follows the liberty of condition.

When a man is under the bondage of the law and under the fear of death with its sting, he does everything with a slavish mind. Where the Spirit of God is, there is the spirit of adoption, the spirit of sons, which is a free spirit. The son does not do his duties to his father out of constraint and fear, but out of nature. God enlarges the hearts of his children. We are redeemed to be a 'peculiar people, zealous of good works' (Titus 2:14). For then we have a low esteem of all things that hinder us from freeness in God's service.

What shall we think, then, of those who, if we get anything of them, it is like a spark out of the flint? Duties come from Christians as water out of a spring, they issue naturally, and are not forced, so far as they are spiritual. I confess that there are remainders of bondage where the Spirit sets at liberty; for while we live in this world there is a double principle of nature and grace. There will be a conflict in every holy duty. When the Spirit would be liberal, the flesh will draw back and say, 'Oh, but I may want!' When the Spirit would be most courageous, the flesh will say, 'But there is danger in it.' We must resist. But still here is liberty to do good, because here is a principle that resists the backwardness of the flesh.

*Glorious Freedom*, pp. 36-37 [40-42]

# Spiritual Liberty (4)

*Now may the God of peace himself sanctify you completely and may your*
*whole spirit and soul and body be kept blameless at the coming of our*
*Lord Jesus Christ.*—1 Thess. 5:23

In a wicked man there is nothing but flesh, and so there is no resistance. We must understand the nature of this spiritual liberty in sanctification. It is not a liberty freeing us altogether from conflict, and deadness, and dullness. It is a liberty not freeing us from combat but enabling us to fight the battles of the Lord against our own corruptions. Freedom from fighting is the liberty of glory in heaven when there will be no enemy within or without.

Therefore, Christians must not be discouraged with the stubbornness and unwillingness of the flesh to good duties. If we have a principle in us to fight against our corruptions, and to get good duties out of ourselves in spite of them, it is an argument for a new nature. God will perfect his own beginnings, and subdue the flesh more and more, by the power of his Spirit. We see what a sweet excuse our blessed Saviour made for his disciples when they were dead-hearted and drowsy, when they should have comforted him in the garden: 'Oh,' said he, 'the spirit is willing, but the flesh is weak' (Matt. 26:41). Sometimes after labour and expenditure of energy, deadness creeps in invincibly, and a man cannot overcome those necessities of nature, so that the spirit may be willing, and the flesh is weak. God knows our necessities. When we are dull, let us strive. Christ is ready to make excuse for us, if our hearts are right: 'The spirit is willing, but the flesh is weak.' I speak this for the comfort of the best sort of Christians, that think they are not set at liberty by the Spirit, because they find some heaviness and dullness in good duties. While we live here there is sin in us, but it does not reign. After a man has the Spirit of Christ, the Spirit of Christ maintains a perpetual combat and conflict against sin. It could subdue sin all at once if God saw it good; but God chooses to humble us while we live here and exercise us with spiritual conflicts.

*Glorious Freedom*, pp. 37-39 [42-43]

# Spiritual Liberty (5)

*And we all, with unveiled face, beholding the glory of the Lord, are being transformed into the same image from one degree of glory to another. For this comes from the Lord who is the Spirit.*—2 Cor. 3:18

By the Spirit of Christ in sanctification we are made kings to rule over our own lusts to some degree. We are not kings to be freed altogether from them, but kings to strive against them. It is a liberty to fight, and in fighting to overcome at last. When the Israelites had a promise that God would give their enemies into their hands, the meaning was not that he would give them without fighting a blow. They would fight, but in fighting they would overcome. The liberty of sanctification, it is not a liberty that ends combat with our corruptions, but a gracious liberty to keep them under, until by subduing them little by little, we have a perfect victory. What greater encouragement can a man have to fight against his enemy, than when he is sure of final victory before he fights!

But this is not all that is in liberty; for the Spirit does not only free us from all that is ill, from sin, but from that which follows it, as fear and terrors of conscience; death and wrath. Where the Spirit is, it frees us from fear; for the same Spirit that tells us in justification that God is appeased, also frees us from the fear of damnation and death and judgment; from the terrors of an evil conscience. Being 'sprinkled with the blood of Christ' (Heb. 10:22), we are freed from fear. And the Spirit not only frees us from the fear of ill things but frees us to do good. Liberty implies two things: a freedom from ill, from a cursed condition, and likewise a liberty to better—a liberty *from* ill and *to* good. We must understand the breadth of Christ's benefits, because they are complete, not only to free us from ill, but to confer all good to us. God will leave no part of the soul unfilled, no corner of the soul empty. By little and little he does it.

*Glorious Freedom*, pp. 39-40 [44-45]

# Spiritual Liberty (6)

*Sanctify them in the truth; your word is truth.*—John 17:17

When we are called out of Satan's kingdom, we are not only called out of that cursed state we are also made a part of a better kingdom; we are made the members of Christ. And so, in justification we are not only freed from damnation, from the justice and wrath of God, but we can use the plea of our righteousness by which we have claim to heaven, which is a blessed privilege and prerogative. We are not only free from the curse of the law, but we have other gracious prerogatives and privileges. We are not only freed from the dominion of sin, but we are set at liberty by the Spirit to do what is good. We have a voluntary free spirit to serve God as cheerfully as we served our lusts before.

That which terrified and frightened us before, now is our direction. A severe schoolmaster to a very young pupil becomes later, as the pupil grows, a wise tutor to guide and direct. So, the law terrified and whipped us when we were in bondage. The law scares us to Christ. Afterwards, the law comes to be a tutor, telling us what we are to do, counselling us and saying this is the best way. And we come to delight in those truths when they are revealed to us inwardly. And the more we know, the more we want to know, because we want to please God every day.

So, besides freedom from what is ill, and its consequences, there is a blessed prerogative and privilege. That is what is meant here by liberty. For God's works are complete. We must know when he delivers from ill, he advances to good. His works are full works always; he does not do things halfway. We have through Christ and by the Spirit not only freedom from what is ill, but advancement to all that is comforting and graciously good.

*Glorious Freedom*, pp. 40-41 [45-46]

# Spiritual Liberty (7)

*And those whom he predestined he also called, and those whom he called he also justified, and those whom he justified he also glorified.*—Rom. 8:30

(4) The Spirit of God glorifies us. Besides liberty in this world, there is a liberty of glory, called 'the liberty of the children of God' (Rom. 8:21). The liberty of our bodies from corruption, the glorious liberty in heaven, when we will be perfectly free. For, alas, in this world we are free to fight, not free from fight. And we are free not from misery, but free from the slavery and control of misery. But in heaven we will be free from the encounter and encumbrance. 'All tears will be wiped from our eyes' (Rev. 7:17). We will be free from all physical pain in sickness and infirmity, and free from all the remainders of sin in our souls. That will be perfect liberty, perfect redemption, and perfect adoption, both of body and soul.

And by the Spirit we have beginnings of this freedom in this world, too. For, what is peace of conscience and joy in the Holy Spirit? Is it not the beginnings of heaven, a grape of the heavenly Canaan? Is not the Spirit that we have here a pledge of that inheritance? It is an earnest payment and an earnest is a piece of the bargain. It is never taken away but is part of the bargain. So, the beginnings of grace and comfort given by the Spirit are the beginnings of that glorious liberty. The earnest assures us of that glorious liberty. For God never goes back on the bargain that he makes with his children. Grace, in some sense, is glory because grace is the beginning of glory. It frees the soul from terror and subjection to sin. So, the life of glory is begun in grace. We have the life of glory begun by the Spirit, this glorious life.

*Glorious Freedom*, p. 48 [53-54]

# Bondage to Freedom (1)

*Now the Lord is the Spirit, and where the Spirit of the Lord is, there is freedom.*—2 Cor. 3:17

The words 'Where the Spirit of the Lord is, there is freedom' imply that we are in bondage before we have the Spirit of the Lord. For outside of Christ we are slaves, the best of us all are slaves. In Christ, the lowest of all is a free man and a king. Out of Christ there is nothing but bondage and slavery. We are under the kingdom of the devil. There is no man who is not a slave until he is in Christ; and the freer a man thinks himself to be, and labours to be, the more enslaved he is.

Take those who labour to have freedom, to do what they choose. They consider it happiness to have their wills over all others, but the more freedom they have in this, the more slavery. Why? The more freedom a man has to lawlessly do what he wills, contrary to justice and equity, the more he sins. The more he sins, the more he is enslaved to sin. The more he is enslaved to sin, the more he is in bondage to the devil and becomes the enemy of God. To pick out the most wretched man in the world, I would pick out the greatest man in the world, if he is wicked, who has the most people under him; he has most freedom and accounts it his happiness. This is the greatest bondage and slavery of all, and it will prove so when he dies and comes to answer for it. If we are not in Christ, we are slaves, as Augustine said in his book *The City of God*, 'He is a slave though he domineers and rules.'

A man till he is in Christ is a slave, he has as many lords as he has lusts. The Scripture speaks of but two kingdoms, the kingdom of Satan and darkness, and the kingdom of Christ. All that are not in the kingdom of Christ must be in the other kingdom of Satan. I mention this briefly as a provocation to stir us up, to get into Christ, that we may have this spiritual freedom.

*Glorious Freedom*, pp. 28-29 [32-34]

## Bondage to Freedom (2)

*Having been set free from sin, we have become slaves of righteousness.*—
Rom. 6:18

Now, where the Spirit of Christ is, there is liberty and freedom from that bondage that we are in by nature and which is strengthened by a wicked course of life. For though we are all born slaves by nature, by a wicked course of life we put ourselves into bonds and entangle ourselves. So many sins and so many repetitions of sin, so many cords—the longer a man lives the greater slave he is. Now when the Spirit of Christ comes, it frees us from all, from both natural and habitual slavery. This liberty is wrought by Christ and applied by the Spirit. What Christ works he makes ours by his Spirit, who takes all from Christ. Yet both have their efficacy—Christ as the meritorious cause, and the Spirit as the applying cause. When Christ and we are one, his sufferings are ours, and his victory is ours, all is ours. Then the Spirit works in us love and other graces. The dominion of sin is broken more and more, and we are set at liberty by the Spirit.

Freedom does not originate with the Spirit, but the grand redeemer is Christ. By paying the price to divine justice, he redeems us, and he alone. We are in bondage to the wrath of God under his justice, and so justice must be satisfied before we can be free. We are freed by a strong hand from bondage to Satan, God's executioner and jailer. Christ frees us by his Holy Spirit, working such graces in us as to make us see the loathsomeness of that bondage, and likewise working grace in us to be in love with that better condition which the Spirit discloses to us. The Spirit brings us out of bondage by revelation and by power. All whom Christ frees by paying the price for their redemption, he perfects that freedom little by little, till he brings them to a glorious freedom in heaven.

*Glorious Freedom*, pp. 29-31 [34-35]

# On Free Will and New Birth (1)

*For freedom Christ has set us free; stand firm therefore, and do not submit again to a yoke of slavery.*—Gal. 5:1

By freedom, I mean the ability and strength to do what is good. Any liberty and ability to that which is good is only from the Spirit. The defence of Martin Luther and others who wrote of this freedom is sound and good, that the will of man is slavish altogether without the Spirit of God.

A liberty to supernatural objects comes from supernatural principles. Nothing moves above its own sphere; nothing is done above the level of activity that God has put into it. A natural man can do nothing except naturally, for nothing can work above itself by its own strength. The soul of man has no liberty at all to that which is spiritually good, without a supernatural principle that raises it above itself. The Spirit of God puts a new life into the soul of a man. When he has done that, that life is preserved against all opposition; and together with preserving that life, it applies that inward life and power to individual works. We cannot perform these works without the inciting power of the Spirit of God. The moving comes from the Spirit of God. As every individual moving in the body comes from the soul, so the Spirit puts a new life, applies that life to the soul, and applies the soul to every action.

Too many divines hold that the Holy Spirit works only by way of persuasion upon the soul, from outside the soul; but he does not enter into the soul or alter it; he does not work as an inward worker, but only as an outward persuader, suggesting and enticing. But this is too shallow a concept for so deep a business as this. He puts a new life into the soul; he takes away the stony heart and gives a fleshly heart (Ezek. 36:26). These phrases of Scripture are too weighty to attach to them such a shallow sense, as only to entreat, as a man would entreat a stone to come out of its place. But the Spirit puts a new life and power, and then acts and stirs that power to all that is good.

*Glorious Freedom*, pp. 42-43 [47-48]

# On Free Will and New Birth (2)

*For the law of the Spirit of life has set you free in Christ Jesus from the law of sin and death.*—Rom. 8:2

Some might object that the work of the Spirit distracts from and overthrows the freedom of the will! By no means! This is not to diminish the liberty of the will, for the Spirit of God is so wise an agent that he works upon the soul while preserving the principles of a man. He alters the judgment by presenting greater reasons and further light than the soul saw before. And then, by presenting to the will greater reasons to be good than ever it had to be ill before, he alters the will, so that we will to do contrary to what we did before. Then when the soul chooses, upon the discovery of light and reason, it chooses freely of its own will. So when the Spirit changes the soul, it presents such strong reasons to come out of its cursed condition and into the blessed state of being in Christ, that the will presently follows what is now understood to be the chief good of all. Grace does not take away liberty. No, it establishes liberty.

What do we pray in the Lord's prayer but for this liberty? 'Your will be done' (Matt. 6:10). That is, 'take me out of my own will more and more; conform my will to yours in all things.' The more I do so, the more liberty I have.

Men are mistaken to think the greatest liberty is to have power to good or evil. Such power is the imperfection of the creature. Man was at the first created free to do either good or evil of himself, that he might fall of himself. This was not strength but followed from a creature that came out of nothing and was subject to fall to his own principles. But the soul established in good, with an understanding so enlightened, and a will so confirmed and strengthened is without danger in temptation. That is glorious freedom. We see clearly, then, that grace does not take away liberty but establishes it.

*Glorious Freedom*, pp. 43-48 [48-53]

# Evidence of Liberty in the Spirit (1)

*For sin will have no dominion over you, since you are not under law but under grace.*—Rom. 6:14

But how will we know whether or not we are set at liberty?

(1) Wherever the Spirit of God is, there is a liberty of holiness, to free us from the dominion of any one sin. We are freed 'to serve him in holiness all the days of our lives' (Luke 1:74, 75). Where the Spirit is, therefore, he will free a man from enslavement to sin, even to any one sin. The Spirit reveals to the soul the odiousness of the bondage. For a man to be a slave to Satan, who is his enemy, a cruel enemy, what an odious thing this is! Now whoever is captive to any lust is in captivity to Satan by that lust. Therefore, where this liberty is, there cannot be slavery to any one lust.

Satan does not care how many sins one forsakes if he still lives in any one sin, for by one sin he has him and can pull him in. Children when they have a bird can let it fly, but it is on a string to be pulled back again. Satan has men on a string if they live in any one sin. The Spirit of Christ is not there, but Satan's spirit, and he can pull them in when he wants. The beast that runs away with a cord about him is caught by the cord again. When we forsake many sins yet still carry his cords about us, he can pull us in when he wants. Such prisoners are at liberty more than others, but they are slaves to Satan by that one sin. And where Satan keeps possession and rules there by one sin, there is no liberty. For the Spirit of sanctification is an antidote to the corruption of nature, and he opposes the old nature in all the powers of the soul. He allows no corruption to have control.

*Glorious Freedom*, pp. 54-55 [60-61]

# Evidence of Liberty in the Spirit (2)

*But love your enemies, and do good, and lend, expecting nothing in return, and your reward will be great, and you will be sons of the Most High, for he is kind to the ungrateful and the evil.*—Luke 6:35

(2) Where this liberty from the Spirit is, there is a blessed freedom to do all duties with a full heart. Those under grace are anointed by the Spirit (Psa. 89:20), and that spiritual anointing makes them active. Now he that is truly anointed by the Spirit is in some degree quick and active in what is good.

One result of anointing is to give agility and strength. Finding cheerfulness and strength to perform holy services, to hear the word, to pray to God, and to perform holy duties—this comes from the Spirit of God. The Spirit sets people at this liberty, because otherwise spiritual duties are as opposite to flesh and blood as fire is to water. When we are drawn to duties out of wrong motives or fear or custom, and not from a new nature, this is not from the Spirit, and their performance is not from the true liberty of the Spirit. For under the liberty of the Spirit, actions come off naturally, not forced by fear or hope or any extra motives. A child does not need other motives to please his father. When he knows he is the child of a loving father, it is natural. There is a new nature in those who have the Spirit of God to stir them up to duty, though God's motives of sweet encouragements and rewards may help. But the principal is to do things naturally, not out of fear or to appease other people.

Artificial things move from a principle outside themselves. Clocks and such things have weights that move all the wheels they go by. So it is with an artificial Christian who sets himself to a course of religion. He moves by weights outside himself and does not have an inward principle of the Spirit to make things natural to him, to excite him and make him do things naturally and sweetly. 'Where the Spirit of God is, there is freedom'—that is, a kind of natural freedom, not forced, not moved by any alien motive.

*Glorious Freedom*, pp. 55-56 [61-62]

# Evidence of Liberty in the Spirit (3)

*We are afflicted in every way, but not crushed; perplexed, but not driven to despair; persecuted, but not forsaken; struck down, but not destroyed.*—2 Cor. 4:8, 9

(3) With the freedom of the Spirit, there is courage and strength of faith against opposition. When the Spirit reveals with conviction the excellence of the state we are in, and the vileness of the state we are moved to by opposition—what is all opposition to a spiritual man? It gives him courage and strength to resist. The more opposition, the more courage he has. When the early Christians had the Spirit of God (Acts 4:29), they resisted opposition, and the more they were opposed, the more they grew. They were cast in prison and rejoiced. And the more they were imprisoned, the more courageous they were still.

There is no setting against this wind or quenching of this fire by any human power; for the Spirit of God, where he truly sets a man at liberty, gathers strength by opposition. See how the Spirit triumphed in the martyrs over fire, and imprisonment, and all opposition. The Spirit in them set them at liberty from such base fears, that he prevailed in them over everything. The Spirit of God is a victorious Spirit, freeing the soul from base fears of any creature. 'If God be for us, who can be against us?' (Rom. 8:31).

It is said of Stephen that they could not withstand the Spirit by which he spoke (Acts 6:10). And Christ promises a Spirit that no enemies will be able to withstand. God's children, in the time of opposition, when they understand themselves and what they stand for, are given by God a Spirit against which no enemies can stand. The Spirit of Christ in Stephen put such a glory upon him that he looked as if he were an angel (Acts 6:15). The Spirit of liberty gives boldness, strength, and courage against opposition. Those, therefore, who are daunted by every small thing when standing in a good cause do not have the Spirit of Christ; for where he is, he frees men from these fears, especially if the cause belongs to God.

*Glorious Freedom*, pp. 56-57 [62-63]

# Evidence of Liberty in the Spirit (4)

*Let us then with confidence draw near to the throne of grace, that we may receive mercy and find grace to help in time of need.*—Heb. 4:16

(4) The Spirit of liberty gives boldness with God himself, who otherwise is a 'consuming fire' (Heb. 12:29). It is in the time of temptation, affliction, and opposition, that a man may best judge who he truly is. When a man is in temptation and can go boldly to God and pour out his soul to God freely as to a father, this comes from the Spirit of liberty. One without the Spirit of Christ can never do this. In extremity, he sinks. But a child of God in extremity goes to God, and cries, '*Abba*, Father.'

Judas, a man of great knowledge, could not go to God. His heart was wicked; he did not have the Spirit of Christ, but the spirit of the devil. If he had said as much to God as he did to the scribes and Pharisees, he might have had mercy in the force of the event. I am speaking not of the decree of God, but of the nature of the act itself: if he had said so much to Christ and to God, he might have found mercy.

So let a man be ever so great a sinner, if he can come in confession and petition and beg mercy of God in Christ to shine as a Father upon his soul, this going to God argues that the Spirit of Christ is there.

In Romans 8:26, which speaks of comfort in afflictions, one comfort among the rest is that the children of God have the Spirit of God, to stir up sighs and groans. God understands the meaning of his own Spirit. A man may know that he has the Spirit of liberty in him, if in affliction and trouble he can sigh and groan to God.

The strong, rebellious, sturdy-hearted persons, who think to work out of their misery by their strength of abilities and friends, die in despair. But when a broken soul goes to God in Christ with boldness, this opening of the soul to God is a sign of the liberty of sons.

*Glorious Freedom*, pp. 57-59 [63-65]

# Evidence of Liberty in the Spirit (5)

*Do not be conformed to this world, but be transformed by the renewal of your mind, that by testing you may discern what is the will of God, what is good and acceptable and perfect.*—Rom. 12:2

(5) Where this Spirit of liberty is, there is a freedom from the prevailing errors and the slavish courses of the times. There are two sorts of wicked persons in the world: one sort counts it their heaven and happiness to domineer over others, so they will sell all to please them. The other sort will sell their liberty, their reason and everything so that they may get anything that they value in the world. Between those two, some domineering and others servile, are a few that live upon the terms of Christianity and are of sound judgment.

Now where the Spirit of God is, there is liberty, that is, a freedom not to enslave our judgments, much less conscience, to any man. Where the Spirit of Christ is, there is a liberty of independence. A man is not dependent upon any other man, beyond what agrees with the rules of religion. He is dependent only upon God and upon divine principles and grounds. So far as a man is 'led by the Spirit' (Rom. 8:14), he discerns things in the light of the Spirit. The apostle does not say there is license to shake off all regulation, for by too much license all liberty is lost. A true Christian is the greatest servant and the greatest freeman in the world. He has a spirit that will yield to none. Yet in the outward life he is a servant to all, to do them good. Love makes him a servant.

The moment a man is in Christ, he has another law in his soul to rule him contrary to that which there was before. Before he was ruled by the law of his lusts, which carried him where it would. But now in Christ he has a new Lord and a new law, and that rules him according to the government of the Spirit. 'The law of the Spirit of life in Christ has freed me from the law of sin and death' (Rom. 8:2).

*Glorious Freedom*, pp. 61-64 [67-71]

# The Three States of a Believer's Life

*Therefore, if anyone is in Christ, he is a new creation. The old has passed away; behold, the new has come.*—2 Cor. 5:17

A man who is on the way to heaven may be in any of three states:

(1) The state of nature, when he cares about neither heaven nor hell, so he may please the sensual nature and go on without fear or wisdom; without grace, he may even satisfy himself in a course of sin. This is the worst state, the state of nature.

(2) But God, if he belongs to him, will not allow him to be in this brutish condition long; he brings him under the law. That is, God sets a man's own corrupt nature before him and shows him the course of his life. Then he is afraid of God: 'Depart from me; I am a sinner' (Luke 5:8). As Adam when he had sinned, ran from God, who was sweet to him before. When a man's conscience is awakened to sin, when he considers that there is but a step between him and hell, and considers what a God he has to deal with and that after death there is eternal damnation, when the Spirit of God has convinced him of this, then he is in a state of fear. In this state, he is unfit to run to God. He uses all his power to move away from God all he can, and hates God, and wishes there were no God, and trembles at the very thought of God and of death.

(3) Oh, but if a man belongs to God, God will not leave him in this condition either. But there is another condition, and that is the condition of liberty, when God by his Spirit reveals to him in Christ forgiveness of sins, the gracious face of God ready to receive him: 'Come unto me, all ye that are weary and heavy laden' (Matt. 11:28), says Christ; and 'where sin has abounded, grace more abounds' (Rom. 5:20). When a man hears this still, sweet voice of the gospel, he begins to take comfort in himself, and he goes to God freely.

*Glorious Freedom*, pp. 59-61 [65-66]

# Grieving the Holy Spirit

*And do not grieve the Holy Spirit of God, by whom you were sealed for the day of redemption.*—Eph. 4:30

When we find the Holy Spirit is touching our souls, oh, give him entrance to come into his own chamber, as it were, to provide a room for him when he knocks. We that live in the church, the heart of each of us, without exception, tells us that we have often resisted the Holy Spirit. Do not grieve the Spirit by any means. The Spirit may be grieved in any of several ways.

(1) The Spirit being a Spirit of holiness, is grieved with unclean words and actions. He is called the Holy Spirit, and he stirs up in the soul holy promptings like himself. He breathes into us holy promptings, and he breathes out of us good and savoury words and stirs us up to holy actions.

(2) Then the Spirit is a Spirit of love, take heed of bitterness and malice. We grieve the Spirit of God by cherishing bitterness and malice one against another. It drives away the sweet spirit of love.

(3) The Spirit of Christ is joined with a spirit of humility. 'God gives grace to the humble' (James 4:6). The Spirit empties the soul of its windy vanity in order to fill it with himself. Those who are filled with vain, high, and proud thoughts grieve and keep out the good Spirit of God.

(4) In a word, any sin against conscience grieves the Spirit of God, and hinders spiritual liberty. When a man sins against conscience he is dead to good actions. Conscience tells him, 'How can you go about that good thing, when you have done this or that bad thing?' He cannot go so naturally to prayer and to hearing from God. Conscience lays a clog upon him. How dare he look to heaven, when he has grieved the Spirit of God, and broken the peace of his conscience?

Let this be a comfort to all struggling and striving Christians that are not yet set at liberty from their lusts and corruptions; that it is the work of Christ by his Spirit to purge the church perfectly. Remember, he will complete his work (Phil. 1:6).

*Glorious Freedom*, pp. 65-67 [71-74]

# A Daily Pursuit

*Not that I have already obtained this or am already perfect, but I press on to make it my own, because Christ Jesus has made me his own.*— Phil. 3:12

If we have all these blessed liberties in this world and in that to come by the Spirit, then we should labour to have the Spirit of Christ, or else we have no liberty at all; and labour every day more and more to get this spiritual liberty in our consciences, to have our consciences assured by the Spirit that our sins are forgiven, and to feel in our consciences a power to bring under sin that has tyrannized over us before. Let us every day, more and more, labour to find this spiritual liberty, and prize daily more the ordinances of God, sanctified to help us know this liberty. Attend upon spiritual means, that God has sanctified, wherein he will convey the Spirit. There were certain times wherein the angel came to stir the waters of the pool of Bethesda (John 5:7). So, the Spirit of God stirs the waters of the word and ordinances and makes them effectual. Attend upon the ordinances of God, the communion of saints, and so on, and the Spirit of God will slide into our souls in the use of these holy means. There is no man who will not find this to be true. He finds himself raised above himself in the use of holy means. The more we know the gospel, the more we have of the Spirit; and the more of the Spirit we have, the more liberty we enjoy. If we prize and value outward liberty, as indeed we do, and we are naturally moved to do so, how should we prize the charter of our spiritual liberty, the word of God, and the promises of salvation, whereby we come to know all our liberty, where we have all the promises opened to us; the promise of forgiveness of sins, of necessary grace; the promise of comfort in all conditions whatsoever. Therefore, let us everyday labour to grow farther and farther both in the knowledge and in the taste and feeling of this spiritual liberty.

*Glorious Freedom*, p. 52 [57-58]

# A Blessed Condition

*Blessed be the God and Father of our Lord Jesus Christ, who has blessed us in Christ with every spiritual blessing in the heavenly places.*—Eph. 1:3

Oh beloved, what a blessed condition it is to have spiritual liberty! Do we see the blessed use and comfort of it in all conditions? In temptations, we have the Spirit of God to free us from temptation; or, if temptation has caught hold of us to sin, we have the Spirit of God to help us fly to the blood of Christ, and lay hold on Christ and to know he has pardoned our sin. In sickness, to consider that there is a glorious liberty of the sons of God, and a redemption of body, as well as of soul, that our base bodies will be like Christ's glorious body; that there is a resurrection to glory and the resurrection will make amends for all these sicknesses and ills of body. In death, when it comes, to know that by the blood of Christ there is a liberty to enter into heaven. In all needs, to think we have a liberty to the throne of grace; we have a freedom in all the promises; what a sweet thing this is, in all wants and needs, to use our spiritual liberty to have the ear of God! Not only to be free from the wrath of God, but to have his favour, to have his care in all our needs: what a blessed liberty this is!

Beloved, it is invaluable. There is not the least branch of this spiritual liberty, but it is worth a thousand worlds. How we should value it and bless God for giving Christ to work this blessed liberty; and for giving his Spirit to apply it to us more and more, and to set us more and more at spiritual liberty. For all three, the Father, the Son, and the Holy Spirit, all join in this spiritual liberty. The Father gives the Son, and the Son gives the Spirit; and all to set us free. It is a comfortable and blessed condition.

*Glorious Freedom*, pp. 53-54 [58-60]

# God's Mercy to Adam *versus* God's Mercy to Sinners

*But God, being rich in mercy, because of the great love with which he loved us, even when we were dead in our trespasses, made us alive together with Christ—by grace you have been saved.*—Eph. 2:4, 5

Adam had the image of God upon him and had communion with God. But there is greater glory now shining in the gospel, in Jesus Christ, to poor sinners. For when man stood in innocence, God did good to a good man, and God was amiable to a friend. Now to do good to one who is good and to maintain sweet communion with a friend is good indeed, and it was a great glory of God's mercy that he would raise such a creature as man to that height. But now in Jesus Christ there is a further glory of mercy, for God does good to evil men, and the goodness of God is victorious over the greatest ill of man. Now in the gospel God does good to his enemies. God set forth and gloriously commended his love, that 'when we were enemies, he gave his Son for us' (Rom. 5:10). Therefore, greater glory of mercy and love shines forth to fallen man in Christ than to Adam in innocence.

But to go higher, consider the angels themselves. It is not the love of angels, but the love of humans, that outshines all. God is not called the lover of angels. He took upon himself not the nature of angels, but the nature of man; and man is the bride of Christ. Nothing is more terrifying than to consider that without regard to Christ, God is a 'consuming fire' (Heb. 12:29). But nothing is sweeter than to consider his glorious mercy in Jesus Christ. For in Jesus Christ God has taken the relation of a Father, 'the Father of mercies, and God of all comfort' (2 Cor. 1:3). The nature of God is lovely in Christ, and our nature in Christ is lovely to him. And this made the angels, when Christ was born, to sing from heaven, 'Glory to God on high' (Luke 2:14). They themselves do not enjoy the grace by Christ but enjoyed increase of glory when Christ was born. What glory? Why, the glory of his mercy, of his love, of his grace to sinful men.

*Glorious Freedom*, pp. 75-76 [82-84]

# Consider God's Mercy More than the Angels Do

*Blessed be the God and Father of our Lord Jesus Christ! According to his great mercy, he has caused us to be born again to a living hope through the resurrection of Jesus Christ from the dead.*—1 Pet. 1:3

Do consider what a loving God we have, who would not be so much in love with his only Son as to keep him to himself; a God that accounts himself most glorious in those attributes that are most for our comfort. He accounts himself glorious not so much for his wisdom, power, or justice, as for his mercy and grace, for his love of man. Will we not be inflamed with a desire to gratify him, who has joined his glory with our salvation; who accounts himself glorious in his mercy above all other attributes? The angels—who do not have that benefit by Christ as we have—sing from heaven, 'Glory to God on high.' Will we who reap the crop be so dead and frozen-hearted as not to acknowledge this glory of God breaking out in the gospel, the glory of his mercy and rich grace?

The apostle is so full when he comes to his theme that he cannot speak without words of amplification, once calling it 'rich grace' (Eph. 1:7), another time standing in admiration: 'Oh, the depth of the riches' (Rom. 11:33). The best testimony that can be given of glorious things is when we admire them. Now is there anything else so admirable about which we could say, 'Oh the height and depth,' as we may of the love of God in Christ? I beseech you, let us often stand in admiration of the love of God to us in Christ. 'God so loved the world' (John 3:16). How? We cannot tell how. 'So' is beyond all expression.

Oh, base nature, that we are dazzled by anything but that which we should most admire. How few of us spend our thoughts considering God's wonderful mercy and grace in Christ, when there is no object in the world so sweet and comforting as this. The very angels desire to pry into the mystery of our salvation by Christ. They are mere students. They pry into the secrets of God's love in bringing his people to heaven. Will they do it, and will we not study and admire these things, that God may have the glory?

*Glorious Freedom*, pp. 77-78 [85-86]

# Never Be Afraid to Return to God

*For God, who said, 'Let light shine out of darkness,' has shone in our*
*hearts to give the light of the knowledge of the glory of God in the face*
*of Jesus Christ.*—2 Cor. 4:6

It is vain for some to think, 'Oh, we must not look to our own salvation so much; this is self-love.' That is true if we sever the consideration
of the glory of God's mercy and goodness from it. We hinder God's glory
if we do not believe his mercy in Christ to us. We wrong both ourselves
and him. Let us yield to him the glory of his mercy, and let us think
that when we sin, we cannot glorify him more than to take recourse
to his mercy. When Satan tempts us to run from God, as he will do at
many times, then keep this in mind: God has set himself to be glorious
in mercy above all other attributes. God will account himself honoured
if we return to him. Let this thought be as a city of refuge. When the
avenger of blood follows you, flee immediately to this sanctuary. Think:
'Let me not deny myself comfort and God glory both at once.' Though
sins, after conversion, stain our profession more than sins before conversion, go still to the glorious mercy of God. To seventy times seventy,
there is yet mercy. 'We beseech you be reconciled' (2 Cor. 5:20), said Paul
to the Corinthians, when they were in the state of grace and already had
their pardon. Let us never be discouraged from going to Christ.

But I have offended often and grievously. With men, offences often
cause permanent alienation, but with God this is not so. As often as we
have spirit to go to God for mercy and spread our sins before him with
broken and humble hearts, we may receive pardon. How does God show
himself and his glory to Moses? 'The Lord, the Lord, gracious, merciful,
long-suffering' (Exod. 34:6). He will be known by those names.

If you find your conscience wounded with any sin, do not hold
back from God any longer. Come and yield, lay down your weapons;
there is mercy ready. It is a victorious, triumphing mercy over all sin and
unworthiness. Look upon God in the face of Jesus Christ. In the face of
Christ God is lovely.

*Glorious Freedom*, pp. 81-83 [88-90]

# See God through the Communion Elements

*For now we see in a mirror dimly, but then face to face. Now I know*
*in part; then I shall know fully, even as I have been fully known.—*
1 Cor. 13:12

While we live on this earth our sight of God is imperfect, as in a mirror. It is nothing compared with seeing him face to face in heaven. We will know this sight better when we are there; we cannot now discover it. It is a part of heaven to know what apprehensions we will have of God there. But surely it will be more excellent than that which is here.

Now while we are here, we are to receive communion. Think of the communion elements as mirrors in which we see the glory of the love and mercy of God in Christ. If we consider the bread alone, and not as representing better things, what is it? And the wine alone, as if it did not represent better things, what is it but an ordinary poor thing? Oh, but take them as a mirror, as things that convey to the soul and represent things more excellent than themselves, and they are a glorious ordinance. Bread and wine must not be taken as naked elements, but as they represent and convey something more excellent: that is, Christ and all his benefits, and the love, mercy, and grace of God in Christ.

I beseech you now, when you are to receive communion, let your minds be more occupied than your senses. When you take the bread, think of the body of Christ broken; and when you think of mixing and uniting the bread into one substance, think of Christ and you made one. When the wine is poured out, think of the blood of Christ poured out for your sin. When you think of the refreshment that wine can bring, think of the refreshing of your spirits and souls by the love of God in Christ, and of the love of Christ that did not spare his blood for your soul's good. Think how Christ crucified and his shed blood refreshes the guilty soul, as wine refreshes the weak spirits! Consider the ordinances as mirrors in which better things are presented, and let your minds as well as your senses be occupied, and then you will be fit receivers.

*Glorious Freedom*, pp. 87-89 [95-97]

# Spiritual Sight (1)

*Father, I desire that they also, whom you have given me, may be with me where I am, to see my glory that you have given me because you loved me before the foundation of the world.*—John 17:24

God puts a spiritual eye by his Spirit into all true believers, by which they behold his excellent glory. This glorious gift was given so that God may have the glory, and we the comfort. There must be a beholding. The Spirit creates and works in us spiritual sight. We see God in several ways:

(1) We see God in his creation, for 'the heavens declare the glory of God' (Psa. 19:1). They are a book in folio. There God is laid open in his creation. That is a pleasing sight. But what is this compared to knowing him in his will to us?

(2) We see God in his will, and in his word and promises. There we see what he is, his grace revealed in Christ, what his good will is to us, and what he wills from us. There we see him as a spouse sees her husband in a loving letter which concerns herself. We see him as the heir sees a deed made to him with an inheritance. It is not a sight only, but a sight with feeling and discovery of a favour. The sight in the word and ordinances is higher than that in the created universe.

(3) Christ was seen when he was in the flesh. When he was covered with the veil of our flesh upon earth, that was a sweet sight. Abraham desired to see it (John 8:56); and Simeon, when he saw it, was willing to depart (Luke 2:29). Yet this outward sight is nothing without an inward sight of faith.

(4) We see by faith, and other sights are to no purpose without this, the sight of God shining in Christ. And it will be perfected in heaven, in the sight of glory, when we shall see him as he is.

There is comfort in all these sights of God in his word and works. It was glorious to see him in his bodily presence, and by faith to see the face of God shining in Christ. Oh, but what is all this to the sight of him hereafter in glory!

*Glorious Freedom*, pp. 90-91 [98-99]

# Spiritual Sight (2)

*Having the eyes of your hearts enlightened, that you may know what is the hope to which he has called you, what are the riches of his glorious inheritance in the saints.*—Eph. 1:18

Knowledge and faith are compared to seeing and beholding, for these reasons:

(1) Sight is the noblest and most glorious sense. It is also the quickest, for in a moment sight apprehends its object in the highest heavens. So it is with faith. It is the noblest sight of all. And it is as quick as sight; for faith is that eagle in the cloud. It breaks through all and sees in a moment Christ in heaven; it looks backward and sees Christ upon the cross; it looks forward and sees Christ to come in glory. Faith is so quick a grace that it presents things past, things above and things to come—all in a moment, so quick is this eagle-eye of faith.

(2) Sight is the broadest sense. We can see almost the whole hemisphere at one view. That a little thing in the eye should apprehend so much in a moment! As it is quick in apprehension, so it is large in comprehension. Sight is the surest sense, surer than hearing, and that is why the divine act of knowledge is compared to seeing. Believing is compared to beholding. When faith looks upon God in the glass of the word and promises, it is as certain as the object itself.

(3) Sight is the sense that works most upon the soul; what the body sees affects and moves the soul. It works upon the affections most. Desire and love rise out of sight. That is why the knowledge that stirs up the affections and works upon the heart is compared to sight. It affects us marvellously: corresponding to our faith, we love, and joy, and delight. Knowledge alters the whole man.

'Faith is the evidence of things not seen' (Heb. 11:1), and it works upon the heart and soul. We should labour to clear the eye of the soul, that we may behold the glory of God in the glass of the gospel.

*Glorious Freedom*, pp. 91-92 [99-101]

# Beholding God's Glory

*And we all, with unveiled face, beholding the glory of the Lord, are being transformed into the same image from one degree of glory to another. For this comes from the Lord who is the Spirit.*—2 Cor. 3:18

How can we make the eye of our souls fit to behold the glory of God? We must fix the eye of the soul; fix our meditation upon the glory of God and the excellency of Christ. A moving, roving eye sees nothing. We must set some time apart to fix our meditations upon the excellent things in the gospel.

We must also labour to have both inward and outward hindrances removed. We must labour that the soul be cleansed from all carnal passions and desires. Only a spiritual soul can ever behold spiritual things. The physical eye cannot apprehend or behold spiritual things. There must be a spiritual eye, and there must be some relation between the soul and spiritual things before the soul can behold them. As the soul must be fixed upon these meditations, so the Spirit of God must sanctify and purge the soul. Sight is also hindered from without by dust in the eyes, cloudiness, and such things. Satan uses the dust of the world to hinder the sight of the soul from beholding the glory of God in the gospel. The apostle says that the god of this world blinds the eyes of men (2 Cor. 4:3, 4). We will not see Christ, and God in Christ, by fixing the soul upon base things below.

We should preserve this sight of faith by hearing. Hearing begets seeing in religion. Death came in by the ear at the beginning, when Adam listened to the serpent who he should not have listened to. Life, too, comes in by the ear. We hear, and then we see; 'As we have heard, so have we seen' (Psa. 48:8). It is also true in religion; most of our sight comes by hearing, which is the sense of learning. God has made it so. We should therefore behold the glory of the Lord all we can in the glass of the word; and to that end hear much. The best picture to see Christ in is the word and the ordinances. And the best eye to see him with is the eye of faith.

*Glorious Freedom*, pp. 92-94 [101-02]

# Unity in the People of God

*Eager to maintain the unity of the Spirit in the bond of peace.*—Eph.
4:3

In Moses' time, he went alone onto the mount and saw God. But now it is 'we all' (2 Cor. 3:18), that is Jews and Gentiles, wherever the gospel is preached. You see that the church is enlarged by the coming of Christ. It was a comfort to Paul and to all good Christians to think of the enlargement of the church by taking in the Gentiles, and it will be a comfort to think of the enlarging of the church by taking in the Jews again. In Christianity, the more the better.

Why is it a privilege for many, why 'we all'? Because in matters of grace and glory there is no envy at all. All may share without prejudice. Here on earth not all can be kings, nor can all be great men, because the more one has the less another has. But in Christ all may have grace. There is no envy, as I said, in grace and glory, where all may share alike. That is why it is always comforting to think of community in faith; it is joined with comfort.

Indeed, it is also comforting to see a communion of many in one. For what is the mystical body of Christ Jesus, but many members joined in one body, under one gracious and glorious head? A divided and disunited body is deformed. That is what the devil rules in: divide and conquer. But God and Christ rule in unity. The same Spirit of God that knits the members to the head by faith, knits the members to one another in love.

Then let us labour to cherish unity and hate division. No one gains by disunion but the devil himself. His policy is always to make any breach greater. But the more who join together in the blessed mysteries of the gospel, the more comfort, and the more glory there is. When all live and join together in the holy things of God, and in sweet love toward one another, it is the glory of that place and society and state.

By love let us labour to bring our hearts to a holy communion.

*Glorious Freedom*, pp. 99-100 [107-09]

# Consider Christ So As to Become Like Him (1)

*Take my yoke upon you, and learn from me, for I am gentle and lowly in heart, and you will find rest for your souls.*—Matt. 11:29

If it is so that we are changed into the image of the second Adam, Jesus Christ, then let us labour every day more and more to study Christ, so that by beholding him we may be transformed into his likeness. The sight of Christ is a transforming sight.

Let us look into his disposition and his conduct as they are set forth in the Gospels. What was his disposition and conduct to his friends, his enemies, and the devil himself?

You see how full of love he was. What drew him from heaven to earth, and so to his cross and to his grave, but love to mankind? You see how full of goodness he was: 'He went about doing good' (Acts 10:38).

See how full of zeal he was! He whipped the buyers and sellers out of the temple (John 2:15).

He was full of goodness. It was his meat and drink to do good (John 4:31-34). It was as natural to him as for a fountain to stream out.

As for his behaviour toward his friends, to those who were good see how sweet and indulgent he was.

Where there was any beginning of goodness, he encouraged it. He never sent any away, but those who went away of their own accord, as the rich young man. Christ did not send him away (Matt. 19:22). He was so full of sweetness to weak Christians; indeed, he revealed himself most to the weakest. He spoke personally with the woman of Samaria, who was an adulteress (John 4:6-26); and Mary, who had been a sinner, how sweetly did he appear to her first (John 20:11-16). How sweet he was to sinners when they repented, how ready to forgive and pardon! See it in Peter. He never reproached him for his apostasy; he never upbraided him for it; he never so much as told him of it. He only 'looked' upon him, and afterward said, 'Do you love me?' (John 21:15).

*Glorious Freedom*, pp. 110-11 [121-22]

## Consider Christ So As to Become Like Him (2)

*For to this you have been called, because Christ also suffered for you, leaving you an example, so that you might follow in his steps.*—1 Pet. 2:21

He would not 'quench the smoking flax, nor break the bruised reed' (Matt. 12:20), so gentle and sweet a Saviour have we. He loved and responded to those who sought him out, as when the rich young man came and said, 'What good thing must I do to inherit eternal life?' (Mark 10:17). So to the Pharisee, he said, 'You are not far from the kingdom of God' (Mark 12:34). He laboured to pull him further. He was of a winning, gaining disposition. Will we not labour to be of his disposition, not to set people further off, but to be of a gaining, winning nature?

See how obedient he was to his Father: 'Not as I will, but as you will' (Matt. 26:39). Both in active and in passive obedience, in all things he looked to his Father's will, being subordinate to him. We see he prayed whole nights (Luke 6:12; 21:37). Wherever there is subordination, there ought to be obedience. We are subordinate to God as our Father in Christ; we should labour to be obedient even to death, as Christ was. Our happiness lies in subordination. The happiness of the inferior is in subjection to the superior that may do him good.

In and of himself, how holy and heavenly he was. He took occasion of vines, of stones, of water, of sheep, and of all things to be heavenly-minded, to raise his soul upon all occasions. And when he rose from the dead and conversed with his disciples, what did he talk about? He spoke all about matters of the kingdom of heaven. So his whole disposition was heavenly and holy in himself, and he was patient in wrongs done to him. He did not return injury for injury. You see how meek he was. He was in himself full of purity and holiness and heavenliness.

*Glorious Freedom*, pp. 111-112 [122-23]

## Consider Christ So As to Become Like Him (3)

*Whoever says he abides in him ought to walk in the same way in which he walked.*—1 John 2:6

How did he behave toward his enemies? Did he call for fire from heaven when they wronged him? He shed tears for those who would shed his blood: 'O Jerusalem, Jerusalem' (Matt. 23:37), who afterward crucified him. And upon the cross you see him saying of his very enemies, 'Father, forgive them, they know not what they do' (Luke 23:34). So then if we will be like Christ, consider how he prayed for his very enemies.

As for the devil himself, deal with him as Christ did, that is, have no terms with him, although he comes to us in our nearest friends. He came to Christ in Peter. And Christ said, 'Satan, get behind me' (Matt. 16:23). If the devil comes to us in our wives, in our children, in our friends, avoid Satan. He comes to us sometimes in our friends, to give corrupt judgment, to promote selfish causes, to do this or that which may crack our conscience. Let us imitate Christ and discern between the love of our friends and the subtlety of the devil in them, and be able to say, 'Get behind me, Satan.' We see that Christ, when he encountered Satan, fought not with Satan's weapons but with the word of God. He did not give reproach for reproach, or lies for lies, but, 'It is written' (Matt. 4:4-10), showing that we must counter Satan with God's armoury, with weapons out of the book of God.

Have nothing to do with those who are manifestly led by the spirit of Satan and would press kindness on us. Those who are led by the spirit of the devil do not lie about everything, but there is deceit in everything. All offers from those who are led by the spirit of Satan we ought to suspect. When Christ was offered a kindness by Satan, he said, 'Be gone!' (Matt. 4:10). Have nothing to do with devilish men. They are always deceivers, though not always liars; and those who see this have least to do with them.

*Glorious Freedom*, pp. 112-114 [123-25]

## Consider Christ So As to Become Like Him (4)

*For those whom he foreknew he also predestined to be conformed to the image of his Son, in order that he might be the firstborn among many brothers.*—Rom. 8:29

So, you have a taste of Christ's behaviour to his friends, to his enemies, to Satan. And as for hypocrites he says, 'Woe to them' (Matt. 23:13). He hated them above all the proud Pharisees. I might spend much time in going over details in the Gospels, to see what expressions there are of Jesus Christ.

When you read in the Gospels of any expression of his love and gentleness, of his obedience and humility, in washing his disciples' feet, for example, or of his saying 'Learn of me, for I am meek' (Matt. 11:29), then think, 'This is the expression of my blessed Saviour, the second Adam, to whose image I must be transformed.' And when you are tempted to sin, from your own corruption or from Satan, reason with yourself: 'Would our blessed Saviour, if he were upon earth, do this? Would he say this? Would he not be ready to do this good turn? Surely he would; and I must be changed into his image and likeness.' Surely our blessed Saviour would not stain and defile his body. He would not make his tongue an instrument of untruth to deceive others. He would not be covetous and injurious.

Are you a Christian or not? If you are, you have the anointing of Jesus Christ. The anointing that was poured on him as the head, runs down to you as a member, as Aaron's ointment ran down to his skirts. If you are only the skirt of Christ, the lowest Christian, you have the same grace. And you must express Christ; as you partake of his name, so you must partake of his anointing. If you are a Christian, why do you do this? Does it agree with what you profess? Do you carry the image of Satan and think you are a Christian? Are you a Christian in name only? Any true Christian is changed into the likeness of Christ, into his image.

*Glorious Freedom*, pp. 114-15 [125-26]

# Consider Christ So As to Become Like Him (5)

*And have put on the new self, which is being renewed in knowledge after the image of its creator.*—Col. 3:10

It is good upon all occasions, every day, to think, 'What would my blessed Saviour say if he were here? What did he do in similar cases when he was upon earth? I must be led by the Spirit of Christ, or else I am none of his.' Let us be ashamed when we are moved by our corruptions and temptations to do anything contrary to this blessed image.

Consider, the more we grow into the likeness of Christ, the more we grow in the love of God, who delights in us as he does in his own Son: 'This is my beloved Son, in whom I am well pleased' (Matt. 3:17). The more we are like Christ, the more he is pleased with us.

And the more we shall grow in love for one another, for the more pictures conform to the original pattern, the more they are like one another. So the more we grow to be like Christ, the more we are like one another; and the more alike, the more love.

Who keeps Christ alive in the world, but a company of Christians, who carry his resemblance? As we say of a child that is like his father. This man cannot die as long as his son is alive because he resembles his father. As long as Christians are in the world, who have the Spirit of Christ, Christ cannot die. He lives in them, and Christ is alive in the world in the hearts of Christians, who have received his grace and who carry the picture and resemblance of Christ in them.

*Glorious Freedom*, p. 115 [126]

# Identifying with Christ's Death and Resurrection

*And we all, with unveiled face, beholding the glory of the Lord, are being transformed into the same image from one degree of glory to another. For this comes from the Lord who is the Spirit.*—2 Cor. 3:18

How are we changed into the likeness of Christ? When we believe in Christ, we are planted into the likeness of his death and his resurrection. This is somewhat mystical, yet it is taught in the Scriptures, especially in Romans 6. How do we come to die to sin by virtue of Christ's death and to live to righteousness by the fellowship of Christ's resurrection? The Scripture says we are transformed into the likeness of Christ. Let us expound these phrases a little.

When Christ died, it was in his own person; Christ died whole and was crucified. But the death itself was limited to the human nature—the human nature died and not the Godhead. Yet by reason of the union, all of Christ died and was crucified: the 'Lord of glory' was crucified (1 Cor. 2:8).

As it was in Christ natural, so it is in Christ mystical. All of Christ mystical was crucified, and all of Christ mystical is risen again, even though the crucifying was confined to Christ the head, not the members. As his death was limited to his human nature, so this crucifying belonged to the head, and the head rose. Yet all believers—all of Christ—as soon as they are one with Christ by reason of the mystical union, are dead and crucified in Christ their head, and they are risen and sit in heavenly places, in Christ their head.

So, a true believer, when he is made one with Christ, reasons: 'My corruption of nature, this natural pride of heart and enmity of goodness, is crucified, for I am one with Christ. I in my head was crucified, and I in my head am now risen and sit in heaven. So now I am in some way glorious and, in my head, I attend to things above. Because the members must conform to the head, I must die to sin more and more, be crucified to sin, and rise by the Spirit of Christ and ascend with him.' The more a believer knows and meditates on this, the more he is transformed into the likeness of Christ's death and resurrection.

*Glorious Freedom*, pp. 116-17 [126-28]

# Looking at the Cross

*How can I who died to sin still live in it?*—Rom. 6:2b

What things in Christ's death especially reveal themselves to us? Three things: wonderful love, that he died for us; wonderful hatred, that he would die for sin; and wonderful holiness and love of grace.

From where does hatred of sin come, but from wondrous purity and holiness that cannot endure sin? And when the soul considers that it is one with Christ, it has the same disposition that Christ had. Christ in love for us died. Can I apprehend that love of Christ when he died and was crucified and tormented for my sin, unless, out of love, I hate sin again? And when I consider how Christ died to purge sin and to satisfy for it, can I, being one with him, have any attitude other than he had upon the cross? I cannot.

I cannot but hate sin; and, hating sin, I must re-enact his part. That is, as he died for sin, so I die to sin; as he was crucified for it, so it is crucified in me; as he was pierced, so he gives corruption a stab in me; as he was buried, so my corruption is buried; and as he died once never to die again, so I follow my sins to the grave, to the death of old Adam, that he never rises again. These and similar thoughts are stirred up in a Christian, which Paul aims at in Romans 6 and other passages. As the power of God's Spirit raised him up when he was at the lowest, after three days in the grave, so the Spirit in every Christian raises him up at the lowest, to comfort, to a further degree of grace, more and more. When Christians are fallen into any sin or any affliction for sin, when they are tripped and undermined by their corruptions, the same power that raised Christ from the grave raises them from their sins daily, that they gather strength against them. And when we are at the lowest, in the grave, the same power will raise us like Christ in every way.

*Glorious Freedom*, pp. 117-18 [128-29]

# Looking at Jesus

*Looking to Jesus, the founder and perfecter of our faith, who for the joy
that was set before him endured the cross, despising the shame, and is
seated at the right hand of the throne of God.*—Heb. 12:2

That we may be changed into the likeness of Christ, let us fix our
meditations upon him, and we will find a change, though we do not
know how it happens. As those who are in the sun for work or play
find themselves lightened and warmed, so let us set ourselves about holy
meditations, and we will find a secret, imperceptible change; our souls
will be altered, we do not know how. There is a virtue that goes with
holy meditation, a changing, transforming virtue. Indeed, we can think
of nothing in Christ without having it change us to the likeness of itself,
because we have all from Christ.

Can we think of his humility and not be humble? Can we think,
'Was God humble, and will base worms be proud? Will I be fierce when
my Saviour was meek?' Can a proud, fierce heart apprehend a sweet,
meek Saviour? No. The heart must be suited to the thing apprehended.
It is impossible that a heart that is not meek, and sweetened, and brought
low, should apprehend a loving and humble Saviour. There must be a
suitability between the heart and Christ. As he was born of a humble
virgin, so he is born and conceived in a humble heart. Christ is conceived
and born and lives and grows in every Christian, and a humble and lowly
heart made like him by his Spirit, that is the womb. The heart that is
suitable is the heart that he is formed in.

*Glorious Freedom*, pp. 120-21 [131-32]

# We Must Be Changed (1)

*That which is born of the flesh is flesh, and that which is born of the Spirit is spirit. Do not marvel that I said to you, 'You must be born again.'*—John 3:6, 7

We must be changed from the state in which we are, as Christ tells Nicodemus (John 3:7), and such a change as a new birth. We must be all new, just as a bell that has even one crack must be newly moulded and recast. It is the same with the soul. Before the soul can make any sweet harmony in the ears of God, there must be a change. There is no coming to heaven without a change.

(1) We are in a state contrary to grace and to God. We are dead. There must be life in us before we come to heaven. We are enemies and must be made friends. How will we be fit for communion with God, in whom our happiness lies, without conformity? Communion is between friends. Before those opposed to each other can be friends, there must be an alteration; and this alteration must be either on God's part, or on ours.

Now, who must change? God, who is unchangeable, or we, who are corrupt and changeable? God will not change. There is no reason he should. He is goodness itself, his perfection unique. Therefore, when there is a difference between God and us, the change must be on our part. We must be changed in the spirit of our minds (Rom. 12:2). We must be wholly moulded anew. On a musical instrument, those strings that are out of tune are adjusted to those that are in tune. In the same way, it is we who must alter, and not God.

We must have new judgements and new desires, new esteem, new affections, new joys and delights, new company. The whole frame and bent of the soul must be new. The face of the soul must look altogether another way. Whereas before it looked to the world, to things below, now it must look to God and heaven. It is a double change, real and gradual. This happens at our conversion when God puts the first form and stamp upon us. The gradual change is from better to better, from glory to glory.

*Glorious Freedom*, pp. 101-03 [112-14]

# We Must Be Changed (2)

*And those whom he predestined he also called, and those whom he called he also justified, and those whom he justified he also glorified.*—Rom. 8:30

(2) We all expect glory in heaven. But how can we reach that unless we are made fit for it? The church is the fitting place for glory. We enter into heaven in the church here. We are hewn and squared here. If we are not holy here, we will never enter into heaven. The change must begin here if ever it is to be perfected in heaven. No unclean thing will come there (Rev. 21:27). As soon as Satan, an angel of light, sinned, he was tumbled out of heaven. It will allow no unclean thing; no unclean thing will ever come there again. Our nature must be altered suitable to that place and glorious condition, before we go to heaven. Unless we are born anew, we cannot enter into the kingdom of God.

But this is forgotten. Men trust to the grace and mercy of God, but do not look for a change; and this prevents many from embracing the whole truth of the gospel and from knowing Christ as the truth is in him. They hear that they must be changed, and they are unwilling. They believe that God is merciful, and that Christ died, and so on. They snatch enough of the gospel to build themselves up in self-love and think all is well. But when they see the kind of grace that must teach them to 'deny ungodliness and worldly lusts' (Titus 2:12), and the grace that must alter them, this they cannot endure. They are content to go to heaven if they may have it on a way to hell, in maintaining their corruptions, being proud and covetous and worldly as they are. This must not be. There must, of necessity, be a change.

*Glorious Freedom*, pp. 103-04 [114]

# We Must Be Changed (3)

*What shall we say then? Are we to continue in sin that grace may abound? By no means! How can we who died to sin still live in it?—* Rom. 6:1-2

*Knowing this, that our old self was crucified with Him, in order that our body of sin might be done away with, so that we would no longer be slaves to sin.—Rom. 6:6*

(3) The soul that truly desires mercy and favour always desires power against sin. Pardon and power go together, both in God's gift and in the desire of a Christian's soul. There is no Christian soul that does not desire the grace of sanctification to change him as much as the grace of pardon. He looks upon corruption and sin as the vilest thing in the world, and upon grace and the new creature as the best thing in the world. There is no one changed who does not also desire sanctification.

Some weak notions would place all the change in justification. They separate Christ's offices, as if he were all priest but not a governing king; or as if he were righteousness but not sanctification; or as if he had merit to die for us and to give us his righteousness, but no efficacy to change our natures; or as if in the covenant of grace God only forgave our sins but did not write his law in our hearts. But in the covenant of grace he does both. Where God makes a combination, we must not break it. Efficacy and merit, justification and sanctification, water and blood, go together. There must be a change.

*Glorious Freedom*, pp. 104-05 [114-15]

# We Must Be Changed (4)

*That according to the riches of his glory he may grant you to be strength-*
*ened with power through his Spirit in your inner being.*—Eph. 3:16

(4) Actions correspond to powers and abilities, and no holy action can come from an unchanged ability. A change in the soul's faculties must precede a change in life and conduct.

In nature we live, and we have the power to move; being and moving go together. So if we have a being in grace, we have a power to move. In the life of grace and sanctification there is an ability to believe in God, to be holy, and to love God and then the actions of love spring from that power. Consider, then, the necessity of a change of the inward man, of the powers of the soul. Can the eye see without a power of seeing? Can the ear hear without a faculty of hearing? Can the soul perform sanctified actions without a sanctified power? It is impossible.

The change is especially in the will, which some would say is not touched. They would say the will is free and would give grace no more credit than necessary. But grace works upon the will most of all. For the bent and desires of the will carry the whole man with it. If the choice and bent are the right way, by the Spirit, it is good. If the will is not inclined and formed to go the best way, there is no work of grace at all. Though all grace first comes in through the understanding being enlightened, it then goes into the will, putting a new taste and relish upon the will and affections.

You see, then, that the grace in the gospel is not mere persuasion and entreaty, but a powerful work of the Spirit entering the soul and changing it and altering the inclination of the will heavenward. The soul is carried up and is shut to things below. We must have great notions of the work of grace. The Scripture has great words of it. It is an alteration, a change, a new man, a new creature, a new birth.

*Glorious Freedom*, pp. 105-06 [115-16]

# We Must Be Changed (5)

*And put on the new self, which in the likeness of God has been created*
*in righteousness and holiness of the truth.*—Eph. 4:24

(5) Finally, whenever God calls and dignifies, he also qualifies. Princes cannot qualify those they raise, but God, whom he advances to glory, he fits and qualifies for glory. Where he bestows his mercies and favours to life everlasting, he calls to great things, and he also changes them. If Saul was changed when he came to be a king, shall we think that God will call any to the participation of his glorious mercy in Christ, in pardoning their sin and accepting them to life eternal, and yet not change them? No. Whoever he calls to glory, he changes and alters their dispositions to be fit for so glorious a condition as a Christian is called to.

Proud men do not like to hear this. It offends their former authority. 'What! I, who was accounted a wise man, now to be a fool. I, who was accounted so and so, must alter all my course and turn the stream another way? The world will say I am mad.' I say, because grace alters everything, 'old things are passed away, and all things are become new' (2 Cor. 5:17). Those that are carnal and proud cannot endure a change because it is an affront to their reputation. But it must be so if they look for salvation.

*Glorious Freedom*, p. 106 [116-17]

# Changed into Christ's Likeness (1)

*Just as we have borne the image of the man of dust, we shall also bear the image of the man of heaven.*—1 Cor. 15:49, 45

The pattern to which we are changed is the image of Christ. It is a true rule that the first in every kind is the measure—the idea and pattern—of all the rest. Now Christ is the first, for he is the 'first-born,' the 'first fruits,' the 'first beloved.' The nearer we come to Christ, the better we are. Before being changed, we are corrupted and depraved according to the likeness of the first Adam after his fall. If Adam had not fallen, we would have been born according to his likeness, that is, good and righteous. But now, being fallen, as soon as we are planted and grafted by faith into the second Adam, we are changed into his likeness. Christ, as it were, is God's masterpiece, that is, the most excellent work and frame of heaven that ever was: such a mediator, to reconcile justice and mercy in bringing God and man into one person. Christ being God's masterpiece, the best and most excellent of all. He is the image, the idea, the pattern of all our sanctification.

We are changed by grace. From the second Adam derives all good, opposite to all the ill we drew from the first Adam. From the first we drew the displeasure of God; by the death and satisfaction of the second we obtain the favour of God. By the wrath of God, we drew corruption from the first Adam; in the second we have grace. From the first Adam we have death and all its attending miseries; in the second Adam we have life and all happiness, until it ends in glory. In a word, whatever ill we have in the first Adam is repaired abundantly in the second.

When you read of the image of God in the New Testament, it must be understood of the image of God in Jesus Christ, the second Adam. This image consists in knowledge, in holiness and in righteousness. Colossians 3 and Ephesians 4 show that these were perfect in Christ, who was the image of his Father. And we must be like Christ, the second Adam, in sanctification.

*Glorious Freedom*, pp. 107-08 [117-18]

# Changed into Christ's Likeness (2)

*Thus it is written, 'The first man Adam became a living being'; the last*
*Adam became a life-giving spirit.*—1 Cor. 15:45

Also, the image of God in the second Adam is more durable. All excellencies and grace are more firmly set on Christ than they ever were upon Adam. They are set upon him with such a character and stamp that they shall never be altered. When God set his image on the first Adam, it decayed and was lost by the malice of the devil because it was not set on so firmly, Adam being a man and a good man, yet changeable. But Christ is the God-man. In one nature God has set such a stamp of grace on the human nature, eternally united to the Godhead, that it could never be altered. We are renewed according to the image of God as it is stamped on Christ, not as it was stamped on the first Adam.

And that is why the state of God's children is unalterable, why being once graced they are so forever. If God set the stamp of the Spirit of Christ on them, it is firm, as it is upon Christ. It never alters in Christ nor in those who are members of Christ, except in growth from better to better. God's children sometimes deface that image by sin. But as a coin that is somewhat defaced, yet still retains the old stamp and is acknowledged for a good coin, so a Christian in all desertions, in the worst state, bears the stamp still. Though darkened by sinfulness, yet after it once receives a fresh stamp, it is an everlasting stamp. When once we are God's coin, we are never reprobate silver. That is all because we are 'renewed according to the image of Christ.' Grace is firmly set in our nature in Christ, so sure that all the devils in hell cannot obliterate it. Christ is the 'quickening Spirit,' able to transform us to his likeness better than the first Adam was. The image of God, then, is the likeness of the second Adam, and we are changed into that.

*Glorious Freedom*, pp. 108-09 [118-19]

# Two Conformities (1)

*And being found in human form, he humbled himself by becoming obedient to the point of death, even death on a cross.*— Phil. 2:8

There are two conformities of exceeding comfort to us, and we must meditate on both.

(1) Christ's conformity to us. He was transfigured into our likeness. In love to us he became man. He took man's nature, and man's base condition (Phil. 2:8). Here is the ground of our comfort, that Christ took our form, he transfigured himself to our lowliness. Will we not labour to be transformed, to be like him, who out of love stooped so low as to be like us? Let us but think of this! Our blessed Saviour took our nature on him pure and holy by his Spirit. He followed sin to death. He was conceived, and lived, and died without sin, to satisfy for sin; and now by his Spirit he cleanses out sin. He pursued and chased out sin from his conception through all the passages of his life; so we should be like him. Drive away sin, get the Spirit, that our nature in us may be as it was in him: holy, pure, and spiritual. Shall he be conformed to us, and we not be conformed to him?

(2) Our conformity to him. Christ, in this work of changing, is all in all. There are many reasons and considerations to move us to be changed into the image of Christ and the reasons inducing us to change are all from Christ. For we are changed not only by power, but by reason. There are the greatest reasons in the world to be a Christian and to come out of the state of nature. When our understanding is enlightened to see the horrible state of nature, and the angry face of God with it, and then to have our eyes opened at the same time to see the glorious and gracious face of God in Jesus Christ, it is the greatest wisdom in the world to come out of that cursed state to a better one.

*Glorious Freedom,* pp. 121-22 [132-34]

# Two Conformities (2)

*So you also must consider yourselves dead to sin and alive to God in Christ Jesus.*—Rom. 6:11

The reasons for this change are from Christ. By knowing Christ, we know the cursed state to be absent from him and see the glorious benefits by Christ's redemption and glorification. These are set before the eye of the soul, and then the heart stirred by reason says: 'If Christ gave himself for me, will I not give myself to Christ?' Paul has this heavenly logic, 'Christ died for us, that we might live to him' (Rom. 6:10, 11).

Since Christ is the image to which we are changed, let us learn, if we would see anything excellent in ourselves, to see it in Christ first. If we would see the love of God, first see the love of God in Christ our head. If we would see the gifts that God has blessed us with, spiritual blessings, it is in Christ. We first have it from our head. God's favour was first in him: 'This is my beloved Son, in whom I am well pleased' (Matt. 3:17). If we would see our evil done away, our sins removed, see it in Christ crucified and made a curse. See them all wiped away in the cross of Christ. If we would see glory upon the removal of our sins, see it in Christ first. He is first risen, and therefore we will rise. He is ascended and sits in heavenly places; therefore, we ascend and sit in heavenly places with him. All the good we have or look to have, see it first in the first pattern, in Christ.

The reason is clear: we are elected and predestined 'to be conformed to the image of his Son' (Rom. 8:29), to be conformed to Christ in all things, to be loved as he is, to be gracious as he is. To rise to be glorious, to be freed and justified afterward from all our sins. We are ordained to be conformed to him in every way. So, in all things we must look to Christ first and he must have the pre-eminence.

*Glorious Freedom*, pp. 122-24 [134-35]

# The Best Subject for Contemplation

*Set your minds on things that are above, not on things that are on earth.*—Col. 3:2

Of all contemplations under heaven, there is no contemplation so sweet and powerful as to see God in Christ and Christ first abased for us, and to see ourselves abased in Christ, and crucified in Christ. Then let us raise our thoughts a little higher, to see ourselves made little by little glorious in Christ; to see ourselves in him rising and ascending and sitting at the right hand of God in heavenly places; to see ourselves, by a spirit of faith, in heaven already with Christ. What a glorious sight and contemplation this is! If we first look upon ourselves as we are, we are as branches cut off from the tree, as a river cut off from the spring, that dies immediately. What is in us, except what we have derived from Christ, who is the first, the spring of all grace, the sum of all the beams that shine upon us? Now to see Christ, and ourselves in Christ, transforms us to be like his image.

We see that this change is brought about by beholding. Beholding the glory of God in the gospel is a powerful beholding. Is not the eye of faith stronger than natural imagination to alter and change? Certainly, the eye of faith, apprehending God's love and mercy in Christ, has a power to change. By it we partake of the divine nature.

This glass of the gospel is excellent and eminent above all other glasses. It is a mirror that changes us. When we see ourselves and our corruptions in the glass of the law, we see ourselves dead. But when we look into the gospel and see the glory of God, the mercy of God, and the gracious promises of the gospel, we are changed into the likeness of Christ. This excellent glass has a transforming power to make us beautiful. Such a glass should be much prized in this proud world; such a glass is the gospel.

Seeing ourselves in the love of God and Christ will naturally stir us up to be like so sweet, and gracious, and loving a Saviour.

*Glorious Freedom*, pp. 124-26 [135-37]

# Grace Brings Transformation (1)

*If the Spirit of him who raised Jesus from the dead dwells in you, he who raised Christ Jesus from the dead will also give life to your mortal bodies through his Spirit who dwells in you.*—Rom. 8:11

How can we know for certain that we see God in Christ and the glory of God in the gospel?

Does this sight have a transforming power in you, to make you like the image of Christ? If it does not, it is a barren, empty contemplation that has no efficacy at all. Insofar as the sight of God's love in Christ breeds conformity to Christ, it is gracious and comforting. No one ever sees the mercy of God in Christ by the eye of faith without being changed. Can you imagine that any soul can see itself in the glass of God's love in Jesus Christ, can see Christ in the gospel, and God reconciled to him in particular, and not love God in return and be altered? It is impossible. It works love, and love works of imitation. Love is full of invention and tries to please the person loved as much as it can in every way.

The adversaries of the grace of God quarrel with us because we preach justification by the free mercy and love of God in Christ. They say this is to deaden the spirits of men, so that they do not care about good works. But can there be any greater incentive and motive in the world to sanctification, to express Christ and to study Christ, than to consider what favour and mercy we have in Christ; how we are justified and freed by the glorious mercy of God in Christ? There cannot be any greater motivation?

The law is a glass too, but the sort of glass that James speaks of. When one looks into it and sees his duty, he goes away and forgets (James 1:23, 24). The law reveals our sin and misery. Indeed, it is a true glass, but this glass does not act upon us. When the gospel glass is held out by the ministers of the word, when people see the love of God in Christ, it changes and transforms them. Is there any study in the world more excellent than that of the gospel, which transforms and changes people from one degree of grace to another?

*Glorious Freedom*, pp. 127-29 [139-40]

## Grace Brings Transformation (2)

*If we say we have fellowship with him while we walk in darkness, we lie and do not practice the truth.*—1 John 1:6

As for those who find themselves to be 'old men' still, who have lived, and still live, in corruption, they must not think they have any benefit by the gospel. If they do, they deceive themselves. For whoever says he has communion with God but walks in darkness is a liar, for God is light (1 John 1:5, 6). How can a man see himself in the love of God and remain in a dark state opposite to love? Will it not alter him? It will not allow him to live in sins against conscience. Let no one who does so think he has benefit by Christ. That knowledge is but a notional knowledge, a speculation. It is not a spiritual knowledge, because wherever the knowledge of God in Christ is real, there is a change and conversion of the whole person. There is a new judgement and new affections. The bent and bias is another way than they were before.

There is a change which in the Scripture is called a turning (Matt. 18:3). Whereas before, they turned their back upon God and good, now they turn their faces to look toward God and heaven and to a better condition; for this change is nothing else but conversion. Those who have seen Christ, the sight makes them differ from themselves; it works a change.

If there were not a change, it would make God swear falsely. For according to the song of Zechariah, 'He has sworn that, being delivered out of the hands of our enemies, we should serve him without fear, in holiness and righteousness, all the days of our life' (Luke 1:73-75). If anyone says he is delivered from his enemies and from the penalty of his sins, and yet does not live in holiness and righteousness, he makes God's oath useless, for God's oath joins both together: deliverance, and serving without fear. All who are in a state of deliverance have grace granted them by which they may serve God in holiness and righteousness all their lives.

*Glorious Freedom*, pp. 129-30 [140-41]

# Grace in Us Is Glorious (1)

*To the praise of his glorious grace, which he has freely given us in the one he loves.*—Eph. 1:6

Grace is glorious. As the wise man says, 'Wisdom makes a man's face to shine' (Eccles. 8:1). Is not wisdom a glorious thing: a wise, understanding man able to guide himself and others? It puts a beauty upon a man, to be wise and understanding. Humility makes a man glorious, for it makes God put glory upon a man, and a man is glorious and does not realize it. Moses, when his face shined, did not know himself that it shined. Many humble men are glorious and do not think so; they are glorious, and they shine, though they do not see it.

Is it not a glorious thing to be taken out of ourselves, to deny ourselves, to offer a holy violence to ourselves and to our corruptions? Is it not glorious, when others lie grovelling like slaves under their corruptions, to stand unmovable in all the changes of the world and in all kinds of trouble, to stand as a rock in the midst of all, founded upon the love of God in Christ and the hope of glory after? Not to be shaken with the wind of temptations from his standing, at least not to be shaken off his standing—this is glorious, to have a constant spirit.

Is it not glorious to have admittance boldly by grace, to go into the presence of God at all times, to prevail with God? Faith overcomes not only the world but God himself. It binds him with his own promise. Is not faith a glorious grace, that triumphs over the great God himself, binding him with his own word and promise?

Is not love a glorious grace, that melts one into the likeness of Christ? It constrains, it has a kind of holy violence in it. We will glory in sufferings for what we love. No water, nothing can quench that holy fire that is kindled from heaven. It is a glorious grace.

Hope, what does it do? When it casts anchor in heaven, it keeps us in all the waves. It purges our natures to be like the thing hoped for.

*Glorious Freedom*, pp. 133-34 [144-45]

# Grace in Us Is Glorious (2)

*Let us then with confidence draw near to the throne of grace, that we may receive mercy and find grace to help in time of need.*—Heb. 4:16

The image of God makes a man glorious. It makes him shine. It is an excellent state to see a man in his place in the commonwealth.

What a glorious sight is it to see a Joseph, a Nehemiah, a Paul, all on fire for the glory of God and the good of the church! The thought of a man shining in grace, what a glorious thought it is!

The same is true in men now living. When wisdom and love tend to the common good, when there is a spirit of mortification, when a spirit of love is not for itself but all for the good of others, as in Christ, who 'went about doing good' (Acts 10:38), it makes them lovely and glorious.

Besides that, it puts an inward glory upon a man, when it makes him rejoice: 'The Spirit of glory rests upon him' (Isa. 61:1). Indeed, in imprisonments and abasements, a good man in any condition is glorious. You will not see flesh and blood, no vengeful mood. When flesh and blood is subdued and nothing appears in a man but the image of Christ, he is a glorious creature, even in the greatest abasement that can be. When Paul was in the stocks, what a glorious condition he was in, when he sang at midnight when the Spirit of glory was upon him!

To see martyrs suffer without revenge, pray for their enemies, show a triumphant spirit that conquered all wrongs, and the fear of death; a spirit raising them above encouragements and discouragements—what a glorious thing this was! A man in his right principles, with the image of God upon him, sees all things here below as beneath him. This is glorious, to see a man who cares no more for the offers of advancement on the one hand or for threatenings on the other. All this is nothing to him. Is this not glorious, to see such a victorious and glorious spirit, above all earthly things?

*Glorious Freedom*, pp. 134-35 [146-47]

# Grace in Us Is Glorious (3)

*For the grace of God has appeared, bringing salvation for all people, training us to renounce ungodliness and worldly passions, and to live self-controlled, upright, and godly lives in the present age.*—Titus 2:11, 12

The church clothed with Christ, who is the glory of the church, tramples all earthly things underfoot. Grace is victorious and conquering, prevailing over those corruptions that prevail over ordinary men. A Christian like David, when he had Saul in the cave, overcomes himself (1 Sam. 24:4). It shows a great strength of grace. Christ overcame himself on the cross. He prayed for his enemies. So when the nature of man is so subject to the power of grace that though there are rebellions in us—and there will be while we are in this world—still they cannot overpower the principle of grace. All this while a man is a glorious Christian, because he is not subject to the common infirmities and weaknesses of men. It makes a Christian glorious when he brings every thought and affection, and every corruption that may be, to the subjection of the Spirit of glory, to the Spirit of Christ in him. Though old Adam stirs in him, he brings him down, so that he does not scandalize the gospel. It will not break out; he subjects these rising thoughts. Here grace is glorious.

Another person cannot do this. He cannot love God; he cannot deny himself; he cannot resist temptations, not inwardly. He may refrain from an action out of fear, but a Christian can love, and fear, and delight in good things. He can resist, and he can enjoy the things of this life, remembering that they are subordinate to better things. A person outside of grace cannot do that. There is a glory upon a Christian, a derivative glory from Christ. For we shine in his beams. We are changed according to his image 'from glory to glory.'

*Glorious Freedom*, pp. 135-36 [147-48]

# God Will Complete His Work in Us (1)

*And I am sure of this, that he who began a good work in you will bring it to completion at the day of Jesus Christ.*—Phil. 1:6

Let no one in whom grace has begun be discouraged.

God will go on with his grace. When he has begun a good work, he will finish it to the day of the Lord (Phil. 1:6). Though grace is little at first, it will not stay there. How it grows we do not know, but in the end, it will be glorious indeed. Until grace has grown it is little distinguished from other things, just as there is little difference between weeds and herbs before they have grown. Grace is little at first, as a grain of mustard seed (Matt. 13:31).

Some Christians of a weaker sort want to be in Canaan just as soon as they are out of Egypt, and I cannot blame them. But they are dissatisfied. As soon as they have grace in them they want out, of covetousness, to advance immediately. 'Oh,' they say 'that I had more knowledge and more victory!' These desires are good; for God does not put desires into the hearts of his children in vain. But they must be content to be led from glory to glory, from one degree of grace to another. Christ himself grew more in favour with God and man. As that little stone grew to a mountain (Dan. 2:35), so we must be content to grow from grace to grace. Progress is gradual in the new creature. We cannot immediately be in Canaan. God will lead us through the wilderness, through temptations and crosses, before we come to heaven. Many who see themselves far short of other, stronger Christians think they have no grace at all.

So, though they are short of many that are before them, let those who are growing not be discouraged with their little beginnings. It is God's way in this world to bring his children by little and little, through many stations. It is one part of a Christian's meekness to be subject to God's wisdom in this respect, and not to complain that they are not as perfect as they would like to be or as they shall be.

*Glorious Freedom*, pp. 150-51 [163-64]

# God Will Complete His Work in Us (2)

*The Lord will fulfil his purpose for me; your steadfast love, O Lord, endures forever. Do not forsake the work of your hands.*—Psa. 138:8

Christians should magnify the mercy of God that there is any change in such defiled and polluted souls; that he has granted any spiritual light of understanding, any love of good things; that the bent of their affections is contrary to what it was; that God has granted any beginnings. Magnify his mercy, rather than quarrel with his dispensation, that he does not do all this at once. And, indeed, if we enter into our own hearts, we find it is our fault that we are not more perfect. But let us labour to be meek, and say, 'Lord, since you have ordained that I will grow from glory to glory, from one degree of grace to another, let me have grace to magnify your mercy that you have given me any goodness, rather than to complain that I have no more.'

Nor may we be discouraged with a seeming interruption in our spiritual growth. God sometimes works by contraries. He makes men grow by their decreasing, and to stand by their falls. Sometimes when God will have a man grow, he will allow him to fall, that by his fall he may grow in a deeper hatred of sin and in jealousy over his own heart, and in a nearer watchfulness over his own ways; that he may grow more in love with God for pardoning him, and stronger in his resolution; and that he may grow more in humility. No one grows so much as those who have their growth stopped for a time.

Let no one be too discouraged who finds a stop. There is no interruption altogether of the Spirit, and this little interruption is like a sickness that will make them grow and shoot up more afterwards. It draws out the toxins that hinder growth. There is such a mystery in the carrying of men from glory to glory, that it makes them more glorious sometimes by base sins. So, I would not have anyone discouraged. God will go through with the work he has begun and will turn everything to good.

*Glorious Freedom*, pp. 151-53 [164-66]

# God Will Complete His Work in Us (3)

*Who will sustain you to the end, guiltless in the day of our Lord Jesus Christ.*—1 Cor. 1:8

To encourage us here, grace begun has the same name as grace perfected. Both are glory. Why does God call them by one name? To encourage Christians. He tells them that if it is begun, it is glory; not that it is already so, but if it is begun it will never end till it comes to heaven. God looks on Christians not as they are in their imperfections and beginnings, but as that which in time he means them to be. He intends to bring them to glory. When God looks upon his children, he looks on them not as children, but as they will be, having come to the perfect stature of Christ. It is all presented to him at once. He gives one name to the whole state of grace; grace and glory; all is glory. If there is any goodness, then, any blessed change in us, let us be comforted, for he who has brought us to the beginnings of glory will never fail until he has brought us to perfect glory in heaven, and there our change shall rest. There is no further change there when we are in our element.

Until that time, there is no creature in the world so changeable as a Christian. For, first, you see he was made in God's image and likeness in his state of standing. After he fell, there was a change to his second state, that of sin. After the fall, there is a change to the state of grace; and after that from one degree of grace to another in this world until he dies. Then the soul is more perfect and glorious. But at the last, when body and soul will be united, there will be an end of all alteration.

So, we see that God intends by his Spirit to bring us, though little by little, to perfection of glory as far as our nature is capable, and this will be at the latter day. Is this not a sweet comfort? Let us comfort ourselves with these things.

*Glorious Freedom*, pp. 153-55 [166-67]

# Grace and Glory

*When Christ who is your life appears, then you also will appear with him in glory.*—Col. 3:4

We see that the state of God's children both here and in heaven is called glory. The children of God are kings here, they will be kings in heaven. They are saints here, as they are saints in heaven. There is an adoption of grace as well as an adoption of glory (Rom. 8). There is a regeneration now of our souls; there is a regeneration then of soul and body. We are new creatures here; and we will be new creatures there.

*Question.* Why do both come under one name, the state of glory in heaven and the state of grace here? Is there no difference?

*Answer.* Yes, but the difference is only in degree, for heaven must be begun here. If we mean ever to enter into heaven hereafter, we enter into the suburbs here. We must be new creatures here. We are kings here; we are heirs apparent here; we are adopted here; we are regenerated here; we are glorious here, before we are glorious hereafter. We may read our future state in our present. We must not think to come out of the filth of sin to heaven, but heaven must be begun here.

Would you like to know what your condition will be afterwards? Read it in your present disposition. If there is not a change, and a glorious change, here, never look for a glorious change hereafter. What is not begun in grace will never be accomplished in glory. Both grace here and glory hereafter come under the same name.

Also, it is a reason for comfort: Why do we have the same term here? When we are in the state of grace, why are we adorned with the same title as we will have in heaven? It is partly for certainty. Grace is glory, and its perfection is glory, to show that where grace is truly begun it will end in glory. All the powers in the world cannot interrupt God's gracious progress. What is begun in grace will end in glory. Where the foundation is laid, God will be sure to put up the roof. He never repents of his beginnings.

*Glorious Freedom,* pp. 143-44 [155-56]

# The Righteous and the Wicked

*The path of the righteous is like the light of dawn, which shines brighter and brighter until full day.*—Prov. 4:18

Solomon said that the righteous are like the sun that grows brighter and brighter until it comes to its full strength (Prov. 4:18). So the state of the godly grows more and more, from light to light, until he comes to full strength.

The state of the wicked is completely contrary. The state of the wicked is like the declining day. The sun goes down to twilight, and then to darkness, and then to utter darkness. Being dark in themselves, they grow from the darkness of misery and terror of conscience to eternal, dismal darkness in hell. But the state of the godly is like the course of the sun after midnight, which is going up and up still, until it comes to midday. The state of the godly is always a growing state; it is a hopeful condition. Let us be assured of eternal glory in the time to come, as we are sure of the beginnings of grace here.

See the main difference between the godly and others. Others grow backward, from worse to worse, till they end in utter desolation and destruction forever. But the godly rise by degrees until they come to that happiness that can admit no further degrees. If men were not spiritually mad, would they not rather be in a condition always growing more and more hopeful, than to be in a condition always declining? A spirit of glory lights and rests on God's children. It does not light upon them and then go away. It is not as a flash or a blaze of flax. But the Spirit rests and grows still upon them 'from glory to glory.' The state of a Christian soundly converted is comforted when he thinks, 'Every day brings me nearer my glory; every day I rise I am somewhat happier than I was the day before, because I am somewhat more glorious and nearer to eternal glory.' Whereas a wretch that lives in sins against conscience may say, 'I am somewhat nearer hell, nearer eclipsing, and ebbing, and declining than before.' So, every day brings comfort to the one, and terror to the other.

*Glorious Freedom*, pp. 144-45 [156-58]

# Grace is Glory Begun

*For if these qualities are yours and are increasing, they keep you from being ineffective or unfruitful in the knowledge of our Lord Jesus Christ.*—2 Pet. 1:8

Let us be exhorted to test the truth of grace in us, and by our care to proceed from glory to glory. Let us not deceive ourselves in our natural condition. Are we content to live the life of a sick man? No, we desire health. And when we have health, is that all? No; when we have health, we desire strength to encounter oppositions. If that is so in nature, is it not much more so in the new creature, in the new nature, in the divine nature? If there is life, there will be a desire to have health, so that our actions are not weak languishing actions. We desire that God, together with pardoning grace, may join healing grace to cure our souls daily more and more. And then, when we have spiritual health, let us desire spiritual strength to encounter oppositions, temptations, and afflictions, to make way through all things that stand in our way to heaven. Let us not deceive ourselves. If there is truth of grace in us, there is still a further desire of grace carrying us to further and further endeavour.

The more we grow in grace the more God smells a sweet sacrifice from us. The more we grow in grace, the more we grow in ability, in nimbleness, and cheerfulness to do others good. That which comes from a strong spirit of love and delight finds more acceptance with others. And the more we grow in grace, the more cheerful we will be with regard to ourselves. God instils the oil of grace further, to give us strength and cheerfulness in good actions, so that they come off with delight. Our own cheerfulness increases as our growth increases.

In a word, you see glory tends to glory, and that is enough to stir us up to grow in it. Seeing that glory here, which is grace, leads to glory in heaven, we should never rest until we come to that perfection. Grace is glory begun, and glory is grace perfected. Let us be always adding grace to grace, and one degree to another (2 Pet. 1:5-7).

*Glorious Freedom*, pp. 157-58 [170-72]

# When You Can't See Growth

*Like newborn infants, long for the pure spiritual milk, that by it you may grow up into salvation.*—1 Pet. 2:2

It will be objected that Christians are sometimes at a standstill, and sometimes they seem to go backward. Some, because they cannot see themselves growing, think they are not growing at all. That is only ignorance: we know that the earth rotates, though we do not see it moving, and we know things grow, though we do not see them growing. So, if we do not perceive our growth from grace to grace, it does not mean we are not growing.

But let's say indeed that Christians decay in their first love or in some grace. It is that they may grow in some other grace. God sees that they need to grow in the root. So he abases them with some infirmity, and then they spring out in full force again. As after a hard winter comes a glorious spring, so after a setback, grace breaks out more gloriously. God shows his powerful rule in our weakness; God's children never hate their corruption more than when they have been overcome by it. Then they know that there is some hidden corruption that they did not discern before and that they had better take notice of. It is profitable for God's children to fall sometimes. Otherwise they would never be as good as they are. They would not wash for the sake of a few spots, but when they see they are foul indeed, they go to wash. But this is a mystery; God wills to have it this way for good ends.

The chief thing in conversion is the desire, the turning of the stream of the will. So when some Christians find their will and their desire good, but their endeavour to fall short of their purposes, they say, 'Surely I have no good, because I do not have what I want to have'—as if they should have heaven upon earth. But we must grow from glory to glory and thank God for that beginning. God looks not to the measure as much as to truth, though it might be ever so little. Let us be comforted in this.

*Glorious Freedom*, pp. 158-60 [172-73]

# In Spiritual Disciplines Remember the Spirit

*It is the Spirit who gives life; the flesh is no help at all. The words that I have spoken to you are spirit and life.*—John 6:63

When you look to have any grace or comfort, then put out of your hearts too much reliance on any outward thing. Do not think that education or steady effort can make us good, or bodily exercise, or listening often to sermons, or conferring often, or taking any pains of our own. Certainly, these are things that the Spirit will be effectual in if we use them as we should. But without the Spirit what are they? 'The flesh profits nothing' (John 6:63). What are the ordinances and the word? Dead things without the Spirit of the Lord. Nothing, no outward thing in the world, can work upon the soul but the Spirit of God. And the Spirit of God works upon the soul by the means of grace, altering and changing it according to the image of Christ, more and more.

In using all these outward things, whatever they are, look up to Christ, who sends the Spirit into our hearts. The Spirit must give life to all these things, and then something will be accomplished by hearing, and reading, and praying, and receiving the ordinances. In all of these first look to the Spirit. We labour in vain if we do not depend wholly upon the Spirit of God and do not trust to a higher strength than our own. It must be a higher strength than our own to work any good in our souls, either grace, or comfort, or peace. And so, as an old proverb says, 'Let the eye be to heaven while the hand is at the helm.' Then we will be transformed and changed by the Spirit of God. Before we set upon anything in which we look for spiritual good, desire God by his Holy Spirit that he would give the substance. Words are wind without the Spirit. The Spirit must give life to the word. So, clothe divine truths with the Spirit, and then it works wonders.

*Glorious Freedom*, pp. 170-72 [184-86]

# We Are Unable

*I can do all things through him who strengthens me.*—Phil. 4:13

Does God expect us to have anything from ourselves? Who expects anything from a barren wilderness? That is what our hearts are like, and God knows it well enough. There is no goodness in us, no more than there is moisture in a stone or a rock. He looks for us to depend upon him to open our eyes with the Spirit of illumination, to reveal his love to us, and then to sanctify us, to work out all corruption little by little, and to work us more and more to glory. He expects us to depend on him for the Spirit in all we do.

Christians, therefore, are much to blame. They try to work and to hew out of their own nature the love of God and keep going by their own efforts, as if they had a principle of grace in themselves. They may work that way for a long time. But that is not the way. Instead we must acknowledge that in and of ourselves, as Paul says, we cannot do anything (Phil. 4:13). We cannot so much, by all the power in the world, as think a good thought. If we should live a thousand years, there cannot rise out of our hearts, of ourselves, a wholly good desire. It is all from outside of ourselves, from the Spirit of the Lord.

It was folly in Peter to presume of his own strength that though all others might forsake Christ, yet he would not (Mark 14:29, 31). God left him to himself, and you see how he fell. So it is with us all, when we presume upon the strength of our own nature and abilities.

We must open as a flower that opens when the sun shines on it. We open as Christ shines on us. As things around us are light only when the sun shines, so we are light and open and flow and are carried only when Christ by his Spirit flows on us. We listen and do good works, but the activity and power and strength all come from the Spirit of God.

*Glorious Freedom*, pp. 173-75 [188-90]

# Consider the Benefits of the Times (1)

*And we all, with unveiled face, beholding the glory of the Lord, are being transformed into the same image from one degree of glory to another. For this comes from the Lord who is the Spirit.*—2 Cor. 3:18

Consider that the glory of the times, and the glory of places and persons, are all from the revelation of Christ by the Spirit. The more God in Christ is laid open, the more the times, places, and persons are excellent. What made the second temple superior to the former? Christ came at the second temple. Though baser in itself, the second temple was more glorious than the first. What made Bethlehem, that little city, glorious? Christ was born there. What makes the heart where Christ is born more glorious than in others? Christ is born there. Christ makes persons and places glorious. What made the least in the kingdom of heaven greater than John the Baptist? He was greater than all that were before him; and all that are after him are greater than he because he did not see the death and resurrection of Christ and the giving of the Holy Spirit. So it is the revelation of Christ and the love of God in Christ that makes times and persons and places glorious.

The glory of these present times comes from a fuller revelation of Christ than in former times. Now there are more converted than in former times because the Spirit goes together with the manifestation of Christ. Why is this kingdom more glorious than any place beyond the seas? Because Christ is here revealed more fully than there. The veil is taken off, and here 'we see the glory of God with open face,' which changes many thousands from glory to glory by the Spirit of God that accompanies the revelation of the gospel. Is there any outward thing that advances our nation above any other nation? No, nothing. They have as much as we do, if not more, in the way of government and riches and outward things. But the glory of places and times is from the revelation of Christ, which has the Spirit accompanying it. That Spirit changes us 'from glory to glory.' Our times are more glorious than they were a century or two ago. Why? Because we see Christ revealed, and the gospel opened, and the veil taken off.

*Glorious Freedom*, pp. 185-86 [199-200]

# Consider the Benefits of the Times (2)

*In their case the god of this world has blinded the minds of the unbe-*
*lievers, to keep them from seeing the light of the gospel of the glory of*
*Christ, who is the image of God.*—2 Cor. 4:4

Now Christ revealed challenges us to acknowledge these blessed
times. What should all this do but stir us up to know the time of our
visitation, and to bless God, who has reserved us for these places and
countries and for this time of glorious gospel light. Now we live under
the gospel, by which 'with open face' (2 Cor. 3:18) we see the glory of the
mercy of God in Christ, the 'unsearchable riches' (Eph. 3:8) of Christ
opened to us. And together with the gospel goes the Spirit. And those
thousands that belong to God are being changed, by the blessing of God,
from glory to glory.

Certainly, if we share in the good of the times, we will have hearts to
thank God and to walk in ways corresponding to it. Since we have the
glorious gospel, we will walk gloriously and not dishonour so glorious
a gospel by base and fruitless lives. Let us remember the times: if we are
no better for these glorious times, if the veil is not taken away, we are
under a fearful judgment. 'The god of this world has blinded our eyes'
(2 Cor. 4:4).

Let us take heed not to while away our time, these precious times
and blessed opportunities. If we do not labour to get out of the state of
nature and into the state of grace, and so to be changed from glory to
glory, God in justice will curse the means we have, that in hearing we
will not hear, and seeing we will not see, and he will secretly and imper-
ceptibly harden our hearts. It is the curse of all curses to grow worse and
duller when we have so much opportunity.

Let us labour for hearts that know the mercies of God in Christ, and
labour to be transformed and moulded into this gospel every day more
and more.

*Glorious Freedom*, pp. 186-87 [200-02]

# Learning Contentment (1)

*Not that I am speaking of being in need, for I have learned in whatever situation I am to be content.*—Phil. 4:11

'I have learned,' said Paul (Phil. 4:11), 'I have been instructed.' It is very emphasized in the original: 'I am consecrated to this knowledge of contentment in all states' (footnote—'I have been fully taught, I have been initiated'). It is a learning not of great persons, nor of learned persons, but of holy persons. It is a mystical knowledge. There is a mystery in it. As all religion is a mystery, 'great is the mystery of godliness' (1 Tim. 3:16). Not only the doctrinal part, but likewise the practical part of it. Repentance is a mystery, faith is a mystery, and this practical part of contentment in all conditions is a great mystery. All the degrees in this world cannot teach this lesson that Paul had learned. He learned it in no school of the world, not at the feet of Gamaliel; he learned it of Christ, and by the blessed experiences in afflictions. Some graces are reserved for some states. He had learned patience and contentment in a variety of states. He had it not by nature, for he said, 'I have learned.' It is a mystical thing, not so easily attained as the world is fond to think. Your ordinary Christian thinks that religion is nothing, that it is easily learned; but what is actually true is that there is no point in religion that is not a mystery. There is no Christian that doesn't find it to be so when he sets himself heartily to go about any religious work; as to humble himself, to repent, to go out of himself, or to cast himself upon the mercy of God in Christ. Oh, he will then say, 'It is a mystery, there is a difficulty in this work that I never thought of until I came to it.' So it is with being content with our condition, whatever it may be, it is a mystery. Nature never teaches this. It is learned in the school of Christ, and not without many stripes. We must be tried and taught a good while before we can truly learn to any degree this one lesson of contentment in any condition.

*The Art of Contentment, Works,* vol. 5, p. 178

# Learning Contentment (2)

*I know how to be brought low, and I know how to abound. In any and every circumstance, I have learned the secret of facing plenty and hunger, abundance and need.*—Phil. 4:12

The Christian can want and can abound, without tainting himself with the sins of those conditions. For instance, he can abound without pride, though this is a hard matter. Abundance works upon the soul of a man. He needs a strong brain who experiences abundance, as it is a wild untamed thing. We see how it wrought upon Solomon and David (1 Kings 11:1; 2 Sam. 11:2). Yet nevertheless the child of God has grace even to overcome the sins that accompany abundance. He has grace to be lowly-minded in a great state; not to trust in uncertain riches; he knows that he has an inheritance of better things in another world, which teaches him to set a small esteem upon all things below.

The same is true of want. The sin that we are subject to fall into in want is putting forth our hands to evil means, to steal. God's child can learn to want without tainting his conscience with ill courses, and then to want without impatience, without too much dejection of spirit, as if all were lost. Indeed, a Christian in a manner is rich in all conditions. For God is his portion, and however a beam may be taken away, the sun is his; take away a stream, the spring is his; in the poorest state, God all-sufficient is his still. God never takes away himself. The Christian knows this, and therefore he can want, he can be abased as long as he has the spring of all. Whereas those that have not been brought up in Christ's school, nor trained up in a variety of conditions, are unable to do this. If they abound, they are proud; if they be cast down, they murmur and fret, and are dejected, as if there were no Providence to rule the world, as if they were fatherless children. This is the excellency of a Christian, that by experience, he knows how to abound with the practice of the graces, and how to want with the avoiding of the snares that usually are in that condition.

*The Art of Contentment, Works,* vol. 5, pp. 179-80

# All Things, Evangelically

*I can do all things through him who strengthens me.*—Phil. 4:13

A Christian is able to do all things through Christ who strengthens him. This must be understood evangelically. Does this verse mean actually, legally, without a flaw? No; 'I can do all things' so far as will show that I am a true Christian; so far as will be beautiful in the eyes of others, to allure them to the embracing of religion; so far as will put the world to silence for reproaching; so far as I will enjoy assurance of the truth of grace; so far as Satan will not get his way in every temptation. Our obedience is evangelical, and not legalistic.

To do all things evangelically is for a man to know that he is in a state of grace. The obedience that is answerable to that condition is a desire to obey God in all things: a grief that he cannot do it so well as he would; a prayer that he might do it so; and an endeavour together with prayer that he may do so, and some strength likewise with endeavour. It is said of gold that even the best gold has an allowance of foreign grains; so take the best Christian, there must be some allowance. He cannot do all perfectly.

The gospel requires truth and not perfection. The perfection that brings us to heaven is in Christ our Saviour. Sincerity is the perfection of Christians. Let not Satan abuse us. We 'do all things,' when we endeavour to do all things, and purpose to do all things, and are grieved when we cannot do better. God pardons that which is ill, for he is a Father. 'I will pity you as a father pities his child' (Psa. 103:13). This, in the covenant of grace, he will do. A Christian can do all then; and wherein he fails, God will pardon him. What is good, God will accept and reward; and what is sick and weak, God will heal, until he has made him complete in Christ. These things must be well and soundly understood, and then we can take no offence at the doctrine.

*The Art of Contentment, Works,* vol. 5, pp. 186-87

# Grace upon Grace

*For from his fullness we have all received, grace upon grace.*—John 1:16

Let us know that outside of Christ there is no grace. There cannot be a beam without the sun; there cannot be a river without a spring; there cannot be a good work without the spring of good works, which is Christ. Also, let us be sure in every action to be poor in spirit. When we have any temptation to resist, any trouble to bear, or any duty to perform, let us empty ourselves. No grace is stronger than humility. No man is weaker than a proud man. For a proud man rests on nothing, yet a humble man who empties himself, he stands upon the Rock. Let us empty ourselves, as the prophet said to the widow; 'Bring empty vessels now, and we will have oil enough' (2 Kings 4:3). There is enough in Christ; but first we must empty ourselves by humility, and then there will be fullness in him. 'Of his fullness we receive grace upon grace' (John 1:16). Let us, as much as we can, empty ourselves of ourselves and stir up the spirit of faith. Go to Christ. If we do but touch him by faith we will have a spring of graces in us answerable to the graces in him (Matt. 9:20).

Come what will, if we be in Christ, either we will be freed from troubles, or we will have grace to bear them. Either we will have that we want, or we will have contentment without it. Is it not better to have grace without the thing? Is it not better to have a glorious Spirit resting on us? Did not the Spirit of glory rest on Paul? Could not God have freed Paul from prison? (Phil. 1:12-14). Yes, but then where would be the demonstration of a contented spirit, of a heavenly mind? Where would be the example of a Christian bearing the cross comfortably? Will we then be afraid of any condition? No! Get the Spirit of God; get the understanding of Christ, get the promises and privileges by him, then let God cast us into whatever condition he will, and we will be safe and well.

*The Art of Contentment, Works,* vol. 5, pp. 191-93

# Why There are False Religions and Heresies

*The natural person does not accept the things of the Spirit of God, for they are folly to him, and he is not able to understand them because they are spiritually discerned.*—1 Cor. 2:14

If the things of the gospel be such, as that without a revelation from God they could not be known, then we see that there is no principle at all of the gospel in nature. There is not a spark of light, or any inclination to the gospel, that is found in nature. For God removes all the natural ways—eye, ear, and understanding—of knowing the gospel. The knowledge of it is only supernatural. For if God had not revealed it, who could ever have devised it? And when he revealed it, to disclose it by his Spirit, it is supernatural. Therefore, you may know the reason why so many heresies have sprung out of the gospel, more than out of the law. There are few or no heresies from the law because the principles of the law are written in the heart. Men naturally know that adultery, filthy living, etc., are sins. Men have not so quenched nature but that they know that those things are evil. There have been excellent lawmakers among the heathens. But the gospel is a 'mystery,' discovered out of the breast of God, without all principles of nature. There are thousands of errors about the nature, the person, and the benefits of Christ; about justification and sanctification, and free will and grace, and such things. What worlds of heresies have proud minds continually started up! This would never have been but that the gospel is a thing above nature. Therefore, when a proud wit and supernatural knowledge revealed meet together, the proud heart storms and loves to struggle, and devises this thing and that thing to commend itself; and hereupon comes heresies, the mingling of natural wit with divine truths. If men had had passive wits to submit to divine truths, and to work nothing out of themselves, there had not been such heresies; but their hearts meeting with supernatural truths, their proud hearts mingling with it, they have devised these errors.

*A Glance of Heaven, Works, vol. 4, pp. 156-59*

# The Gospel Revealed in Three Degrees

*Now to him who is able to strengthen you according to my gospel and
the preaching of Jesus Christ, according to the revelation of the mystery
that was kept secret for long ages.*—Rom. 16:25

There are three degrees of revelation.

(1) There must be a revelation of the things themselves, by word,
writing, speech, and the like. There must be a revelation of these things,
or else we could never have devised how to reconcile justice and mercy by
sending a mediator to procure peace, the God-man, to work our salvation. This is the first degree, that we may call revelation by Scripture, or
by the doctrine of the gospel. Who could disclose those things but God
himself?

(2) When they are revealed by the word of God, and by men that
have a function to unfold the unsearchable riches of Christ by the ministry of the gospel, yet they are hidden riddles still to the company of
carnal men. Suppose the veil be taken off from the things themselves, yet
if the veil be over the soul, the understanding, will, and affections, there
is no apprehension of them. There must be a revelation by the Spirit of
God. Of necessity this must be as Paul said in 1 Corinthians 2:11, 'None
know the mind of man but the spirit that is in man, so none know the
mind of God but the Spirit of God.' What is the gospel, without the
Spirit of Christ to disclose the mind of God to us? We know in general
that such things are revealed in Scripture. But what is that to us if Christ
be not our Saviour and God our Father. Therefore, you see a necessity of
revelation by the Spirit.

(3) A higher revelation in heaven. That which is revealed here is but
in part; and if we believe, we believe but in part. If our knowledge, which
is the ground of all other graces and affections, be imperfect, all that
follows must be imperfect also. John said, 'We know that we are the sons
of God, but it appears not what we shall be' (1 John 3:2). In heaven our
eyes will see, our ears hear, and our hearts will conceive those things that
now we neither can see, nor hear, nor understand.

*A Glance of Heaven, Works,* vol. 4, pp. 158-59

# How to Study the Bible and Understand the Gospel

*Open my eyes, that I may behold wondrous things out of your law.—*
Psa. 119:18

Here is direction on how to read and study holy truths, especially the sacred mysteries of the gospel. We think to break into them with the engine of our intelligence, and to understand them, and never come to God for his Spirit. God will curse such proud attempts. In studying the gospel, let us come with a spirit of faith, and a spirit of humility and meekness. There is no breaking into these things with the strength of our parts. That has been the ground of so many heresies as have been in the church. Only Christ 'has the key of David, that shuts, and no man opens; and opens, and no man shuts' (Rev. 3:7). He has the key of the Scripture, and the key to open the understanding. If 'eye has not seen, nor ear heard, nor has entered into the heart of man to conceive' the things of the gospel (1 Cor. 2:9), without the revelation of the Spirit, then we must come with this mind when we come to hear the things of the gospel. 'Lord, without your Holy Spirit they are all as a clasped book; they are hidden mysteries to me, though they be revealed in the gospel. If my heart be shut to them, they are all hidden to me.'

The course that God takes with his children is this. Those that he means to save, he first inspires into their hearts some desire to come to hear and attend upon the means of salvation, to understand the gospel. Then under the means of salvation he shines into the understanding and inspires into the will and affections some heavenly inclination to the truth of the gospel. Under these means the soul comes to relish and to understand these mysteries. A believing man, that has his heart subdued by the Spirit of God relishes the point of forgiveness of sins; he relishes the point of sanctification; he studies it daily more and more; he relishes peace of conscience and joy in the Holy Spirit; they are sweet things. Must not the heart be new-moulded again if the former frame be not sufficient for these things?

*A Glance of Heaven, Works,* vol. 4, pp. 160-61

# Value That Which Is Most Valuable (1)

*No eye has seen, nor ear heard, nor the heart of man imagined, what*
*God has prepared for those who love him.*—1 Cor. 2:9

If eye has not seen, nor ear heard, nor has entered into the heart of man to conceive those things that God has prepared for him, then let us make this the rule of our esteem of anything that is good, or anything that is ill; make it a rule of valuation. We grieve at the fever, and at the gallstone, and the gout; they are grievous things indeed. But what be these things that we feel and see, to those in another world, that we cannot apprehend! The torments of hell, we cannot conceive and understand them here; for it is indeed to be in hell itself to conceive what hell is. Also, it is the same with the greatest good. Christ could see through all the glory in the world that the devil showed him (Matt. 4:8). These are things that we can hear of. They are not the greatest good. There are more excellent things than the things of this world. There be things that the eye has not seen, nor ear heard, nor the soul conceived; and these be the joys of heaven. Is not this desperate folly, to venture the loss of the best things, of the most transcendent things, that are above the capacity of the greatest reaches of the world? Will I lose all for petty poor things that are within my own reach and compass?

How foolish are those that are given to pleasures! They feel the pleasure indeed, but the sting comes after. They delight in those ill things that they can see and hear, and never think of the excellent things that the eye has not seen nor ear heard. Let this make us to love divine truths in the Scripture, the gospel, that part of the Scripture that promises salvation by Christ, and all the graces and privileges of Christianity. These are above our reach. We study other things which we can reach. We can reach the mysteries of the law by long study, and the mysteries of physics, and the mysteries of trades by understanding. To be wise to salvation is the best wisdom.

*A Glance of Heaven, Works, vol. 4, pp. 162-63*

# Value That Which Is Most Valuable (2)

*For I consider that the sufferings of this present time are not worth com-
paring with the glory that is to be revealed to us.*—Rom. 8:18

What a pity, that God should give us our understandings for better
things than we can see or hear in this world, yet we employ them in
things of the world wholly. Let us not do as some shallow, proud heads,
that regard not divine things. The Scriptures they will not vouchsafe
to read once a day, perhaps not once a week; some scarce have a Bible
in their studies. 'Learn on earth that which will abide in heaven,' said
Augustine. Let us be stirred up to value the Scriptures and the mysteries
of salvation in the gospel that breeds an inward peace and joy that is
unspeakable and glorious. All that we have in the world is not worth
those little beginnings that are wrought by the hearing of the word of
God. If the firstfruits here be joy 'unspeakable and glorious' (1 Pet. 1:8),
what will the consummation of these things be at that day?

Here you see a ground of the wonderful patience of the martyrs. You
wonder that they would suffer to have their souls severed so violently
from their bodies. Cease to wonder; when they had a sense wrought in
them by the Spirit of God of the things that eye has not seen nor ear
heard. If a man should have asked them why they would suffer their
bodies to be misused, when they might have redeemed all this with a
little quiet, they would have answered presently, as some of them have
done: 'We suffer these things in our bodies and in our senses, for those
things that are above our senses. We will have more glory in heaven than
we can have misery here. For we can see this, and there is an end of it;
but we will have joy that eye has not seen, nor ear heard.' As Paul said in
Romans 8:18, the things that we suffer here are not 'worthy of the glory
that will be revealed.' Let us not wonder so much at their patience as to
lay up this ground of patience against an evil day when we might have to
seal the truth with our blood.

*A Glance of Heaven, Works,* vol. 4, pp. 163-64

# Why Only a Glimpse of Heaven?

*But according to his promise we are waiting for new heavens and a new earth in which righteousness dwells.*—2 Pet. 3:13

Reasons why God hides from us the glory that will be. We must be modest when we speak of God's counsels and courses.

(1) God will have a difference between the warring church and the triumphing church. This life is a life of faith and not of sight. Why? Partly to try the truth of our faith, and partly for the glory of God, that he has such servants in the world that will depend upon him, upon terms of faith. If a man should see hell open, and the terrors there, for him then to abstain from sin, what glory would it be? The sight would force abstinence. If he should see heaven open, and the joys of it present, it would be no commendation to believe, for again, sight would force it.

(2) God will have a known difference between hypocrites and the true children of God. If heaven were upon earth, and nothing reserved in faith and in promise, everyone would be a Christian. But now the greatest things being laid up in promises, we must exercise our faith to wait for them. Only a true Christian will venture the loss of these things here for those in heaven.

(3) Our bodies could not contain it. We are incapable; our brain is not strong enough for these things. As we see Peter was not himself at the transfiguration; he forgot himself because of what he saw on the mount. He knew not what he said, when he said, 'Master, let us make three tabernacles' (Mark 9:5). Nor Paul when he saw things in heaven above expression, that might not be uttered, could not digest them (2 Cor. 12:4). They were so great, that if he had not had something to weigh him down, to balance him, he would have been overturned with pride. Therefore, there was a 'thorn in the flesh' sent to Paul, to humble him (2 Cor. 12:7). Are we greater than Peter and Paul? Our capacities now are not capable, our affections will not contain those excellent things. God trains us up by little and little to the full fruition and enjoying of them.

*A Glance of Heaven, Works,* vol. 4, pp. 168-69

# Humility and Thankfulness because of the Hope of Heaven

*Let us hold fast the confession of our hope without wavering, for he who promised is faithful.*—Heb. 10:23

We must humble ourselves and say with the psalmist, 'Lord, what is man, that you are mindful of him?' (Psa. 8:4). We who lost our first condition and betrayed you; yet you have advanced us to the state, 'that neither eye has seen, nor ear heard, neither has entered into the heart of man' (1 Cor. 2:9). Will we talk of merit? Surely grace never entered into that man's heart, that has such a conceit to entertain merit. Will a man think by a penny to merit a thousand pounds; by a little performance to merit things that are above the conception of men and angels?

With that humiliation, take that which always goes with it: thankfulness. When Peter thought of the 'inheritance immortal and undefiled,' he began, 'Blessed be God, the Father of our Lord Jesus Christ' (1 Pet. 1:3, 4). He could not think of these things without thankfulness to God. Now if we were in heaven already, we should praise God, and do nothing else. Faith making us sure to the soul, as if we had them, sets the soul on work to praise God. We should cheer our hearts in the consideration of these things in all conflicts and desolations. We little think of these things, and that is to our fault. Like little children that are born to great matters but carry not themselves answerable to their hopes. But as they grow in years, the more they grow in spirit and conception fitting the estates they hope for. So it is with Christians at the first; when they are weak and troubled with this loss or that cross; but when a Christian grows to a full stature in Christ, every cross does not cast him down. He thinks: 'Will I be dejected with this loss when I have heaven reserved for me? Will I be cast down with this cross when I have things that eye has not seen nor ear heard prepared for me?' He will not. He makes use of his faith to fetch comfort from the things that are reserved for him, that are inexpressible and inconceivable.

*A Glance of Heaven, Works*, vol. 4, p. 171

# Pity and Wonderment

*Blessed be the God and Father of our Lord Jesus Christ! According to his great mercy, he has caused us to be born again to a living hope through the resurrection of Jesus Christ from the dead.*—1 Pet. 1:3

Let us comfort ourselves in all the slightings of the world. A man that has great hopes in his own country, if he be slighted abroad, he thinks to himself, I will have a different manner of respect when I come home. Should not we be content as unknown men here, when God the Father and Christ our Saviour are unknown? There are better things reserved at home for us. Let us not envy them their condition, for use it as they will, there is a date when all will be done. All their happiness it is but a measured happiness; their eyes can see it and their ears can hear it, and when they can neither see nor conceive more in this world, then there will be an end of all their sense-derived happiness. Will we envy, when they will shortly be turned out of this world to the place of torment? They should be objects of pity, even the greatest men in the world, if we see by their lives they be void of grace.

But what affection is due and suitable to the state of a Christian? If we would have the right affection, it is wonderment. What is wonderment? It is the state and disposition of the soul toward things that are new and rare and strange. A Christian cannot but wonder because the things prepared are beyond his reach. Yea, when he is in heaven, he will not be able to conceive the glory of it. He will enter into it; it will be beyond him; he will have more joy and peace than he can comprehend. It will be a matter of wonder even in heaven itself, much more should it be here below. The holy apostles, when they spoke in the Scriptures of these things, it was with terms of wonderment, 'joy unspeakable and glorious' (1 Pet. 1:8), and 'peace that passes understanding' (Phil. 4:7); and 'marvellous light' (1 Pet. 2:9). 'Behold what love the Father showed us, that we should be called the sons of God' (1 John 3:1). To be called, and to be, one with God; both are beyond expression.

*A Glance of Heaven, Works, vol. 4, pp. 171-72*

# Wrong Hope for a Wrong Heaven

*And everyone who thus hopes in him purifies himself as he is pure.—*
1 John 3:3

It is impossible for a man, if he be not truly renewed, to desire heaven. He may wish for it under the notion of a kingdom, a pleasure, or the like; but as heaven containing a state of perfect holiness and freedom from sin, he cares not for it. A man that is out of relish with heavenly things, and can taste only his worldly sins, cannot relish heaven itself. His own heart tells him, I would rather have this world's pleasure and honour than to have those of heaven. Swine love mud better than a garden. They are in their element in these things. Take a swinish, worldly person, he loves to wallow in this world. Tell him of heaven, he has no desire for it.

Yet, there are none of us, but we desire, at least we pretend that we desire, heaven; but most men conceive it only as a place free from trouble and annoyance. But except you have a holy, gracious heart, and desire heaven that you may be free from sin, and have communion with Christ and his saints, to have the image of God, the divine nature perfect in you; you are a hypocrite and you carry a presumptuous conception of these things. Your hope will delude you; it is a false hope. 'Everyone that has this hope purifies himself' (1 John 3:3). Everyone, he excludes none. Do you defile yourself, and live in a sinful way, and have you this hope? You have a hope, but it is not this hope; for everyone that has this hope purifies himself. Even the greatest man living, if he be a sinful man, is frightened by death, 'the king of fears.' He thinks, 'I may have some trouble in this world, but there is worse to come'; things that he is not able to conceive of. Let us not therefore delude ourselves. There is nothing that will bring confidence but being a new creation in Christ. Then we may without presumption hope for the good things 'that neither eye has seen, nor ear heard, neither has entered into the heart of man' (1 Cor. 2:9).

*A Glance of Heaven, Works*, vol. 4, pp. 176-77

# How to Know if You Love God (1)

*Whom have I in heaven but you? And there is nothing on earth that I desire besides you.*—Psa. 73:25

(1) There must be an esteem of God and Christ. A high esteeming and prizing of God and his love above all things in the world.

*a*. This valuing is known by choice. What a man esteems and values highly he chooses above all things in the world and what a man chooses is seen by his life and actions. We see this in Moses. He had a high esteem of the state of God's afflicted people. Upon his estimation he made a choice: 'He chose rather to suffer afflictions with the people of God, than to enjoy the pleasures of sin for a season' (Heb. 11:26). His choice followed his esteem. If we value and love God above all things, we will choose the Lord. As Peter said when Christ asked them, 'Will you also forsake me?' he said, 'Lord, where shall we go? You have the words of eternal life' (John 6:68). Have you with Mary chosen the better part? (Luke 10:42).

*b*. Our esteem is known by our willingness to part with anything for that which we esteem. As a wise merchant does sell all for the pearl (Matt. 13:46). If we sell all for the truth of God, and part with all, and deny all for the love and obedience of it, it is a sign we have an esteem answerable to his worth. Those that will part with nothing for God when they are called to it, do they talk of love to God? They have no love because they have no esteem.

*c*. What we esteem highly of we speak largely of. A man is always eloquent in what he esteems. You never knew a man in want of words for what he prized. When we are in want of words to praise God, and to set out the value of the best things, it is an argument we have poor esteem of them. If a man esteems the best things, he will be often speaking of them.

*d*. Esteem likewise carries our thoughts. Would you know what you esteem highly? What do you think of most and highest? You may know it by that.

*A Glance of Heaven, Works*, vol. 4, pp. 183-84

# How to Know if You Love God (2)

*Jesus answered him, 'If anyone loves me, he will keep my word, and my Father will love him, and we will come to him and make our home with him.'*—John 14:23

(2) Where there is true love and affection, there is a desire of union. Love is that kind of affection; it draws the soul all it can to the thing loved. If there be the love of God, there will be a desire of fellowship and communion with him by all means.

*a.* A desire of union will breed a desire of communion. We will open our souls often to him in prayer, and we will desire that he will open himself in speaking to our hearts by his Spirit. Those that make no habit of hearing the word and of free access to the throne of grace, they love not God and Christ. Strangeness is opposite to love, and it dissolves affections. When we are strange to God, that we can go from one end of the day or week to the other, and not be acquainted with God, and not open our souls to him, it is a sign we have no love.

*b.* Where we love we consult and rest in that advice, as coming from a loving person. In all our decision-making, we will go to God and take his counsel; and will account it the counsel of one that is wise and loving.

*c.* A man who loves God, acquaints himself with his God and will not lose that communion he has with God for all the world. As Daniel, they could not get him from his prayers with the hazard of his life (Dan. 6:11).

*d.* Where this desire of union and joining is, there is a desire even of death itself, that there may be a fuller union, and a desire of the consummation of all things. To fear the sweet and eternal communion we will have in heaven, where we will have all things in greater excellency and abundance, it is from want of faith and love. Paul said, 'I desire to depart, and to be with Christ, for that is much better for me' (Phil. 1:23). We should rejoice to think there are happier times to come, where there will be an eternal meeting together that nothing shall dissolve.

*A Glance of Heaven, Works*, vol. 4, pp. 184-86

# How to Know if You Love God (3)

*But godliness with contentment is great gain.*—1 Tim. 6:6

(3) It is in the nature of love to place contentment in the thing we desire. Now we may know if God is our contentment by the inward quiet and peace of the soul in all conditions. He is able to satisfy all the delights and desires of our soul. Where else could we go for contentment? Why should we go out of religion to content ourselves in vain recreations and pleasures of sin for a season, when we have abundance in God? Where there is contentment in God, there will be trusting in him and relying upon him. A man will not rely upon riches, or friends, or anything; we repose our confidence and trust in him. He will be our rock and castle and strength. Would you know whether you rest in him or not? In the time of danger, where does your soul run? He that is a child of God flies to him for refuge, and there he covers himself, and is safe (Psa. 61:3). He enters into those chambers of divine providence and goodness, and there he rests in all troubles. He has God reconciled in Christ, and in his love he plants himself in life and death. He makes God his habitation and his castle. 'I love the Lord dearly, my rock and my fortress' (Psa. 18:2). A Christian has his contentment and his habitation in God; he is the house he dwells in, his rock, his resting-place, his centre in which he rests. 'Come unto me, and you will find rest for your souls' (Matt. 11:28). In losses and crosses you have contentment in God, you will fetch what you lose out of the love of God. You will say, 'This and that is taken from me, but God is mine; I can fetch more good from him by faith than I can lose in the world.' As Augustine said to God, 'Take all from me, so you leave me yourself.' Where will a man have comfort in the many passages of his life, if he finds it not in God?

*A Glance of Heaven, Works,* vol. 4, pp. 186-87

# How to Know if You Love God (4)

*For this is the love of God, that we keep his commandments. And his commandments are not burdensome.*—1 John 5:3

(4) Where the true affection of love to God is, it stirs up the soul to do all things that may please him. Isaac's sons saw that their father loved venison, therefore they provided venison for him (Gen. 25:28). Does God delight in a meek, broken, humble spirit? Then it will be the desire of a Christian to have such a spirit. Search in God's word for what he delights in and let us labour to bring ourselves to such a condition as God may delight in us. Love stirs up the affections of the party to remove all things that are distasteful to the party it loves. It will purge the soul; it will work upon the soul a desire to be clean as much as can be, because God is a pure, holy God, and it will 'have no fellowship with the works of darkness' (Eph. 5:11). As much as human frailty will permit, it will study purity, to keep itself 'unspotted of the world' (James 1:27). It will not willingly cherish any sin that may offend the Spirit. God hates pride and idolatry. A man that loves God will hate idols and all false doctrine. His heart will rise against them because he knows God hates it. He observes what is most offensive to God, and he will avoid it and seek what is pleasing to him. God and Christ are wondrously pleased with faith. Therefore, let us labour for faith, for all graces. Let us labour to be furnished with all things that he loves. Especially those graces that have some excellencies set upon them in the Scripture. Show me in your life what you do to please God. If you live in ways that are condemned, never talk of love. It is a pitiful thing to see in the bosom of the church, under the glorious revelation of divine truth, that men should live openly and impudently in sins against conscience, that glory in their shame. It is a strange thing that they should glory in their profaneness; that they should glory in a kind of atheistic life.

*A Glance of Heaven, Works*, vol. 4, pp. 187-89

# How to Know if You Love God (5)

*We love because he first loved us.*—1 John 4:19

Oh, let us labour to have this affection of love planted in our hearts; that God by his Spirit would teach us to love him. It is not a matter of the brain to teach. God only is the great schoolmaster and teacher of the heart.

The soul that loves God and Christ says, 'Are there any other people who carry the image of God and Christ?' That soul will be sure to love them also. Undoubtedly if we love God, we will love his children, and anything that has God's stamp upon it. We will love his truth, his cause, his religion, and whatever is divine and touches upon God.

Love for God will make us please him in all things. As Christ describes it out of Moses, to 'love God with all our mind, with all our soul, and with all our strength' (Deut. 6:5; Luke 10:27). Where love is, it sets all on work to please. It sets the mind to study. It will study God's truth, and not serve him by our own inventions. If he be a magistrate, with the strength of his magistracy; if he be a minister, with the strength of his ministerial calling. In any condition I must love him, with all that that condition enables me to.

Much might be said to this purpose to test ourselves, whether we love God or not. It is the command of both the Old and New Testaments. 'I give you a new command,' said Christ (John 13:34). Yet it is no new command, but old and known. But it is commanded now in the gospel; it is renewed by new manifestations of God's love in Christ, 'that we should love him, as he has loved us' (John 15:12). This affection the Holy Spirit sets out as the disposition and qualification of those for whom God has prepared great things: 'eye has not seen, nor ear heard, nor has entered into the heart of man, the things which God has prepared for those that love him' (1 Cor. 2:9).

*A Glance of Heaven, Works,* vol. 4, pp. 189-91

## Simple Yet Growing Love for God

*That your faith might not rest in the wisdom of men but in the power of God.*—1 Cor. 2:5

It may be asked again, as indeed we see it is true, what is the reason that sometimes lowly, simple Christians have more loving souls than great scholars? One would think that knowledge should increase love and affection? So it does, if it be a true knowledge. But great thinkers and great scholars busy themselves about questions and intricacies and are not so much about the affections. A lowly, simple Christian ofttimes takes those things for granted that scholars study, and dispute, and question. There is a heavenly light in the simple soul that God is my Father in Christ, and Christ is my Mediator. He takes it as truth, and so his affections are not troubled. Whereas the other, having corruption answerable to his parts, he is tangled with doubts and arguments. The scholar studies to inform his brain; the simple soul to heat his affections. Instead of disputing, he believes, and loves, and obeys; and that is the reason that many a lowly, simple soul goes to heaven with a great deal of joy, when others are tangled and wrapped in their own doubts.

At the same time, it is our duty to aim at the highest pitch of love that we can, and not to rest in the lowest pitch. The lowest pitch of loving God is to love God because he is good to us. The Scriptures stoop so low as to allow that God would have us love him and holy things for the benefit we have by them. But that is mercenary if we rest there. We must love God, not for ourselves, but labour to rise to this pitch, to love ourselves in God, and to see that we have happiness in God, and not in ourselves. Our being is in him. We must love ourselves in him and be content to be lost in God. Do others what they will, we will love him, and ourselves for his excellencies, and because we see ourselves in him and are his children. We must labour to rise to that, and that is the highest pitch that we can attain.

*A Glance of Heaven, Works,* vol. 4, p. 194

# Where to Place Our Love

*Do not love the world or the things in the world. If anyone loves the world, the love of the Father is not in him.*—1 John 2:15

Like the fire of the sanctuary that never went out, so is the affection of love for God, that if it be once kindled in the heart it will never go out. It is a kind of miracle in reverse when we love other things besides God, baser than ourselves; it is as much as if a river should turn backward. For man that is an excellent creature, to be carried with the stream of his affection to things worse than himself, it is a kind of monster for a man to abuse his understanding so. Our love is the best thing in the world, and who deserves it better than God and Christ? We can never return anything, but this affection of love we may return. Can we place it better than upon divine things, whereby we are made better ourselves?

Does God require our affections only for himself? No. It is to make us happy. It advances our affection to love him; it is the turning of it into the right stream. It is for the making of us happy that God requires it. What is any sin but the abuse of love? For the crookedness of this affection turns us to present things and that is the cause of all sin. For what is all sin, but pleasure, profit, and honour (1 John 2:16), the three idols of the world? And what are all good actions but love well placed? The well ordering of this affection is the well ordering of our lives; and the misplacing of this affection is the cause of all sin.

To make us the more careful, consider the vanity of placing our affections upon anything other than God. We lose our love and the thing and ourselves. For whatsoever else we love, if we love not God in it, nor love it for God, it will perish and come to nothing ere long. The affection perishes with the thing. We lose our affections and the thing; and lose ourselves too, in the misplacing of our love.

These are forcible considerations for understanding persons.

*A Glance of Heaven, Works*, vol. 4, p. 199

# All Die

*And just as it is appointed for man to die once, and after that comes judgment.*—Heb. 9:27

The righteous die in the same manner outwardly as the wicked do. For Christ, in his first coming, came not to redeem our bodies from death, but our souls from damnation. His second coming will be to redeem our bodies from corruption and raise them in glorious liberty. Wise men die as well as fools. Those whose eyes and hands have been lifted up to God in prayer, and whose feet have carried them to the holy place, as well as those whose eyes are full of adultery, and whose hands are full of blood, they all die alike. Often it looks the same in the eye of the world when death comes upon good and bad alike. But the difference is that to those in grace their death is for their greater glory; for the shell must be broken before they come to the pearl. Death fits them for the blessed life, after the body has laid a while in the grave, the soul being in the hands of God. Death also makes an end of sin, that brought death. Holy and gracious men are happy in their lives. While they live they are the sons of God, the heirs of heaven; they are set at liberty; they have access to the throne of grace; all things work for their good; they are the temples of the Holy Spirit. But they are more happy in their dying, and most happy and blessed after death.

Considering we have no long continuance here, while we are here, we must do that for which God put us here. Let us consider that we are sent here to get into a state of salvation, to furnish our souls with grace, to fit us for our dissolution to come. Let us do the work that God has put into our hands quickly and faithfully, with all our might. 'The time is short, therefore let those that use the world be as if they used it not' (1 Cor. 7:29-31). Let us beg of God to help us rightly use this fading condition.

*Balaam's Wish, Works*, vol. 7, pp. 3-4, 6

# The Death of the Righteous

*Who can count the dust of Jacob or number the fourth part of Israel? Let me die the death of the upright, and let my end be like his!*—Num. 23:10

The soul continues after death. In Numbers 23:10, Balaam wishes to die the death of the righteous, not for anything excellent in their deaths, but regarding the existence and continuance of their souls after death. Scripture, reason, and nature enforce this, that the soul has a life of itself, distinct from the life it communicates to the body. Now when the life it communicates to the body is gone to dissolution, the soul has a life in heaven. The life of the soul is the whole man. Abraham was Abraham after he was dead, when his soul was in heaven, and his body in the grave.

Let us know what our best part is, namely, the soul that has a being after death, that we do not employ it in lower uses, for which it was not made nor given us. Do we think that these souls of ours were made and given us to scrape wealth or to travel in our affections to the lower things of this world? Are they not capable of supernatural and excellent things? Are they not capable of grace and glory, of communion with God, of the blessed stamp of the image of God? Let us use them, therefore, to the end that God gave them. What is the life of most men but a purveying and prowling for the body? Were our souls given us for this end? And especially considering this, that our souls are immortal, that they will never die, but live forever. Let us not waste the precious time that has been given us to save our souls, and to get the image of God stamped upon them. Let us not spend this precious time in things that will leave us when our souls live on. The souls of such men that seek the things of this life will have a being in eternal misery. These souls of ours, next to angels, are the most excellent creatures of God, and all the more excellent if they get the image of God stamped upon them, become new creations, and have the life of grace within them.

*Balaam's Wish, Works,* vol. 7, pp. 4-5

# Choices and Desires

*I am hard pressed between the two. My desire is to depart and be with Christ, for that is far better. But to remain in the flesh is more necessary on your account.*—Phil. 1:23, 24

Paul's soul was as a ship, between two winds, tossed up and down, and as iron between two loadstones, drawn first one way, then another; the one loadstone was his own good, to be in heaven; the other was the good of God's people, to abide still in the flesh. Observe that the servants of God are oftentimes in great straits. Some things are so exceedingly bad that, without any deliberation or delay at all, we ought presently to abominate them, as Satan's temptations to sin, to distrust, and despair. Some things also are so good that we should immediately cleave unto them, as matters of religion and piety. There should be no delay in these holy businesses. Deliberation here, argues weakness. Some things, however, are of an ambiguous and doubtful nature, requiring our best consideration. Such was Paul's strait in this place. He had reasons swaying him on both sides; and such is the happy estate of a Christian, that whatever he had chosen would have been well for him.

(1) Paul's desire was spiritual, not after happiness, so much as holiness. His desire of death was to be freed from the body of sin (Rom. 7:24), more than to be taken out of the flesh; and his desire of holiness, to have Christ's image stamped on his soul, was more than of eternal happiness.

(2) This desire came from a taste of sweetness in communion with Christ.

(3) It was a constant desire. He does not say, 'I have a feeling,' but, 'I desire,' and that carried him to a love of Christ and his members.

(4) It was efficacious, not a mere inclination, but a strong desire, carrying him even through death itself to Christ. Desires thus qualified are blessed desires. As where we see vapours arise, there are springs usually below them, so where these desires are, there is always a spring of grace in that soul. Nothing characterizes a Christian so much as holy and blessed desires.

*Christ is Best*, pp. 3-7

# Paul's Desire to Depart

*My desire is to depart.*—Phil. 1:23

*I desire to depart.* There must be a parting and a departing; there must be a parting in this world with all outward excellencies, from the sweet enjoyment of the creatures; there must be a departing between soul and body, between friend and friend, and whatever is near and dear to us. Here we cannot stay long; away we must; we are for another place. How far we are from making right use of the mysteries of salvation. Moses, considering the suddenness of his departure, begged of God to teach him to number his days, that he might apply his heart unto wisdom (Psa. 90:12). Death is but a departing; like loosening a ship from the shore or moving a ship to another coast (2 Tim. 4:6; Phil. 1:23). We must all be unloosened from our houses of clay, and be carried to another place, to heaven. Paul labours to sweeten so harsh a thing as death, by comfortable expressions of it. It is but a sleep (1 Cor. 15:20), a going home (2 Cor. 5:8), a laying aside our earthly tabernacle (2 Cor. 5:1), to teach us this point of heavenly wisdom, that we should look on death as it is now in the gospel, not as it was in the law and by nature. To be with Christ is a thing desirable of itself; but because we cannot come to Christ but by the dark passage of death, said Paul, I desire to depart, that so my death may be a passage to Christ; so that death was the object of Paul's desire so far as it made way for better things. To be with Christ that came from heaven to be here on earth with us, and descended that we should ascend; to be with him, that has done and suffered so much for us; to be with Christ that delighted to be with us; to be with Christ that emptied himself, and became of no reputation, that became poor to make us rich; to be with Christ our husband, now contracted here, that all may be made up in heaven, this was the thing Paul desired.

*Christ is Best*, pp. 8-10

# Death Is the Suburbs of Heaven

*And if I go and prepare a place for you, I will come again and will take you to myself, that where I am you may be also.*—John 14:3

Heaven is not heaven without Christ. It is better to be in any place with Christ than to be in heaven itself without him. Paul loved to see Christ, to embrace him, and enjoy him that had done so much and suffered so much for his soul. To be with Christ is to be at the springhead of all happiness. Every creature thinks itself best in its own element, that is the place it thrives in, and enjoys its happiness in; now Christ is the element of a Christian. Again, it is far better, because to be with Christ is to have the marriage consummated. Is not marriage better than the contract? Is not home better than absence? To be with Christ is to be at home. Is not triumph better than to be in conflict? But to be with Christ is to triumph over all enemies, to be out of Satan's reach. Is not perfection better than imperfection? Here all is but imperfect, in heaven there is perfection. Here the grace in a man is with combat of flesh and spirit, but in heaven there is pure peace, pure joy, pure grace. Grace indeed is glory here, but it is glory with conflict. Is it not much far better to die, that we may be with Christ, than to live a conflicting life here? Death is but a grim sergeant that lets us into a glorious palace, that takes off our rags, that we may be clothed with better robes, that ends all our misery, and is the beginning of all our happiness. Why should we be afraid of death? It is but a departure to a better condition. It is but as Jordan to the children of Israel, by which they passed to Canaan. Of itself it is an enemy indeed, but now it is harmless, nay, now it has become a friend. It is one part of the church's journey. It ends all our misery and sin; and it is the suburbs of heaven. It is a shame for Christians to be afraid of that which Paul makes the object of his desire (Phil. 1:23).

*Christ is Best*, pp. 11-15

## The Fear of Death

*As it is my eager expectation and hope that I will not be at all ashamed,*
*but that with full courage now as always Christ will be honoured in*
*my body, whether by life or by death.*—Phil. 1:20

May a good Christian fear death? I answer, 'No,' so far as a Christian is led with the Spirit of God and is truly spiritual; for the Spirit carries us upward. But as far as we are earthly and carnal, and biased downward to things below, we are loath to depart here. In some cases, God's children are afraid to die, because their accounts are not ready. Though they love Christ, and are in a good way, yet notwithstanding, because they have not prepared themselves by care, they say, 'Oh stay away awhile that I may recover my strength, before I go hence and be no more seen' (Psa. 39:13). But as far as we are guided by the Spirit of God sanctifying us, so far the thoughts of death ought not to be terrible to us. Beloved, there is none but a Christian that can desire death; because it is the end of all comfort here, it is the end of all callings and employments, of all sweetness in this world. If another man who is not a Christian, desires heaven, he desires it not to be with Christ as Christ; he desires it under some notion suitable to his corruption. Heaven is no place for such. None but a child of God can desire that; for if we consider heaven, and to be with Christ, to be perfect holiness, can he desire it that hates holiness here? Can he desire the communion of saints in heaven, yet hate Christian fellowship now? Can he desire to be free from sin, who engulfs himself continually in sin? He cannot, and therefore as long as he is under the dominion of any lust he may desire heaven indeed, but it is only so far as he may have his lusts there, his pleasures, honours, and riches there too. If he may have heaven with that, he is contented; but alas, heaven must not be so desired. Paul did otherwise; he desired to depart, to be with Christ (Phil. 1:23). Paul desired it as the perfection of the image of God, under the notion of holiness and freedom from sin.

*Christ is Best*, pp. 15-18

## The Best for Last

*But as it is, they desire a better country, that is, a heavenly one. There-
fore, God is not ashamed to be called their God, for he has prepared
for them a city.*—Heb. 11:16

We see that God reserves the best for the last. God's last works are his
best works. The new heaven and the new earth are the best; the second
wine that Christ created himself was the best; spiritual things are better
than natural. A Christian's last is his best. God will have it so, for the
comfort of Christians, that every day they live, they may think, 'My best
is not behind, my best is to come.' That every day they rise, they may
think, 'I am one day nearer heaven than I was before.' What a solace this
is to a gracious heart! A Christian is a happy man in his life, but happier
in his death, because then he goes to Christ; but happiest of all in heaven,
for then he is with Christ. How contrary to a carnal man, that lives
according to the sway of his own lusts! He is miserable in his life, more
miserable in his death, but most miserable of all after death. I beseech
you, lay to heart that death is but a way for us to be with Christ, which
is far better, this should sweeten the thinking of death to us.

But how shall we attain this sanctified sweet desire that Paul had, to
die, and be with Christ (Phil. 1:23)?

(1) Let us carry ourselves as Paul did, and then we shall have the same
desires. Paul, before death, in his lifetime, had his heart and mind on
heaven (Col. 3:1, 2). There is no man's soul that comes into heaven, but
his mind is there first. It was an easy matter for him to desire to be with
Christ, having his heart and mind in heaven already.

(2) Paul had loosed his affections from all earthly things; therefore,
it was an easy matter for him to desire to be with Christ. 'I am crucified
to the world, and the world is crucified to me' (Gal. 6:14). If once a
Christian comes to this pass, death will be welcome to him. Those whose
hearts are fastened to the world, cannot easily desire Christ.

*Christ is Best*, pp. 19-21

# A Good Conscience

*Pray for us, for we are sure that we have a clear conscience, desiring to act honourably in all things.*—Heb. 13:18

Paul laboured to keep a good conscience in all things. 'Herein I exercise myself, to have a good conscience towards God and men' (Acts 24:16). It is easy for a man to desire to depart, who has his conscience sprinkled with the blood of Christ (Heb. 10:22), free from a purpose of living in sin. But where there is a stained, defiled, polluted conscience, there cannot be this desire; for the heart of man, naturally, as the prophet said, 'casts up mire and dirt' (Isa. 57:20). It casts up fears, and objections, and murmurings. Oh, beloved, we think not what mischief sin will do when we suffer it to seize upon our consciences. When it is once written there with the claw of a diamond, and with a pen of iron (Jer. 17:1), who shall get it out? Nothing but great repentance and faith, applying the blood of Christ. When conscience is not appeased, there will be all clamours within. It will fear to appear before the judgment seat. A guilty conscience trembles at the mention of death. I wonder how men who live in looseness, in filthiness, in debauchery of life, who labour to satisfy their lusts and corruptions, I wonder how they can think of death without trembling, considering that they are under the guilt of so many sins. You have a company of wretched persons, proud enough in their own conceits, and censorious. Nothing can please them, whose whole life is controlled by the lusts of their flesh, and they do nothing but build the sting of death every day. They arm death against themselves, which when once it appears, their conscience, which is a hell within them, is wakened, and where are they? They can stay here no longer; they must appear before the dreadful Judge; and then where are all their pleasures and satisfactions, for which they neglected heaven and happiness, peace of conscience, and all? Oh, therefore let us walk wholly with our God, and maintain inward peace all we can, if we desire to depart here with comfort.

*Christ is Best*, pp. 21-24

# Paul's Strait

*I am hard pressed between the two. My desire is to depart and be with Christ, for that is far better. But to remain in the flesh is more necessary on your account.*—Phil. 1:23, 24

Will a man leave the prison when he knows he will be carried to execution? Oh, no; he had rather be in the dungeon still. So for those with guilt on the soul and no assurance of salvation; they would rather abide in the flesh if they could, forever, for all eternity. Therefore, if we would come to Paul's desire, labour to come to the frame of the apostle's spirit. He knew whom he had believed; he was assured that nothing could separate him from the love of God, neither life, nor death, nor anything whatsoever that could befall him (Rom. 8:38, 39). Paul had an art of sweetening the thoughts of death. When death was presented to him as a passage to Christ, it was an easy matter to desire the same. It should be the art of Christians to present death as a passage to a better life, to labour to bring our souls into such a condition, as to think death not to be a death to us, but the death of itself. Death dies when I die, and I begin to live when I die. It is a sweet passage to life. We never live until we die. Would we cherish a desire to die, Let us look on death as a passage to Christ, and look beyond it to heaven. All of us must go through this dark passage to Christ, which when we consider it as Paul did, it will be an easy matter to die.

I come now to the next words, 'But to remain in the flesh is more necessary on your account.' This is the other desire of Paul, that brought him into this strait. He was troubled whether he should die, which was far better for himself, or live, which was more needful for them; but the love of God's people did prevail in Paul, above the desire of heaven. Oh, the power of grace in the hearts of God's children, that makes them content to be without the joys of heaven for a time, that they may do God's service, in serving his church here upon earth.

*Christ is Best*, pp. 25-28

# Worthy Leaders

*Remember your leaders, those who spoke to you the word of God. Consider the outcome of their way of life and imitate their faith.*—Heb. 13:7

The lives of worthy leaders, especially officials and ministers, are very needful for the church of God. The reason is because God often conveys good to people by the means of worthy leaders. If we consider the great benefit that comes by them, we will easily agree; for what a great deal of sin does a good official stop and hinder! When there were good judges and good kings in Israel, see what a reformation there was. When they were removed, there was a floodgate opened for all manner of sin and corruption to break in. There is an abundance of good that comes in by gracious persons.

(1) By their counsel; 'The lips of the righteous feed many' (Prov. 10:21).

(2) By their reformation of abuses, by planting God's good orders. They stand in the gap and stop evil. They reform it, and labour to establish that which is pleasing to God.

(3) Gracious persons, in whatever position they are, carry the blessing of God with them.

(4) They do good by their pattern and example. 'They are the lights of the world' (Phil. 2:15), that give aim to others in the darkness of this life.

(5) They can by their prayers bind God, as it were, that he will not inflict his judgments. They do a world of good by this way. A praying force and army is as good as a fighting army. Moses did as much good by prayer, as the soldiers in the valley when they fought with Amalek.

If this be so, then we may lament the death of worthy leaders, because we lose part of our strength in the loss of them. When there is scarcity of good leaders, we should say with Micah, 'Woe is me, the godly have perished from the earth' (Mic. 7:2). For all of us, once we are in Christ, we live for others, not for ourselves. A father is kept alive for his children's sake; good officials are kept alive for their subjects' sake; a good minister is kept alive out of the present enjoying of heaven for his people's sake.

*Christ is Best*, pp. 28-33

# Life is Sacrifice

*For you were bought with a price. So, glorify God in your body.—*
1 Cor. 6:20

A Christian is a consecrated person and he is not his own. He is a sacrifice as soon as he is a Christian. He belongs to Christ (2 Cor. 8:5).

(1) Beloved, that we had the spirit of Paul, and the Spirit of Christ, to set us at work to do good while we are here, 'to deny ourselves' (Titus 2:12). Consider all the capacities and abilities we have to do good, this way and that way, in this relation and that relation, that we may be trees of righteousness. God will mend his own trees. He will purge them and prune them to 'bring forth more fruit' (John 15:2). God cherishes fruitful trees. God spares a fruitful person until he has done his work. Sometimes one poor wise man delivers the city (Eccles. 9:15). We see for one servant, Joseph, Potiphar's house was blessed (Gen. 39:8). They carry God's blessing wherever they go, and they think in every situation that they are there to do good, as it says in Esther 4:14, 'God has called me to this place, perhaps for this end.' Now, that we may be fruitful as Paul was, let us labour to have humble spirits. God delights to use humble spirits, that are content to stoop to any service for others.

(2) Get loving hearts. Love is full of creativity. How shall I glorify God? How shall I do good to others? How shall I bring to heaven as many as I can? Love is a sweet and boundless affection.

(3) Labour to have sufficiency in our places. When ability and sufficiency meet together with a gracious heart, what a deal of good is done then!

(4) Labour to have a sincere aim in what we do to please God, and then resolve to do all the good we can. Those that are fruitful in their places never want for arguments of good assurance of salvation. It is the lazy, lukewarm Christian that wants assurance. I beseech you, be stirred up and labour to be useful in your place in the world all you can.

*Christ is Best*, pp. 38-44

# Start Now to Die Well

*O Lord, make me know my end and what is the measure of my days; let me know how fleeting I am! Behold, you have made my days a few handbreadths, and my lifetime is as nothing before you. Surely all mankind stands as a mere breath!*—Psa. 39:4, 5

In this moment let us provide for eternity. Out of eternity before, and eternity after, issues this little spot of time to do good in. Let us sow to the Spirit, count all time lost which we either do not or take not, good in. Time is short, but opportunity is shorter. Let us catch all opportunities. This is the time of worship. Oh, let us sow now. Will we go to sowing then when the time comes that we should reap? Some begin to sow when they die, but that is the reaping time. While we have time let us do good to all, but especially to those who are of the household of faith. (Gal. 6:10). Consider the standings and places that God has set us in; consider the advantages in our hands, the price that we have; consider that opportunity will not stay long. Let us do all the good we can, and so if we do, beloved, we will come at length to reap. If we desire to end our days in joy and comfort, let us lay the foundation of a comfortable death now. To die well is not a thing of that light moment as some imagine: it is no easy matter. But to die well is a matter of every day. Let us daily do some good that may help us at the time of our death. Every day by repentance pull out the sting of some sin, so that when death comes, we may have nothing to do but to die. To die well is the action of the whole life. He never dies well for the most part that dies not daily, as Paul said of himself, 'I die daily' (1 Cor. 15:31); he laboured to loosen his heart from the world and worldly things. If we loosen our hearts from the world and die daily, how easy will it be to die at last! He that thinks of the vanity of the world, and of death, and of being with Christ forever, and is dying daily, it will be easy for him to end his days with comfort.

*Christ is Best*, pp. 57-59

# The Ministry of Angels

*But Mary stood weeping outside the tomb, and as she wept, she stooped to look into the tomb. And she saw two angels in white, sitting where the body of Jesus had lain, one at the head and one at the feet.*—John 20:11, 12

As Mary wept at the tomb of Jesus, she stooped down and looked into the sepulchre, and there saw two angels in white: a colour of glory, purity, and joy, because it was a time of joy. They were one at the head, and the other at the feet. As in the law, when the mercy-seat was made, two cherubim were also framed, and placed one at the one end, and the other at the other end, with their faces looking one towards another (Exod. 25:20). And when Christ was risen, there were two angels, one at the head, another at the feet, to show that peace was to be expected in the true propitiatory, Jesus Christ.

One at the head, the other at the feet of the body of Jesus. And they sat there. It was a time of peace. Peace was made between heaven and earth, God and man; and here is a posture of peace, 'They sat quietly.' In Christ, angels and we are at one; God, and we, and all. There is a recapitulation and gathering of all things in heaven and earth (Col. 1:20).

The angels, they attended on Christ in all the passages of his life and death till they brought him to heaven. They brought news of his birth, comforted him in his agony; they were at his resurrection, and you see here they attend. At his ascension they accompany him. And as they did to the Head, so they will to the members. In our infancy, they take charge of our tender years; in our dangers, they pitch their tents about us; in our deaths, they carry our souls to Abraham's bosom, a place of happiness. At our resurrection, their office is to gather our bodies together. That service and attendance they afforded the Head they afford to the members, to the spiritual Christ as well as the actual Christ. Therefore, let us comfort ourselves in the service they did to Christ.

*A Heavenly Conference*, pp. 2-3

# Why Does Christ Hide Himself at Times?

*I will wait for the Lord, who is hiding his face from the descendants of Jacob. I will put my trust in him.*—Isa. 8:17

Why does Christ conceal himself at times? Four reasons why:

(1) To see whether we can live by faith, or whether we be altogether addicted to sense, as the world is, who live altogether by sense and not by faith.

(2) He would have our patience tried to the utmost. He would have 'patience have its perfect work' (James 1:4).

(3) Christ will stir up and quicken zeal and fervency in his children; and therefore he seemed to deny the woman of Canaan (Mark 7:27, 28); first, he gives no answer but a harsh answer, 'A dog.' And she works upon it: 'Though I am a dog, yet dogs have crumbs.' All which denial was only to stir up zeal and earnestness. And therefore, though Christ does not manifest himself to us at first, he does so to stir up zeal and affection to seek him more earnestly. There is a notable passage of this (Song of Sol. 3:1-4). The soul sought Christ, and sought long, and sought in the use of all means; but at length she waited, and in waiting she found him.

(4) Christ does this to set a better price upon his presence when he comes; to make his presence highly valued when he does reveal himself. Things long desired please more sweetly; as warmth after cold, and meat after hunger, and so in every particular of this life. And therefore God, to set a greater price on his presence, defers for a long time. Long deferring of a thing does but enlarge the soul. Now, when we want what we love, that empties the soul marvellously much; it mortifies affection. When God keeps off a long time, and we see it is God only must do it, then affection is taken off from earthly things, and the heart enlarged to God by the want of the thing we love. It is very beneficial to us. We lose nothing. We have it at last more abundantly. Certainly, this comes from God, and God should have all the glory. God is wise; and therefore, makes us wait a long time for what we do desire.

*A Heavenly Conference*, pp. 17-19

## Beware of Spiritual Apathy

*Then you will call upon me and come and pray to me, and I will hear you. You will seek me and find me when you seek me with all your heart.*—Jer. 29:12, 13

Take heed of such a temper of soul, as cares not whether we find Christ or no. Oh take heed of that! If we will seek him, seek him as Mary did on that first resurrection morning. She sought him early in the morning; she broke her sleep and sought him with tears. If there be anything to be sought with tears, it is Christ and communion with him. She sought him so, that no impediment could hinder her, she was full of grief and love (Matt. 28:1; Mark 16:9; Luke 24:1; John 20:1). She sought him with her whole heart, she waited in seeking. That is the way to find Christ. Seek him early, in the early times of each day, in the morning of our years. Oh, that we could seek Christ as we seek our pleasures. We should find more pleasure in Christ than in all the pleasures of the world if we could persuade our base heart so much. Seek him above all other things. Awake with this resolution in our hearts, to find Christ, never to be quiet until we may say with comfort, 'I am Christ's and Christ is mine.' When we have him, we have all. Seek him with tears, at length we are sure to find him. He has bound himself, that if we knock, he will open; and if we seek, we will find. Seek Christ for Christ, and then we will be sure to find him.

*A Heavenly Conference*, pp. 20-21

## Mary Proclaims the Resurrection

*Jesus said to her, 'Do not cling to me, for I have not yet ascended to the Father; but go to my brothers and say to them, "I am ascending to my Father and your Father, to my God and your God."' Mary Magdalene went and announced to the disciples, 'I have seen the Lord.'*—John 20:17, 18

Jesus said to Mary, 'Go to my brethren.' I have another work for you to do, 'Touch me not.' You clasp about me as if you had nothing to do. There is another work to do that pleases me better: to comfort them that are in distress, my poor brethren and disciples. And therefore 'Go to my brethren …' Those poor souls are mourning and disconsolate for me, as if I were clean taken away; go to them and prevent their further sorrow. God has a wonderful respect of others. So, a work of charity and love is preferred before a duty and compliment to himself. Let us show our love to God by our love to man. Observe the circumstances, it is worth your consideration.

(1) Who is sent? A woman. A woman to be the apostle of apostles, to be the teacher of the great teachers in the world. Mary Magdalene was sent to instruct the apostles in the great articles of Christ's resurrection and ascension to heaven. She stood out when the rest went away (John 19:25). She was constant and broke through all difficulties; and then God honoured her to be the first preacher of his resurrection.

(2) To whom must she go? 'Go, tell my brethren,' the apostles. Go to the apostles, who are disconsolate men, now orphans, deprived of their Master and Lord. Disconsolate men, and not in vain, not without cause; for they had reason to be discomforted, not only for their want of Christ, but for their own ill carriage towards Christ. One of them denied him, and the rest forsook him; and yet 'my brethren,' 'go tell my brethren.'

(3) When did he speak this? After his resurrection, in the state of glory; in the beginning of it, and when he is ascending to heaven; and yet he owns them as brethren, though such brethren as had dealt most unbrotherly with him.

*A Heavenly Conference*, pp. 32-34

## Christ Calls Us Brothers and Sisters

*The Spirit himself bears witness with our spirit that we are children of God, and if children, then heirs—heirs of God and fellow heirs with Christ, provided we suffer with him in order that we may also be glorified with him.*—Rom. 8:16, 17

How can it be that we are considered Christ's brothers? Christ is the first-born of many brethren (Rom. 8:29). He is the Son of God by nature; and all others are his brothers and sisters by grace and adoption (Rom. 8:17). Christ is the first-born among many brethren; and in Christ we have one Father with Christ. 'If sons, then heirs' (Gal. 4:7). Now we are all in Christ sons of God, heirs with him. He took our nature; and therefore, having our flesh, he is our brother (Heb. 2:14). It is a ground of comfort that he is a man as we are. But that is not the main thing to consider. He is our brother in a spiritual respect, in regard to adoption. He is the first Son of God, and we in him are sons. He is the first heir of God, and we in him are heirs. Beloved, it is a point of marvellous comfort, that Christ is not ashamed to call us brethren (Psa. 22:22): 'I will declare your name among my brethren,' says Christ. He is 'a second Adam,' and therefore a father in that regard. The first Adam is the father of all that perish; the second Adam is the father of all that will be saved. He is our head, husband, friend, father, brother, and whatsoever can convey comfort to us.

And the truth of it is, he is these things more truly than any relation is made true on earth. For these relations of husband and wife, and brother and sister, and father and child, are but shadows of that everlasting relation that Christ has taken upon himself. We think there is no brother but the brother in flesh, no father but the father in flesh. Alas! These are but shadows and quickly cease: 'the fashion of the world passes away' (1 Cor. 7:31). These do but represent the best things that are in heaven. Christ is the father, brother, friend, and whatsoever is comforting in heaven. When he out of his free love will own us as brethren, will not we own him?

*A Heavenly Conference*, pp. 35-39

# God's Love Never Changes

*No, in all these things we are more than conquerors through him who loved us. For I am sure that neither death nor life, nor angels nor rulers, nor things present nor things to come, nor powers, nor height nor depth, nor anything else in all creation, will be able to separate us from the love of God in Christ Jesus our Lord.*—Rom. 8:37-39

*We love because he first loved us.*—1 John 4:19

Beloved, let us not lose the comfort of the constancy and immutability of God's love. Let us conceive that all the sweet links of salvation are held strong on God's part, not on ours; the firmness is on God's part, not on ours.

Election is firm on God's part, not on ours. We choose indeed as he chooses us, but the firmness is of his choosing; so, he calls us, we answer, but the firmness is of his action. He justifies; we are made righteous, but the firmness is of his imputation. Will he forgive sins today, and bring us into court and damn us tomorrow? No. The firmness is of his action. We are ready to run into new debts every day, but whom he justifies he will glorify. The whole chain so holds, that all the creatures in heaven and earth cannot break a link of it. Whom he calls he will justify and glorify. Therefore, never doubt of continuance, for it holds firm on God's part, not yours. God embraces us in the arms of his everlasting love, not that we embraced him first.

When the child does not fall it is from the mother's holding the child, and not from the child's holding the mother. So, it is God's holding of us, knowing of us, embracing of us, and justifying of us that makes the state firm, and not ours; for ours is but a reflection and result of his, which is invariable.

The sight of the sun varies, but the sun in the firmament always keeps its constant course. So, God's love is as the sun, invariable, and forever the same. I only begin to touch it, as the foundation of wonderful comfort.

*A Heavenly Conference*, pp. 53-54

# The Advantage of the Spirit

*Nevertheless, I tell you the truth: it is to your advantage that I go away,*
*for if I do not go away, the Helper will not come to you. But if I go, I*
*will send him to you.*—John 16:7

*Truly, truly, I say to you, whoever believes in me will also do the works*
*that I do; and greater works than these will he do, because I am going*
*to the Father.*—John 14:12

He ascended to leave his Spirit, that he might send the Comforter. He went away himself, who was the great Comforter while he was below. But Christ ascended to heaven that they might have comfort through the God of comfort, the Spirit of comfort, the Holy Spirit: 'I will send the Comforter' (John 14:16).

And though there was no loss by the ascension of Christ, they might fear by losing Christ that all their comfort was gone. But Christ tells them, 'I go to prepare a place for you.' He goes to take up heaven for his church, and then to send his Spirit. What a blessed intercourse is there now between heaven and earth! Our body is in heaven, and the Spirit of God is here on earth. The flesh that he has taken into heaven is a pledge that all our flesh and bodies will be where he is before long. In the meantime, we have the Spirit to comfort us, and never to leave us until we are brought to the place where Christ is. This is great comfort and might well come now in more abundance than before, because by the death of Christ all enemies are conquered, and by the resurrection of Christ it was revealed that God was appeased. The resurrection of Christ manifested to the world what was done by death; and now, all enemies being conquered, and God being appeased, what remains but the sweetest gift next to Christ, the Holy Spirit? And that is the reason why the Holy Spirit was more abundant after Christ's resurrection, because God was fully satisfied, and declared by the rising of Christ to be fully satisfied, and all enemies to be conquered.

*A Heavenly Conference*, pp. 68-69

# Christ's Work of Intercession

*Consequently, he is able to save to the uttermost those who draw near to God through him, since he always lives to make intercession for them.*—Heb. 7:25

He is there to plead our cause. He is there as our surety to appear for us, and not only so, but as a counsellor to plead for us; and not only so, but one of us, as if a brother should plead for a brother; and not only so, but a favourite brother too. All favourites are not so excellent at counselling perhaps, but we have one that is favourite in heaven, and is excellent at pleading, who can non-suit all accusations laid against us by the devil. Let us think of the comforts of it. He pleads before God the Father, who sent him to take our nature, die, and ascend into heaven for us, to sustain the persons of particular offences. He must hear Christ, that sent him for that purpose. Where the judge appoints a counsel, it is a sign he favours the cause. Perhaps we cannot pray, are disconsolate, and vexed with Satan's temptations. The poor client has a good cause but cannot make a good cause of it. But if he gets a skilful lawyer, that is favourable to him, and being before a favourable judge, his comfort is that his advocate can make his cause good. So, we confess our sins, as we must do; and we lay open ourselves to God; and desire God to look upon us, and Christ to plead our cause for us and answer Satan. And when Satan is very malicious and subtle, as he is a very cunning enemy to allege all advantages against us, to make us despair, remember this: we have one in heaven who is more skilful than he 'that is the accuser of the brethren' (Rev. 12:10), that accuses us to God and to our own souls, that accuses every man to himself and makes him an enemy to himself. But we have a pleader in heaven who will take our part against the accuser of our brethren, and quiet us at length in our consciences. Perhaps we may be troubled for a while, to humble us; but remember that he is in heaven purposely to plead our cause.

*A Heavenly Conference*, pp. 73-74

## A Present Application of Christ's Ascension

*Jesus said to her, 'Do not cling to me, for I have not yet ascended to the Father; but go to my brothers and say to them, "I am ascending to my Father and your Father, to my God and your God."'*—John 20:17

Jesus told Mary to tell his disciples, 'I ascend.' He speaks of that as present which was surely to be. So, we should think of our future state as if we were presently to go to heaven. Faith has this force, to make things to come present. If we could keep it in us, and exercise it, could we live in any sin? But that it is distant, that is the cause of sinning. We put off things in a distance. If it be at the day of judgment, that is far off; and therefore, they will not leave their present pleasure for that which is coming they know not when. But look on things in the word of a God who is Jehovah, who gives being to all, who has spoken of things to come as if present, and then you will be of another mind. Faith is the privilege of a Christian, which makes things far off present. Believe God on his word, that these things shall be. Another man lives all by sense; but the Christian will trust God on his word.

We must not think of the ascension of Christ as a severed thing from us, but if we would have the comfort of it, we must think of it as ourselves ascending with him. Think of Christ as a surety for us, and then we will have great comfort in that, that he said, 'I ascend.' God prepared paradise before he made the creatures. He would have him to come into a place of honour and pleasure. And so, God, before ever we were born, provided a place and paradise for us in heaven, that we might end our days with greater comfort. We may be in duress here. Many a good Christian has scarce a place to lay his head; but Christ is gone to prepare a place for them in heaven.

*A Heavenly Conference*, pp. 77-78

# Christ Our Advocate

*My little children, I am writing these things to you so that you may not sin. But if anyone does sin, we have an advocate with the Father, Jesus Christ the righteous.*—1 John 2:1

This may comfort us in the consideration of all our sins: for sin past, and for corruption present, and sin that we may commit in the time to come. For anything that is past, if we confess our sins to God, he will forgive them. 'The blood of Christ cleanses us from all sins' (1 John 1:7). We have one that stands between God and us as a surety; and he will give us his Spirit to subdue our corruptions, and at length make us like himself, a glorious spouse (Eph. 5:27). If we were perfect men, we would not need a mediator. Instead, we have one to make our peace; if we sin, we have an advocate (1 John 2:1). When Christ taught us to pray, 'Forgive us our trespasses,' he supposed we should run daily into sins (Matt. 6:12). We have an advocate in heaven every day to stand between God and us, to undertake that at length we should cease to offend him; and for the present, we are those he shed his precious blood for; and he appears for us by virtue of his death, which is a marvellous comfort. If all things were made up between God and us, would there be need of an intercessor? But God knows well enough we run into daily sins, by reason of a spring of corruption in us. Therefore, we may daily go to God in the name of our advocate, and desire God for Christ's sake to pardon us. There is not a Christian but will be in himself apprehensive because there is a spring of corruption in him. We must live by faith in this branch of Christ—his mediation—and make use of it continually. And if we sin every day, go to God in the name of Christ, and desire him to pardon us. When we be in heaven, we will need a mediator no longer, for we will be perfectly holy. We cannot think of these things too much. They are the life of religion and of comforts; and it may teach us to make a true use of Christ in all our conditions.

*A Heavenly Conference*, pp. 78-79

# The Fatherhood of God (1)

*I will be a father to you, and you shall be sons and daughters to me, says the Lord Almighty.*—2 Cor. 6:18

What we may expect from God being a father:

(1) We may expect whatever a child may expect from a father. God takes not upon him empty names. He says he will be a father, not only called a father. Fathers on earth are but poor fathers, yet they are reflections of the fatherly affection that is in God. God will let us see by these reflections of compassion what real compassion he bears to us. As a father pities his child, so God will pity us (Mal. 3:17). Will a father cast off his child? No, he will cleanse the child. So, God will take away our abominations, and purge us when we defile ourselves. We may expect from him indulgence; and it is an indulgence of indulgence. Can we pity and pardon a child? And will not God pardon and pity us? Why should we conceive worse of him than of ourselves? Think not that God will cast us off. God pardons us, and heals our infirmities, and pities us as a father pities his own child (Psa. 103:13). It is a name under which no man must despair. What! Despair of mercy when we have a father to go to? The poor prodigal, when he had spent his inheritance, his good name, had lost all, yet he had a father, and 'I will go to him' (Luke 15:18). Likewise, when we are at our last, and have spent all, we have a father. Therefore, go to him. What says God's people? 'Though our righteousness be as a filthy rag, and we be defiled, yet you are our Father; we are the clay, you are the potter' (Isa. 64:6, 8). As the father of the prodigal, God runs to us, and is ready to meet us, when we begin to repent of sin and are sensible of our faults. He is more ready to pardon than we to ask pardon. May you remember these things against the evil day and hour of temptation. He takes not on himself the relation of a father for naught but will fill it up to the uttermost.

*A Heavenly Conference*, pp. 82-84

# The Fatherhood of God (2)

*Yet for us there is one God, the Father, from whom are all things and for whom we exist, and one Lord, Jesus Christ, through whom are all things and through whom we exist.*—1 Cor. 8:6

(2) *Father*, a name of comfort. It is the speech of a natural man, 'A little punishment is enough from a father.' 'He knows whereof we are made; he remembers we are but dust' (Psa. 103:14); he knows we are not iron or steel; and therefore, he will deal gently with us when he corrects us. It is as necessary as our daily bread to have gentle correction, to wean us from the world. A little punishment will serve from a gracious father.

(3) *Father*, a name of provision. That he will in all our necessities provide for us whatever is needful. What says our Saviour Christ to the poor disciples doubting of want? 'It is your Father's good will to give you the kingdom.' What then? 'Fear not, little flock' (Luke 12:32). He who will give you a kingdom, will not he give you daily bread and provision for a journey? Therefore, in the Lord's prayer, before all petitions, as a ground of all, he puts in 'our Father.' Christ took effort to persuade his disciples that they should not want necessaries; and therefore, he made whole sermons to strengthen their faith in this: 'Your heavenly Father knows what you stand in need of' (Matt. 6:8). The Father can interpret any sigh, any groan, and knows what we would have. And therefore, we may fetch provision from him in all conditions.

(4) *Father*, a name of protection. Therefore, make this use of it. In the temptations of Satan, lie under the wing of our Father. We have a father to go to; make use of his protection, that God would shield us, that he would be a tower, as he is a tower, and 'the righteous man may fly to him' (Prov. 18:10). Lie under his wings. He is a gracious father, and he has taken this sweet relation on himself for this purpose, that we may have comfort in all conditions. You see then what we may expect from God, by this sweet relation he has taken on him in Christ, to be our Father.

*A Heavenly Conference*, pp. 84-86

# The Fatherhood of God (3)

*If you then, who are evil, know how to give good gifts to your children, how much more will your Father who is in heaven give good things to those who ask him!*—Matt. 7:11

The word *father* is a word of relation. It binds God to us and us to God. We are to honour him as our Father. This one word is sufficient to express our duty to a father: reverence; for it includes a mixed affection of fear and love. Reverence is an affection of an inferior to a superior. He is great, therefore we ought to fear him. He is good, therefore we ought to love him. There is with him beams of majesty and a heart of compassion. As there are beams of majesty, we ought to fear him; as a heart of compassion, we ought to love him. If we tremble and are afraid to go to him, we know not he is loving. If we go to him over-boldly and saucily, we forget that he is great. Therefore, we must think of his greatness, that we forget not his goodness. We must so think of his goodness, that we forget not his greatness.

In the word 'Father,' there is more saving power than in ten thousand. If God be our Father, go to him boldly; but with reverence go with trust. What cannot we look for from him, that majesty that has condescended to be called 'Father,' and to be a Father to us in all our necessities? Either we will have what we want and lack, or else we will have that which is better. He is a wise Father. He answers not always according to our wills, but always according to our good. Come to him boldly therefore, under the name of a Father, that he may move, and he surely will hear us. For in Psalm 27:10, when all forsook me, 'My father and mother forsook me, but the Lord took me up.' He is an eternal Father. He was our Father before we had a father in the world, and he will be our Father when we will cease to be in the world. Therefore, never be disconsolate, but remember, he was our Father from eternity in election; he will be our Father to eternity in glorification.

*A Heavenly Conference*, pp. 86-89

# The Fatherhood of God (4)

*For I am sure that neither death nor life, nor angels nor rulers, nor*
*things present nor things to come, nor powers, nor height nor depth,*
*nor anything else in all creation, will be able to separate us from the*
*love of God in Christ Jesus our Lord.*—Rom. 8:38, 39

Beloved, live upon this. Here is the love of God the Father, who is content to be a Father even in our sinful condition. If be a Father to us, as to Christ, then let not our hearts be discouraged in afflictions, persecutions, temptations. God was a Father to Christ in his desertion. God leaves us to ourselves sometimes, and we fear we have lost his love. Did not he leave his own Son upon the cross—'My God, my God, why have you forsaken me?' (Matt. 27:46)—and yet he did not cease to be his Father. For persecution from enemies: was not Christ's whole life filled up with persecution, and yet a Son? For temptations: you are tempted, and think you are not one of God's children. Satan tempted our blessed Saviour, that he might be a merciful Saviour, and know how to succour you in times of temptation. Therefore, be not discouraged. Say not, when you are deserted, persecuted, afflicted, tempted, God is not your Father; for by that reason you may argue, God was not Christ's Father. God was Christ's Father, notwithstanding his desertion for a time, and notwithstanding his afflictions in the world, his persecutions of all sorts by men, and notwithstanding his temptations, God was his Father still. This we must observe, 'father' is not a relation today, gone tomorrow. It is an eternal relation. *'Dum percutis, pater es; dum castigas, pater es,'* wrote: 'While you strike us, you are our Father; while you correct us, you are our Father.' Parents are tender to their weakest and sick children; and God is most tender of all to them that are weak. We cannot be in a condition wherein, on any sound grounds, we may run from God.

*A Heavenly Conference,* pp. 97-98

# Christ First, Then Us

*'Go to my brothers and say to them, "I am ascending to my Father and your Father, to my God and your God."'*—John 20:17

This is a weighty point for directing our devotion, that we may know in what order to look on God. See God in Christ; see all things in Christ first, and then in us. Look upon him as Father to Christ, and then to us. Look on him as God to Christ first, and in Christ God to us. Look on him as having elected us but elect in Christ first. See ourselves justified, but see Christ justified first from our sins, and his justification declared by his resurrection. When we consider any spiritual blessing, say with the apostle, 'Blessed be God, that has filled us with all spiritual blessings in Christ' (Eph. 1:3). Whatsoever is derived from God to us is through Christ. It is for our comfort that it is so, that God's love is to Christ first. The love and care and fatherly disposition of God towards us is sweet to us, because it is tender to his Son. He can as soon cease to love his Son, as cease to love us. For with the same love, he loves all of Christ's spiritual body, head and members. There is not the least finger of Christ, the least despised member of Christ, but God looks on him with that sweet eternal tenderness with which he looks upon his Son. Oh, this is a sweet comfort, that now all the excellent privileges of a Christian are set on Christ and then on us; and we should not lose them, for Christ will lose nothing. Whatever we see in Christ, think: This will belong to us. As verily as he ascended, we shall ascend; as verily as he rose, we shall arise; as verily as he is at God's right hand, we will be there too. Therefore, when we are to deal with God, be sure to go through Christ. If we stagger, and doubt to receive anything at God's hand, we wrong not only God's bounty, but Christ the mediator. I beseech you, let us not lose the comfort of these things, since our Saviour Christ intended them for comfort.

*A Heavenly Conference*, pp. 105-11

# God Is Our God

*I will make my dwelling among them and walk among them, and I will
be their God, and they shall be my people.*—2 Cor. 6:16

I beseech you, do not lose the comfort of it, that in Christ, God is
our God. Perhaps we cannot say, great houses are ours, or friends are
ours, or inheritances ours. That is no matter. We can say, that is ours
which is infinitely more than that. We can say, God is ours in Christ. If
God be ours, then all else is ours too. What does that include?

(1) If God be ours, his wisdom must be ours, to find out ways to do
us good; for his infinite wisdom has found out a way in Christ to bring
us to heaven.

(2) If we are in danger, his power is ours, to bring us out of it.

(3) If we have sinned, his mercy is ours, to forgive us.

(4) In any want, his all-sufficiency is ours, to supply it or to turn it
to good.

(5) In a word, God being ours, whatever is in God, whatever God
can do, whatever he has, is ours, because he is ours.

Therefore, I beseech you, make this use of it, to get into Christ by
faith; to be one with Christ, that God may be our God. Now, when we
have God to be our God, he is able to fill the soul. He is larger than the
soul, and he is able to quiet the soul; he is the rest of the soul, the place
of quiet. Though a man continues many thousand years in the world, yet
he will be weary of all things in the world, because there is no freshness in
them. But in God is a spring of fresh comforts to everlasting. Consider,
again, the things that enable him to be our God, to fill the soul, and to
be larger than the soul; to quiet and calm the soul in all the troubles of
it; and then to have fresh springs of comfort. What a comfort is this: to
have God for their God! Let it therefore raise up our souls to labour after
God, and never rest till we have some interest in this great portion, of
God being our God.

*A Heavenly Conference*, pp. 117-20

# Is God Our God?

*And he said to him, 'You shall love the Lord your God with all your heart and with all your soul and with all your mind. This is the great and first commandment.'*—Matt. 22:37, 38

What is it for us to make God our God? It is this: to set up God a throne in our hearts; to give him a sovereignty over all things in the world, that we may say in truth of heart, God is our joy, God is our comfort, God is our rock, God is all in all to us. For all to whom he is a God in the covenant of grace, and have hearts to make him so, the Spirit raises up their affections to make him God to themselves. It is said of old, 'what we love most is our god.' What we joy most in is our god, what we rely on and trust in most is our god, as it was said of the 'wedge of gold' (Job 31:24). It is a query of the greatest concern in the world to put to our hearts. What do I make my god? As David put the query to himself: 'Now, Lord, what is my hope? is it not in thee?' (Psa. 39:7).

And so, put this query to ourselves: Lord, what is my joy, what is my hope, what is my trust, what is my comfort? Is it not in you? If our hearts cannot make an answer to this in some sincerity, surely yet we have not made God our God. But until, by the Spirit of God, we be brought to see an emptiness and vanity in the creature, and nothingness in all in comparison of God, that we can say, 'Whom have I in heaven but thee?' We have not comfort, because we do not make him ours. Alas! We may be ashamed of it; those best do often forget themselves. Oh, how do men value the favours of a man; and how does it grieve them to have the frowns of flesh and blood, the frowns of greatness! But when their consciences tell them they are under guilt of many sins, and God is not in good terms with them, how does this affect them? It is of greatest concern that we take God to be our God.

*A Heavenly Conference*, pp. 121-22

# One with God

*So in Christ Jesus you are all children of God through faith, for all of you who were baptized into Christ have clothed yourselves with Christ. There is neither Jew nor Gentile, neither slave nor free, nor is there male and female, for you are all one in Christ Jesus.*—Gal. 3:26-28

Who gives us a being to be Christians, to have a new nature, but God? Who maintains and preserves that being but God? And who keeps and preserves us until we are changed into a glorious being in heaven but God, who is all-sufficient, self-sufficient, sole-sufficient, and only-sufficient? This God is our God now in Christ. Man has a reasoning soul and is fitted by nature to have communion with God. If God be our God in Christ, we have a spiritual being, which is as much above the dignity and prerogative of our natural being as our being by nature is above the basest creature in the world. However, the world takes no notice of them because their excellency is seen with another eye than the world has. 'The God of the world blinds the eyes of unbelievers' (2 Cor. 4:4). They cannot see into the excellency of God's children, no more than they know God himself and Christ himself. In this our excellency consists, that God is our God in Christ, who was God; and that he might bring God and us to good terms together; that he might make God our God. He was Immanuel, God with us—God with us in favour and love. God in Christ is so near our nature, that there is a oneness in union. By reason of this near union of the Godhead to our nature comes that comfort whereby God has sweet communion and interaction with us in Christ. God by his Spirit is graciously one with us as his children. Now we may say, God is our God; and upon good grounds, because God is Christ's God, and in him our God, which is a point of singular comfort.

*A Heavenly Conference*, pp. 123-26

# Inner Comfort

*Call upon me in the day of trouble; I will deliver you, and you shall glorify me.*—Psa. 50:15

Beloved, what cannot we expect from God, who is now our God! What he is, what he is able to do, what he has, all is ours. The wise merchant in the gospel sold all for the field wherein the treasure was (Matt. 13:44). We have the field itself in having God, and having God we have all.

However, if God be ours, and all things else, how comes it that we want so many things? It is our own fault for the most part. If God be our God and Father in Christ, why have we sins? Why vexed with the devil? Why persecuted from men? Why frightened thus, and thus, and thus? All this is for our good. God is our God in the midst of these; and is never more our God than in the greatest extremity of all. When we have nothing to go to but God there is a sweet communion and the sweetest comfort. We have inward comforts when outward ones have deserted. God was never more near our blessed Saviour than on the cross, when he cried, 'My God, my God,' for then he found invincible strength supporting him in the great undertaking under the wrath of his Father. We never have sweeter comforts than in the want of all outward comforts, when nothing else can comfort us but the presence of God. We must know that the state of a Christian in this world is a hidden condition; for it is to the eye of faith, not of sense. Who observes the influence of the sun? Light we see, but there is a secret influence pierces deeper than the light, to the very depths of the earth. Where no light comes, still there is an influence, though not discerned. Much more can there be spiritual influences of strength and power and hidden comfort, though there be no sight. Cannot God be our God though there be no visible and sensible comfort, though even we see it not? Certainly, the soul is upheld by an invincible strength in the worst condition that can be.

*A Heavenly Conference*, pp. 126-29

# Assurance of Salvation (1)

*The Spirit himself bears witness with our spirit that we are children of God.*—Rom. 8:16

Knowing you are a true believer:

(1) Those that belong to God, the Spirit of God witnesses to them that they are sons. There will be some intimations, and insinuations, and hints, though the Spirit of adoption witnesses not fully and gloriously to the soul always, because we are not fitted for it. There is something in us renewed by the Spirit; there is something of the new creature. When a Christian cannot hear God say to his soul, 'I am thy salvation,' yet a man may see a work of grace. There is a love to God, to the ordinances, to the people of God; a mourning because he cannot mourn; a sighing, because he has not a heart pliable. There is a work of the Spirit that helps him in his worst condition. Besides, there is a spirit of supplication in some measure. Though he cannot make set discourses to God, yet he can in a manner lay open his sorrow and grief to God. They be broken words, perhaps, but God can pluck sense out of them. Again, a Christian in the worst condition, God not only shines on him through the cloud, but there is a spirit in him that sighs to go through all thick clouds to God. It is promised. 'The Spirit will help our infirmities when we know not how to pray' (Rom. 8:26). Communion with God is never broken off where there is the Spirit of adoption. If they could embrace Christ, they would not leave him. If they could not embrace Christ, they would touch the hem of his garment. They will not yield to the stream altogether but strive against it. And though they be carried away with the strength of the stream, and see no goodness in themselves, yet they that be with them shall see a spirit striving to another condition than they are in. Something of Christ's, something of God's Spirit there will be in them. And take them at the worst, they will appear better than the natural man, that thinks himself a glorious man, though he has nothing but for show and fashion.

*A Heavenly Conference,* pp. 101-03

# Assurance of Salvation (2)

*Examine yourselves, to see whether you are in the faith. Test yourselves.*
*Or do you not realize this about yourselves, that Jesus Christ is in*
*you?—unless indeed you fail to meet the test!*—2 Cor. 13:5

(2) Likewise, we may know those who belong to God by our sympa-thy and antipathy—our sympathy with them that be good, and antipathy to that which is wicked. There is a love of that which is good. So good things are natural to a good man. There is a relish in good company and good things. As there is sweetness in the best things, so there is something in the children of God that is answerable to the God whom they serve. He is never so out of taste, but he finds his chief comfort in these things, and he is never himself so much as when he is conversant in these things, though in different measure: sometimes more, and sometimes less. On the other hand, there is an inward antipathy to God in a proud carnal man that has not his heart subdued by grace; there is a contrariness to the power of that grace which outwardly he professes, and a sympathy with the world and the spirit of the world. Take a good Christian at the worst, he is better than another at the best.

I beseech you, therefore, examine your dispositions; how you stand affected to things of a higher nature than the things of the world; to spiritual things, how you can relish spiritual things, God's ordinances, and anything that is holy. Surely if there be the life of God and Christ in you, there will be a kind of naturalness and suitableness of taste to the sweetness that is in holy things.

*A Heavenly Conference*, pp. 101-03

## Assurance of Salvation (3)

*For I am sure that neither death nor life, nor angels nor rulers, nor things present nor things to come, nor powers, nor height nor depth, nor anything else in all creation, will be able to separate us from the love of God in Christ Jesus our Lord.*—Rom. 8:38, 39

That we may maintain our assurance of salvation, see the grounds of it. It is not in our perfection, for then the poor disciples, where had they been? Alas! They had dealt unfaithfully with Christ. But the ground of assurance is on God's side, the certainty is on God's part, not ours. Though we make breaches every day God breaks not, as Malachi 3:6, 'Verily, I the Lord am not changeable; and therefore, you are not consumed.' We change, ebb and flow, are to and fro, up and down every day, varying in our dispositions. Though there be some root and seed of grace in us always, yet there is a change in our dispositions every day; but it holds on God's part. Christ names not any qualification in them to build comfort on but that God will yet maintain the relation of a Father to you. So that we maintain not our assurance on any part in us, but on God's love. 'Whom he loves, he loves to the end' (John 13:1). Our God unchangeably loves us, in whom there is not so much as a shadow of change. In the last of the Hebrews it is called an 'everlasting covenant.' 'The God of peace that brought again from the dead our Lord Jesus, the great Shepherd of the sheep, through the blood of the everlasting covenant' (Heb. 13:20). By the blood of Christ there is an everlasting covenant. God will be our God to death, and in death, and forever. For this relation being on God's part, extends itself from forgiveness of sins to life everlasting. It is always. The blood of Christ is the blood of an everlasting covenant. 'I will marry you to me forever' (Hos. 2:19). It holds sure on God's part.

*A Heavenly Conference*, pp. 155-56

# Assurance of Salvation (4)

*Therefore, brothers, be all the more diligent to confirm your calling and election, for if you practice these qualities you will never fall.—* 2 Pet. 1:10

As for the assurance of salvation, we must do our part too, though it begins with God. He loves us first and embraces us first; and we must love in return and embrace in return. Lord, you must begin. The covenant consists of two sides. Yet, desire God, by his grace, to enable us to do our side, for he does both. And desire him, according to his promise, to teach us to love him, and 'to write his law in our hearts' (Jer. 31:33). Lord, you have made a covenant with us; we cannot keep it without you. And this God will do. Let us labour to get into Christ, for it is in him that God is our Father. To grow up in Christ, to grow more and more in faith and in all grace. A gracious Christian is never lacking arguments of the assurance of salvation. It is the dead-hearted Christian, the careless Christian. Labour daily to choose God to be your God. If we say, we are God's, let us make choice of him at the same time. There is renunciation of all others. I have served other gods, the world, the flesh, and the favour of man, but they will be my god no more. If we be tempted to any sin, say; 'Why, I am not mine own, I am God's. I have chosen him to be my God; I have renounced all other; I have offered myself to him; therefore, what have I to do with sin, with this temptation? It is contrary to the state I am advanced to, and contrary to my relation. God is my Father and my God, and therefore I must be his; and what have I to do with sin?' Further, what has pride to do with a heart given to God? What has lust and filthiness? What has injustice, or anything else that is sinful to do in a heart that has dedicated and consecrated itself to God. Therefore, let us make use of these and like things to do our part in the assurance of salvation.

*A Heavenly Conference,* pp. 156-60

## Assurance of Salvation (5)

*In him you also, when you heard the word of truth, the gospel of your salvation, and believed in him, were sealed with the promised Holy Spirit, who is the guarantee of our inheritance until we acquire possession of it, to the praise of his glory.*—Eph. 1:13, 14

The assurance of salvation is wrought by the sealing of the Spirit and the sanctifying of us. Take heed we grieve not the Spirit of God. God's Spirit moves our hearts oftentimes in hearing the word, or reading, or praying; and therefore do not grieve the Spirit of God, whose office is 'to seal us to the day of redemption,' to assure us God is our God and our Father in Christ. Grieve him not, lest he grieve us, by racking and tormenting our consciences. Take heed of crossing the Spirit, especially by any sin against conscience. Conscience is God's deputy. Grieve not the Spirit and grieve not conscience. The conscience is a little god within us. And therefore, if we will not alienate God from us, to whom we have given ourselves if we be true believers, do nothing against the Spirit that sanctifies and seals us to the day of redemption. Beloved, favour cannot be maintained with great persons without much industry, respect, and observance of distance. Shall we think then to preserve respect with God without much industry and holiness? It cannot be. 'And therefore, give all diligence,' not a little, 'to make your calling and election sure' (2 Pet. 1:10). It requires all diligence, but it is worth your pains. Why do not Christians enjoy the comforts of this, that God is their God in Christ, more than they do? The reason is, they be negligent to maintain communion between God and them. A loose Christian can never enjoy the comforts of God. He is so great, and we so fallen, we ought to reverence him, we ought to 'love him with fear, and rejoice with trembling' (Psa. 2:11). Humble thyself to walk with your God. Where there is a great deal of humility, it maintains friendship. We must acknowledge ourselves to be 'dust and ashes,' know him in his greatness, and ourselves in our fallenness. Surely, he that delights himself in the prosperity of his servants will delight to make himself more and more known to us, that we may be assured of our salvation.

*A Heavenly Conference*, pp. 160-63

# In Trouble? Pray!

*The name of the Lord is a strong tower; the righteous man runs into it and is safe.*—Prov. 18:10

Prayer is a product or branch of faith. God gives faith to make use of prayer. God will not give this great privilege without hearts to make use of it. As soon as Paul was a believer, presently after his conversion, 'behold he is praying' (Acts 9:11). The child cries as soon as born, and the child of God is known by his praying; as soon as he is converted, an intercourse is opened between God and the soul, which a Christian soul will never neglect. If they are placed in the worst condition, they will pray to God, or at least sigh and groan, which is a prayer that God can make sense of.

Those that have any strong places of defence, in trouble they will be sure to fly there; in times of war they will betake them to their castle and place of munition. And so, they that be God's, in time of danger run presently to God; he is their rock, their refuge, and place of defence. They run to him by faith and prayer. A man may know what his god is by who he runs to in times of extremity. The carnal man runs to his friends or to his purse to bring him through. He will go to that which his instinct will specially lead him to in times of trouble. Every creature has received an instinct from God to go to the place of refuge wherein it is safe. The rabbits, poor weak creatures, hide themselves most strongly, out of instinct they have of their own weakness. Likewise, God's child, being knowledgeable of his weakness, and need of support and strength, has the strongest support that may be, and runs to his God. Worldly men have many schemes, as the wily fox has; but a Christian has but one, but that is a great one: he goes to his God in time of need. In times of extremity, no man but a Christian can pray with any comfort, with any sweet familiarity, 'Abba, Father.'

*A Heavenly Conference*, pp. 130-32

# How We Can Know That God Has Chosen Us

*We love because he first loved us.*—1 John 4:19

We can know that God has chosen us and called us effectually if we have grace to choose him for our God. When he bids us believe he gives an influence of power to be able to say, 'I believe; Lord, help my unbelief' (Mark 9:24). We may know he loves us, when we reflect love back, and love him. We may know he delights in us when we delight in him and his servants. Where is the strength of this argument? From this. All good things, whatsoever we do, are from God. God shines on us first and God owns us for his first. God being the spring of all goodness, he must begin. 'We love him because he loved us first' (1 John 4:19), else we could never love him. Therefore, if we love him and truth, he loves us. Surely, he owns us, because in order of causes we can have nothing but from him first. God sometimes will let us see things in the effect and hide them in the cause. Perhaps he will not persuade by his Spirit that he loves us, has chosen us, and that we are his; but he will work something in our hearts, some good thing, some love. Surely then God is theirs. Though there be not an open voice, yet they may know God has loved this soul and spoken peace to that soul, because we can return nothing to God, but he must shine on us first. Let us not deceive ourselves, but if we find some beginnings of grace, and can say without arrogancy or usurpation, 'Doubtless you are our Father, our God' (Isa. 63:16); we are not worthy to be yours, but we are yours; if we find something that castaways cannot have, some grief over a heart for sin, some faith, some little measure of love, and some love of truth, then we may come boldly to increase our familiarity and communion with God.

*A Heavenly Conference*, pp. 139-42

## Invitation to Salvation

*But to all who did receive him, who believed in his name, he gave the right to become children of God.*—John 1:12

Let me speak a word to the many who yet have their choice to make, who have other lords and other gods to rule over them. Let them consider what a fearful state it is not to be able to say; 'God is my God and my Father.' They can say they be God's creatures; but what a fearful condition is it not to be able to say, God is my Father. Will not these know that to the one whom he is not a God to in favour, he will be a God to in vengeance? He must be a friend or enemy. There is no third position. If you do not belong to God, you belong to the devil. Yet God is daily pulling men out of the kingdom of the devil, by opening their eyes to see their miserable condition. If you cannot say, God is your God, then the devil is your god; and what a fearful condition is it to be under the god of this world! And perhaps you may die so. If God be not our God, he is our enemy; and then creatures, angels, devils are against us, conscience is against us, and the word is against us. If he be for us, who is against us? If he be against us, who is for us? A terrible condition, and therefore get out of it, I beseech you.

You may say, 'How can I? Is there mercy for such a wretch?' Yea, he offers himself to be your God if you will come in. What is the purpose of our ministry and the word of grace, but to preach life to all repentant sinners? He entreats you to come in. You be rebels, not only against him, but enemies to your own souls if you do not. He thought of you when you could not think of yourselves. How many encouragements have you to come in! Take God's gracious offer. He gives you time. Make your peace. It is nothing but wilful rebellion to stand out against God.

*A Heavenly Conference*, pp. 163-66

# The Sun of Righteousness Heals (1)

*For you who fear my name, the Sun of Righteousness will rise with heal-ing in his wings.*—Mal. 4:2a

*Because of the tender mercy of our God, whereby the sunrise shall visit us from on high.*—Luke 1:78

If Christ is the Sun of Righteousness, we should, when we are spirit-ually cold and numb, retreat to him, and know that he has exactly what we need. Are we dark? He is light. Are we sick? He can heal us. Are we dying? He is life. Are we in discomfort? He is the fullness of love. He is the Sun, we should seek him, and make him our all in all. Make him our Prophet, to direct us by his light; our Priest, to make atonement for us; our King, to help us overcome all our corruptions, and to make us more than conquerors. Malachi tells us, 'the Sun of Righteousness will rise with healing in his wings.' We understand the word *wings* as beams of the sun, for beams spread from the body of light, as wings from the body; and Christ, though but one, can spread all his graces to all parts of the world. Also, wings have the power to keep warm, and comfort the young ones; and God is said to gather his children as a hen gathers her chickens (Matt. 23:37). Further, in the beams there is a healing nature. The Sun of Righteousness will be a healing Sun.

For by nature we are all sick and wounded. Some see and feel their diseases and pain, others do not; but those that do not are the most dangerously afflicted. We are all sick with a general spreading leprosy of sin; but we also have, every one of us, our particular diseases. Some swell with pride; others who are covetous have an ever-supposed hunger, always crying for more. Some burn with anger, as men do in a hot fever. We are all sick and have a need of the healing that is found and accom-plished only in Christ.

In a wonderful manner, Christ calls to us, 'Come to me, all you that are weary' (Matt. 11:28). Doctors usually heal by applying natural drugs and medicines; but Christ heals with the ointment of his own blood. By his wounds and stripes are we healed (Isa. 53:5).

*Sun of Righteousness, Works,* vol. 7, p. 171

# The Sun of Righteousness Heals (2)

*Behold, I will bring to it health and healing, and I will heal them and reveal to them abundance of prosperity and security.*—Jer. 33:6

By his Spirit he heals and enlightens our understanding, which by nature is dark, and so easily led astray to mistake light for darkness, and darkness for light. This he heals by his word, creating in us sound affections and judgments, by which we value things as they truly are.

He heals our wounds of conscience that Satan makes by his darts and sharp temptations, by which he makes us think that we are still reprobates, and that God is angry with us. Against these Christ strengthens our faith and trust in God.

The soul that hungers after comfort will find it; for Christ is a universal healer, healing both the bodies and souls of men, and healing them from all evil, from both blindness and deafness of the heart; the very dead heart he can restore to life. This should teach us to take notice of our diseases in time, and to go to the healing God, as he terms himself (Exod. 15:26), and lay open ourselves to him, and confess, as David did, 'Heal me, Lord, for I have sinned against you' (Psa. 41:4). What comfort there is for a poor miserable wretch, but to be well grounded in the knowledge of his Physician, and to be assured of his healing power, he who has cured innumerable souls.

We should also take heed of ignorance; for many, when temptations come, have not the least knowledge of any healing power in Christ, and so they go on until death, and they die like blocks. We should meditate on his commandments and promises; on his goodness and nature; on his encouragement to come to him, 'Come to me, all you who are weary' (Matt. 11:28). Christ has a medicine of his own that is able to cure any disease no matter how desperate, any person no matter how sick; Mary Magdalene as well as Paul; Zacchaeus as well as Manasseh; all come from him having been made whole. When Satan would tempt us to despair, we should call to mind that we have a merciful God that 'forgives all our sins and heals all our infirmities' (Psa. 103:3).

*Sun of Righteousness, Works*, vol. 7, pp. 171-73

# Questions About the Spiritual Life in Christ (1)

*For you who fear my name, the Sun of Righteousness will rise with heal-
ing in his wings.*—Mal. 4:2a

*Who forgives all your iniquity, who heals all your diseases.*—Psa. 103:3

Why are we not healed all at once and completely? What does
it mean that we are still subject to these infirmities of ours? Some of
Christ's works of healing are perfectly done all at once, but some are
done by degrees, little by little. Christ heals the soul of guiltiness all
at once, but there remains the corruption and the dregs of this disease
for heavenly purposes. He heals by not healing and leaves infirmities to
cure enormities. He allows us to be humbled by our infirmities, lest we
should be exalted above measure, as he dealt with Paul (2 Cor. 12:7).
Peter benefited more spiritually when he fell (Mark 14:72), than when
he presumed (Mark 14:29). We should retort Satan's accusations when he
tempts us to despair because of our sins, by reasoning this way: because
we have infirmities, therefore we will pray the more earnestly, 'forgive us
our trespasses' (Matt. 6:12); because we are sick, we will go to Christ that
took our nature not to cure everyone but to help the weak. Christ does
not immediately and perfectly cure our weaknesses, because he will have
us live by faith, every day going to the throne of grace, and depending
on his promise for the forgiveness of our sins, assuring ourselves that
the Spirit in us. Like David's house, we will grow stronger and stronger,
while the house of Saul is weaker and weaker (2 Sam. 3:1). Be assured, if
the flesh begins once to fall, it will surely fall.

*Sun of Righteousness, Works*, vol. 7, p. 173

# Questions About the Spiritual Life in Christ (2)

*You will go free, leaping with joy like calves let out to pasture.*—Mal. 4:2b

*The righteous flourish like the palm tree and grow like a cedar in Lebanon.*—Psa. 92:12

Does a Christian perpetually grow? Not at all times, in all parts. Trees we know, in wintertime, grow in the root. Christians do not grow always in all graces, but only in some one radical grace, as in faith or humility. If there is any stop, it is to further his speediness afterwards, as we see in those that stumble in their course, and as water stopped, breaks out more outrageously. This is how it was in the failings of David and Peter. God's children, after times of falling, are as a broken bone after it is set. The bone grows stronger in that part than in any other.

Why, at times, can I not perceive any spiritual growth in me? We perceive not when the corn grows, nor when the shadows move, yet in the passing of time we see that the corn has grown, and the shadow has moved. So, though we perceive it not, yet every act of repentance and faith strengthens us. There may be many cloudy times in every Christian's life. David, a man after God's own heart, had many infirmities. These times may cloud a man's eyes, so that he may think he is going backward. But these times should not hinder our faith in God's love; for God does not call every slip in a man's life to reckoning. Any traveller may set his foot awry and may go out of his way, yet at length he gets home; and God judges us not by single acts, but by the tenor and direction of our lives.

*Sun of Righteousness, Works,* vol. 7, pp. 175-76

# Kingdom Violence (1)

*From the days of John the Baptist until now the kingdom of heaven has suffered violence, and the violent take it by force.*—Matt. 11:12

Those that intend to enter the kingdom must strive to enter; and when they are in, they must keep it with violence. This violence is necessary for all who desire to enter the kingdom of heaven, for these reasons:

(1) Between us and our blessed state in heaven there is much opposition; and there must be violence. The state of the church here, the state of grace and the enjoyment of the means of grace, are all in a state of opposition. Good people and good things are opposed in this world. The means and graces of salvation are opposed in every way, within us and without us. Where there is opposition we must break through the opposition with violence.

(2) The graces of salvation are opposed from within us and that is the worst opposition. For Satan holds communication within us, in our own traitorous flesh. In all the stages of salvation there is violence. In effectual calling, when we are called out of the kingdom of Satan, he is not willing to let us go; he seeks to keep us. When we come to have our sins forgiven in justification, there is opposition; our proud flesh will not yield to the righteousness of the gospel; it will not rest in Christ; it will seek what it needs from in itself. In sanctification there is opposition between the flesh and the Spirit. In every good work we know there are many carnal reasonings that arise from our flesh. If a man wants to give to another, the flesh suggests, 'I may want that someday for myself.' If he is led to reform abuses in others, he is quick to think, 'Others will have something to say against me and I will just be offensive to those I desire to help.' The affection of earthly things chains us to the things below, and self-love prompts a man to remain unaltered. A man cannot come to the state of grace without breaking through these things. We must offer violence to ourselves, to our own fleshly reasoning, to our own wills and to our affections.

*Victorious Violence, Works,* vol. 6, pp. 300-01

# Kingdom Violence (2)

*But though we had already suffered and been shamefully treated at Philippi, as you know, we had boldness in our God to declare to you the gospel of God in the midst of much conflict.*—1 Thess. 2:2

(3) There is opposition from the world. On one side there are the snares and delights of the world, to quench the delight in the good things of the Spirit. On the other side are fears, terrors, and scandals, to scare us from doing what we know we ought to do.

(4) There is opposition from Satan in every good action. He besets us in prayer and in our duties with distracted thoughts, for he knows these tend to the ruin of him and of his kingdom. There is no good action that isn't opposed from both within us and without us. The means of salvation and our attention to them are not without slander and disgrace in the world.

(5) God will have this violence and striving as a character of difference, to show who are false professors and who are true. True followers of Jesus must endure the cost and charges and sometimes even to sacrifice life itself; yielding whatever is dear and precious in the world. A man must be so violent that he is willing to go through all, even death itself, though it be a bloody death, for Christ. This reveals all lukewarm, carnal professors, who avoid this violence. God requires this violence even in the most peaceful times. In times of peace the truth and religion are tolerated by the laws of the land, yet the influence of truth is much opposed by many. Those in Christ will bear the scorn that is cast upon the gospel, they will 'go with Christ outside the gate, bearing his reproach' (Heb. 13:13). It is an easy thing to have as much of Christianity as will be acceptable to our feelings or our pleasure; but to have as much as will bring glory to heaven, is always hard for the church.

(6) God will have us grow in grace with violence that we may set a higher price on the things of grace. When we have things that are gotten by violence and difficulty, oh how much more we value them!

*Victorious Violence, Works, vol. 6, pp. 301-02*

# Kingdom Violence (3)

*Strive to enter through the narrow door. For many, I tell you, will seek to enter and will not be able.*—Luke 13:24

(7) The excellency of something demands violence. It is appropriate that excellent things should have answerable affections. It is the kingdom of heaven, what affection is answerable but a violent, strong affection?

(8) Together with the excellency is the necessity of it; for the kingdom of heaven is a place of refuge as well as a kingdom to enrich us. There were cities of refuge among the Jews. When a man was followed by the avenger of blood, he would run as fast as he could to the city of refuge, and there he was safe. So when a guilty conscience pursues us or when God's judgments awaken us and hell is open; when a man apprehends his state and is convinced who he is and what he deserves, of necessity he will fly to the city of refuge; and where is that but in the grace found in the church? Happy is he that gets in at the gate of this kingdom. But there must be a striving 'to enter in at the gate' (Luke 13:24). In this respect the kingdom of heaven suffers violence. It is compared to some great, rich city, that has some great treasure and riches in it; and the city must be besieged for a long time, and those that are able to enter it are there forever. It is like the gate of a large city where there is striving and thronging, and where there are also enemies, and if men do not strive against the throng they are cut, mangled, and killed. So, it is in the state of God's kingdom. When a man's eyes are opened, he sees the devil and hell behind him, and either he must enter or be damned. He is strongly moved to offer violence on both sides. If he looks behind him there is the kingdom of Satan, darkness, misery, and damnation. Before him there is the kingdom of happiness and glory. The fear of what follows him and the hope of what is set before him, makes him strive to enter the gate of that city.

*Victorious Violence, Works*, vol. 6, pp. 301-02

# Kingdom Violence (4)

*So flee youthful passions and pursue righteousness, faith, love, and peace,
along with those who call on the Lord from a pure heart.*—2 Tim.
2:22

Compare your efforts toward the good things of heaven with
your efforts toward the things of the world. If there is a hope of being
preferred, the doors of great men are sure to suffer violence from those
seeking to get ahead. The courts of justice suffer violence from those
demanding their rights in earthly things. If a man could but observe the
courses of men in the city, he would see one violent for his pleasures,
running to the house of the harlot 'as a fool to the stocks' (Prov 7:22);
another to the exchange, to increase his estate; another to the place of
justice, to undermine his neighbour or to get his own right. These places
suffer violence. But what violence does the poor gospel endure? Alas! it
is slighted; and men will regard it when they can spare the time. It is not
regarded according to its worth and value. If ever we look to receive good
from the gospel, our dispositions must be violent, in some proportion
answerable to the excellency of it.

We may justly turn the complaint on ourselves, that while we spend
our strength in violence about the fallen and ordinary things of this life,
the kingdom of heaven offers violence to us, and yet we will have none
of it. How God beseeches us in the ministry! 'We beseech you to be
reconciled' (2 Cor. 5:20); and 'Why will ye die, O house of Israel?' (Ezek.
18:31). God comes and offers these appeals to us, and yet we refuse them.
We are so far from offering violence to the gospel and to grace, that God
offers violence to us, as if we should do him a favour to receive the gospel
and do good to our own souls; and yet the vile and proud hearts of men
will not regard and receive these heavenly things. How it will justify
God's sentence on the day of judgment, when he will declare that there
was a presenting of such things to you, and instead of violence in seeking
them, you slighted and neglected them.

*Victorious Violence, Works,* vol. 6, pp. 302-03

# Kingdom Violence (5)

*For if we are beside ourselves, it is for God; if we are in our right mind,*
*it is for you.*—2 Cor. 5:13

There is a blessed violence that will stand under judgment. A man must not be violent and wise in the things of this world; much less after filthy pleasures. Instead, a man 'must become a fool' (1 Cor. 3:19) in these things. But in respect of heavenly things, a man may be violent and wise; for there is such a degree of excellency in the things that no violence can be too much. Men talk of being too strict and too holy. Can there be too much of that which we can never have enough of in this world? I speak of this to confound the evil judgment the world has of a holy disposition. They are thought to be fanatics, to be out of their minds, as they thought Paul was; but he answers, 'If we are out of our wits, it is to God' (2 Cor. 5:13). Christ himself had hands laid on him, as if he had been out of his mind (John 10:20). As Festus told blessed Paul, 'that much learning had made him mad' (Acts 26:24), when he saw him eager in the cause of Christ. So many, when they see a man earnest in the matters of God, think surely these men have lost their discretion. No; it is the highest discretion in the world to be eager and violent for things that are invaluable. It is the violent that have eyes in their heads, violence guided with judgment, from knowing the excellency of the good things of the gospel.

Let us not be frightened by the ill reports of those with idle brains and rotten hearts, those who know not the things that belong to the kingdom of heaven. Is there anything that a man should be earnest for if not for the things of God? Were our souls created to pursue the things that are earthly and fallen? Were our minds made only to plod in the temporal, and to neglect our heavenly calling? If anything is to challenge the best of our endeavours, the marrow of our labours, the utmost of our spirits and minds, certainly it is grace and glory.

*Victorious Violence, Works*, vol. 6, pp. 303-04

# Kingdom Violence (6)

*Because you are lukewarm, and neither hot nor cold, I will spit you out*
*of my mouth*—Rev. 3:16

We see then the disposition of true disciples, they are violent in respect of heavenly things. Those that are not earnest in the cause of religion, when the state of things requires it, they have no religion in them, they are not in the state of grace. We must be earnest against our own sins. Violence must begin there, to subdue all to the Spirit of Christ, to allow nothing else to rule in our hearts. There is also violence to maintain the cause of Christ. 'To contend earnestly for the faith once delivered to the saints' (Jude 3), and if it be opposed to vindicate it. Christ cannot abide those who are lukewarm. His stomach cannot bear them. 'I will spit you out. I would you were hot or cold' (Rev. 3:15, 16). It would be better for a man to be nothing in religion than to be lukewarm. If a man will have any good from religion, he must be in earnest in it: 'If Baal be God, stand for him, if you would have good by him: if the Lord be God, stand for him' (1 Kings 18:21). There is no good received by religion if we be not earnest for it. Religion is not a matter to play with.

Religion does not take away the earnestness of the affections. Instead, it directs them to better things. It takes not away anything in us but turns the stream another way. Violence requires the height and strength of the affections. If a stream violently runs one way, if it be, by skill and cunning, turned to another way, it will run as fast that way as it did before. So it is with the heart of man. Religion takes nothing away that is good but lifts it up; it elevates and advances it to better objects. There are honours, and pleasures when a man is in Christ, but they are of a higher kind. They draw greater affections than all other things. But these affections are purified, they run in a better, in a clearer channel. He that was violent before is as violent still, only the stream is turned.

*Victorious Violence, Works*, vol. 6, pp. 304-05

# Kingdom Violence (7)

*Hope does not put us to shame, because God's love has been poured into our hearts through the Holy Spirit who has been given to us.*—Rom. 5:5

Consider Paul for an instance. He was as earnest when he was a Christian as before he was a Christian. He was never more eager after shedding of the blood of Christians and breathing out slaughter against them, as he was afterwards in breathing after the salvation of God's people and a desire to enlarge the gospel. Zacchaeus was never so covetous of the world before, as he was desirous of heaven when he became a Christian. I say religion takes nothing away, it only turns the stream. But it is a miracle for the stream to be turned. It was God that turned the Jordan River (Josh. 3:16). It is a greater work than man can do to turn the streams of a man's affections, to make them run upward. It is only God's work. This is the excellency of religion. It ennobles our nature. That which was natural is made heavenly and spiritual.

It would be of little comfort to hear of the excellency and necessity of these heavenly things if there were no hope of them. Hope stirs up diligence and endeavour in the things of this world. What makes men adventure to the east or west? They hope for a voyage that will enrich them for their whole life. Hope in doubtful things stirs up industry. What makes the poor farmer diligent to plough and sow? The hope that he will have a harvest, but a harvest is not always the certain outcome. But spiritual things are certain. Hope in spiritual things stirs up endeavour. We need not call them into question. As it stirs up diligence, so it stirs up the use of the means; to not give up until we see our hopes fulfilled. It also stirs up the hope of success, that we will not lose our labour, it enables and strengthens us to bear the tediousness of the time and the encumbrance of afflictions.

*Victorious Violence, Works,* vol. 6, pp. 305-07

# Affections Rightly Placed

*Do not love the world or the things in the world. If anyone loves the world, the love of the Father is not in him. For all that is in the world—the desires of the flesh and the desires of the eyes and pride in possessions—is not from the Father but is from the world. And the world is passing away along with its desires, but whoever does the will of God abides forever.*—1 John 2:15-17

A great light being near a little one, draws away and obscures the flame of the other. So it is when the affections are taken up higher to their fit object; they die unto all earthly things, while that heavenly flame consumes and wastes all base affections and earthly desires. Among the ways of mortification, there are two that stand out:

(1) By embittering all earthly things to us, whereby the affections are deadened to them.

(2) By showing more noble, excellent, and fit objects, that the soul, issuing more largely and strongly to them, may be diverted, and so by degrees die to other things.

The Holy Spirit has chosen the later way, by elevating and raising our affections and love, to take it off other things, so that it might run in its right channel. It is a shame that a sweet stream should not rather run into a garden than into a mud puddle. Likewise, what a shame it is that man, having in him such excellent affections as love, joy, delight, should cleave to dirty, base things, that are worse than himself, so becoming debased like them! Therefore, the Spirit of God, out of mercy and pity to man, would raise up man's affections, by making comparison with earthly things, leading them to higher matters, that only deserve love, joy, delight, and admiration. Let God's stooping to us occasion our rising up to him.

*The Love of Christ* (*Bowels Opened*), pp. 2-3

# God's Wind on the Church (1)

*Awake, O north wind, and come, O south wind! Blow upon my garden, let its spices flow. Let my beloved come to his garden and eat its choicest fruits.*—Song of Sol. 4:16

(1) We see here that Christ sends forth his Spirit, with command to all means, under the name of 'north and south wind,' to farther the fruitfulness of his church. What winds are to the garden, that the Spirit of Christ, in the use of means, is to the church. In comparing how Christ commands the winds, we may observe that all creatures stand in obedience to Christ, as ready at a word, whenever he speaks to them. They are all, as it were, asleep until he wakes them. He calls the wind out of his treasures when he pleases.

(2) We see here that Christ speaks to winds contrary one to another, both in regard of the coasts from whence they blow, and in their quality. Both are necessary for the garden: where we see that the courses that Christ takes, and the means that he uses with his church, may seem contrary; but by a wise ordering, all agree in the wholesome issue. A prosperous and an afflicted condition are contrary: a mild and a sharp course may seem to cross one another; yet sweetly they agree in this, that as the church needs both, so Christ uses both for the church's good.

Hence it is that the manifold wisdom of Christ makes use of a variety of conditions, that the Spirit of Christ is mild in some men's ministries and sharp in others. Sometimes the people of God need purging, and sometimes refreshing. Whereupon the Spirit of God carries itself suitably to both conditions. The Spirit in the godly draws good out of every condition, sure as they are that all winds blow them good. If Christ can bind up or let loose all kind of winds at his pleasure, then if means be wanting or fruitless, it is he that says to the clouds, 'Drop not,' and to the winds, 'Blow not.' Therefore, we must acknowledge him in want or plenty of means. The Spirit of Christ in the use of means is a free agent, sometimes blowing strongly, sometimes more mildly, sometimes not at all. It is wisdom to yield to the gales of the Spirit.

*The Love of Christ (Bowels Opened)*, pp. 5-7

# God's Wind on the Church (2)

*The wind blows where it wishes, and you hear its sound, but you do not*
*know where it comes from or where it goes. So it is with everyone who*
*is born of the Spirit.*—John 3:8

In spiritual things there is a chain of causes and effects: prayer comes
from faith (Rom. 10:14); faith from the hearing of the word; hearing
from a preacher, by whom God by his Spirit blows upon the heart; and a
preacher from God's sending. If the God of nature should but hinder and
take away one link of this chain, the whole frame would be disturbed.
We need this blowing, otherwise our spirits will be becalmed and stand
at a standstill and Satan will have his bellows blowing up the seeds of
sinful lusts in us. For there are two spirits in the church, the one always
blowing against the other. The best had need to be stirred up; otherwise,
with Moses (Exod. 17:12), their hands will be ready to fall, and abate in
their affection. We need blowing:

(1) In regard of our natural inability.

(2) In regard of our dullness and heaviness, cleaving to nature
occasionally.

(3) In regard of the contrary winds from without. Satan has his
bellows filled with his spirit, that hinders the work of grace all he can;
so that we need not only Christ's blowing, but also his stopping other
contrary winds (Rev. 7:1).

(4) In regard to the state and condition of the new covenant, wherein
all beginning, growth, and ending, is from grace, and nothing but grace.

(5) Because old grace, without a fresh supply, will not hold against
new crosses and temptations.

Therefore, when Christ draws, let us run after him; when he blows,
let us open ourselves to him. It may be the last blast that we will ever
have from him. And let us set upon duties with this encouragement, that
Christ will blow upon us, not only to prevent us from falling, but also to
maintain his own graces in us. Where is the stirring up of ourselves, and
one another, upon these grounds?

*The Love of Christ* (*Bowels Opened*), pp. 9-10

# With Christ's Help Pursue Fruitfulness

*Whoever believes in me, as the Scripture has said, 'Out of his heart will flow rivers of living water.'*—John 7:38

If the church is a separated portion, then we should walk as people of a separated condition from the world. To ensure this we must be subject to his pruning and dressing. It is so far from being an ill sign that Christ follows us with afflictions, it is rather a sure sign of his love. Men care not for heath and wilderness, upon which they bestow no effort. So, when God prunes us by crosses and afflictions, and sows good seed in us, it is a sign he means to dwell with us, and delight in us.

Let us bless God that our lot has fallen into such a pleasant place, to be planted in the church, the place of God's delight. This should move us to be fruitful. For men will endure a fruitless tree in the waste wilderness, but not in their garden. It is strange to be fruitless and barren in this place that we live in, being watered with the dew of heaven. How fearfully a fruitless state is threatened by the Holy Spirit, that 'it is near unto cursing and burning' (Heb. 6:8). Visible churches, if they prosper not, God will remove the hedge, and lay them waste, preferring a garden elsewhere. Sometimes God's plants prosper better in Babylon than in Judea. We must learn from him how and where to please him. Obedience from a broken heart is the best sacrifice. Let us then strive and labour to be fruitful in our places and callings. The blessed man is said to be 'a tree planted by the waterside, that brings forth fruit in due season' (Psa. 1:3).

The church may seem to lie open to all incursions, but it has an invisible hedge about it, a wall without it, and a well within it. God himself is a wall of fire about it (Zech. 2:5), and his Spirit a well of living waters running through it to refresh and comfort it. This is a good plea for the church: 'The church is yours; fence it, water it, defend it, keep the wild boar out of it.'

*The Love of Christ (Bowels Opened)*, pp. 12-14

# With the Spirit's Help Pursue Multiplication (1)

*Awake, O north wind, and come, O south wind! Blow upon my garden,*
*let its spices flow.*—Song of Sol. 4:16

Good things lie in us dead and bound up, unless the Spirit brings them out. There are gracious good things in the church, but they want further spreading, from this we may observe:

(1) We need not only grace to put life into us at first, but likewise grace to draw forth that grace. Here is the difference between man's blowing and the Spirit's. Man, when he blows, if grace be not there before, spends all his labour upon a dead coal, which he cannot make take fire. But the Spirit first kindles a holy fire, and then increases the flame. Christ begins the work of grace on the church, and now further promotes his own work. The wind first blows, and then the spices of the church flow out. We are first sweet in ourselves, and then sweet to others.

(2) It is not enough to be good in ourselves, but our goodness must flow out; that is, grow more strong, useful to continue and stream forth for the good of others. We must labour to be, as was said of John the Baptist, burning and shining Christians (John 5:35). For Christ is not like a box of ointment shut up and not opened, but like that box of ointment that Mary poured out, which perfumes all the whole house with its sweetness (John 12:3). For the Spirit is like wind; it carries the sweet savour of grace to others. A Christian, so soon as he finds any rooting in God, is of a spreading disposition, and makes the places he lives in the better for him. The whole body is the better for every good member, as we see of Onesimus (Philem. 11). The very naming of a good man casts a sweet savour, as presenting some grace to the heart of the hearer. For then we have done what we were meant for, that others have occasion to bless God for us, for conveying comfort to them by us. The winds are called upon to awake and blow upon Christ's garden, 'that the spices thereof may flow out' (Song of Sol. 4:16).

*The Love of Christ (Bowels Opened)*, pp. 14-15

# With the Spirit's Help Pursue Multiplication (2)

*Now may the God of peace who brought again from the dead our Lord Jesus, the great shepherd of the sheep, by the blood of the eternal covenant, equip you with everything good that you may do his will, working in us that which is pleasing in his sight, through Jesus Christ, to whom be glory forever and ever. Amen.*—Heb. 13:20, 21

(3) That where once God begins, he goes on, and delights to add encouragement to encouragement, and does not only give them a stock of grace at the beginning, but also helps them to trade in grace. He is not only Alpha, but Omega, to them, the beginning, and the ending (Rev. 1:8). He does not only plant graces, but also waters and cherishes them. Where the Spirit of Christ is, it is an encouraging Spirit; for not only does he infuse grace, but also stirs it up, that we may be always prepared for every good work, otherwise we cannot do that which we are able to do. The Spirit must bring all into exercise, else the habits of grace will lie asleep. We need a present Spirit to do every good; not only the power to will, but the will itself; and not only the will, but the deed, is from the Spirit, which should stir us up to go to Christ, that he may stir up his own graces in us, that they may flow out.

Let us labour, then, in ourselves to be full of goodness, that we may be fit to do good to all. As God is good, and does good to all, so must we strive to be as like him as may be. For others' sakes, we must pray that God would make the winds to blow fully upon us, 'that our spices may flow out' (Song of Sol. 4:16) for their good. For a Christian in his right temper thinks that he has nothing good to purpose, but that which does good to others.

*The Love of Christ (Bowels Opened), pp. 15-16*

# God Loves Our Changed Lives (1)

*I appeal to you therefore, brothers, by the mercies of God, to present your*
*bodies as a living sacrifice, holy and acceptable to God, which is your*
*spiritual worship.*—Rom. 12:1

God accepts the graces of his children, and delights in them.

(1) Because they are the fruit that comes from his children, his spouse, his friend. Love of the person wins acceptance of that which is presented from the person. What comes from love is lovingly taken.

(2) They are the graces of his Spirit. If we have anything that is good, all comes from the Spirit, who is first in Christ and then in us. Christ sees his own face, beauty, glory, in his church; he looks in love upon her, and always with his looks conveys grace and comfort. Christ loves the reflection of his own graces in his children and accepts them.

(3) His kindness is such that he accepts all. Both we ourselves are sacrifices, and what we offer is a sacrifice acceptable to God, through him that offered himself as a sacrifice of sweet-smelling savour. God accepts of Christ first, and then of us, and what comes from us in him. We may boldly pray, 'Lord, remember all our offerings, and accept all our sacrifices' (Psa. 20:3). Paul does will us 'to offer up ourselves a holy and acceptable sacrifice to God' (Rom. 12:1), when we are once in Christ. In the Old Testament we have many manifestations of this acceptance. He accepted the sacrifice of Abel, as it is thought, by fire from heaven, and so the sacrifices of Elijah and Solomon by fire (1 Kings 18:38; 1 Chron. 21:26). So, in the New Testament he showed his acceptance of the disciples meeting together, by the sound of a mighty wind, and then filling them with the Holy Spirit (Acts 2:3). But now the declaration of the acceptance of our persons, graces, and sacrifices that we offer to him, is most in peace of conscience and joy in the Holy Spirit, and from a holy fire of love kindled by the Spirit, whereby our sacrifices are burned. In the incense of prayer, how many sweet spices are burned together by this fire of faith; as humility and patience in submitting to God's will, hope of a gracious answer, holiness, and love to others.

*The Love of Christ (Bowels Opened)*, pp. 42-43

# God Loves Our Changed Lives (2)

*For it is God who works in you, both to will and to work for his good pleasure.*—Phil. 2:13

If it is so that God accepts the performances and graces, especially the prayers of his children, let it be an argument to encourage us to be much in all holy duties. It would deaden the heart of any man to perform service where it should not be accepted. But when all that is good is accepted, and what is amiss is pardoned, when even a cup of cold water will not go unnoticed nor unrewarded (Matt. 10:42), what can we desire more? It is infidelity, which is dishonourable to God and uncomfortable to us, that makes us so barren and cold in duties.

Only let our care be to approve our hearts unto Christ. When our hearts are right, we cannot but think comfortably of Christ. Those that have offended some great persons are afraid when they hear from them, because they think they are in a state displeasing to them. So, a soul that is under the guilt of any sin is so far from thinking that God accepts of it, that it looks to hear nothing from him but some message of anger and displeasure. But one that preserves acquaintance and due respect to a great person, hears from him with comfort. So, as we would desire to hear nothing but good news from heaven, and acceptation of all that we do, let us be careful to preserve ourselves in a good state. Every child of God is beloved and accepted of him. This made his presence so desired in the gospel with those that had gracious hearts. They knew all was the better for Christ, even the company better, for he never left any house or table where he was, but there was an increase of comfort and grace. As it was in his personal presence, so it is in his spiritual presence. He never comes, but he increases grace and comfort. Let us be stirred up to have communion with Christ. Let us labour to be such as Christ may delight in and where he tastes sweetness, he will bring more with him.

*The Love of Christ (Bowels Opened)*, pp. 43-45

## Rejoicing in the Graces of Others

*Just so, I tell you, there is joy before the angels of God over one sinner who repents.*—Luke 15:10

What a happy condition when God's glory, the church's comfort and strength, and our own joy, meet. We ought to take notice of the works of God in creation and providence, when we see plants, stars, and such like, or else we dishonour God. What then should we do for his gifts and graces in his children, that are above these in dignity? Should we not take notice of what is graciously good, and praise God for it? That is what they did for Paul's conversion, 'they glorified God.' For when they saw that Paul, once a wolf had become not only a sheep, but a shepherd and leader of God's flock, 'they glorified God' (Gal. 1:24). So, the believing Jews, when the Gentiles were converted, they glorified God, that he had taken the Gentiles to also be his people (Acts 11:18). When Paul and others had planted the gospel, and God gave increase, the godly Jews rejoiced at that good. So, we that are Gentiles, should rejoice to hear of the conversion of the Jews, and pray for it; for then there will be a general joy. Want of joy shows want of grace. There is not a surer character of a devilish disposition, than to look on the graces of God's children with a malignant eye. Those that speak evil of the graces of God in others, and cloud them with disgraces, that they may not shine, and will not have the sweet ointment of their good names to spread, but cast dead flies upon it, show that they are of his disposition who is the accuser of the brethren. All that have grace in them, are of Christ's and of the angels' disposition. They joy at the conversion and growth of any Christian. They are called friends and beloved; and none but friends and beloved can love as Christ loves, and delight as Christ delights.

*The Love of Christ (Bowels Opened)*, pp. 47-48

# Spiritual Sleepiness

*So then let us not sleep as others do but let us be alert and sober.—*
1 Thess. 5:6

Signs of a spiritually sleepy state:

(1) We know that sleep is creeping upon us, by comparing our present condition with our former, when we were in a more wakeful frame and the graces of God's Spirit were in exercise in us.

(2) Compare us again with that state and frame that a Christian should be in; for sometimes a Christian goes under an uncomfortable condition all the days of his life, so that he is not fit to make himself his pattern. The true rule of a waking and living Christian is the description that is in the word. As, for instance, a Christian should walk 'in the comfort of the Holy Spirit' (Acts 9:31), live and walk by faith and depend upon God. Our hope, if it be waking, will purge us, and make us suitable to the condition we hope for in heaven, and the company we hope to have fellowship with there.

(3) Look to the examples of others who are more gracious. They enjoy no more means than I; and yet they abound in assurance and are comfortable in all conditions. A man may discern he is asleep, by comparing himself with others who are better than himself.

(4) It is evident that we are growing on to a sleepy condition when we find a backwardness to spiritual duties, as to prayer, thanksgiving, and spiritual gatherings. It should be the joy of a Christian to come into the presence of Christ. When what is spiritual in a duty does not sit well with us, it is a sign our souls are in a sleepy temper.

(5) When the soul begins to admire outward excellencies; when it awakes much to profits, pleasures, and honours; when men admire great men, rich men, great places. The strength and fat of the soul are consumed by feeding on these things so that when it comes to spiritual things it is faint and drowsy. By these signs, let us labour to search the state of our souls.

*The Love of Christ (Bowels Opened)*, pp. 72-73 [71-73]

# Avoiding Spiritual Sleepiness (1)

*But stay awake at all times, praying that you may have strength to escape all these things that are going to take place, and to stand before the Son of Man.*—Luke 21:36

Motives against sleepiness:

(1) Consider the danger of a sleepy state. The devil labours all he can to cast men into this temper, which he must do before he can make him fall into any gross sin. The devil has a faculty this way, to make outward things look great that are worth nothing, and to make sins seem little that if we were awake, would frighten us. He works strongest upon the imagination when the soul is sleepy or a little drowsy. There is no man that comes to gross sin suddenly. But he falls little by little; first to slumber, from slumber to sleep, and from sleep to false security. Sleepiness is the inlet to all sins, and the beginning of all danger. The Lord takes a contrary course with his own. When he would preserve a state or person, he plants in them first a spirit of faith, to believe that there is such a danger, or such a good to be apprehended; and second, if it be a matter of threatening, he stirs up fear, which wakes up care and diligence.

(2) A man in his sleep is fit to lose all. A sleepy hand lets anything go with ease. A man who has grace and comfort lets it go in his spiritual sleepiness. Through their carelessness they allow themselves to be robbed of first beginnings, by yielding to delights, company, and contentment. The better a man is, the more unquietly will he sleep in such a state. He will feel startlings and frights in the midst of his carnal delights if he belongs to God.

(3) God meets them with some crosses in this world, that they will gain nothing from sleepiness. There is none of God's children that ever gained by yielding to any corruption, or drowsiness, though God saved their souls. It is always true, a sleepy state is a sure forerunner of some great cross, or some great sin. It must be distasteful to God when we go drowsily and heavily about his work. 'Cursed is he that does the work of the Lord with slackness' (Jer. 48:10).

*The Love of Christ (Bowels Opened)*, pp. 73-75 [73-74]

# Avoiding Spiritual Sleepiness (2)

Therefore stay awake—for you do not know when the master of the house will come, in the evening, or at midnight, or when the rooster crows, or in the morning—lest he come suddenly and find you asleep.—Mark 13:35, 36

(4) Sleepiness is an odious temper to God. For, does he not deserve cheerful service at our hands? Does not his greatness require that our senses be all waking? Does not his mercy deserve, that our love should take all care, to serve him who is so gracious and good to us? Is it not the fruit of our redemption to serve him without fear, in holiness and righteousness all the days of our lives (Luke 1:14, 15)?

(5) Sleepiness is a state not only odious to God, but irksome to our own spirits. The conscience is never fully at peace in a drowsy state or in drowsy performances. Likewise, it is not graceful to others. It breeds in others a dislike for good things. Let carnal men see a Christian not carry himself in a wakeful way, as he should, though they be a thousand times worse themselves, yet they think it should not be so. Let a man consider why God has given the powers of the soul and the graces of the Spirit. Are they not given for exercise, and to be employed about their proper objects? A Christian is not a Christian, when he is not waking. Why has God given us understanding, but to conceive the best things? Why have we judgment, but to judge aright between the things of heaven and earth? Why do we have love planted in us, but to set it on lovely objects? Why faith, but to trust God over all? Why hatred, but to fly from ill? Why do we have affections, but for spiritual things? Why are all graces planted in the soul, as faith and love, and hope and patience, but to be in exercise, and waking? A Christian, in his right temper, should be in the act and exercise of what is good in him, upon all occasions. What a world of good might Christians do if they were in a right temper! What a great deal of ill might they escape and avoid if they would rouse up their souls to be as Christians should be!

*The Love of Christ (Bowels Opened)*, pp. 75-76

# The Heart

*Keep your heart with all vigilance, for from it flow the springs of life.—*
Prov. 4:23

The word *heart* includes the whole soul, for the understanding is the heart, 'an understanding heart' (Job 38:36). To 'lay things up in our hearts' (Luke 2:51) is memory; and to cleave in heart is to cleave in the will (Acts 11:23). To 'rejoice in heart' (Isa. 30:29) is the affection. So that all the powers of the soul, the inward man, as Paul calls it (2 Cor. 4:16), is the heart. In all the powers of the soul there is something good and something ill, something flesh, and something spirit.

A Christian may know how it is with himself. Though he be a mix of flesh and spirit, he has a distinguishing knowledge and judgment whereby he knows both the good and evil in himself. A man who has the Spirit knows both; he knows himself and his own heart. The Spirit has a light of its own, even as reason has. How does reason know what it does? By reflection, which is inbred in the soul. Will a man who is natural consider his state, and know what he knows, what he thinks, what he does, and may not the soul that is raised to a higher state know as much? Undoubtedly it may. Besides, we have the Spirit of God, which is light, and self-evidencing. The work of the Spirit may sometimes be hindered, as in times of temptation. But a Christian, when he is not in such a temptation, he knows his own state, and can distinguish between the principles in him of the flesh and spirit, grace and nature. As the church is determined to confess that which is amiss, so she must be as true in confessing that which is good in her. We must not bear false witness, against others, much less against ourselves. Many help Satan, the accuser, and plead his case against the Spirit, their comforter, in refusing to see what God sees in them. We must make note of this, to know the good as well as the evil, though it be so little.

*The Love of Christ (Bowels Opened)*, pp. 77-79 [77-78]

# The Conscience

*The aim of our charge is love that issues from a pure heart and a good conscience and a sincere faith.*—1 Tim. 1:5

The heart is often taken for the conscience in Scripture. A good conscience, called a merry heart, is 'a continual feast' (Prov. 15:15). Now, the conscience of God's children is never so sleepy, but it awakens in some measure. Though perhaps it may be deadened in a particular act, yet there is so much life in it that there will be an opening of it, and a yielding at length to the strength of spiritual reason. His conscience is not seared. David was but a little roused by Nathan, yet you see how he presently confessed openly that he had sinned (2 Sam. 12:13). When David had numbered the people, his conscience presently smote him (2 Sam. 24:10); and when he resolved to kill Nabal and all his family, which was a wicked and carnal passion, in which there was nothing but flesh; yet when he was stopped by the advice and discreet counsel of Abigail, we see how presently he yielded (1 Sam. 25:32). There is a kind of perpetual tenderness of conscience in God's people.

Answerable to these inward powers of conscience is the outward obedience of God's children. In their sleepy state they go on in a course of obedience. Though deadly and coldly, and not with the glory that may give others good example or yield themselves comfort, yet there is a pattern of good duties. His usual way is good, however he may misstep. In Christ he is awake, this is his state as a Christian; but his sleepiness may result in missteps out of which he recovers himself.

*The Love of Christ (Bowels Opened)*, pp. 80-81 [79-80]

# God's Love Never Fails and the Eternal Security of the Saints

*I give them eternal life, and they will never perish, and no one will snatch them out of my hand.*—John 10:28

Let us magnify the goodness of God that God's children never totally fall from grace. Though they sleep, yet their heart is awake. The prophet Isaiah, speaking of the church and children of God said 'It will be as a tree, as an oak whose substance is in them, when they cast their leaves,' (Isa. 6:13). Though you see neither fruit nor leaves, yet there is life in the root. Peter, when he denied his Master, was like an oak that was weather-beaten; yet there was life still in the root (1 Pet. 1:3; Matt. 26:31, 32). For undoubtedly Peter loved Christ from his heart. Sometimes a Christian may be in such a poor state, as the spiritual life runs all to the heart, and the outward man is left destitute; as in wars, when the enemy has conquered the field, the people run into the city, and if they be beaten out of the city, they run into the castle. The grace of God sometimes fails in the outward action, in the field, when yet it retires to the heart, in which fort it is impregnable. When the outward man sleeps, and there are weak, dull performances, and perhaps actions amiss, too, yet the heart is awake. It is said in the Scripture of Eutychus 'his life is in him still,' though he seemed to be dead (Acts 20:10). As Christ said of Lazarus in John 11:4, so a man may say of a Christian in his worst state, 'he is not dead, but sleeps.'

This is a sound doctrine and comfortable, agreeable to Scripture and the experience of God's people. We must not lose it but make use of it against the time of temptation. There are some pulses that reveal life in the sickest man, so are there some breathings and spiritual motions of heart that will comfort in such times. These two never fail on God's part, his love, which is unchangeable, and his grace, a fruit of his love. As Christ never dies in himself, after his resurrection, so he never dies in his children.

*The Love of Christ (Bowels Opened)*, pp. 81-82

# Heart and Actions

*The good person out of the good treasure of his heart produces good, and the evil person out of his evil treasure produces evil, for out of the abundance of the heart his mouth speaks.—Luke 6:45*

A Christian is what his heart and inward man is. Grace is at the centre, and from there it goes to the circumference. Let the church value herself by the disposition and temper of her heart. To evaluate our spiritual states, we must look into our consciences and souls. Do we allow the ways of God in the inward man? How is it with our affections and bent to good things? God must first have our hearts and then our hands. A man otherwise is but a ghost in religion, which goes up and down; a picture that has an outside and is nothing within. Let us look to our hearts. 'Oh, that there was such a heart in this people,' said God to Moses, 'to fear me always, for their own good' (Deut. 5:29). This is what God's children desire, that their hearts may be aright set. 'Wash your heart, O Jerusalem,' said the prophet, 'from your wickedness' (Jer. 4:14).

However, God is not content with the heart alone. God, as the maker of both soul and body, he must and will have all. Yet, in times of temptation the chief trial is in the heart. A sound Christian does what he does from the heart. What good he does he loves in his heart first, judges it to be good, and then he does it. A hypocrite would do ill, and not good, if it were in his choice. The good that he does is for by-ends, for reputation, or conformity with the times, to cover his designs under formality of religion; that he may not be known outwardly, as he is inwardly, an atheist and a hypocrite. A Christian, by the power of God's Spirit, is sensible of the contradictions in himself, complains, and is ashamed of them. But a hypocrite is not so; he is not sensible of his sleepiness. He does not complain of his sleepiness but composes himself to slumber, and seeks darkness, which is a friend of sleep. He would willingly be ignorant, to keep his conscience as dull as he can, that it may not upbraid him.

*The Love of Christ* (*Bowels Opened*), pp. 83-85

## Preserving Spiritual Wakefulness (1)

*For the weapons of our warfare are not of the flesh but have divine power to destroy strongholds. We destroy arguments and every lofty opinion raised against the knowledge of God and take every thought captive to obey Christ.*—2 Cor. 10:4, 5

To preserve the soul, especially in these drowsy times:

(1) Propose to our souls, wakeful considerations. What causes our sleep but want of matters of more serious observation? None will sleep when a thing is presented of excellency. We never fall to sleep in earthly and carnal delights, till the soul lets its hold go of the best things and ceases to think of them. Make the heart think of the shortness and vanity of this life, with the uncertainty of the time of our death; and of what wondrous consequence it is to be in the state of grace before we die. Stir up our hearts to consider the terror of the Lord; to think that before long we will all be drawn to an exact account, before a strict, precise judge. Will our eyes then be sleeping and careless? These and such considerations out of spiritual wisdom we should propose to ourselves, that so we might have waking souls, and preserve them in a right temper.

(2) Keep faith awake. Now it is the nature of faith to make things powerfully present to the soul (Heb. 11:1). Faith is an awakening grace. Keep faith awake, and it will keep all other graces awake. When a man believes that all these things will be on fire before long; that heaven and earth will fall in pieces; that we will be called to give an account; when faith apprehends, and sets this to the eye of the soul, it affects the same marvellously. Let faith set before the soul some present thoughts according to its temper. Sometimes terrible things to awaken it out of its dullness; sometimes glorious things, promises and mercies, to waken it out of its sadness. When we are in a prosperous state let faith make present all the sins and temptations that usually accompany such a state, as pride, security, self-applause, and the like. If in adversity, think also of what sins may beset us there. This will awaken up such graces in us, as are suitable to such a state, and so keep our hearts in 'exercise to godliness' (1 Tim. 4:7).

*The Love of Christ (Bowels Opened)*, pp. 85-87

# Preserving Spiritual Wakefulness (2)

*Besides this you know the time, that the hour has come for you to wake from sleep. For salvation is nearer to us now than when we first believed.*—Rom. 13:11

(3) Labour for an abundance of the Spirit of God. What makes men sleepy, and drowsy? The want of the Spirit. We are dull, and overladen with gross passions, whereby the strength sinks and fails. Christians should know that there is a necessity, if they will keep themselves awake, to keep themselves spiritual. Pray for the Spirit above all things. He is the life of our life, the soul of our soul. What is the body without the soul, or the soul without the Spirit of God? Even a dead lump. Let us keep ourselves in such good ways, as we may expect the presence of the Spirit to be about us, which will keep us awake.

(4) We must keep ourselves in as much light as possible. For all sleepiness comes with darkness. Let us keep our souls in a perpetual light. When any doubt or dark thought arises, upon yielding comes a sleepy temper. Sleepiness in the affections arises from darkness of judgment. The more we labour to increase our knowledge, and the more the spiritual light of it shines in at our windows, the better it will be for us, and the more we will be able to keep awake. What makes men in their corruptions to avoid the ministry of the word, or anything that may awaken their consciences? It is the desire they have to sleep. They are aware, that the more they know, the more they must practice, or else they must have a galled conscience. A gracious heart will be desirous of spiritual knowledge especially, and not care how near the word comes, because they honestly and freely desire to be spiritually better. They make all things in the world yield to the inward man. They desire to know their own corruptions and evils more and more. They love the light 'as children of the light, and of the day' (1 Thess. 5:5). Sleep is a work of darkness. Men of dark and drowsy hearts, desire darkness, so their consciences may sleep.

*The Love of Christ* (*Bowels Opened*), pp. 87-88 [88-89]

# Preserving Spiritual Wakefulness (3)

*The Lord commanded us to do all these statutes, to fear the Lord our God, for our good always, that he might preserve us alive, as we are this day.*—Deut. 6:24

(5) Labour to preserve the soul in the fear of God because fear is a waking affection, yea, one of the most wakeful. Naturally we are more moved with dangers than stirred with hopes. Preserve the fear of God by all means. It is one characteristic of a Christian, who, when he feels he has lost almost all grace, yet the fear of God is always with him. He fears sin, and the consequence of it. God makes that awe the bond of the new covenant 'I will put my fear into their hearts, that they will never depart from me' (Jer. 32:39). Of all Christians, mark those that are most gracious, spiritual, and heavenly, they are the most fearful and careful of their speeches, courses, and demeanours, tender even of offending God in little things. Sometimes a good Christian may in a state of sleepiness be faulty some way. But as he grows in the sense of the love of God, he is afraid to lose that sweet communion in any way, or to grieve the Spirit of God. Let us preserve by all means this awe-filled affection, the fear of God. Let us then often search the state of our own souls; how it is between God and our souls; how fit we are to die, and to suffer; how fit for the times that may befall us. Those that will keep wakeful souls, must consider the danger of the place where they live, and the times; what sins reign, what sins the company they converse with are subject to, and their own weakness to be led away with such temptations. There is no Christian, but he has some special sin, to which he is more prone than to another. Here now is the care and watchfulness of a Christian spirit, that knowing by examination, and trial of his own heart, his weakness, he does especially fight against that which he is most inclined to; and is able to bring the strongest arguments to dishearten himself and others from the practice of it.

*The Love of Christ* (*Bowels Opened*), pp. 88-90 [88-91]

# Preserving Spiritual Wakefulness (4)

*Not neglecting to meet together, as is the habit of some, but encouraging one another, and all the more as you see the Day drawing near.—* Heb. 10:25

(6) In the last place it is a thing of no small consequence, that we keep company with wakeful and faithful Christians, such as neither sleep themselves nor do willingly allow any to sleep that are near them. It is one of the best fruits of the communion of saints, and of our spiritual good acquaintances, to keep one another awake. It is an unpleasing work on both sides. But we will one day cry out against all of them that have pleased themselves and us, in rocking us asleep, and thank those that have pulled us 'with fear' out of the fire (Jude 23), though against our wills. Certainly, a drowsy temper is the most ordinary temper in the world. What do worldly men mean when they fear not to lie, dissemble, and rush upon the pikes of God's displeasure? Were they awake, would they ever do this? Will not a fowl that has wings, avoid the snare? Or will a beast run into a pit when it sees it? They will catch drowsy tempers, as our Saviour said, of those latter times: 'For the abundance of iniquity, the love of many will grow cold' (Matt. 24:12). A chill temper grows ever from the coldness of the times that we live in. The life of many, we see, is a continual sleep. Let us especially watch over ourselves, in the use of liberty and such things as are in themselves lawful when done in a moderate use. Recreations are lawful; who denies it? To refresh a man's self, is not only lawful, but necessary. God knew it well enough, therefore he allotted time for sleep, and the like. But we must not turn recreation into a calling or spend too much time in it. It is true for the most part, more men perish in the church of God by the abuse of lawful things, than by unlawful. Let us keep awake, that we may carry ourselves so in our liberties, that we condemn not ourselves in the use of them.

*The Love of Christ (Bowels Opened)*, pp. 90-92 [89-91]

# The Awake Christian Is Prepared

*Be sober-minded; be watchful. Your adversary the devil prowls around like a roaring lion, seeking someone to devour.*—1 Pet. 5:8

Consider the excellence of an awake Christian. When he is in his right temper, he is a prepared person, fit for all assaults. He is impregnable. Satan has nothing to do with him, for he, as it is said, is then a wise man, and 'has his eyes in his head' (Eccles. 2:14). He knows himself, his standing, his enemies, the snares of prosperity and adversity, and of all conditions. He, being awake, is not overcome by the evil of any condition, and is ready for the good of any state. He that has a wakeful soul, he sees all the advantages of good, and all the snares that might draw him to ill (Mark 13:37). What a blessed state this is! In all things watch, in all conditions, in all times, and in all actions. There is a danger in everything without watchfulness. There is a scorpion under every stone, a snare under every blessing of God, and in every condition, which Satan uses as a weapon to hurt us; adversity to discourage us, or prosperity to puff us up. If a Christian has not a waking soul, Satan has him in his snare, in prosperity to be proud and secure; in adversity to murmur, to complain, and to be dejected and call God's providence into question. When a Christian has a heart and grace to be awake, then his love, his patience, his faith is awake, as it should be. He is fit for all conditions, to do good in them, and to take good by them. Let us labour to preserve watchful and waking hearts continually, so that we may be fit to live, to die, and to appear before the judgment seat of God; to do what we should do, being prepared for all.

*The Love of Christ (Bowels Opened)*, p. 92 [91–92]

# Ministers and Ministry

*He gave the apostles, the prophets, the evangelists, the shepherds and teachers, to equip the saints for the work of ministry, for building up the body of Christ.*—Eph. 4:11, 12

There is a knocking that Christ uses in the church, his ministerial knocking. When he was here in the days of his flesh, he was a preacher and prophet himself, and now that he is ascended into heaven, he has given gifts to men, and men to the church (Eph. 4:11), whom he speaks by, to the end of the world. In preaching and unfolding the word they are but Christ's mouth and his voice. Now he is in heaven, he speaks by them, 'He that hears you hears me, he that despises you despise me' (Luke 10:16). Christ is either received or rejected in his ministers. They are as ambassadors of Christ. 'We, therefore, as ambassadors, beseech and entreat you, as if Christ by us should speak to you; so, we entreat you to be reconciled unto God' (2 Cor. 5:20). You know what heart-breaking words the apostle uses in all his epistles, especially when he writes to Christians in a good state, as to the Philippians, 'If there be any affection of mercy, if there be any consolation in Christ,' then regard what I say, 'be of one mind' (Phil. 2:1). Among the Thessalonians he was as a nurse to them (1 Thess. 2:7). So, Christ speaks by them, and puts his own affections into them, that as he is tender and full of affection himself, so he has put the same affection into those that are his true ministers. He speaks by them, and they use all kind of means that Christ may be received into their hearts; sometimes threatenings, sometimes entreaties, sometimes they come as 'sons of thunder' (Mark 3:17), sometimes with the still voice of sweet promises. And because one man is not so fit as another for all varieties of conditions and spirits, therefore God gives variety of gifts to his ministers, that they may knock at the heart of every man by their several gifts. For some have more rousing, some more insinuating gifts; some more legal, some more evangelical spirits, yet all for the church's good. All kind of means have been used in the ministry from the beginning of the world.

*The Love of Christ (Bowels Opened)*, pp. 104-05

# The Conscience and the Trinity

*For when Gentiles, who do not have the law, by nature do what the law requires, they are a law to themselves, even though they do not have the law. They show that the work of the law is written on their hearts, while their conscience also bears witness, and their conflicting thoughts accuse or even excuse them.*—Rom. 2:14, 15

Besides his Spirit, God has planted in us a conscience to call upon us, to be his vicar; a little god in us to do his office, to call upon us, direct us, check and condemn us, which in great mercy he has placed in us. In this we see what means Christ uses—his voice, works, and word; works of mercy and of correction; his word, together with his Spirit, and the conscience, that he has planted, to be, as it were, a god in us; which together with his Spirit may move us to duty. This Augustine speaks of when he says, 'God spoke in me often, and I knew it not.' He means it of conscience, together with the Spirit, stirring up motives to leave his sinful courses. 'God knocked in me, and I considered it not.' While Christ knocks all the three persons are said to do it. For as it is said, 'God was and is in Christ reconciling the world' (2 Cor. 5:19). For whatever Christ did, he did it as anointed, and by office. Therefore, God does it in Christ, and by Christ, and so in some sort God died in his human nature, when Christ died. So here the Father beseeches when Christ beseeches, because Christ beseeches only what is sent from and anointed of the Father. And God the Father stoops to us when Christ stoops, because Christ is sent of the Father, and does all by his Father's command and commission (John 5:27). So, besides his own affection, there is the Father and the Spirit with Christ, who does all by his Spirit, and from his Father, from whom he has commission. Therefore, God the Father, Son, and Holy Spirit knock at the heart. 'Open to me, my love, my dove, my undefiled' (Song of Sol. 5:2) but Christ especially by his Spirit, because it is his office.

*The Love of Christ (Bowels Opened)*, pp. 106-07

# The Christian's Two Natures

*And we all, with unveiled face, beholding the glory of the Lord, are being transformed into the same image from one degree of glory to another. For this comes from the Lord who is the Spirit.*—2 Cor. 3:18

We should have a double eye: one eye to see that which is amiss in us, our own imperfections, thereby to carry ourselves in a perpetual humility. Another eye of faith, to see what we have in Christ, our perfection in him, and glory in this our best being—such a one whereby God esteems us perfect, and undefiled in him. The one sight should force us to the other, which is one reason why God, in this world, leaves corruption in his children. Is there any harbour for me to rest in my own righteousness? No! It drives a man out of that harbour. Nay, I will rest in that righteousness which God has wrought by Christ. The sight of our own unworthiness should not be a ground of discouragement, but a ground to drive us completely out of ourselves, that by faith we might renew our title to that righteousness, wherein is our glory. Why should we not judge ourselves as Christ does? Notwithstanding all he sees, he accounts us as undefiled.

Since he accounts us undefiled, because he means to make us so, it shall not thus be always with us. Oh, this flesh of mine will become weaker and weaker as Saul's house (2 Sam. 3:1), and the Spirit at last will conquer! Imperfection should not discourage us. Let us rejoice, in that we are chosen to sanctification, which is a little begun, being an earnest of other blessings. Let us not rest in the earnest, but labour for a further pledge of more strength and grace. For those that have the Spirit of Christ, will strive to be as much unspotted as they can, to fit themselves for that heavenly condition as much as may be. When, because they cannot be in heaven, yet they will converse there as much as they can; and because they cannot be with such company altogether, they will be as much as they may be; labouring to be that which they will be hereafter. Imperfection contents them not, and therefore they pray still in the Lord's prayer, 'Your kingdom come' (Matt. 6:10).

*The Love of Christ (Bowels Opened)*, pp. 150-52 [150-51]

# Christ's Presence: Felt and Not Felt

*You make known to me the path of life; in your presence there is fullness of joy; at your right hand are pleasures forevermore.*—Psa. 16:11

There is a double presence of Christ: felt and not felt.

Christ's felt presence is when he is graciously present and is also pleased to let us know, which is a heaven upon earth. My soul is in paradise when I feel 'the love of God shed abroad in the heart' (Rom. 5:5), and the countenance of God shining upon me. Then I despise the world, and all, and walk as if I were half in heaven already.

Christ's unfelt presence is a presence of Christ that is secret; when he seems to draw us one way, and to drive us another, that we are both driven away and drawn in at once. When we find our souls go to Christ, there is a drawing power and presence; but when we find him absent, here is driving away. As we see in the woman of Canaan (Matt. 15:21, 22). We see what an answer she had from Christ, at first none, and then an uncomfortable one, and lastly a seemingly unkind answer. 'We must not give the children's bread to dogs' (Matt. 15:27). Christ seemed to drive her away, but, at the same time, he by his Spirit draws her to himself, and was thereby secretly present in her heart to increase her faith. It is good to observe this type of Christ's dealing with us because it will keep us from being discouraged when we feel him absent. If we find the Spirit of God moving us to love the word and ordinances, to call upon him by prayer, and to be more instant, certainly we may gather there is a hidden, secret presence here that draws us to these things. Nay, more, that the end of this is to draw us nearer and nearer, and at length to draw us into heaven to himself. God's people are gainers by all their losses, stronger by all their weaknesses, and the better for all their crosses. It should teach us to depend upon him, 'though he slay me,' as Job did (Job 13:15). Our souls should never give up on seeking Christ, praying, and endeavouring, for there is true love.

*The Love of Christ (Bowels Opened)*, pp. 206-08 [204-06]

# Christ Is Altogether Lovely

*He is altogether desirable. This is my beloved and this is my friend, O daughters of Jerusalem.*—Song of Sol. 5:16b

Was he lovely when he was nailed on the cross, hung between two thieves, when he wore a crown of thorns, whipped, when he sweat water and blood? Oh! yes; then he was most lovely of all to us, by how much the more he was abased for us. This makes him more lovely that out of love he would abase himself so low. When greatness and goodness meet together, how goodly it is! That Christ, so great a majesty, should have such compassion! It was so beyond comparison lovely in the eyes of the disciples, that they stood and wondered to see him, who was the eternal Word of the Father, condescend to talk with a poor Samaritan woman (John 4:6, 7). What loveliness of carriage was in him to Peter, undeserving, after he had denied him, yet to restore him to his former place, loving him as much as ever he did before! In a word, what sweetness, gentleness, meekness, pity, and compassion did he reveal to those that were in misery! There is a remarkable passage in the story of Alphonsus the king, not very well liked of some. When he saw a poor man pulling his beast out of a ditch, he put out his hand to help him; after which, as it is recorded, his subjects ever loved him the better. Is it not as wonderful that the King of heaven and earth should stoop so low as to help us poor worms out of the ditch of hell and damnation and advance us to such a state and condition as is above our admiration, which neither heart can conceive nor tongue express? Is not this wonderful condescension?

Let us labour to place all our sweet affections upon this object, this lovely deserving object, Christ. Let the whole stream of our affections be carried unto Christ. For he, being altogether lovely, all that comes from him is lovely. His promises, his directions, his counsels, his children, his ordinances, are all lovely. Whatever has the stamp of Christ upon it, let us love it. We cannot bestow our hearts better.

*The Love of Christ (Bowels Opened)*, pp. 292-94 [288-90]

# Evidence of Loving Christ

*If you love me, you will keep my commandments.*—John 14:15

Let us labour to kindle in our hearts an affection for Christ. We may judge our love by our esteem.

(1) How do we value Christ? What place should he have in our hearts? If he be the chief of ten thousand, let us rather offend ten thousand than offend him. Let us say, with David, 'Whom have I in heaven but you?' (Psa. 73:25).

(2) Are we ready to suffer for Christ? Are we resolved not to give in though the world disgraces and censures us? No, we love Christ the more, and stick to his truth the faster. Certainly, where the love of Christ is, there is a spirit of fortitude. You have some who, for frowns from greatness, fear of loss, or for hope of rising, will warp their conscience, and do anything. Where is love to Christ? He that loves Christ, loves him the more for his suffering, as the Holy Spirit has recorded of some, that they 'rejoiced that they were thought worthy to suffer for Christ' (Acts 5:41). So, the more we suffer for him, the dearer he will be to us.

(3) Where love is, there it enlarges the heart, which being enlarged, enlarges the tongue also. The church has never enough of commending Christ, and of setting out his praise. The tongue is loosed because the heart is loosed. Love will alter a man's disposition. Let a man love Christ, and though before he could not speak a word in the commendation of Christ, yet if the love of Christ be in him, he will speak and labour earnestly in the praises of God.

(4) The church is never content until she finds Christ. It is with a Christian; if he has lost, by his own fault, his former communion with Christ, he will not rest nor be satisfied; but searches. He runs through all God's ordinances and means until he finds Christ. Nothing in the world will content him, neither honour, riches, place, or friends, until he finds that which he once enjoyed, the comfort and assurance of God's love in Christ.

*The Love of Christ (Bowels Opened)*, pp. 294-97 [290-92]

# Jesus Is Each Stage of Our Salvation (1)

*Beloved, we are God's children now, and what we will be has not yet appeared; but we know that when he appears we shall be like him, because we shall see him as he is. And everyone who thus hopes in him purifies himself as he is pure.*—1 John 3:2, 3

How is Christ our life?

Christ is in every way the cause of the life of grace and glory. Not only the cause, but the root and spring as well. We have spiritual life from Christ and in Christ. We have it in Christ as a root, and from Christ as the working cause, and by Christ as the mediator. For Christ procured our life at God's hands by his sacrifice and death. We have it in Christ as a head, from him as a cause, together with both the other persons of the Trinity; and through him as mediator, who by his death made the way to life, appeasing the wrath of God. Christ is not only our life, but also is the matter of our life that we feed on.

After he has wrought spiritual life in us, the soul lives by faith in Christ, and feeds upon him. For as food nourishes the body, so the soul, when it experiences daily temptations, afflictions, troubles, and discomforts, must out of necessity be forced to look to Christ every day, and spiritually feed upon Christ. For he is a mediator forever; and he is in heaven to make good what he has done by his death; and he maintains the life he has begun.

Then after being justified by faith, we have the life of sanctification and holiness. For God out of his love, when he has pardoned our sin, he gives his Spirit as the best fruit of his love; and we having our consciences absolved and acquitted by the Spirit of God, through the obedience of Christ, we love God. With the stream of mercy open, there is a way made for another life, the life of sanctification by the Spirit. Upon pardon of our sins he gives the Spirit; and we, feeling that love, have love wrought in us to him again, and that love stirs up every Christian to obedience.

*The Hidden Life, Works, vol. 5, p. 209*

# Jesus Is Each Stage of Our Salvation (2)

*May the God of hope fill you with all joy and peace in believing, so that by the power of the Holy Spirit you may abound in hope.*—Rom. 15:13

After he has acquitted us by his all-sufficient satisfaction, being God and man, and has given us his Spirit, there is another life, the life of comfort, which is the life of our life, in peace of conscience and joy unspeakable and glorious. This life issues from the former. For when we find our conscience appeased, that God said to our souls he is 'their salvation' (Psa. 35:3), and find a newness wrought in our nature by the Spirit of God, and some strength to obey him, then we begin to have a sweet peace, as the children of God find in themselves, and joy unspeakable and glorious.

This is the ultimate life of this life. Having union with Christ and his righteousness and Spirit, we have a peace, which is the way to glory and the beginning of it. As we were dead in nature, so we have a life in sanctification. As we were dead in despair, and ran into terrors of conscience; so we have a life of joy and peace.

But all those in this life are imperfect because there is only a union of grace here, until we come to the union of glory in heaven. At the day of judgment there will be a perfect justifying of us. We will not only be acquitted in our conscience, as we are now, but we will be acquitted before angels and devils and men, and Christ will acknowledge us. 'These are they for whom I died. These are they for whom I made intercession in heaven.' On that day, the life of sanctification, that is now in part, will be perfect, and likewise the peace that now 'passes understanding' (Phil. 4:7) will be full; and our joy will be full by Christ who is our life.

*The Hidden Life, Works*, vol. 5, pp. 209-10

# The Return of Christ (1)

*For you have died, and your life is hidden with Christ in God. When Christ who is your life appears, then you also will appear with him in glory.*—Col. 3:3, 4

'When Christ who is your life appears.' There are two appearings. His first appearing was to work our salvation; his second will be to accomplish and finish what he has begun to work. His first appearing was to redeem our souls from death, and his second will redeem our bodies from the corruption of the grave. His second appearing will be to accomplish all the good that he came to do and to work by his first. As verily as Christ has come in his first appearing, so verily and certainly he will appear the second time. As it was the description of holy men before his first coming to wait for him, 'to wait for the consolation of Israel' (Luke 2:25), so should Christians now wait. Those blessed souls that have the hope and confidence in his second appearing, they wait for the coming of Christ.

There were all kinds of witnesses of his first coming: angels, men, women, shepherds, the devils themselves. The Trinity from heaven witnessed of him. For his second coming there will be witnesses. Christ himself said he will come. The angels said, 'This Jesus that you see go up will come again' (Acts 1:11). It is an article of our faith that he will come. The Spirit of God in every Christian says 'Come,' and that is not in vain. The desires of the Spirit of God must be fulfilled. Therefore, Jesus will come. And the Spirit of God stirs up our spirits to say 'Come.'

Christ will appear, and 'you also will appear with him in glory.' We will appear, and appear with him, and appear in glory with him. Christ's glory is in some way hid now. For though he be king of the church, yet we see what enemies are in the church; and Satan disrupts the church a great while, and the nearer he is to his end the more he rages, so that Christ's glory seems to be hid. But Christ will then appear, and his church will appear with him in glory

*The Hidden Life, Works*, vol. 5, pp. 211-12

# The Return of Christ (2)

*I charge you in the presence of God and of Christ Jesus, who is to judge the living and the dead, and by his appearing and his kingdom: preach the word; be ready in season and out of season; reprove, rebuke, and exhort, with complete patience and teaching.*—2 Tim. 4:1, 2

Christ will appear in glory as certainly as he appeared in his first coming; and we will appear with him in glory. Why should we doubt it? Has not that which is even greater been already done? Has not God himself become man? Has not God humbled himself in his first coming and died? Is not that more wondrous than that a man should become like God in his second coming? What is greater, for God to become man, or for men to be raised out of their graves and become glorious? Certainly, the latter is the lesser. Let us encourage our hearts with this, that as verily as he came in humility to work our salvation, so verily he will come and raise us to glory.

We would never be lacking in grace nor comfort if we often thought of and applied this truth to our hearts. Let us bring ourselves to this light; let us often think of the blessed times to come: in so doing could we be unfruitful? This made Paul charge the Thessalonians, 'I beseech you, by the coming of our Lord Jesus Christ' (2 Tim. 4:1, 2). Further, 'I need no greater argument to press you, than as verily as Christ will come in glory, you will be gathered to him, so hear what I say' (2 Thess. 2:1). This promise will move a man's conscience and carry him to his duty. Let us think seriously on this, Christ will come with thousands of his angels in glory and majesty; glorious in his company, glorious in himself, glorious in his enemies. And we will come to the same glory. Let us think of this, it will quicken and inspire all our courses and actions with a spiritual kind of light, making them acceptable to God. All should be done in sincerity, constancy, abundantly, cheerfully, readily, and willingly; for God requires these qualities in what we do. What makes a man sow his seed, that he scarcely can spare, but the hope of a harvest? Be constant, 'for in him you will receive the reward if you faint not' (Gal. 6:9).

*The Hidden Life, Works*, vol. 5, pp. 214-15

# Confront Your Soul and Remember God's Mercy

*Why are you cast down, O my soul, and why are you in turmoil within me? Hope in God; for I shall again praise him, my salvation and my God.*—Psa. 42:11

What if our condition is so dark that we cannot read in ourselves any evidence of grace? Here look up to God's infinite mercy in Christ, as we did at our conversion, when we found no goodness in ourselves. That is the way to recover whatever we think we have lost. When the waters of sanctification are troubled and muddy, let us run to the witness of blood. God seems to walk sometimes contrary to himself; he seems to discourage, when secretly he does encourage, as the woman of Canaan in Matthew 15:21-28. Faith can find out these ways of God, and untie these knots, by looking to the merciful nature of God. Let our foolish and rebellious flesh murmur as much as it will, 'Who are you?' and 'What is your worth?' yet a Christian 'knows whom he believes' (2 Tim. 1:12). Faith has learned to set God against all. We must go on to add grace to grace. A growing and fruitful Christian is always a comfortable Christian. Christ is first a king of righteousness, and then a king of peace (Heb. 7:2).

Another thing that hinders the comfort of Christians is, that they forget what a gracious and merciful covenant they live under, in which the perfection that is required is found in Christ. Perfection in us is sincerity; what is the end of faith but to bring us to Christ? Now imperfect faith, if sincere, knits us to Christ, in whom our perfection lies.

There is no portion of Scripture more often used to fetch up drooping spirits than this: 'Why are you cast down, O my soul?' (Psa. 42:11). It is figurative, and full of rhetoric, and enough to quietly persuade the perplexed soul to trust in God; which, without this retiring into ourselves and checking our hearts, will never be brought to pass. As David acquainted himself with this form of dealing with his soul, so let us, demand a reason of ourselves, 'Why we are cast down?' Which will at least check and put a stop to the distress and make us fit to consider more solid grounds of true comfort.

*The Soul's Conflict with Itself, Works*, vol. 1, pp. 124-25

# Cast Down? Diagnosing Spiritual Discouragement (1)

*And about the ninth hour Jesus cried out with a loud voice, saying, 'Eli, Eli, lema sabachthani?' that is, 'My God, my God, why have you forsaken me?'*—Matt. 27:46

Causes of spiritual discouragement.

(1) God himself sometimes withdraws the beams of his countenance from his children, whereupon the soul of even the strongest Christian is disquieted. The child of God, when he sees that his troubles are mixed with God's displeasure, and perhaps his conscience tells him that God has a just quarrel against him; this anger of God puts a sting into all other troubles. When the Son of God himself, having always enjoyed the sweet communion with his Father, complained in all his torments of nothing else, but 'My God, my God, why have you forsaken me?' (Matt. 27:46). So, when the soul, raised up and upheld by the beams of his countenance, feels that God has left, it presently begins to sink. We see when the body of the sun is partially hid from us in an eclipse by the body of the moon, that there is a drooping in the whole frame of nature; so it is with believers, when there is anything that comes between God's gracious countenance and the soul.

(2) If we look down to inferior causes, the soul is often cast down by Satan. For being a cursed spirit, cast and tumbled down himself from heaven, where he is never to come again, he is full of disquiet, carrying a hell about himself. All that he labours for is to cast down and disquiet others, that they may be, as much as he can procure, in the same cursed condition as himself. He thinks Christ's members never low enough, until he can bring them as low as himself. By his envy and subtlety we were driven out of paradise at the first, and now he envies us the paradise of a good conscience; for that is our paradise until we come to heaven, into which no serpent will ever creep to tempt us. When Satan sees a man strongly and comfortably walking with God, he cannot endure that a creature of lower rank by creation than himself should enjoy such happiness. It is his continual trade and course to seek his rest in our disquiet.

*The Soul's Conflict with Itself, Works*, vol. 1, pp. 133-34

# Cast Down? Diagnosing Spiritual Discouragement (2)

*There is one whose rash words are like sword thrusts, but the tongue of the wise brings healing.*—Prov. 12:18

(3) What Satan cannot do himself by immediate suggestions, he then labours to work by his instruments; as those in the psalm who cry, 'Down with him, down with him, even to the ground' (Psa. 137:7). A character of these men's dispositions we have in Psalm 102:8, 'My enemies,' said David, 'reproach me all day.' As sweet and as compassionate a man as he was, to pray and put on sackcloth for them (Psa. 35:13), yet he had enemies. David's enemies did not only have their malice boiling in their own breasts, but they also reproached him in words. Neither did they go behind his back but were so impudent to say it to his face. A malicious heart and a slandering tongue go together, their insolence spoke much to David's heart (Psa. 109:1-5). Their malice was unwearied, for they spoke daily against him. Malice is an insatiable monster and it ministers words. But what was it they said so reproachfully and daily? 'Where is your God now?' (Psa. 42:3). They reproached him for his singularity, they did not say, 'Where is God?' but 'Where is your God that you boast so much on, as if he had some special interest in you?' Here we see that the scope of the devil and wicked men is to shake the faith of the godly and their confidence in their God.

How was David affected by these reproaches? Their words were as swords in his bones (Psa. 42:10). They cut him to the quick when they touched him in his God. Touch a true, godly man in his religion, and you touch his life and his best possession. We see David, therefore, upon this reproach, call out himself for it, 'Why are you so cast down and disquieted, O my soul' (Psa. 42:5, 11). This bitter taunt ran so much in his mind, that he expressed it twice in this psalm. We see by daily experience, that there is a special force in words uttered from a subtle head, a false heart, and a smooth tongue. Words that can weaken the hearts of believers.

*The Soul's Conflict with Itself, Works*, vol. 1, pp. 134-35

# Cast Down? Diagnosing Spiritual Discouragement (3)

*Examine yourselves, to see whether you are in the faith. Test yourselves.*
*Or do you not realize this about yourselves, that Jesus Christ is in*
*you?—unless indeed you fail to meet the test!*—2 Cor. 13:5

(4) We need go no farther than ourselves to find causes of discouragement; there is a seminary of them within us. Consider these discouragements in ourselves.

(4a) When there is a lack of true knowledge, this ignorance, being darkness, is full of false fears. Our forefathers in times of ignorance were frightened by everything. Some spiritual leaders keep people in darkness, that they might make them fearful and might heal them with false cures.

(4b) When the soul is not ignorant, yet if it be forgetful and mindless, as Hebrews 12:5 says, 'you have forgotten the consolation that speaks to you.' We have no more present actual comfort than we have remembrance. Help a godly man's memory, and you help his comfort. Like charcoal, which, having once been kindled, is easier to take fire. He that has formerly known things, takes ready acquaintance of them again, as old friends.

(4c) The lack of setting due price upon comforts as the Israelites did when they set no value on the pleasant land. It is a great fault when, as they said to Job, 'the consolation of the Almighty seems light and small to us' (Job 15:11).

(4d) Add to this a childish kind of peevishness when they don't have what they want, like children, they throw away all. Abraham himself, wanting children (Gen. 15:2), undervalued all other blessings. Jonah, because he was angry about his gourd plant, was weary of his life. The same may be said of Elijah, flying from Jezebel. This peevishness is increased by a flattering of their grief, so far as to justify it. Like Jonah, 'I do well to be angry even to death' (Jonah 4:9). Some, with Rachel, are so overtaken, that they 'will not be comforted' (Jer. 31:15), as if they were in love with their grievances. There are no men more subject to discontentment than those who would have all things after their own way.

*The Soul's Conflict with Itself, Works,* vol. 1, pp. 135-37

# Cast Down? Diagnosing Spiritual Discouragement (4)

*Therefore, brothers, be all the more diligent to confirm your calling and election, for if you practice these qualities you will never fall.—* 2 Pet. 1:10

(4e) One main ground is false reasoning. Thinking we have no grace when we feel none. Feeling is not always a fit rule to judge our states by. Thinking that God has rejected us because we are confused by things which issue from God's wisdom and love. There are many who imagine their failings to be fallings, and their fallings to be fallings away; that every sin against conscience, to be the sin against the Holy Spirit. Satan, as a cunning debater, here enlarges the fancy, to apprehend things bigger than they are, abuses confident spirits in another contrary way; to apprehend great sins as little, and little as none. Some also think that they have no grace, because they have not grown as Christians, even though they have been several years in Christ. Some are so desirous after what they have not, that they mind not what they have.

(4f) Some are much troubled because they proceed by a false method and order in judging of their state. They begin with election, which is the highest step of the ladder; when they should begin with a work of grace wrought within their hearts, from God's calling them by his Spirit, and their answer to his call. By so doing they raise themselves upward to know their election by their answer to God's calling. 'Give all diligence,' said Peter, 'to make your calling and election sure' (2 Pet. 1:10), your election by your calling. God descends down to us from election to calling, and so to sanctification; we must ascend to him, beginning where he ends. Otherwise it is as great a folly as removing a pile of wood by beginning at the lowest first. This great secret of God's eternal love to us in Christ is hidden in his breast, and does not appear to us, until in the use of means God by his Spirit reveals the same to us. We know God must love us before we can love him, and yet we often first know that we love him (1 John 4:19).

*The Soul's Conflict with Itself, Works,* vol. 1, pp. 137-38

# Cast Down? Diagnosing Spiritual Discouragement (5)

*The aim of our charge is love that issues from a pure heart and a good conscience and a sincere faith.*—1 Tim. 1:5

(4*g*) Another cause of disquiet is, that men seek for their comfort in much sanctification, neglecting justification, relying too much upon their own performances. Paul was of another mind, accounting all but dung and dross, compared to the righteousness of Christ (Phil. 3:8, 9). Why did the apostles in the prefaces of their letters join grace and peace together, but that we should seek for our peace in the free grace and favour of God in Christ?

Those who hold salvation by works will always find some flaw even in our best performances. Thus, the doubting and misgiving soul comes to make this absurd demand, 'Who shall ascend to heaven?' (Psa. 24:3). The truth is, if we believe in Christ we are as sure to come to heaven as Christ is there. Neither height nor depth can separate us from God's love in Christ (Rom. 8:39). But we must remember, though the main pillar of our comfort be in the free forgiveness of our sins, yet if there be a neglect in growing in holiness, the soul will never be soundly quiet, because it will be prone to question the truth of justification, and it is as proper for sin to raise doubts and fears in the conscience, as for rotten flesh and rotting wood to breed worms.

(4*h*) The neglect of keeping a clear conscience is another cause of a lack of peace. Sin, like Achan, or Jonah in the ship, is that which causes storms within and without. Where there is not a pure conscience, there is not a pacified conscience; and therefore though some, thinking to save themselves by justification alone, neglect sanctification and the cleansing of their natures and ordering of their lives, yet in time of temptation they will find that course more troublesome than they think. A Christian is a new creature and as far as he walks according to the Scriptures, peace is upon him (Gal. 6:16). Loose walkers who regard not their way, must expect sorrows instead of peace. Watchfulness is the preserver of peace.

*The Soul's Conflict with Itself, Works,* vol. 1, pp. 138-39

# Cast Down? Diagnosing Spiritual Discouragement (6)

*Through sloth the roof sinks in, and through indolence the house leaks.*—Eccles. 10:18

(4*i*) Some reap the fruit of their ignorance of Christian liberty, by unnecessary scruples and doubts. It is both unthankfulness to God and wrong to us, to be ignorant of the extent of Christian liberty. It makes melody to Satan to see Christians troubled with what they neither should nor need to be troubled about. Yet there is danger in stretching Christian liberty beyond the bounds. For a man may condemn himself in what he approves, as in not walking circumspectly in regard of circumstances, and so breed his own disquiet, and give scandal to others.

(4*j*) Sometimes also, God suffers men to be disquieted for want of employment. Those who shun labour, bring trouble upon themselves. By not doing that which is needful, they are troubled with that which is unnecessary. An unemployed life is a burden to itself. God is a pure act, always working, always doing; and the nearer our soul comes to God, the more it is in action and the freer from disquiet. Men by experience feel that comfort in doing that which is theirs to do. A heart not exercised in some honest labour works trouble out of itself.

(4*k*) Omission of duties and services of love often troubles the peace of good people; for even in time of death, when they look for peace and desire it most, they look back upon former failings, and see lost opportunities for doing good. From these memories they can be much disquieted, and so much the more because they see now no hope to make things right. A Christian life is full of duties, and the peace of it is maintained by much fruitfulness and being aware of the needs around us. The debt of duty is a disquieting thing to an honest mind. Paul lays the charge 'that we should owe nothing to any man but love' (Rom. 13:8).

*The Soul's Conflict with Itself, Works,* vol. 1, pp. 139-40

# Cast Down? Diagnosing Spiritual Discouragement (7)

*Surely a man goes about as a shadow! Surely for nothing they are in turmoil; man heaps up wealth and does not know who will gather!—* Psa. 39:6

(4*l*) One special cause of much disquiet is the lack of firm resolution in good things. The soul cannot but be disquieted when it knows not what to cleave to, like a ship tossed by contrary winds. 'If God be God, cleave to him' (1 Kings 18:21). If the duties of religion bring peace of conscience, then with intention practice them in every passage of life. We should labour to have a clear judgment, and a resolved purpose. A wavering-minded man is inconsistent in all his ways (James 1:6). Uncertain men are always unquiet men, and giving too much way to passion makes men unsettled.

(5) Reasons that come from specific personal actions.

(5*a*) It breeds disquiet when men lay up their comfort too much on outward things, which are subject to much inconstancy and change. We are cast down by the disappointing of our hopes, as we were too much lifted up in expectation of good from them. From misplaced hopes proceed these complaints: A friend has failed me; I never thought to have fallen into this condition; I had set my joy in this child, in this friend, etc. But this is to build our comfort upon things that have no firm foundation. We should follow Agur's example and desire God 'to remove from us vanity and lies' (Prov. 30:8). Confidence in vain things makes a vain heart. We may say of all earthly things as the prophet speaks, 'here is not our rest' (Micah 2:10). It is no wonder that worldly men are often cast down and disquieted, when they walk in a vain shadow (Psa. 39:6). Men given much to recreations can be subject to passionate distempers because things fall out other than they looked for. Likewise, men that grasp more businesses than they can discharge bear both the blame and the grief of losing or marring many businesses, it being almost impossible to do many things well. It is the covetous and over-busy men that bring trouble both to their hearts and their houses.

*The Soul's Conflict with Itself, Works,* vol. 1, p. 140

# Cast Down? Diagnosing Spiritual Discouragement (8)

*Not by the way of eye-service, as people-pleasers, but as bondservants of Christ, doing the will of God from the heart.*—Eph. 6:6

(5*b*) Another source of spiritual discouragement is when we depend too much upon the opinions of other men. Often, even good men are too much troubled with the unjust censures of others. It is the vain man who lives more to other's opinion of them than to conscience. It cannot be that he should long enjoy settled quiet, because those in whose good opinion he desires to dwell, are ready often to take up contrary opinions of him for the slightest grounds.

(5c) Another cause for spiritual discouragement is when we look too much and too long upon the ill in ourselves and others. We may even fix our eyes too long upon sin itself. Much more may we err in poring too much upon our afflictions. We naturally mind one hardship more than a hundred favours, dwelling over long upon the sore.

Similarly, our minds may be taken up in the consideration of the miseries of the times at home and abroad, as if Christ did not rule in the midst of his enemies and would not help all in due time. Christians forget that their perfect rest is kept for the hereafter, in heaven. But now for the most part we are in an afflicted and conflicted condition. Here we are in a sea, where nearly all we can look for are storms. At times we usurp God and take his office upon ourselves by predicting the outcome of things. Our part is only to do our work and be quiet, as children when they please their parents take no further thought.

*The Soul's Conflict with Itself, Works,* vol. 1, p. 141

# Strong Reasons against Spiritual Discouragement (1)

*Rejoice always, pray without ceasing, give thanks in all circumstances;*
*for this is the will of God in Christ Jesus for you.*—1 Thess. 5:16-18

There is no reason, which the wisdom from above allows to be a reason, why believers should be discouraged. There is not only no reason for it, but there are strong reasons against it. Consider:

(1) Discouragement indisposes a man to all good duties; it makes him like an instrument out of tune, and like a body out of joint, that moves painfully. It makes one unfit for duties to God, who loves a cheerful giver, and especially a thanks-giver. Also, in our duties to men, if the spirit be dejected, they are unwelcome, and lose the greatest part of their life and grace; a cheerful and a free spirit in duty is that which is most accepted. We observe not so much what is done, as from what affection a thing is done.

(2) Spiritual discouragement is a great wrong to God himself, and it makes us think dark thoughts of him, as if he were an enemy. It is like injuring and calling into question a generous father, who has given many gracious evidences of his favour and love!

(3) So it makes a man forgetful of all former blessings and stops the influence of God's grace for the time present and for that to come.

(4) So, again, for receiving of good, it makes us unfit to receive mercies. A quiet soul is the seat of wisdom; therefore, meekness is required for the receiving of that 'engrafted word which is able to save our souls' (James 1:21). Until the Spirit of God meekens the soul, say what you will, it minds nothing; the soul is not quiet enough to receive the seed of the word. It is useless to sow in a storm; so, a stormy spirit will not allow the word to take root. When we cast ourselves down sullenly, and neglect our spiritual comforts, or undervalue them, it proceeds from pride. When we think to ourselves, 'Why should it be so with us?' As if we were wiser to dispose of ourselves than God is. Satan has never more advantage than when we are discontent.

*The Soul's Conflict with Itself, Works,* vol. 1, pp. 143-44

# Strong Reasons against Spiritual Discouragement (2)

*But exhort one another every day, as long as it is called 'today,' that none*
*of you may be hardened by the deceitfulness of sin.*—Heb. 3:13

(5) Spiritual discouragement keeps beginners from progressing on
and growing in the ways of God. It brings an ill report upon religion. It
dampens, the spirits of those that walk the same way with us, when we
should, as good fellow-travellers, cheer up one another both by word and
example. In such a case the wheels of the soul are taken off, or else, as it
were, want oil, making the soul pass on very heavily, and no good action
able to come from it, which breeds not only uncomfortableness, but
unsettledness in good courses. For a man will never go on comfortably
and constantly in that which he heavily undertakes. That is the reason
why uncheerful spirits seldom hold out as they should. Peter knew this
well, and therefore he wills that there should be 'quietness and peace
between husband and wife, that their prayers be not hindered' (1 Pet.
3:7). Their prayers are hindered by family breaches. There is nothing
more required for the performing of holy duties than uniting of spirits,
and therefore God would not have the sacrifice brought to the altar
before reconciliation with our brother (Matt. 5:24).

Therefore, we should all endeavour and labour for a calmed spirit,
that we may better serve God in praying to him and praising of him; and
serve one another in love, that we may be fitted to do and receive good,
that we may make our passage to heaven more cheerful. So much as we
are quiet and cheerful upon good grounds, so much we live, and are, as
it were, in heaven. So much as we yield to discouragement, we lose so
much of our life and happiness. Cheerfulness being, as it were, that life
of our lives and the spirit of our spirits by which they are more enlarged
to receive happiness and to express it.

*The Soul's Conflict with Itself, Works*, vol. 1, p. 144

# When in Solitude

*I bless the Lord who gives me counsel; in the night also my heart instructs me, I have set the Lord always before me; because he is at my right hand, I shall not be shaken.*—Psa. 16:7, 8

We see here again that a godly man can make a good use of solitude. When he is forced to be alone, he can talk with his God and himself; one reason for this is that his heart is a treasury and storehouse of divine truths, from this storehouse he can speak to himself, by way of correction or encouragement. He has a Spirit over his own spirit, to teach him to make use of that store he has laid up in his heart. The Spirit is never nearer him than when by way of witness to his spirit he is thus comforted. This is one way the child of God differs from another man, who cannot endure solitariness, because his heart is empty; he was a stranger to God before, and God is a stranger to him now, so that he cannot go to God as a friend.

We read of great princes, who after some bloody designs were as terrible to themselves as they were formerly to others, and therefore could never endure to be awaked in the night, without music or some like diversion. We may be cast into such a condition, where we have none in the world to comfort us; as in contagious sickness, when none may come near us, or we may be in such a state where no friend will own us. Therefore, let us labour now to be acquainted with God and our own hearts, and acquaint our hearts with the comforts of the Holy Spirit. Then, though we have not so much as a book to look on, or a friend to talk with, yet we may look with comfort into the book of our own heart and read what God has written there by the finger of his Spirit. All books are written to amend this one book of our heart and conscience. By this means we shall never lack a divine to comfort us, a physician to cure us, a counsellor to direct us, a musician to cheer us, a controller to check us, because, by help of the word and the Spirit, we can be all these to ourselves.

*The Soul's Conflict with Itself, Works,* vol. 1, pp. 148-49

# Pride

*Pride goes before destruction, and a haughty spirit before a fall.*—Prov. 16:18

Pride, with a desire of liberty, makes men think it to be a diminishing of greatness and freedom either to be curbed, or to curb ourselves. We love to be absolute and independent; but as it brought ruin upon our nature in Adam, so it will upon our persons. Men, as Luther said, are born with a pope in their belly, they hate to give an account, even to themselves, their wills are a kingdom to them.

Let us, therefore, when any lawless passions begin to stir, deal with our souls as God did with Jonah, 'Do you well to be angry' (Jon. 4:4), that you should fret this way? This will be a means to make us quiet; for what weak reasons have we often of such strong emotions. We think, 'Such a man gave me no respect, another looked kindlier upon someone else than upon me,' etc. You have some of Haman's spirit that for a little neglect would ruin a whole nation (Esth. 5:13). Passion presents men that are innocent as guilty to us, and because we will not seem to be mad without reason, pride commands the mind to justify anger, and so one passion maintains and feeds another. It would prevent much trouble in us and others, if at the first beginnings of any unruly passions and affections, they would be taken control over. Like ill-nurtured children, who, being not chastened in time, that it is often above the power of parents to bring them in order. A child set at liberty, said Solomon, 'breeds shame, at length, to his parents' (Prov. 29:15). It is a great fault in bringing up children, for fear of taking down their spirits, not to take down their pride, and get victory of their affections.

A proud, unbroken heart brings more trouble often than all the world beside. It is better to be taken down in youth, than to be broken in pieces by great crosses in age. Early in life or later, self-denial and victory over self is absolutely necessary; otherwise faith, which is a grace that requires self-denial, will never rule in the soul.

*The Soul's Conflict with Itself, Works,* vol. 1, pp. 146-47

# Soul Care (1)

*For what will it profit a man if he gains the whole world and forfeits his soul? Or what shall a man give in return for his soul?*—Matt. 16:26

A godly man's care and trouble is especially about his soul. When God touches our bodies, our estates, or our friends, he aims at the soul in all. God will never remove his hand, until something be wrought upon the soul. In sickness, or in any other trouble, it is best the divine should be before the physician, and that men begin where God begins. In great fires, men look first to the jewels, and then to their lumber; so our soul is our best jewel. A carnal, worldly man is called, and well called, a *fleshly* man, because his very soul is flesh, and there is nothing but the world in him. When all is not well within, he cries out, 'My body is troubled, my state is broken, my friends fail me.' But all the while, there is no care for the poor soul, to settle a peace there.

The possession of the soul is the richest possession, no jewel so precious. The account for our own souls and the souls of others, is the greatest account, and therefore the care of souls should be the greatest care. What an indignity it is that we should forget such souls to satisfy our lusts! To have our wills! To be vexed with any, who by their judgment, example, or authority, stop, as we suppose, our courses! Is it not the greatest plot in the world, first, to have their lusts satisfied; secondly, to remove, either by fraud or violence, whatever stands in their way; and, thirdly, to put colours and pretences upon this to delude the world and themselves. Employing all their carnal wit and worldly strength for their carnal aims, and fighting for that which fights against their own souls? For, what will be the issue of this but certain destruction?

*The Soul's Conflict with Itself, Works,* vol. 1, pp. 149-50

# Soul Care (2)

*And do not fear those who kill the body but cannot kill the soul. Rather fear him who can destroy both soul and body in hell.*—Matt. 10:28

We should set ourselves to have most care of that which God cares most for. That which he breathed into us at first, set his own image upon, gave so great a price for, and values above all the world besides. Will all our study be to satisfy the desires of the flesh, and neglect the soul?

Is it not a vanity to prefer the casket before the jewel, the shell before the pearl, the gilded potsherd before the treasure? Is it not much more vanity to prefer the outward condition before the inward? The soul is that which Satan and his has most spite at, for in troubling our bodies or estates, he aims at the vexation of our souls. As with Job, his aim was to abuse that power God had given him over his children, body, and goods, to cause Job, by a disquieted spirit, to blaspheme God. It is an ill method to begin our care in other things, and neglect the soul, as Ahithophel, who set his house in order, when he should have set his soul in order first (2 Sam. 17:23). Wisdom begins at the right end. See that all be well within, and then all troubles from without cannot much annoy us.

Grace will teach us to reason in this way—God has given my enemies power over my liberty and condition, but will they have power and liberty over my spirit? It is that which Satan most seeks for; but never yield. By not yielding a godly man will become more than a conqueror; when in appearance he is conquered, his spirit prevails, and is undaunted. A Christian is not subdued until his spirit is subdued. This torments the proud, worldly ones, to see godly men enjoy a calm and resolute frame of mind in the midst of troubles; when their enemies are more troubled in troubling them than they are in being troubled by them.

*The Soul's Conflict with Itself, Works,* vol. 1, pp. 150-51

# Aiming Our Complaints (1)

*Why are you cast down, O my soul, and why are you in turmoil within me? Hope in God; for I shall again praise him, my salvation and my God.*—Psa. 43:5

We see here how to frame our complaints. David complains not of God, nor of his troubles, nor of others, but of his own soul; he complains of himself to himself. As if he said, 'Though all other things be out of order, yet O my soul, you should not trouble me too, you should not betray yourself to troubles, but rule over them.' A godly man complains to God, yet not of God, but of himself. A carnal man is ready to justify himself and complain of God, he complains not to God, but of God. He complains of the grievance that lies upon him, but never regards what is amiss within himself. Openly he cries out about bad fortune, yet secretly he strikes at God; while he quarrels with that which is nothing, he attacks him that is the cause of all things. Like a man with gout who complains of his shoe, or an anguished man of his drink, when the cause is from within. Likewise, men are disquieted with others, when they should rather be disquieted and angry with their own hearts.

We condemn Jonah for contending with God, and justifying his unjust anger, yet the same risings are in men naturally if shame would allow them to give vent to their secret discontent. Their heart speaks what Jonah with his tongue spoke. Oh, but here we should lay our hand upon our mouth, and adore God, and command silence to our souls.

*The Soul's Conflict with Itself, Works*, vol. 1, p. 151

# Aiming our Complaints (2)

*But each person is tempted when he is lured and enticed by his own desire. Then desire when it has conceived gives birth to sin, and sin when it is fully grown brings forth death.*—James 1:14, 15

No man is hurt but by himself first. We are drawn to evil and allured from a true good to a false by our own lusts; 'God tempts no man' (James 1:13). Satan has no power over us further than we willingly lie open to him. Satan works upon our affections, and then our affections work upon our will. He does not work immediately upon the will. We must thank ourselves in willingly yielding to our own passions for all the ill Satan or his instruments draws us into. Saul was not vexed with an evil spirit (1 Sam. 16), until he gave way to his own evil spirit of envy. The devil did not enter Judas (Matt. 27:3), until his covetous heart made way for him. The apostle strengthens his convictions against rash and lasting anger by knowing that unrighteous anger is giving way to the devil (Eph. 4:27). It is a dangerous thing to pass from God's government and come under Satan's.

Satan mingles himself with our own passions, therefore we should blame ourselves first, be ashamed of ourselves more, and judge ourselves most severely. But self-love teaches us a contrary method, to transfer all to others, and it robs us of a right judgment of ourselves. Though we desire to know all diseases of the body by their proper names, yet we will conceive of sinful passions of the soul under milder terms; as lust under love, rage under just anger, murmuring under just displeasure, etc. Sin has not only made all creatures enemies to us, but ourselves the greatest enemies of all. We should begin our complaints against ourselves and discuss ourselves thoroughly. In all discouragements a godly man has most trouble with his own heart.

*The Soul's Conflict with Itself, Works, vol. 1, pp. 151-52*

# Wisdom for When We Excessively Grieve Over Sin

*Against you, you only, have I sinned and done what is evil in your sight, so that you may be justified in your words and blameless in your judgment.*—Psa. 51:4

When grieving for our sin becomes too much.

(1) Excessive grieving for our sin is wrong when it takes the soul from minding what it should and distracts us from the duties of our callings. Christ upon the cross was grieved to the utmost, yet it did not take away his care for his mother (John 19:26, 27). At times the grieving may be so extreme that all we can do is quietly submit to God and desire to be carried unto Christ by the prayers of others.

(2) We grieve over sin to an extreme when we forget the grounds of comfort and allow our mind to run only upon the present transgression. It is a sin to dwell on sin and turmoil our thoughts about it when we are called to be thankful for our forgiveness in Christ. Grief for sin often comes upon us during seasons when we should be expressing joy. God has made some days for joy, and joy is the proper work of those days. 'This is the day which the Lord has made' (Psa. 118:24). Some in a sick distemper desire that which increases their sickness; so some that are deeply cast down, desire whatever may cast them down more, when what they should do is meditate upon comforts, and get some sweet assurance of God's love. Joy is the constant temper which the soul should be in. 'Rejoice evermore' (1 Thess. 5:16). We should think of such truths as may raise up the soul and sweeten the spirit.

(3) We grieve too much when it inclines the soul to inconvenient courses. Excessive grief over sin is a poor counsellor, when either it hurts the health of our bodies, or draws the soul to ease itself by some unlawful liberty. When grief keeps such a noise in the soul, it doesn't allow the soul to hear what the messengers of God, or the still voice of the Spirit says. As in explosions, loud cries are scarce heard, so in such cases the soul will neither hear itself nor others. The fruit of this overmuch trouble of spirit is increase of trouble.

*The Soul's Conflict with Itself, Works,* vol. 1, pp. 156-57

# The Storms and Calms of Life

*I have said these things to you, that in me you may have peace. In the*
*world you will have tribulation. But take heart; I have overcome the*
*world.*—John 16:33

Here is the life of a Christian in this world. (1) He is in great danger
if he be not troubled at all. (2) When he is troubled, he is in danger to
be over-troubled. (3) When he has brought his soul in tune again, he is
subject to new troubles.

Between this ebbing and flowing there is very little quiet. Now
because this cannot be done without a great measure of God's Spirit, our
help is to make use of that promise of giving 'the Holy Spirit to them
that ask it' (Luke 11:13). It is the Spirit who will teach the heart how long,
and how much to grieve; and when, and how long, and how much to
rejoice. As the Spirit moved upon the waters before the creation, so he
must move upon the waters of our souls. For we do not have command
of our own hearts. Every man without the Spirit is carried away with his
flesh and passions, upon which the devil rides, and carries him wherever
the devil wishes. But a godly man is not a slave to his carnal affections.
The soul bred from heaven desires to be, like heaven, above all storms,
uniform, constant; not as things under the sun, which are always in
change, constant only in being inconstant. Affections are the wind of the
soul. The soul is carried as it should be, when it is neither so becalmed
that it moves not when it should, nor yet tossed with tempests to move
disorderly. Our affections must not rise to become unruly passions, for
then as a river that overflows its banks, they carry much slime and soil
with them. Though affections be the wind of the soul, yet unruly passions
are the storms of the soul, and will overturn all if they be not suppressed.
Even the best, if they do not steer their hearts aright, are in danger of
sudden gusts. A Christian must neither be a dead sea, nor a raging sea.
Instead, he does as David did and labours to bring into captivity the first
motions of sin in his heart (Psa. 51:1, 2).

*The Soul's Conflict with Itself, Works*, vol. 1, pp. 159-60

# Two Natures Within

*Or do you not know that your body is a temple of the Holy Spirit within*
*you, whom you have from God? You are not your own.*—1 Cor. 6:19

God, when he will humble a man, need not fetch forces from without. If he but let our own hearts loose, we will have trouble enough. If there were no enemy in the world, nor devil in hell, we carry enough within us, that, if it be let loose, will trouble us more than all the world besides.

We see the necessity of having something in the soul above itself. It must be a partaker of a more divine nature than itself; otherwise, when the most refined part of our souls, the very spirit of our minds, is out of frame, what will bring it in again? We must recognize in a godly man, a double self, one which must be denied, the other which must deny; one that breeds all the disquiet, and another that stills what the other has raised. The way to still our corrupt self, is not to parley with it, and divide government for peace's sake, as if we should gratify the flesh in something, to allow liberty to the spirit in other things; for we will find the flesh will be too encroaching. We must strive against it, not with subtlety and discourse, so much as with peremptory violence to silence and restrain it. An enemy that parleys will yield at length. Grace is nothing else but that blessed power by which our spiritual lives make progress against our carnal selves. Grace labours to win ground from the old man, until at length it be all in all. A good man has something in him that is wiser than himself, holier than himself, stronger than himself; there is something in him more than a man.

That which most troubles a good man in all troubles is himself, he is more disquieted with himself than with all troubles outside of himself. Where the spirit is enlarged, it cares not much for outward bondage; where the spirit is settled, it cares not much for outward changes; where the spirit is sound, it can bear outward sickness. Nothing can be very ill with us when all is well within.

*The Soul's Conflict with Itself, Works*, vol. 1, pp. 160-61

# Deal with Sin Quickly

*But each person is tempted when he is lured and enticed by his own desire. Then desire when it has conceived gives birth to sin, and sin when it is fully grown brings forth death.*—James 1:14, 15

It is best to prevent, as much as in us is possible, the very first risings of sinful passions, before the soul be overcast. Passions are but little motions at first, but grow as rivers do, greater and greater, the farther they are carried from their spring. The first risings must be looked to, because there is most danger in them, and we have least care over them. Sin, like rust, or a canker, will little by little eat out all the graces of the soul. All sin is easier kept out than driven out. If we cannot prevent wicked thoughts, yet we may deny them lodging in our hearts. What we are afraid to do before men, we should be afraid to think before God. It would much further our peace to keep our judgments clear, as being the eye of the soul, whereby we may discern in every action and passion what is good and what is evil. When the heart begins once to be kindled, it is easy to smother the smoke of passion, which otherwise will fume up into the head, and gather into so thick a cloud as we will lose the sight of ourselves and what is best to be done. Little risings neglected cover the soul before we are aware. If we would check these risings, and stifle them in their birth, they would not break out afterwards to the reproach of religion, to the grief of God's Spirit in us, to the disturbance of our own spirits in doing good, to the disheartening of us in the troubling of our inward peace, and the weakening of our assurance. Let us stop sin's beginnings as much as may be possible. So soon as they begin to rise, let us begin to examine what raised them, and where they are about to carry us (Psa. 4:4). The way to be still is to examine ourselves first, and then censure what stands not with reason. As David does, when he had given way to unbefitting thoughts of God's providence, 'So foolish was I,' he said, 'as a beast before you' (Psa. 73:22).

*The Soul's Conflict with Itself, Works,* vol. 1, p. 166

# The Comfort of Christian Friends (1)

*Two are better than one, because they have a good reward for their toil.*—Eccles. 4:9

It is a course that will have a blessing attending it, for friends to join in league, one to watch over another, and observe each other's ways. It is a usual course for Christians to join together in other holy duties, as hearing the word, receiving of the ordinances, and prayer; but this fruit of holy fellowship which arises from a mutual observing of one another is much lacking. This is why so many believers droop and are so uncheerful in the ways of God, and are groaning under the burden of many cares, and are battered with so many temptations, because they are left alone to their own spirits. What an unworthy thing it is that we should pity a beast overladen, and yet take no pity of a brother! There is no living member of Christ who does not have divine spiritual love infused into him and some ability to comfort others. Dead stones in an arch uphold one another, and will not the living stones? (1 Pet. 2:5). It is the office of the Holy Spirit to be the Comforter, not only immediately, but by breathing comfort into our hearts through the comforting words of others. There is a sweet sight of God in the face of a friend. God has promised a blessing to the functioning of the communion of saints performed by one private man towards another. Mercy shown to the souls of men is the greatest mercy, and wisdom in winning of souls is the greatest wisdom in the world, because the soul is the essence of the man, and upon the goodness of the soul the happiness of the whole man depends. What shining and flourishing Christians would we have if these duties were performed! As we have a portion in the communion of saints, so we should labour to have humility to take good from one another, and the wisdom and love to do good to one another. A Christian should have feeding lips and a healing tongue. The very words of the righteous have a curing virtue in them.

*The Soul's Conflict with Itself, Works,* vol. 1, pp. 191-92

# The Comfort of Christian Friends (2)

*For if they fall, one will lift up his fellow. But woe to him who is alone*
*when he falls and has not another to lift him up!*—Eccles. 4:10

Some will show a great deal of humanity in comforting others, but little Christianity; for as kind men they will utter some cheerful words, but as Christians they lack wisdom from above to speak a gracious word in season (2 Tim. 4:2). Nay, some there are who hinder the saving working of any affliction upon the hearts of others by unseasonable and unsavoury discourses, either by suggesting false remedies, or else diverting men to any false contentment, and so become spiritual traitors rather than friends. Happy is he that in his way to heaven meets with a cheerful and skilful guide and fellow traveller who carries cordials with him against any fainting of spirit. It is a part of our wisdom in salvation to choose such a one as may further us in our way. An indifference for any company shows a dead heart. How many have been refreshed by one short, apt, savoury speech, which has produced new spirits in them.

In ancient times, as we see in the story of Job, it was the custom of friends to meet together to comfort those who were in misery, and Job takes it for granted, that 'to him that is afflicted, pity should be showed from his friends' (Job 6:14). For besides the presence of a friend, which has some influence of comfort in it, friends can express loving affection which has a cherishing sweetness in it. Friends also can add wholesome words that bring comfort and peace to the heart of a troubled patient. When these actions of friends meet together in one, then is comfort sealed up to the soul. Sympathy has a strange force, as we see in the strings of an instrument, which being played upon, as they say, the strings of another instrument are also moved with it. After love has once kindled love, then the heart, being melted, is fit to receive any impression. Unless both pieces of the iron be red hot, they will not join together. Two spirits warmed with the same heat will easily solder together.

*The Soul's Conflict with Itself, Works*, vol. 1, pp. 192-93

# When Christians Find No Peace Within (1)

*Why are you cast down, O my soul, and why are you in turmoil within me? Hope in God; for I shall again praise him, my salvation and my God.*—Psa. 43:5

What if neither the words of others nor the rebuke of our own hearts, will quiet the soul? Is there no other remedy left? That is when we must look up to God, the father and fountain of comfort. It is what David did when he sought to recover himself by laying a charge upon his soul to trust in God.

(1) A Christian, when he is beaten out of all other comforts, yet has a God to run to. A wicked man beaten out of earthly comforts is as a naked man in a storm, or an unarmed man in the battlefield, or a ship tossed in the sea without an anchor which presently dashes upon rocks. But a Christian, when he is driven out of all comforts below, when God seems to be angry with him, he can appeal from God-angry to God-appeased. He can wrestle and strive with God by God's own strength, fight with him with his own weapons, and plead with God by his own arguments. What a happy state this is! A Christian has something to rely on when all else fails! There can never be any true, settled peace until the soul sees and resolves to rest upon God alone.

(2) We see here that there is a sanctified use of all troubles to God's children. First, they drive them out of themselves, and then draw them nearer to God. Crosses, indeed, of themselves estrange us more from God, but by an overruling work of the Spirit they bring us nearer to him. The soul of itself is ready to give up, as if God had too many controversies with him. Satan knows that nothing can stand and prevail against God, or a soul that relies on God, therefore he labours to breed and increase an everlasting division between God and the soul. Let Christians not muse so much upon their trouble, but see whither it carries them, whether it brings them nearer to God or not. This shows that one loves God, and is called of him, that they believe 'all things work together for the best' (Rom. 8:28).

*The Soul's Conflict with Itself, Works*, vol. 1, pp. 197-99

# When Christians Find No Peace Within (2)

*When I remember God, I moan; when I meditate, my spirit faints.*—
Psa. 77:3

(3) When the soul finds no rest the Spirit of God awakens the soul and keeps it in the holy pursuit of stirring up the grace of faith to its proper function. It is not so much the having of grace, as grace in exercise, that preserves the soul. We should 'stir up the grace of God in us' (2 Tim. 1:6), that it may be kept working in vigour and strength. It is the waking Christian, that has his attention and his grace ready about him, who is the safe Christian. Grace dormant, without the use of it, does not secure us. The soul without action is like an instrument not played upon, or like a ship always in the haven. Even life itself is made livelier by action. The Spirit of God, by whom his children are led, is compared to things of the quickest and strongest actions, as fire and wind. By stirring up the grace of God in us, sparkles come to be flames, and all graces are kept bright.

(4) We see another use of speaking to our own hearts. When the soul sees itself out of order, it then enjoins itself the duty of trusting in God. The soul works as it should, by reflecting on itself, gathering some profitable conclusion, and leaving itself with God. David, upon reflecting on himself, found nothing but discouragement; but when he looked upward to God, there he found rest. This is one reason why God allows the soul to tire and beat itself, that, finding no rest in itself, it might seek him. Let no man, truly religious, use as an excuse his temper or provoking circumstances, for grace raises the soul above nature. Though holy men be subject to 'like passions with others' (James 5:17), as it is said of Elijah, yet they are not so enthralled by them that they carry them wholly away from their God; but they hear a voice of the Spirit within them, calling them back to their former communion with God; and so grace takes occasion, even from sin, to exercise itself.

*The Soul's Conflict with Itself, Works*, vol. 1, p. 199

# When Christians Find No Peace Within (3)

*I will arise and go to my father, and I will say to him, 'Father, I have sinned against heaven and before you. I am no longer worthy to be called your son. Treat me as one of your hired servants.'*—Luke 15:18, 19

(5) Observe further, that distrust is the cause of all disquiet. The soul allows itself by something here below to be drawn away from God but can find no rest until it returns to him. It is God's mercy to us, that when we have let go of our hold of God, we should find nothing but trouble and unquietness in anything else, so that we might remember from where we have fallen and return home. It is a good trouble that brings us back to the most comfortable rest. It is but an unquiet quiet, and a restless rest which is out of God. The soul that has had a saving work upon it, will always be impatient until it recovers its former sweetness in God. After God's Spirit has once touched the soul, it will never be quiet until it stands pointed God-ward.

(6) It is no easy thing to bring God and the heart together. As one striving to get to the harbour in a storm is driven back by the waves, but recovering himself, gets forward still, and after much beating back, at length obtains the wished for and restful haven, so much and more is there to bringing the soul to God, the harbour of true comfort. It would be an easy thing to be a Christian if religion stood only in a few outward works and duties, but to take the soul to task, and to deal roundly with our own hearts, and to let conscience have its full work, and to bring the soul into spiritual subjection to God, this is not so easy a matter, because the soul out of self-love is loath to enter into itself, lest it should have other thoughts of itself than it would have. The soul so far as it is gracious commands, so far as it is rebellious resists. The soul naturally sinks downward, and therefore has need often to be wound up.

*The Soul's Conflict with Itself, Works,* vol. 1, pp. 199-201

# When Christians Find No Peace Within (4)

*You will keep in perfect peace those whose minds are steadfast, because they trust in you.*—Isa. 26:3

(7) We should therefore labour to bring our souls to a firm and peremptory resolution, and not remain wavering, as if it were equally balanced between God and other things. We must enforce our souls. We will get little ground over infidelity in no other way. Drive your souls to this issue, either to rely upon God, or else to yield up itself to the present grievance. If by yielding, it resolves to be miserable, there's an end, but if it desires rest, then let it resolve upon this only way, to trust in God. Well may the soul so resolve, because in God there are grounds of quieting the soul, above all that may unsettle it; in him there is for the soul both worth to satisfy, and strength to support. The best way to maintain inward peace is to settle and fix our thoughts upon that which will make us better, until we find our hearts warmed and wrought upon. Then, 'God will keep us in perfect peace' (Isa. 26:3). Come to this point once, trust God I ought, therefore, trust God I will, come what may. It is good to renew that resolution again and again: for every renewal brings the soul closer to God and brings fresh strength from him. If we neglect our resolution, our corruption, joining with outward hindrances, will carry us further backward, and this will multiply our trouble and grief. We have both wind and tide against us, we are going up hill, therefore, we need to arm ourselves with resolution. Since the fall, the motion of the soul upward is violent, because of our corruption which weighs it downward. If we resolve in God's power and not our own, and be 'strong in the Lord' (Eph. 6:10), and not in ourselves, then it matters not what our troubles or temptations are either from within or without, for trust in God at length will triumph. 'Turn us again,' said the psalmist, 'cause your face to shine upon us, and we will be saved' (Psa. 80:19).

*The Soul's Conflict with Itself, Works*, vol. 1, pp. 201-02

# When Christians Find No Peace Within (5)

*Why are you cast down, O my soul, and why are you in turmoil within me? Hope in God; for I shall again praise him, my salvation.*—Psa. 42:5

(8) David does not only resolve to turn to God, but presently takes up his soul before it strayed too far from God. The further and the longer the soul wanders from God, the more it entangles itself, and the thicker darkness will cover the soul, yea, the loather it is to come to God again, being ashamed to look God in the face after discontinuing our acquaintance with him; nay, the stronger the league grows between sin and the soul, and the more there grows a kind of suitableness between the soul and sin. If ever we mean to trust God, why not now? The sooner we give up ourselves to the Lord, the sooner we know upon what terms we stand, and the sooner we provide for our best security. Time will salve up grief in the meanest of men; reason, in those that will allow themselves to be ruled thereby, will cure, or at least stay the fits of it; but faith, if we stir it up, will give our souls no rest, until it has brought us to our true rest, that is, to God.

(9) Lastly, we see, that though the soul be overcome by passion for a time, yet if grace has once truly seasoned it, it will work itself into freedom again. Grace, as oil, will be above. The eye when any dust falls into it, is not more tender and unquiet, until the dust be removed, than a gracious soul is, being once troubled. The spirit, as a spring, will be cleansing of itself more and more. Whereas the heart of a carnal man is like a standing pool, whatever is cast into it, there it rests. Trouble and unquietness in him are in their proper place. God has set it down for an eternal rule, that vexation and sin will be inseparable. Happiness and rest were severed because of sin in heaven when the angels fell, and in paradise when Adam fell (Gen. 3) and will remain forever separated until the breach be made up by faith in Christ.

*The Soul's Conflict with Itself, Works,* vol. 1, p. 202

# God's Providence (1)

*He is before all things, and in him all things hold together.*—Col. 1:17

The consideration of God's continual providence is a great stay to our faith. It is good to know that God's providence is extended as far as his creation. Every creature, in every element and place receives a powerful influence from God, who does what pleases him, both in heaven and earth, in the sea, and all places. We must know that God does not put things into being, and then leave them to their own motion, as we do clocks, after we have once set them right, and ships, after we have once built them, commit them to wind and waves; but as he made all things, and knows all things, so, by a continued kind of creation, he preserves all things in their being and working, and governs them in their ends. He is the first mover that sets all the wheels of the creature working. One wheel may move another, but all are moved by the first. If God moves not, the clock of the creation stops. If God should not uphold things, they would presently fall to nothing, from where they came. If God should not guide things, Satan's malice, and man's weakness, would soon bring all to a confusion. The wise providence of God keeps everything on its right hinges. All things stand in obedience to this providence of God, and nothing can withdraw itself from under it. If man, the most unruly and disordered creature of all, withdraw himself from God's gracious government of him to happiness, he will soon fall under God's just government of him to deserved misery. If he shakes off God's sweet yoke, he puts himself under Satan's heavy yoke, who, as God's executioner, hardens him to destruction. While he rushes against God's will, he fulfils it; and while he will not willingly do God's will, God's will is done upon him against his will.

The most casual things fall under providence, yea, the most disordered thing in the world, sin, and, of sins the most horrible that ever the sun beheld, the 'crucifying of the Lord of life' (Acts 3:15), was guided by a hand of providence to the greatest good.

*The Soul's Conflict with Itself, Works, vol. 1, pp. 204-05*

# God's Providence (2)

*The king's heart is a stream of water in the hand of the Lord; he turns it wherever he will.*—Prov. 21:1

Though man has a freedom in working, and of all men the hearts of kings are most free, yet even these are guided by an overruling power (Prov. 21:1), as the rivers of water are carried in their channels wherever skilful men divert them.

There is nothing so high, that is above his providence; nothing so low, that is beneath it; nothing so large, but is bounded by it; nothing so confused, but God can order it; nothing so bad, but he can draw good out of it; nothing so wisely plotted, but God can disappoint it; nothing so simply and poorly carried out, but he can give a prevailing success to it; nothing so natural, but he can suspend it in regard of operation, as heavy bodies from sinking and fire from burning.

It cannot but bring strong security to the soul, to know that in all variety of changes and intertwining of good and bad events, our God has a disposing hand. Whatsoever befalls us, all serves to bring God's electing love, and our glorification. God's providence serves his purpose to save us. All sufferings, all blessings, all graces, all common gifts, nay, our very falls, yea, Satan himself with all his instruments, as over-mastered, and ruled by God, have this injunction upon them, to further God's good intentions to us, and a prohibition to do us harm. Augustus taxed the world for civil ends, but God's providence used this as a means for Christ to be born at Bethlehem (Luke 2:4). Xerxes could not sleep and calls for the chronicles, the reading of which occasioned the deliverance of the Jews (Esth. 6:1). God often disposes little occasions to great purposes. Proud men have tried to withstand God's counsels, but they actually fulfilled them, as we see in the stories of Joseph and Moses and those who sought to harm them.

*The Soul's Conflict with Itself, Works,* vol. 1, pp. 205-07

# God's Providence (3)

*All the inhabitants of the earth are accounted as nothing, and he does according to his will among the host of heaven and among the inhabitants of the earth; and none can stay his hand or say to him, 'What have you done?'*—Dan. 4:35

God's ways seem often to us full of contradictions because his course is to bring things to pass by contrary means. There is a mystery not only in God's decree concerning man's eternal state, but likewise in his providence, as why he should deal unequally with men otherwise equal. His judgments are a great depth, which we cannot fathom, they will swallow up our thoughts and understandings. God often wraps himself in a cloud and will not be seen until afterward. Where we cannot trace him, we ought, with Paul, to admire and adore him. When we are in heaven, it will be one part of our happiness to see the harmony of those things that seem now confused to us. All God's dealings will appear beautiful in their due seasons, though we for the present see not the continuity and linking together of one with another.

The way to submit patiently to God's will is to be in the habit of doing so. He that endures anything will endure it quietly, when he knows it is the will of God, and considers that whatever befalls him comes from his good pleasure. Those that have not accustomed themselves to the yoke of obedience, will never endure the yoke of suffering; they fume and rage 'as a wild boar in a net' (Isa. 51:20). It is worth the considering, to see two men of equal parts under the same cross, how quietly and calmly the one that establishes his soul on Christ will bear his afflictions, whereas the other rages as a fool, and is more beaten.

Let us lay our hand upon our mouths, and command the soul to holy silence, not daring to yield to the least rising of our hearts against God. David said, 'I was dumb, and opened not my mouth, because you did it' (Psa. 39:9). In this silence and hope is our strength.

*The Soul's Conflict with Itself, Works, vol. 1, pp. 207-08*

# God's Providence (4)

*The Lord has established his throne in the heavens, and his kingdom rules over all.*—Psa. 103:19

Nothing should displease us that pleases God, and neither should anything be pleasing to us that displeases him. This conformity is the ground of comfort. 'If we acknowledge God in all our ways, he will direct our paths, and lead us the way that we should go' (Prov. 3:6). The quarrel between God and us is removed when his will and our will are one; when we have sacrificed ourselves and our wills to God; when, as he is highest in himself, so his will has the highest place in our hearts. We find by experience that, when our wills are so subdued, that we delight to do what God would have us do, and to be what God would have us be, then sweet peace presently rises to the soul.

When we can say, 'Lord, if you will have me poor and disgraced, I am content to be so. If you will have me serve you in this condition I am in, I will gladly do so. It is enough to me that you would have it so. I desire to yield readily, humbly, and cheerfully to your disposing providence.' A godly man says amen to God's amen and puts his will and assent to God's. As the sea turns all rivers into its own relish, so he turns all and makes whatsoever befalls him an exercise of some virtue. A heathen could say that calamities did rule over men, but a wise man has a spirit overruling all calamities, much more a Christian. For a man to be in this state, is to enjoy heaven in the world under heaven. God's kingdom comes where his will is thus done.

It is good to observe the particular signals and signs of providence, how things join and meet together. Fit occasions and suiting of things are intimations of God's will. Providence has a language which is well understood by those that have a familiar acquaintance with God's dealing; they see a train of providence leading one way more than to another.

*The Soul's Conflict with Itself, Works*, vol. 1, pp. 208-11

# The Nature, Providence, and Promises of God

*By which he has granted to us his precious and very great promises, so that through them you may become partakers of the divine nature, having escaped from the corruption that is in the world because of sinful desire.*—2 Pet. 1:4

For the better settling of our trust in God, a further discovery is necessary than of the nature and providence of God; for though the nature of God is written in the book of creation in such great letters, as he that runs may read, and though the providence of God appears in the order and use of all things, there is another book whereby we know the will of God towards us, and our duty towards him. We must have a knowledge of the promises of God. For though God has revealed himself most graciously in Christ, yet had we not a word of promise, we could not have the boldness to build upon Christ. From the same reasoning that there must be a God, there must also be a revealing of the will of God. For how else can we ever have any firm trust in him without him offering himself to be trusted? Therefore God has opened his heart to us in his word, and reached out to us by many sweet promises for us to lay hold on. For promises are the stay of the soul in an imperfect condition, and so is faith in them until all promises end in performance, and faith in sight, and hope in possession.

Note of these promises: (1) The spring from whence they proceed—the free engagements of God, for if he had not bound himself, who could? (2) Their value—precious. (3) Their extent—large, even to include all things that contribute to true happiness. (4) The benefit they produce—quickening and strengthening to the soul. (5) Their certainty—as sure as the love of God in Christ is, upon which they are founded, and from which 'nothing can separate us' (Rom. 8:39). For all promises are either Christ himself, the promised seed, or else they are the good things made to us in him and for him and accomplished for his sake.

*The Soul's Conflict with Itself, Works*, vol. 1, p. 212

# Remember and Tell

*Come and hear, all you who fear God, and I will tell what he has done*
*for my soul.*—Psa. 66:16

For our better encouragement in these sad times, and to help our trust in God, we should often call to mind the former experiences, which either ourselves or others have had of God's goodness, and make use of them for our spiritual good. As the Psalmist did, 'our fathers trusted in you and were not confounded' (Psa. 22:4). God's truth and goodness is unchangeable, 'he never leaves those that trust in him' (Psa. 9:10). Likewise, in our own experiences, we should take notice of God's countless dealings with us, how many ways he has refreshed us, and how good we have found him in our worst times. After we have once tried him and his truth, we may safely trust him. God will stand upon his credit, he never failed any yet, and he will not begin to break with us. If his nature and his word and his former dealing have been sure and square, why should our hearts waver? 'Your word' wrote the Psalmist, 'is well tried, therefore your servant loves it' (Psa. 119:140). The word of God is 'as silver tried in the furnace, purified seven times' (Psa. 12:6). Experience is nothing else but a multiplied remembrance of former blessings, which will help to multiply our faith. Tried truth and tried faith in truth, sweetly agree, and answer one another. It strengthens the faith of Christians when they would communicate to each other their mutual experiences. This has formerly been the custom of God's people, 'Come and hear, all you that fear God, and I will declare what he has done for my soul' (Psa. 66:16); and David urges this as a reason for the deliverance that came from God's hand. Then 'the righteous would encompass him about' (Psa. 142:7), to rejoice in the experience of God's goodness to him. The want of this makes us upon any new trial, to call God's care and love into question, as if he had never formerly been good to us. Every experience of God's love should refresh our faith for any new onset of trouble or distress.

*The Soul's Conflict with Itself, Works*, vol. 1, pp. 216-17

# Death—the Greatest Trial of Trust

*For if we live, we live to the Lord, and if we die, we die to the Lord. So then, whether we live or whether we die, we are the Lord's.*—Rom. 14:8

The greatest trial of trust is in our last encounter with death, where we will find not only a deprivation of all comforts in this life, but a confluence of all ill at once. But we must know that God will be the God of his own unto death, and not only unto death, but in death. We may trust God the Father with our bodies and souls which he has created; and God the Son with the bodies and souls which he has redeemed; and the Holy Spirit with those bodies and souls that he has sanctified. We are not disquieted when we take off our clothes and go to bed, because we trust God's providence to raise us up again. Why should we be disquieted when we take off our bodies and sleep our last sleep, considering we are more sure to rise out of our graves than out of our beds? We are raised up already in Christ our Head, 'who is the resurrection and the life' (John 11:25), in whom we may triumph over death. Death is the death of itself, and not of us.

In regard of our state after death, a Christian need not be disquieted, for the angels are ready to do their office in carrying his soul to paradise, to those 'mansions prepared for him' (John 14:2). His Saviour will be his judge, and the Head will not condemn the members; then he is to receive the fruit and end of his faith, the reward of his hope. How strong are the helps we possess that uphold our faith in those great things! Does he not keep our place for us? Is not our flesh there in him and his Spirit below with us? Have we not some first-fruits and earnest of it beforehand? Whatever we experience in this world that comes between us and heaven, such as desertions, inward conflicts, outward troubles, and death at last; are not all of these making us fit for a better condition hereafter, and by faith to stir up a strong desire for it? 'Comfort one another with these things' (1 Thess. 4:18).

*The Soul's Conflict with Itself, Works*, vol. 1, pp. 241-42

# The Christian's Privileged Position

*And God is able to make all grace abound to you, so that having all sufficiency in all things at all times, you may abound in every good work.*—2 Cor. 9:8

Do not lose any measure of the comfort that is found in the sweet privilege that whatsoever is in God is mine. If I am in a perplexed condition, his wisdom is mine; if in great danger, his power is mine; if I be sighing under the burden of sin, his grace is mine; if in any want, his all-sufficiency is mine. 'My God,' said Paul, 'will supply all your wants' (Phil. 4:19). What is religion but a spiritual bond whereby the soul is tied to God as its own. 'Lord, you have made yourself to be mine, therefore show yourself and be exalted in your goodness and power, for my defence. I need wisdom to go in and out innocently before others, furnish me with your Spirit. You who are the God of all consolation, bestow it on me.' In time of desertion put Christ between God and your soul and learn to appeal to God in Christ. 'Lord, look upon my Saviour, your Son who is near you and near to me as my brother, and who now intercedes at your right hand for me.' When we are in any trouble, let us wait on him, and never let him go until he casts a gracious look upon us.

Further, when we can say, God is our God, it is more than if we could say, heaven is mine; or whatever good this world can give is mine. If God be ours, goodness itself is ours. If he be not ours, though we had all things else, yet before long nothing would be ours. What a wondrous comfort is this, that God has made it possible for him to be ours! A believing soul may say with greater confidence that God is his than he can say his house is his, his treasure is his, or his friends are his! Nothing is so much ours as God is ours, because by his being ours in covenant; and if God be once ours, well may we trust in him that he will always be. God and us, being united by grace, makes up the full comfort of a Christian.

*The Soul's Conflict with Itself, Works,* vol. 1, pp. 271-72

# God Gives Us Himself

*My flesh and my heart may fail, but God is the strength of my heart and my portion forever.*—Psa. 73:26

In the division of things, God gives himself to those who are his and when he does, he gives the best portion he could possibly give. There are many good things in the world, but none of these are a Christian's portion. God supplies all earthly good until the time comes that we stand in need of no other good outside of him. It is our chief wisdom to know him, our holiness to love him, our happiness to enjoy him. There is in him to be had whatever can truly make us happy. We go to our treasure and our portion in all our wants; we live by it and value ourselves by it. God is such a portion, that the more we spend on him the more we may. 'Our strength may fail, and our heart may fail, but God is our portion forever' (Psa. 73:26). Everything else teaches us, by the vanity and vexation we find in them, that our happiness is not in them. They send us to God; they may make us worse, but they cannot make us better. If God be once ours, he goes forever along with us, and when earth will hold us no longer, heaven will. Who that has his senses about him would perish for want of water when there is a fountain by him? Or for hunger when there is at a feast? God alone is a rich portion. O, then, let us labour for a large faith, as we have a large object. When the prophet came to the widow's house, as many vessels as she had were filled with oil (1 Kings 17:14). We are limited in our own faith, but not limited in our God. It happens often in this world that God's people are like Israel at the Red Sea, surrounded with dangers on all sides. What course have we to take, but only to look up and wait for the salvation of our God? Here is great consolation; let us teach our hearts to draw comfort from it.

*The Soul's Conflict with Itself, Works*, vol. 1, pp. 273-74

# God—the Chief Good

*Why are you cast down, O my soul, and why are you in turmoil within me? Hope in God; for I shall again praise him, my salvation and my God.—Psa. 42:11*

We should seek for no blessing of God so much as for himself.

What is there in the world of equal goodness to draw us away from our God? If to preserve the dearest thing we have in the world, we break with God, God will take away the comfort we look to have by it, and it will prove but a dead contentment, if not a torment to us. Whereas, if we care to preserve communion with God, we will be sure to find in him whatsoever we deny for him, honour, riches, pleasures, friends, all; so much the sweeter, by how much we have the more immediately from the spring-head. We will never find God to be our God more than when, for making of him to be so, we suffer anything for his sake. We enjoy never more of him than then.

At the first we may seek him because he is rich to supply our wants, or as a physician to cure our souls and bodies; but here we must not rest until we come to rejoice in him as our friend, and from there rise to an admiration of him for his own excellencies. We should delight in the meditation of him, not only as good to us, but as good in himself; because goodness of bounty springs from goodness of disposition. He does good because he is good.

A natural man delights more in God's gifts than in his grace. But, alas! what are all other goods, without the chief good? They are but as flowers, which are long in planting and growing, but short in enjoying the sweetness of them. David joys in God himself; he cares for nothing in the world but what he may have with his favour; and whatever else he desires he desires only that he may have the better ground from where to praise his God (Psa. 42:11).

*The Soul's Conflict with Itself, Works,* vol. 1, p. 278

# Looking to God's Provision

*I trust in the Lord that shortly I myself will come also.*—Phil. 2:24

God's providence extends to every particular thing. He guides our incomings and our outgoings; he disposes of our journeys; his providence extends to the smallest things, to the sparrows and to the hair of our heads; he governs every particular passage of our lives.

This should teach us to set upon our affairs with looking up to heaven for permission, power, and endurance. James enforces this by reproving the contrary, 'Come now, you who say, "Today or tomorrow we will go,"' he adds for our instruction, 'instead you ought to say, "If the Lord wills we will live and do this or that"' (James 4:13-15). Let us therefore in all our affairs be holy, and not bind or limit our holiness only to coming to church; but seeing at all times and in all places we are Christians, and ever in the presence of God, let us place ourselves always in his eye, and do nothing but that we would be willing God to see; and labour to behold him in every good thing we have, and give him thanks in all the good we enjoy.

It also should give us warning, that we ought not to set upon anything, wherein we cannot expect God's guidance; and so consequently cannot trust on him for a blessing upon what we do. For if we do, we must look to meet the Lord standing in our way, as Balaam did, in opposing our lewd and wicked intentions.

It also ought to teach us to take nothing but that for which we may give God the thanks and praise; as contrarily many do, who may thank the devil for what they have gotten, and yet make God implicitly the giver of their most unjust transactions.

*Of the Providence of God, Works,* vol. 5, pp. 35-36

# God's Ministers (1)

*I have thought it necessary to send to you Epaphroditus my brother and*
*fellow worker and fellow soldier.*—Phil. 2:25

Paul calls Epaphroditus his 'fellow labourer,' in regard of the pains he endured; and 'fellow soldier,' in regard of the perils and dangers he jointly did undergo with the apostle. The doctrine that arises is, that ministers are fellow labourers. They are not, or should not be, fellow loiterers, as many are. The Scriptures compare them to the most painful and laborious professions; to farmers, whose labour is circular, every year renewing as the year does renew. Such is the ministers' labour, converting and strengthening others. It is a great labour to break the shell of the word; to lay open the right interpretation. It is as the peril of women in travail; 'My little children, of whom I travail in birth till Christ be formed in you' (Gal. 4:19).

If ministers are labourers, you to whom we preach are God's orchard; you must submit yourselves to be wrought on. If ministers are farmers, you must be the 'ground,' and such ground that brings forth fruit to perfection, or else all their labour and pains are in vain (Heb. 6:7). If ministers are builders, you must be lively stones of this building. You must suffer yourselves to be squared, and cut, and made fit for this building while you are here.

It is observable here, that he doesn't allow his faithful labourers to be alone. Christ sends them out by 'two and two' (Mark 6:7). So that they might be a mutual aid, strengthening and comforting one another. It is what Christ did in the old times, and it is what he does in these later times. Observe God's wisdom in sending men of diversity of gifts: Jerome, severe and powerful; Augustine, meek and gentle; Luther, hot and fiery; Melanchthon, of a soft and mild spirit; one to temper the other's over-forwardness, and thereby to prevail with some that didn't like the strictness of the other. By this means God sent teachers suitable to the natures and fitting the several humours of men, among whom some desire to hear the 'sons of consolation,' others the 'sons of thunder.'

*Of the Providence of God, Works, vol. 5, pp. 37-38*

# God's Ministers (2)

*We destroy arguments and every lofty opinion raised against the knowledge of God and take every thought captive to obey Christ.—* 2 Cor. 10:5

Every man's life is a warfare, but most of all and above all, the minister is continually in war and strife. They are soldiers, leaders; they carry the standard. They of all others are in the most danger, they stand in the brunt of the battle. The reason: the devil has malice against the whole church in general, but he specially aims at those who pull men out of his service into the church. It is the minister that treads on the serpent's head: no marvel, then, if the devil endeavours to bite them by the heel. It is how he dealt with Christ when he first set upon his office of mediator; also, how he dealt with Moses and Paul, in the main plots contrived against them. Such as those are great eyesores to Satan, and this it is that makes them soldiers and captains. But how? I answer, as Paul did in 2 Corinthians 10:4, 5, that ministers do fight against the strongholds of corruption within us, against natural reason, corrupt affections, proud conceits; they fight against these imaginations, and in them, against the devil himself, who uses these instruments to bring his purposes to pass. In ministers, it is required they be knowledgeable in the stratagems of the devil, especially in those among whom they should serve; by observing the corruptions of the times, place, and customs. He who would be a good soldier must be continually resident in his charge; for once the devil gets a hold, he seeks to sing them asleep with 'Soul, you have much goods' (Luke 12:19). This is dangerous. The minister must look to it; for men do soothe themselves up in pleasure, thinking that religion may well abide with the love of the world. The watchman must tell them plainly, 'You cannot serve God and mammon' (Matt. 6:24).

If ministers be soldiers for us, let us help them by our prayers. Seeing we are here in a working state, no, in a warring state.

*Of the Providence of God, Works,* vol. 5, pp. 38-39

# Why Sickness?

*For he [Epaphroditus] has been longing for you all and has been distressed because you heard that he was ill.*—Phil. 2:26

Observe here how one wave follows another. After Epaphroditus had endured a long and dangerous voyage, he meets with a long and dangerous sickness. It is the nature of us. Let us not dream of any immunity. God's children are subject to sicknesses while they live. Daily experience proves it. Their heaven is not here. As the outward man is weakened, so is the inward man renewed (2 Cor. 4:16). For by sickness we are put in mind to make even our accounts with God, and by it he also makes the pleasures of this world to be bitter to us, that we may the more willingly part with them.

(1) God often allows his children to come to extremities, yea, even to death itself. He allowed Hezekiah, Job, Jonah, David, Daniel, and the 'three in the furnace' to run into the jaws of death. By this it comes to pass that when all natural and ordinary means fail God's children, their trust is not placed on the means, but on some more durable and constant help, upon God's own good will and power. God is jealous of our affections.

(2) God allows his children to fall into extremities, to the end that having experienced God's helping hand in them, we might come to rely more confidently on him in all adversities. He allows us to receive the sentence of death in us, to the end that we should not trust in ourselves, but in God (2 Cor. 1:9). For God is never nearer than in extremities.

(3) God allows us to fall into extremities that he might try what is in us, and that he might exercise the graces in us. Afflictions are called trials because they try our graces. For if it were not for them, we should not know what faith, patience, hope, or grace are.

(4) Sickness causes the communion between God and us to be more sincere. For when there is nothing to rely on, that is when we come sensibly and experimentally to taste, see, and feel God's comfort. When ordinary helps fail, God's help begins.

*Of the Providence of God, Works,* vol. 5, pp. 40-41

# Before Sickness (1)

*Indeed he was ill, near to death. But God had mercy on him, and not only on him but on me also, lest I should have sorrow upon sorrow.*—Phil. 2:27

Seeing then we cannot avoid sickness nor death, let us consider briefly how to fit ourselves for it beforehand.

(1) Before sickness labour to make God your friend, who is Lord of life and death. Is there any hope of pardon for a prisoner who abuses the judge continually? How can he imagine that a man who all his lifetime followed his own wilful courses of sin, and persecuted, by scandalizing and slandering good men; who continually blasphemed God and abused him by his words; how can this man think to demand comfort in sickness? How can he think God will be pleased with him? No. All such repentance in sickness may justly be suspected to be hypocritical, that it is made rather for fear of punishment than loathing of sin. God often leaves such men to despair. See what he said in Proverbs 1:25, 26, 'Because I have called, and you refused; I have stretched out my hand, and no man regarded; I will laugh at your calamity, and mock when your fear comes.' It is just with God, seeing when he called you would not answer, that when you call, he should not answer. Be wise therefore to foresee the time to come.

(2) If you would find comfort in your sickness, disease not your soul beforehand. Those that will avoid sickness, they will abstain from such meats and other things as may increase their malady. Let it be thus in our soul sickness; find what you are sick from and take heed of hunting after such temptations and occasions as may inflame your soul. Take away the strength and power of sickness.

(3) Wean your affections from the earth or else when any cross comes, we will not be able to endure. In what proportion a man loves this world too much, in that proportion he grieves too much at his departure from it. It is an easy matter for one to die who has died in heart and affection already. Consider the uncertainty and vanity of these things, and how unable they will be to help you when you will stand most in need of help.

*Of the Providence of God, Works*, vol. 5, pp. 42

# Before Sickness (2)

*The Lord sustains him on his sickbed; in his illness you restore him to full health.*—Psa. 41:3

(4) Make up your accounts daily, that when sickness and weakness come, we have not our greatest and most laborious work to do. It is an atheistic folly to put off all until sickness, whereas they know not but God may call them by sudden death, or if he warns them by sickness, God may suffer their understanding and senses to be so troubled as they shall neither be able to conceive or judge. What madness it is to put off our hardest works to our weakest state.

(5) While you are in health, lay a foundation and ground of comfort for sickness; and still be doing something that may testify of the reconciliation between God and you. A good death is ever laid in a good life. We spend all our wits and powers to get a little worldly capital; and will we think to go to heaven, and to be carried there through pleasures and ease? It is the good that we do in our health that comforts us in our sickness, by considering how it has pleased God not only to put into our minds but into our wills to do this or that good. We think of it as an evidence of God's Spirit in us. Contrarily, when we think how brave our appearance has been, how gallant our company, what pleasing plays and spectacles we have seen, how can this comfort us? Will it not discomfort us to consider we have spent our means and time unprofitably; we have delighted in worldly delights? How shall I account with that just Judge for my time and means ill spent? Does not this argue want of grace, want of God's Spirit? Be wise therefore with Joseph against times of famine, of sickness, of death; prepare such cordials as may strengthen you.

*Of the Providence of God, Works,* vol. 5, pp. 42-43

# When Sick (1)

*Come, let us return to the Lord; for he has torn us, that he may heal us;*
  *he has struck us down, and he will bind us up.*—Hos. 6:1

Consider how we are to behave ourselves in sickness.

(1) Know and consider, 'Sickness comes not from the dust' (Job 5:6); but consider your ways, especially your antecedent course of life, which of late you have passed over right before your sickness. For God corrects not for sin in general so much as for the sin that rules. If it appears not, pray to God to help you in your search: and when you have found out the Achan that troubles you, then judge yourself and justify God.

(2) 'Judge yourselves, that you be not judged of the Lord' (1 Cor. 11:31); lay yourself open by confession; renew your repentance, and confess yourself thoroughly, and spare not yourself. It is cruelty to be merciful to yourself in this thing. And justify God; say with the holy prophet, 'Just are you, O Lord, and righteous are your judgments' (Psa. 119:75). God uses it as a messenger to call us to meet with him. Until David confessed his sin, 'his bones waxed old with roaring, and his moisture was turned to the drought of summer.' But when he confessed his sins, 'You forgave the iniquity of my sin' (Psa. 32:3-5). For indeed the sickness of the body begins from the iniquity of the soul. Begin with it; look to heal it, and comfort in your bodily state will follow.

(3) Look for the evidence of comfort. Desire God to witness to your soul his peace; and upon every warning of sickness, look for your evidence afresh. This will strengthen you as it did Job. Whatever discomforts he saw, 'yet I know my Redeemer lives, and that I will see him' (Job 19:26).

(4) Labour for love. Consider how the world is with us. Begin with justice, in giving every man his own, and then with bounty; then forgive. We cannot go to heaven with anger. It is what Christ did, 'Father, forgive them' (Luke 23:34); and Stephen, 'Lord, lay not this sin to their charge' (Acts 7:60). Be far from revenge. This is hard to fleshly minds, but it must be done.

*Of the Providence of God, Works*, vol. 5, pp. 43-44

# When Sick (2)

*Even though I walk through the valley of the shadow of death, I will fear no evil, for you are with me; your rod and your staff, they comfort me.*—Psa. 23:4

(5) Labour for patience. Consider that the sickness is from God, who is powerful. We will get nothing by striving or murmuring; he will have his will fulfilled in us. Then consider it comes from God, who is your Father who loves you. Know also, that all the circumstances of your sickness are ordered by him, the degree and time are limited by him, he knows what is needful and fitting. Consider that you deserve much worse; cast yourself on his mercy. Consider what will be the fruit and end of all troubles, even the quiet fruits of righteousness. Though it be bitter, God is working my good. Though I feel it not now, later I will in his good time.

(6) Be heavenly-minded, thinking on nothing but that which may bring spiritual comfort. It is not fit that our minds should be on earthly things when our souls are going to heaven. If we would have a pattern of dying well, look on Christ; before his death, when he was troubled, he would have his disciples with him. So, when we are vexed with any temptation or trial, use such company as may bring spiritual comfort and strength to us. As Christ left his peace behind him (John 14:27), let us seek to preserve peace after our departure. As Christ studied how to do all his work, we should endeavour to do what we have to do, that with a clear conscience we may say as Christ did, 'Father, I have done the work you gave me to do' (John 17:4). Christ cared for his disciples and friends and his mother before he died (John 15:26; 19:27). We also ought to be careful for the well-leaving of them whom God has committed to our care. Christ was not vindictive; 'Father, forgive them' (Luke 23:34). So, we must forgive all the world, yea, our enemies. Lastly, Christ commends his soul to God, 'Father, into your hands I commend my spirit' (Luke 23:46). We ought to imitate him and die in faith. When we die, we will die with comfort.

*Of the Providence of God, Works,* vol. 5, pp. 44-45

# Whether We Live or Die All Is God's Mercy

*For if we live, we live to the Lord, and if we die, we die to the Lord. So then, whether we live or whether we die, we are the Lord's.*—Rom. 14:8

God's mercy extends to this temporal life. We think his mercy is only for things that belong to the life everlasting. No! The same love and mercy that gives us heaven, is the same that gives us our daily bread. It is the same faith we have in God for the things of this life that we have in him for the other life in heaven. So did the saints before us, as we see in Hebrews 11.

Life is to be desired as a blessing from God that we might do good; for after death we are receivers only, and not doers. All the good we convey to others we must do it while we live here. It is not unlawful to desire to live to see your children brought up in the fear of God, and yet let that be with a resignation to God's will and purpose. If you be well, rejoice in it, and count it as God's blessing. If you be sick, patiently submit yourself to God's will, and count it as his merciful dealing with you. As we look on death being an enemy to our nature, and a destroyer, we desire it not. Yet, considering it as God's decree and will, say still, 'Your will be done, O Lord, and not mine.' Paul considered for himself it was better to die, but looking to the Philippians, 'nevertheless, to abide in the flesh is better for you' (Phil. 1:24). Learn the sweet state of God's children; whether we live or die, all is mercy; and this we have by being assured that we are in the covenant of grace. Labour therefore to find an interest therein for yourself. God does good to us in this life by others. Let us therefore praise him for parents, friends, benefactors; for by them God has mercy on us. God uses man for the good of man, that he might knit the communion of saints together more straightly. We ought to acknowledge God's mercy on us, by taking mercy on others.

*Of the Providence of God, Works*, vol. 5, pp. 46-47

# Risking Our Lives for Christ's Work

*For he nearly died for the work of Christ, risking his life to complete what was lacking in your service to me.—Phil. 2:30*

For the work of Christ, Epaphroditus was nigh to death. This work of Christ especially aims at works of mercy to Paul while he was in prison and his long and tedious journey. From these he took a sickness, and thereby was nigh to death. These are called 'the works of Christ' because in the doing of them the aim is Christ's honour. All our actions must be done with having an eye on and a respect to Christ. What if you do any good thing with an eye on credit, or to get popular applause or a good name, without respect of Christ's command, example, and obedience? All that you do in this manner cannot merit the name of a work of Christ. Let us do all things commanded in the second table of the Ten Commandments, as in obedience of the first, to glorify God. Let us do good works thoroughly, though they cost us labour, money, and danger. 'Cursed is he that does the work of the Lord negligently' (Jer. 48:10). Give freely to everyone that Christ sends to you a-begging. 'This is pure religion before God and undefiled, to visit the fatherless and widows' (James 1:27). These things done as they ought to be, will comfort us on our deathbed, and be an assurance to our consciences of our faith.

It may seem Paul was ill advised of the work of Epaphroditus, that he called it a work of Christ, when it might have cost him his life. Yet it ought not to seem strange, for by this very pattern we learn not to avoid or fly from the doing of any work of Christ, though by doing of it we incur danger of our lives. For the best good must take the chief and first place with us; and by how much the soul is more excellent than the body, by so much is the good of the soul to be preferred before the good of the body. God would have us exercise our judgments in these things beforehand, that we may go about all such things with a holy and zealous resolution.

*Of the Providence of God, Works, vol. 5, pp. 51-52*

# Persecution and Martyrdom (1)

*Blessed are you when others revile you and persecute you and utter all kinds of evil against you falsely on my account. Rejoice and be glad, for your reward is great in heaven, for so they persecuted the prophets who were before you.*—Matt. 5:11, 12

Questions concerning times of persecution:

(1) Whether we ought to lose our lives or deny the truth? To this I answer: We ought rather to lose our lives than deny the truth; for God's truth is better than our lives. It was commendable in Priscilla and Aquila that they laid down their necks for Paul's life (Rom. 16:3, 4); much more is the truth of God's word to be esteemed above man's life. They are counted wise that have this esteem; as the martyrs, whose state is accounted a blessed state.

(2) Whether a minister ought to leave his congregation in the time of pestilence, or not? I answer: Upon the same ground as above, he ought not; for he is not, in regard of the work of God, to esteem his own life. But he is not bound to a particular visitation of everyone whom it has pleased God to visit with sickness, neither ought the sick party to require this at the hands of the pastor; but rather to reserve him to the general good of all of them, and to spare him. In the law the leprous person was to go about and to cry 'Unclean, unclean' to the end that others might not unawares be polluted by him.

(3) Whether a man may equivocate to save his own life? I answer: If a man be lawfully called to answer for himself, he must know that he ought to tell the truth, and not to be ashamed thereof. Why do men live but to live honestly, and to keep a good conscience? It is more necessary that truth should flourish and be cleared than that you should live. Those that now are ashamed to confess the truth, the God of truth will be ashamed of them hereafter.

*Of the Providence of God, Works*, vol. 5, pp. 52-53

# Persecution and Martyrdom (2)

*Then they will deliver you up to tribulation and put you to death, and*
*you will be hated by all nations for my name's sake.*—Matt. 24:9

(4) Whether a man may break out of prison to save himself? I answer: You ought not to do anything that may endanger another man to save your own life. You may not, by breaking out of prison, endanger the jailor's life to save yourself. For it shames the truth of your cause. When the prison doors were opened Paul would not fly (Acts 16:28). Peter did it indeed, he came out of prison; but it was an extraordinary and miraculous deliverance by the command of the angel (Acts 12:11). Also, it is a contempt of the government and the law; for every man is to be governed by and to submit himself to the law.

(5) Whether a minister may flee from persecution? I answer: We may flee for our own safety; and a minister may, if there be those good shepherds left who will stand for the flock, that it be not scattered. Yet if God gives you a spirit of courage to hold out, consult with God by earnest prayer for the direction of his Holy Spirit. If out of your own confidence you should stand out, and afterward give back, it would weaken and discourage others.

In all these situations, you must labour to have your judgment enlightened, correctly discerning the order of things. A Christian can rightly account his life, when he knows that it is 'but a vapour that soon vanishes' (James 4:14). He knows the world cannot be worth a soul. These things being truly learned, we will be ready to deny father, mother, yea, our very life, if they once oppose Christ. We should get a resolution beforehand by daily considering these things, and have a mind truly prepared for all trials. To that end put cases to yourself; what would you do or suffer rather than be drawn to offend God, if the time of trial were to come now? The peace of conscience is above all good that can be desired. Remember that your life is not your own.

*Of the Providence of God, Works, vol. 5, pp. 53-54*

# Opposition

*For Demas, in love with this present world, has deserted me and gone to Thessalonica.*—2 Tim. 4:10

Paul sets down the diverse assistance he found from both God and man in the preaching of the gospel. As for men, when Paul was most in need of comfort, he found that they dealt unfaithfully with him. Demas, a man of great note, in the end forsook him. Alexander the coppersmith did him most harm. And weaker Christians forsook him as well. But mark the wisdom of God in the apostle in his different reactions towards these people. Demas, because his fault was greater by reason of the eminence of his profession, Paul brands him to all posterity by saying he went back to the world (2 Tim. 4:10). Alexander's opposition, because it sprung from an extreme malice towards the professing of godliness, Paul curses, 'the Lord reward him according to his works' (2 Tim. 4:14, 15). The weaker Christians, who failed him because they lacked a measure of courage yet retained a hidden love to the cause of Christ, their names Paul concealed and prayed that God would not lay their sin to their charge (2 Tim. 4:16). Yet see what large encouragement he had from heaven! Though all forsook him, 'God did not forsake me, but stood by me, and I was delivered out of the mouth of the lion' (2 Tim. 4:17).

Sometimes God allows his children to be forsaken, that they might fly to Christ. Our hearts do not naturally cling to God and are soon ready to join with anyone or anything else. We must see the excellencies of Christ and cling and adhere to him. This will soon take the soul away from resting upon lesser props. David said, 'My hill is strong, I will never be moved,' then almost immediately he cried 'my soul was troubled' (Psa. 30:6-10). Earthly things, such as riches, honours, and friends are not given to us to be a sure foundation to rest upon, but for comforts on our way to heaven. Whatever comfort there is in the earthly things the soul will spend quickly and still look for more; whereas the comfort that we have in God, 'is undefiled, and fades not away' (1 Pet. 1:4).

*Experience Triumphing, Works, vol. 7, pp. 408-09*

# Soul-Sight and True Happiness

*And Jesus, looking at him, loved him, and said to him, 'You lack one thing: go, sell all that you have and give to the poor, and you will have treasure in heaven; and come, follow me.'*—Mark 10:21

God has planted the grace of faith in us, that our souls might be carried to himself, and not rely upon earthly things, which are only as good as we do not trust in them. If we trust in friends, or estates, more than God, we make them idols. There is still left in man's fallen nature a desire for pleasure, profit, and whatever the natural self esteems as good. Because the soul is infected with a contrary taste, the desire of gracious comforts and heavenly delights is altogether lost. Man has a soul capable of excellency, and desirous of it, and the Spirit of God in and by the word reveals where true excellency is to be had; but man's fallen nature has left God and seeks its satisfaction elsewhere, in carnal friendship and the like. The soul goes against its own God-given desires, until the Spirit of God reveals where these things are to be truly had. By grace God turns the stream of a man's soul into its right current and man's nature is brought to its right frame again. Grace and sinful nature seek the same general object of comfort, only the sinful nature seeks comfort in broken cisterns, and grace in the fountain. The beginning of our true happiness is in the discovery of true and false objects, and as the soul clearly sees what is best and safest, and steadfastly relies upon it. For the soul is as that which it relies upon; if on vanity, it becomes vain; if upon God and Christ, it becomes a spiritual and heavenly soul. It is no small privilege which the Lord grants to some, when he crosses their greedy appetites after earthly comforts, so that he may refresh them with pleasures of a higher nature. Alas! What is the delight that we have in friends or children and the like, compared to the joy of God's presence and the pleasures at his right hand forevermore (Psa. 16:11)?

*Experience Triumphing, Works*, vol. 7, pp. 409-10

# Persevere as God Preserves (1)

*Teach me your way, O Lord, that I may walk in your truth; unite my heart to fear your name.*—Psa. 86:11

How to persevere in goodness:

(1) Labour for true grace. What is sincere, is constant. That is true grace which the Spirit of God works in us, and is not built on false grounds, as to have respect for this or that man, or ends of our own. Now, that we may have true grace, let us labour to be thoroughly convinced of sin, after which grace will follow. To which end we should pray earnestly for the Spirit, who will 'convince us of all sin' (John 16:8, 9), and work this grace of constancy, and all other graces in us. For where the Spirit is, there is a savour and relish in all the ways of God. How sweet to a spiritual heart is the goodness of God in our redemption, justification, and preservation!

(2) Seek a strong resolution against all oppositions, for, know this, scandals will come, difficulties will arise, but firm resolution will carry us through all. Those who go forth to walk for pleasure, if a storm comes, they return in again presently; whereas he that sets out on a journey, though he meets with many storms and tempests, yet he will go through all, because he has resolved beforehand.

(3) Labour for the obedience of faith, to believe the truth and to obey it in practice. Labour to know and obey that you may be built on the rock Christ Jesus. If you fall, it is your own fault for building on the sand. Often put these questions to your soul: 'Is this truth that I hold? Is this truth I would die for?' If so, then hold it fast, otherwise suspect the soundness of your faith.

(4) Above all things, get the love of God in your heart. This will constrain you to obedience. If you always look upon your discouragements, you will soon falter and fall away. But if you eye your encouragements, it is impossible that you would desert Christ, or his truth. Who would not hold out, having such a captain, and such a cause as we fight for? Where the truth is loved and received and practiced, there is constancy.

*Experience Triumphing, Works,* vol. 7, pp. 410-11

# Persevere as God Preserves (2)

*Let us hold fast the confession of our hope without wavering, for he who promised is faithful.*—Heb. 10:23

(5) Strive to grow daily in the denial of yourself. No one can come to heaven who does not first strip himself of himself. He must not trust in his own wisdom, will, or affections. He must deny himself in all his aims after the pleasure, profit, or preferment of the world. A religion that vacillates in what it holds as most valuable is never a sound religion. A true Christian has a single eye; he serves God for God himself. A man that has worldly aims has a double eye as well as a double heart; such a one cannot help but vacillate. Bring therefore a single eye, a single heart, and a single aim to receive the word. It is said of Israel that they brought Egypt into the wilderness (Num. 11:18). So it is with most men, they want to have religion and their lusts together; but whatever begins in hypocrisy will end in apostasy. He that has religion must not turn back to his old aims and company. For he now has acquaintance with God and an eternal inheritance to aim at.

(6) Labour to have divine truth engrafted in you; not to hold it loosely, for then it will never grow. We should embrace truth inwardly. For then God's children will have truth that belongs to them. As a wife receiving a letter from her husband, says, 'This is sent to me, it belongs to me.' So we should say of God's truth; 'This was penned for me, and directed to my soul in particular.'

(7) To grow deeper in religion, we must grow deeper and deeper in humility. A man is humble when he accounts sin his greatest evil and grace his greatest good. Such a one will hold out in time of trial. If temptations come on the right hand, he says, 'Christ is better to me!' If sin comes on the left hand, to draw him aside, he says, 'This is the vilest thing in the world; it is the worst of all evils, I will not yield to it.'

*Experience Triumphing, Works*, vol. 7, pp. 411-12

## Two Masters

*Do not love the world or the things in the world. If anyone loves the world, the love of the Father is not in him.*—1 John 2:15

*No one can serve two masters, for either he will hate the one and love the other, or he will be devoted to the one and despise the other. You cannot serve God and money.*—Matt. 6:24

The love of Christ and the love of the world cannot lodge together in one heart. For they are two masters who rule by contrary laws. Christ was resolved to suffer, but the world said, 'Spare yourself' (Matt. 16:22). How can these agree? I do not deny that a man may be truly religious and abound with all outward blessings; but the love of the world and the love of Christ cannot harbour in one breast. When the love of the world entered into Judas, it is said the devil entered into him (John 13:2). Christ and Satan are contrary to each other. Where religion is, it carries the soul upwards to heaven and heavenly things; but where the love of the world is, it brings the soul downward to the earth and things below.

This reveals the gross hypocrisy of men who labour to bring God and the world together, which cannot be. When the world has possession of the heart, it makes us false to God and false to each other. It makes us unfaithful in our callings, and false to religion itself. Labour to have the world in its rightful place, which is under your feet. For if we love the world, we will break with religion, with the church, and with God himself. We see how it hindered the rich man, in the Gospels, from blessedness. As soon as Christ told him to 'sell all that he had and give it to the poor' he went away sorrowful 'for he had great possessions' (Matt. 19:22). Oh, how these things steal the good word out of our hearts, as the birds did the seed that was on the path (Matt. 13:4). It even chokes the word, as the tares choked the corn when it had sprung up (Matt. 13:26). Where the love of the world is, there can be no true profession of Christ.

*Experience Triumphing, Works*, vol. 7, p. 412

# Guard against False Loves (1)

*You adulterous people! Do you not know that friendship with the world is enmity with God? Therefore whoever wishes to be a friend of the world makes himself an enemy of God.*—James 4:4

How can I know if I love the world?

What we love will be seen by observing the bent of our heart if it is swayed toward God and his service or toward things below. When two masters are separated, their servants will be known by whom they serve and whom they follow. In these days we enjoy both religion and the world together; but if times of suffering should begin, then it would be known whose servants we truly are. Consider therefore beforehand what you would do. If trouble and persecution should arise, would you stand up for Christ, and let go of liberty, riches, honour, and all in comparison to him?

We must know it is not simply the world that draws our hearts from God, but the love of the world. Worldly things are good in themselves and are given by God to sweeten our passage to heaven. It is your falseness that makes them hurtful, in loving them too much. Use the world as a servant and not as a master, and you will have comfort in this life. It is not the world properly used that hurts us, but our setting our hearts upon it. When God should be in our thoughts, our spirits are drunk with the cares below. Thorns will not prick by themselves, but when they are grasped in a man's hand they prick deep. So this world and the things of the world are all good, and were all made by God for the benefit of his people. Is it not our immoderate affection for them that makes them hurtful? When once a man's heart is set upon the world, how does he shine as a light for God? He breaks with God, his truth, his religion, and his all, to satisfy a lust! It is where we place our love that reveals whether we are good or bad. We are not as we know, but as we love. Our affections are the things which declare who we are. If we do not love God and the things of God, it does not matter what we know or how we talk of them.

*Experience Triumphing, Works, vol. 7, pp. 412-13*

# Guard against False Loves (2)

*As we look not to the things that are seen but to the things that are unseen. For the things that are seen are transient, but the things that are unseen are eternal.*—2 Cor. 4:18

Labour to know the world in truth so that you may detest it. In the things of God, the more we know the more we will love. With worldly things, the more we truly know the less affection we will have for them. Like some pictures, from a distance they look good, but come near to them and they do not. Let us see what the world truly is. It is but the present world which will vanish away suddenly. In seeking these things, we lose ourselves and the world too; but a Christian never loses that which he seeks after: God, Christ, and the things of a better life. The more we know of the vanities of the world and the excellencies of grace, the more we will love the one and hate the other.

Labour also for faith, that you may overcome the world. It was an excellent question of Christ when he sent forth his disciples, 'Did you lack anything?' and they said, 'Nothing at all' (Luke 22:35). Labour therefore for faith to rely on the promise of provision, protection, and all things needful. If God be our shepherd, we are sure to lack nothing. Cherish a waking heart. The way to get this is not to be drunk on the world, but by being wise, redeeming your time; and comparing these earthly things with the heavenly. Recognize what these fading comforts are to eternity (2 Cor. 4:18). We must let our affections run the right way and have Abraham's eyes to see afar off (Heb. 11:10), and feed our meditations with the things which will last forever, as Moses did (Heb. 11:24-28).

*Experience Triumphing, Works*, vol. 7, p. 413

# Mere Knowledge versus Growing in Godliness

*His divine power has granted to us all things that pertain to life and godliness, through the knowledge of him who called us to his own glory and excellence.*—2 Pet. 1:3

What makes a true Christian? When he simply believes the grounds of divine truth, the articles of the faith, when he can recite them over—does that make a true Christian? No! It is when these truths take root and work godliness. For religion is a truth according to godliness not according to mere knowledge or thought. Wherever these fundamental truths are embraced, there is godliness with them; a man cannot embrace religion in truth and not be growing in godliness. A man knows no more of Christ and divine things, than he values and esteems and allows to make affect and brings the whole inward man into a frame to be like the things. If they carry not the soul to trust in God, to hope in God, to fear God, to embrace him, to obey him, that man is not yet a true Christian; for Christianity is not a simple knowledge of the truth, but godliness.

Religious evangelical truth is wisdom, and wisdom is a knowledge of things that leads to practice. The gospel is a divine wisdom, teaching practice as well as knowledge. It works godliness, or else a man has but a human knowledge of divine things. He that is godly, believes aright and practices aright. He that believes ill can never live well, for he has no foundation. He makes an idol of some thought he has, and he that lives ill, though he thought well, will be damned too. A true Christian gets godly principles out of the gospel, and a godly lifestyle suitable to those principles. Can a man know God's love in Christ incarnate, and Christ's suffering for us, and his sitting at the right hand of God, the infinite love of God in Christ, and not be carried in affection back to God, in love and joy and true allegiance, and to whatever makes up the respect of godliness? It cannot be. Therefore, being a Christian is not a cold, simple apprehension, but a spiritual knowledge, when the soul is stirred up to a suitable disposition and lifestyle that makes godliness.

*The Fountain Opened, Works,* vol. 5, p. 461

# Mystery (1)

*Great indeed, we confess, is the mystery of godliness: He was manifested in the flesh, vindicated by the Spirit, seen by angels, proclaimed among the nations, believed on in the world, taken up in glory.*—1 Tim. 3:16

The whole evangelical truth is a mystery, for these reasons:

(1) It was hidden from all men until God brought it out of his own bosom. First to Adam after the fall; and more clearly later to the Jews; and in Christ's time even more fully to Jews and Gentiles. It was not a thing framed by angels or men. It was Christ who brought it out of the bosom of his Father. 'No man has seen God at any time; Christ the only begotten Son, in the bosom of the Father, he has made him known' (John 1:18). The reconciling of justice and mercy, it is a mystery of heavenly wisdom that the creature could never think of.

(2) When it was revealed, it was revealed only to a few. It was revealed at first only to the Jews and to them it was wrapped in ceremonies and types and in general promises. It was quite hidden from most parts of the world.

(3) When Christ came and the gospel was preached in the church, it was a mystery to carnal men who heard the gospel, and yet did not understand it because they had a veil over their hearts. It is 'hidden to them that perish' (2 Cor. 4:3), though it be open to those who believe.

(4) Though we see some part of it, yet we see not the whole gospel. We see not all, nor wholly. 'We see but in part and know but in part' (1 Cor. 13:9). It is a mystery in regards of the full accomplishment of it.

(5) It is a mystery regarding what we do not know but will hereafter know. How do we know divine truths now? In the mirror of the word and the ordinances. We know not Christ by sight. That manner of knowledge is reserved for heaven. So here we know as it were in a kind of mystery. This seeing compared to the old covenant is 'seeing the face of God in Christ' (2 Cor. 4:6)—a clear sight. But compared to that which we will see, it is seeing only as in a glass or mirror.

*The Fountain Opened, Works,* vol. 5, pp. 462-63

# Mystery (2)

*Therefore, if anyone is in Christ, he is a new creation. The old has passed away; behold, the new has come.*—2 Cor. 5:17

Is the doctrine of the gospel the only mystery?

No. All the graces are mysteries, every grace. Let a man once know it and he will find that there is a mystery in faith; that the earthly soul of man should be carried above itself, to believe supernatural truths, and to depend upon what he sees not, to sway the life by reasons spiritual; that the heart of man should believe; that a man in trouble should carry himself quietly and patiently from supernatural supports and grounds, it is a mystery. That a man should be as a rock in the midst of a storm, to stand immoveable, is a mystery. That the direction of the soul should be turned universally another way; that the judgment and affections should be turned backward, as it were; that he who was proud before should now be humble; that he who was ambitious before should now despise the vain world; that he who was given to his lusts and vanities before should now, on the contrary, be serious and heavenly-minded: here is a mystery indeed when all is turned backward. Therefore we see how Nicodemus, as wise as he was, it was a riddle to him when our blessed Saviour spoke to him of the new birth, that a man should be wholly changed and new-moulded; that a man should be the same and not the same. The same man for soul and body, yet not the same in regard of a supernatural life and that life being put into him, leading him in another manner, by other rules and respects, as much different from other men as a man differs from a beast. For a man to be content with his condition and to have a mind immoveable, it is a mystery. Paul said, 'I have learned the secret of facing plenty and hunger' (Phil. 4:12). It is a mystery for a man to be tossed up and down in life, and yet to have a contented mind.

*The Fountain Opened, Works*, vol. 5, pp. 463-64

# Mystery (3)

*That their hearts may be encouraged, being knit together in love, to reach all the riches of full assurance of understanding and the knowledge of God's mystery, which is Christ, in whom are hidden all the treasures of wisdom and knowledge.*—Col. 2:2, 3

In Christ all is mystery. Christ possessing two natures, God and man, in one person; mortal and immortal; greatness and baseness; infiniteness and finiteness, in one person.

The church itself is a mystery. For under all its fallenness and the scorn of the world, what is hid? A glorious people. The state of the church in this world is like a tree that is weather-beaten. The leaves and fruit are gone, but there is life in the root. What is the church? A company of people that are in the world without glory, without comeliness and beauty; yet notwithstanding, they have life in the root, a hidden life: 'Our life is hid with Christ, in God' (Col. 3:3). The church has a life, but it is a hidden, mystical life. They seem to die to the world, but they are alive. This is excellently and theoretically followed by Paul: 'As dying, and yet we live; as poor, yet making many rich' (2 Cor. 6:9). A strange kind of people, poor and rich, living and dying, glorious and fallen. Yet this is the state of the church here in this world. They are an excellent people, but they are veiled under infirmities of their own, and the disgraces and persecutions of the world.

So, we see that the doctrine itself, and the graces, and the head of the church, and the church itself, are nothing but mysteries.

*The Fountain Opened, Works,* vol. 5, p. 464

# Believing God's Mysteries (1)

*To bring to light for everyone what is the plan of the mystery hidden for ages in God, who created all things.*—Eph. 3:9

How can we come to know the mysteries of God?

(1) Whenever we take the Bible in our hands, when we come to hear the word, hear of God the Spirit, we must remember what God said, 'My house will be called the house of prayer' (Isa. 56:7). His house is not only to be the house of hearing divine truths but also the house of prayer. It is impudence and presumption to come to these things without lifting up our souls to God. There is so little profit under the hearing of these glorious mysteries because there is so little prayer and lifting up the heart to God. We should go to Christ, who 'opens, and no man shuts; and shuts, and no man opens' (Rev. 3:7). Go to him, therefore, that he would both open the mysteries and open our hearts, that they may understand.

In Revelation 5:4, John wept when the book with seven seals could not be opened. He wept that the prophecy was so obscure, that it could not be understood; but then Christ takes the book and opens it. When we cannot understand divine mysteries, let us groan and sigh to Christ. He can open the book and he can lay open all the mysteries as far as it concerns us to know.

From this also comes the necessity of the ministry; for if the gospel be a mystery then there must be some to help make it known. God has therefore established an office in the church, with which he joins his own Spirit, that both ordinance and Spirit joining together, the veil may be taken off. 'How can they understand without a teacher?' (Rom. 10:14). 'To us is committed the grace to preach the unsearchable riches of Christ,' said Paul (Eph. 3:6-8). Profane people think they know enough, they need not be taught. This spirit argues a profane and wicked heart. Sometimes God denies his Spirit in hearing because he will have us read; and denies it in that because he will have us confer and practice the communion of saints; to apprehend this glorious, excellent mystery.

*The Fountain Opened, Works*, vol. 5, pp. 468-70

# Believing God's Mysteries (2)

*He leads the humble in what is right and teaches the humble his way.*—
Psa. 25:9

(2) If we would understand these mysteries, let us labour for humble spirits; for the Spirit works that disposition in the first place: 'The humble, God will teach' (Psa. 25:9). Now this kind of humility here required, it is a denial of our own wisdom. We must be content 'to become fools, that we may be wise' (1 Cor. 4:10). We must deny our own understanding and be content to have no more understanding in divine things than what we can get out of God's word. We must bring this humility if we want to understand this mystery.

(3) Bring along a serious desire to know, with a purpose to be moulded to what we know, and to be delivered to the obedience of what we know, for then God will reveal it to us. Together with prayer and humility, let us bring a purpose and desire to be taught, and we will find divine wisdom. None ever miscarry in the church but those that have false hearts. They do not have humble and sincere hearts, willing to be taught. Let a man have a wicked heart, and he will find flatterers to build him up in all violent and wicked courses. God in judgment will give him teachers that will suit his disposition. But if he be a child of God, and have a sincere heart to know the truth, he will meet with some that will in sincerity tell him the truth. Therefore, we should pity men less when we see them run into errors. God sees that they have wicked dispositions. God will have mercy on them if they be sincere, though they be in error. But if we see men who may know the truth, and yet run into errors, know that such a man has a poisonous heart, a malicious bent of heart against the truth. Where God gives a willing mind, there he opens his meaning. Wisdom is easy to him that wills to understand.

*The Fountain Opened, Works,* vol. 5, p. 470

# Believing God's Mysteries (3)

*I will give them a heart to know that I am the LORD, and they shall be*
*my people and I will be their God, for they shall return to me with*
*their whole heart.*—Jer. 24:7

(4) Take heed of passion and prejudice, of carnal affections that stir
up passion; for they will make the soul not able to see the mysteries that
are plain in themselves. As we are strong in any passion, so we judge;
and the heart, when it is given up to passion, transforms the truth to
its own self. When the taste is distorted, it tastes things, not as they are
in themselves, but inaccurately. So corrupt hearts transform the sacred
mystery to their own liking, and often force the Scriptures to defend
their own sin, and their corrupt state. The corrupt will believe according
to their leanings. What it loves, it will force itself to believe—although
it be contrary to divine mysteries—when the heart is deeply engaged
in any passion or affection. Let us labour to come with purged hearts
to receive God's mysteries. They will lodge only in clean hearts. Let us
labour to see God and Christ with a clear eye, free from passion, covetousness, and vainglory. We see a notable example of this in the scribes.
When they were not led with passion, covetousness, and envy against
Christ, how right they could judge of the gospel, and the unfolding of
the prophecies to the wise men. They could tell aright that he should be
born in Bethlehem (Matt. 2:5, 6). But when Christ came among them,
and opposed their lazy, proud kind of life, that kept people in awe of
their ceremonies, then they sinned against the Holy Spirit, and against
their own light, and maligned Christ, and brought him to his end. So it
is with men. When their minds are clear, before they are overcast with
passion and strong affections to the world, they judge clearly of divine
things; but when those passions prevail with them, they are opposed to
the truth that they saw before. Men are also unsettled. Sometimes they
will grant truths, sometimes they will not, as their passions lead them.
Therefore, it is of great consequence to come with clean hearts and minds
to the mysteries of God.

*The Fountain Opened, Works,* vol. 5, pp. 470-71

# Knowledge and Affections

*Oh how I love your law! It is my meditation all the day.*—Psa. 119:97

When we have the truths of religion revealed to us by the ministry of others or by reading on our own, let us ask our souls, 'Are these things so or not? Do I believe them to be so or not?' If I do believe them, then I must consider what my affections and inward disposition are, whether they are suitable to such things. We must work upon our hearts that our knowledge may be an affecting knowledge, a knowledge that sinks even to the very affections, that pierces through the whole soul. Let us never cease until there is a correspondence between the affections and truth. Are they true? Believe them. Are they good? Embrace them. Let us think there is a defect in our apprehension if the affections embrace them not. Let us never think our state good until we find our hearts warmed with the goodness of divine supernatural truths. 'Oh! how I do love your law!' said David (Psa. 119:97). Let us labour to have great affections, consistent with the truth; and never stop until we can love them and joy and delight in them as the greatest things. Like Paul, account 'all as dung and dross, in comparison to them' (Phil. 3:8). The knowledge that is a saving knowledge is that which works the heart to a love, to a joy and delight, that works the whole man to practice and obedience. All other knowledge serves for nothing but to prove God correct in our damnation: when knowing these things, we do not work our hearts to love them, but we rest in the barren knowledge of them. Therefore, we should labour to see spiritual things in a spiritual light, for where spiritual light is there is always spiritual heat. Where spiritual evidence is in the understanding there is spiritual embracing in the affections. Supernatural light and supernatural life go together. Let us labour that our comprehension of these great mysteries may be supernatural and spiritual, and then as our minds comprehend them to be true, and our affections are present, we will believe them and live by them.

*The Fountain Opened, Works*, vol. 5, p. 476

# Christic in Human Flesh

*Therefore he had to be made like his brothers in every respect, so that*
*he might become a merciful and faithful high priest in the service of*
*God, to make propitiation for the sins of the people.*—Heb. 2:17

By *flesh* is meant human nature, the property of human nature, both body and soul. By flesh is also understood the infirmities and weakness of man. So, 'He was manifested in the flesh' (1 Tim. 3:16) means in our nature and the properties of it, he put it all on; our infirmities, and weaknesses, our miseries. What is more, he took our flesh when it was tainted with treason, not when it was innocent in the garden but after it was fallen. All of this is a wondrous product of his love, causing him to be full of pity and compassion (Heb. 2:17, 18; 4:14, 15).

You might say, 'How can he be truly full of pity? There are many infirmities that he did not take upon himself.' I answer, by comparison to those that he did take, he knows how to be full of pity to those experiencing things he did not take. He is infinitely wise. He knows how to make the correlation.

But some will say, 'He took my nature and the general infirmities, as weariness, and hunger; but I am also sick and troubled in my mind and conscience.' I answer, for the trouble of mind, he knew it in that great desertion, when he cried out, 'My God, my God, why have you forsaken me?' (Matt. 27:46). He was not sick himself; but by the experience of labour, and thirst, and the like, he knows what it is to be sick. He knew not what it is to sin and to be troubled for sin, because he did not sin himself; but being our surety for sin, and feeling the wrath of God for it, he had the experience of that so that he can be compassionate to us. He was weary, to pity those who are weary; he was hungry, to pity those who are hungry; he was poor, to pity those who are poor; he was misused and reproached, to pity those who are in like condition. You can name nothing, but he can out of his own experience be merciful and full of pity to those experiencing it.

*The Fountain Opened, Works,* vol. 5, pp. 479-80

# Think Often of the Incarnation of Christ

*That which was from the beginning, which we have heard, which we have*
*seen with our eyes, which we looked upon and have touched with our*
*hands, concerning the word of life—the life was made manifest, and*
*we have seen it, and testify to it and proclaim to you the eternal life,*
*which was with the Father and was made manifest to us.—*1 John 1:1, 2

To think of God absolutely, without God in the flesh, he is 'a consuming fire' (Heb. 12:29), every way terrible; but to think of God in our nature, we may, with boldness, securely go to him, as a brother. Think of God born of a virgin, of God lying in the cradle, sucking the breast! Think of God going up and down teaching and doing all good! Think of God sweating for you, hanging on the cross, shedding his blood, lying in the grave, raising himself again, and now in heaven as our intercessor 'seated at the right hand of God' (Eph. 1:20). To think of God alone swallows up our thoughts but to think of God in Christ, of God in the flesh is a comfortable consideration. To see the sun alone in itself, in the glory and lustre of it, it is impossible without hurting the eye; but to see the sun in water, or in an eclipse, we may do it. So, we cannot conceive of God alone, absolutely; but to conceive of God in our flesh is to look upon the sun as it were in the water. God tells Moses, 'None can ever see God and live' (Exod. 33:20), that is, see God absolutely. Oh, but God, made manifest in our flesh, we may see; and it will be our happiness in heaven to see him there, to see 'God in our flesh face to face' (Exod. 33:11).

We cannot too often meditate on these things. It is the marrow of the gospel. It is the wonder of wonders. We need not wonder at anything after this. It is no wonder that our bodies will rise again; that mortal man should become immortal in heaven, since the immortal God has taken man's nature and died in it. All the articles of our faith and all miracles yield to this grand thing, 'God manifested in the flesh' (1 Tim. 3:16). Believe this and believe all other. Therefore, let us often have cherishing thoughts of God in our flesh, that it may strengthen and nourish our faith, especially in the time of temptation.

*The Fountain Opened, Works*, vol. 5, pp. 484-85

# Persecution of the Church (1)

*I charge you in the presence of God, who gives life to all things, and of Christ Jesus, who in his testimony before Pontius Pilate made the good confession, to keep the commandment unstained and free from reproach until the appearing of our Lord Jesus Christ, which he will display at the proper time—he who is the blessed and only Sovereign, the King of kings and Lord of lords.*—1 Tim. 6:13-15

Some may say, 'How does it appear that Christ is King of the church? We see how the church is trampled on these days. Where is the life and glory of the church? What! The church is his spouse, and thus used! What! His turtle, and thus polluted and plucked by the birds of prey!'

I answer, look with the eye of faith, and then you will see a spring in the winter of the church. The church is now abased and eclipsed, yet she will be justified; and it will be known that Christ does regard his church and people and children more than all the world besides.

It was fit there be a time of Christ's abasement or how else should he have suffered? The world would never have been able to crucify God. Therefore, he was abased; he veiled his Godhead under his manhood, under a base condition, to pass through suffering. So it must be in the body of Christ. It must pass through the veil of infirmities, of weakness, affliction, and disgrace. How else should she be conformable to Christ? If Christ had justified himself at all times in his humiliation, he could not have suffered; if we should be justified now and appear to all the world who we are, who would persecute us? Therefore let us quietly and meekly for a while endure these things, knowing this, that as he was justified by little and little, until he was perfectly justified when he was raised from the dead, so we will be perfectly justified and freed from all accusations at the last day, when by the same Spirit that raised him we will be raised up too.

*The Fountain Opened, Works,* vol. 5, p. 491

# Persecution of the Church (2)

*Beloved do not be surprised at the fiery trial when it comes upon you to test you, as though something strange were happening to you. But rejoice insofar as you share Christ's sufferings, that you may also rejoice and be glad when his glory is revealed. If you are insulted for the name of Christ, you are blessed, because the Spirit of glory and of God rests upon you.*—1 Pet. 4:12-14

In this world, when it is for his glory and for our good, he will bring our righteousness to light as the noonday (Psa. 37:6). He will free us from the accusations that the world lays on us. Then the world will see that we are not the profane, bitter, malicious persons, led by the spirit of the devil, that they charge us to be.

Let us take no indignation at the present afflictions of the church. Christ will justify his mystical body by his glorious power in good time. Antichrist will not always swagger in the world. Christ will be shown to be the King and Ruler of the world. 'All authority has been given him' (Matt. 28:18). But we see antichrist raging in the world, and the church seems to be under siege. Let us comfort ourselves, beloved. Christ justified himself by his Spirit, and will he not justify his poor church, and free it from the tyranny of antichrist? He will advance those that are trodden on now and made as the dirt in the street, so that 'they will shine as the sun' (Dan. 12:3). Therefore, when you hear of the dejected state of the churches abroad, do not be dismayed. Consider there is a glorious King who rules the world, and he will make it known before long. He is wise and he is working his own work. He corrects and rules and purges his church in the furnace of affliction. But be sure the time will come that he will bring the cause of religion to light, and he will show what side he owns; he will tread Satan and all his members underfoot. The present condition of things will not hold long. As verily as Christ is in heaven, as verily as he has conquered in his own person, so he will by his Spirit conquer for his church.

*The Fountain Opened, Works*, vol. 5, p. 492

# Walk Worthy (1)

*For the kingdom of God does not consist in talk but in power.*—1 Cor. 4:20

True religion is not a matter of form, but of spirit. Let us not show our religion only by word, but by the fruit of the Holy Spirit, by love, mercy, meekness, and zeal. The whole life of a Christian, as far as he is a Christian, gives evidence that he is a Christian. Let us ask ourselves, 'We profess to be the children of God, what shows that in our lives?' A true Christian can answer, 'I can justify it by the Spirit; I find I do things from other principles and motives than the world does. I find I do things out of the assurance that I am a child of God and live in obedience to him.'

Alas! I cannot but lament the poor profession of many. How do they make good that they have the Spirit of God raising them above other men, when they live no better than pagans, nay, sometimes not even as well? Would pagans live as many Christians do? Do they not keep their words better? Are they so loose in their lives and conversations, and so licentious? Many ordinary Christians are worse than pagans. If the heathen should see them, they would not say, 'You talk of religion, but if you had the power of it, you would express it more in your fidelity, honesty, mercy, love, and sobriety.' The kingdom of God, that is, the manifestation of the government of Christ, 'is not in talk but in power' (1 Cor. 4:20). Therefore, let us labour to justify that we are subjects of that kingdom, by the power of it.

Paul said of mere moral people, they 'have a form of godliness, but deny the power of it' (2 Tim. 3:5). A form is easy, but the power of it is not so easy. Let us show our religion by our lifestyles. Let us justify the preaching and hearing of the word of God, by reverence in hearing it as the word of God, and labour to express it in our lives and conversations; showing that we are true members of Christ, that we are like Christ.

*The Fountain Opened, Works,* vol. 5, pp. 494-95

# Walk Worthy (2)

*So as to walk in a manner worthy of the Lord, fully pleasing to him:*
*bearing fruit in every good work and increasing in the knowledge of*
*God.*—Col. 1:10

Beloved, it is a great power that must make a true Christian, no less than the same 'power of the Spirit, that raised Christ from the dead' (Eph. 1:20). Paul prays that they might 'feel the power that raised Christ from the dead' (Eph 1:19). It is no less power for Christ to shine in our dark hearts, than to 'make light to shine out of darkness' (2 Cor. 4:6).

Now, what power is in the lives of most moral men? The 'power that raised Christ from the dead'? Certainly no! What power is there in now and then speaking a good word, or now and then to doing a slight action? Is this the 'power that raised Christ from the dead,' when by the strength of nature men can do it? There must be something above nature to justify a sound, spiritual Christian. We must have something to show that we have our spirits raised up by the Spirit of Christ. In prosperity, to show that we have a spirit above prosperity, that we are not proud of it. In adversity, that we do not sink under it. In temptation by arming ourselves with a spirit of faith, to beat back the 'fiery darts of Satan' (Eph. 6:16). When all things seem contrary, let us cast ourselves, by a spirit of faith, upon Christ. Doing so argues a powerful work of the Spirit, when we can, in contraries, believe contraries.

We show we are Christians when we look with the eye of faith through all discouragements and clouds, and see God reconciled in Christ. Let us labour, not only for slight outward performances that are easy for anyone to do, but by an inward frame of soul, and by a carriage and conversation becoming our profession, let us 'walk worthy of our calling' (Eph. 4:1), fruitfully and watchfully, carefully and soberly, as becomes a Christian.

*The Fountain Opened, Works*, vol. 5, pp. 495-96

# Angels: God's Messengers—Our Attendants (1)

*Are they not all ministering spirits sent out to serve for the sake of those who are to inherit salvation?*—Heb. 1:14

A Christian has angels to remove the hindrances that are between heaven and him, and that keep him from Christ.

When Christ rose there were angels who told Mary that he was risen. Then at his ascension the angels told the disciples that Christ would come again. From the annunciation of his conception to his ascension angels saw him, and attended on him, and witnessed of him. As soon as he was born, the angels appeared to the shepherds. What a glorious hymn they sang! 'Glory to God on high, peace on earth, good will to men' (Luke 2:14). How joyful they were of the incarnation of Christ, and the great work of redemption wrought by him! They did not only see these things, but they wondered at the love, mercy, and wisdom of God in the Head and members of the church. 'We preach the gospel, which things the angels desire to look into' (1 Pet. 1:12). The very angels desire to pry and look with admiration into the wondrous things of the gospel, and into the 'manifold wisdom of God' (Eph. 3:10) in his governing of the church and his electing and restoring his people. The angels see and wonder at the love and wisdom of God in joining things irreconcilable to man's comprehension, infinite justice with infinite mercy in Christ. Will they wonder at it, and joy and delight in it, and will we slight those things that are the wonderment of angels? There is a company of profane people—I would there were not too many among us—who will hardly ever look into these things. They can wonder at a story, or a poem, or some trivial device not worthy to be reckoned. But as for the great mysteries of salvation, the great works of the Trinity, they slight them and never talk seriously of these things, except with a graceless slighting and scorn. These things we dally and trifle with when we should take up our time in studying these transcendent things that go beyond the capacity of the very angels.

*The Fountain Opened, Works*, vol. 5, pp. 496-501

# Angels: God's Messengers—Our Attendants (2)

*For it is written: 'He will command his angels concerning you to guard you carefully; and they will lift you up in their hands, so that you will not strike your foot against a stone.'*—Luke 4:10, 11

It is a great comfort to us that Christ was seen, attended on, and admired by angels. For it is the ground of all the attendance and comfort that we have from the angels. This is a rule in divinity, that what is true for the Head is also true for the members. Therefore, what comfort and attendance Christ had, who is the Head, the church, which is the body, has the same, only with some differences. They attended upon him immediately for himself, they attend upon us for his sake. For whatever we have of God, we have it second-hand. We receive the attendance of angels, for the attendance they yielded to Christ first; they attend upon us, by his direction, commission, and charge. But surely, whatever they did to him they do to us, because there is the same respect to Head and members. The devil was not mistaken when he alleged, 'He will give his angels charge over you, that you dash not your foot against a stone' (Psa. 91:11). He was right in applying that to Christ. And what is true for Christ will be true for Christians as well. For 'he that sanctifies, and they that are sanctified, are all one' (Heb. 2:11).

The angels will forever be attendants to us because their love and respect to us is founded upon their love and respect to Christ. When the favour that a king or a great person bears to one is founded on the love of his own son; he loves the other because he loves his son; so it is perpetual and sound, because he will ever love his son. The angels will forever love, honour, and attend us. What ground do they have to respect us at all? It is in Christ, whose members and spouse we are. So long as the church has any relation to Christ, so long will the angels respect the church; and the church has relation to Christ forever. Therefore, the respect that the blessed angels have to Christ and to the church is forever.

*The Fountain Opened, Works*, vol. 5, pp. 496-501

# Angels: God's Messengers—Our Attendants (3)

*Bless the LORD, all his angels mighty in strength, who do his word, who hearken to the voice of his command.*—Psa. 103:20

Let us think and make use of this; that now in Christ we have the attendance of angels. We do not see them, as in former times, before Christ's incarnation. It is true; because now, since Christ has come in the flesh the rule of Christ is spiritual; and we are not supported with those glorious manifestations, instead they are about us in an invisible manner. We have 'Elisha's guard' (2 Kings 6:17) about us continually, but we see them not. There were more appearances in the infancy of the church because the plan and work of Christ then was according to the weak state of the church. But now Christ has come in the flesh and has been received up in glory and there is more abundance of the Holy Spirit. We should be more spiritual and heavenly-minded, and not look for the visible appearance of angels; but be content that we have a guard of them about us. 'Despise not,' said Christ, 'these little ones for their angels behold the face of your heavenly Father' (Matt. 18:10). There are angels even of children. Let a man be poor, even as Lazarus, yet he has the attendance of angels, in life and death (Luke 16:22). There is no Christian of low degree, of the lowest degree, that can think himself neglected of God, for the very angels attend him.

Likewise, this may comfort us in all our extremities, in all our desertions. The time may come when we may be deserted by the world and deserted by our friends, so that we have nobody in the world near us. But if a man be a true Christian, he has God and angels about him always. A Christian is a king; he is never without that invisible guard of angels. If a man has nobody by him when he dies but God and his good angels, is he neglected? Every Christian, if he has no one else with him, he has God, the whole Trinity, and the guard of angels, to help and comfort him, and to convey his soul to the place of happiness.

*The Fountain Opened, Works*, vol. 5, pp. 496-501

# Angels: God's Messengers—Our Attendants (4)

*Just so, I tell you, there is joy before the angels of God over one sinner who repents.*—Luke 15:10

When we look upon all the passages of our life, we see how ready we are to fall into danger. In our infancy, in our tender years, we are committed to their custody. In our dangers, 'the angels of the Lord pitch their tents about those that fear the Lord' (Psa. 34:7). In our conversion they rejoice. 'There is joy in heaven at the conversion of a sinner' (Luke 15:10). At the hour of death, as we see in Lazarus, they are ready to convey our souls to the place of happiness. Lazarus' soul 'was carried by angels into Abraham's bosom' (Luke 16:22). 'Christ will come with a multitude of heavenly angels' (Matt. 24:30, 31) at the day of judgment, 'when he will come to be glorified in his saints' (2 Thess. 1:10). Then saints and angels together, will glorify God forever in heaven. We have association with them from our infancy until we be in glory. Indeed, they are as nurses: 'They will carry you, that you dash not your foot against a stone' (Psa. 91:12). They keep us from many inconveniences.

But you ask, 'God's children fall into inconveniences; how then are they attended by angels?' I answer: God's angels preserve those who are his from many inconveniences that they know not of. And certainly, we have demons about us continually, and there is a conflict between good angels and demons about us continually. If they keep us not from evil, they will keep us while in it, and deliver us out of evil at length. If we suffer in the custody of angels any inconvenience, it is that we may be tried by it, that we may be exercised and bettered by it. There is nothing that falls upon God's children in the world, but they gain by it, whatever it is.

*The Fountain Opened, Works*, vol. 5, pp. 496-01

# Angels: God's Messengers—Our Attendants (5)

*Of the angels he says, 'He makes his angels winds, and his ministers a flame of fire.'*—Heb. 1:7

Let us comfort ourselves in all conditions. Even when the enemies are thousands more than we, many thousands and millions; yet, if we be in the covenant of grace, and in good terms with God, we have angels to fight for us. You know Elisha's servant, when he saw the multitude of enemies, his eyes were opened to see a company of angels; and said the prophet, 'There are more for us than against us' (2 Kings 6:17). Let us have Elisha's eye, the eye of faith, and we will have his guard about us always. This should comfort us.

We must also learn not to grieve these good spirits. It is a wondrous humility that they stoop to be servants to us, who are of a weaker, baser nature than they (Psa. 8:5). It is a wondrous patience, that they continue to guard us even when we do that which grieves them. Let us consider when we are alone—it would keep us from many sins—no eye of man sees; but God sees, and my conscience within sees, and angels are witnesses. They grieve at our sin, and the demons rejoice at it. These thoughts will help us when we are tempted to sin.

Let us learn to magnify God, who has honoured us; not only by taking our nature upon himself, but also to give us his own attendants, his own guard, a guard of angels. Indeed, he did not take upon himself the nature of angels, but of men. His plan is that those glorious creatures should be our attendants for our good; and they do not find this attendance distasteful. What care God has over us, and what love he bears us; that he has honoured us with creatures of a more excellent rank than we, the angels, who are at service to us in Christ. All this should cause us to be full of thankfulness.

*The Fountain Opened, Works*, vol. 5, pp. 496-501

# Angels: God's Messengers—Our Attendants (6)

*For he will command his angels concerning you to guard you in all your ways.*—Psa. 91:11

It should teach us not to despise the meanest Christians, seeing angels do not despise to attend them. Oh, the pride of man's nature! When the more glorious angels disdain not to be our servants, and not only to great and noble men, but to little ones, even to Lazarus. What a devilish quality is envy and pride, that stirs us up to disdain to be useful one to another, especially to those who are inferiors! God himself disdains not to look on things below (Psa. 113:6). Because God became a man, will we wonder that angels should attend upon the nature that God has so honoured? The angels rejoice at the salvation of a sinner (Luke 15:10). Will we despise the work of regeneration and the image of God in another? Will the welfare and thriving of others spiritually or outwardly be the joy of the angels and not our joy?

The angels are described with wings to fly to show their delight in their attendance; and wings to cover their faces and their feet, to show their adoration and reverence of God (Isa 6:2). The nearer they come to God, the more reverence. Is there no Christian, who like the angels, the nearer he comes to God, the more he abases himself and adores God? Let us imitate the angels in this. The angels have a double office: a superior office and an inferior. The superior office they have is to attend upon God, to serve God and Christ, to minister to our Head. The inferior office is to attend his church, and to do battle with the evil angels that are about us continually.

It is good for us to know our privilege and our strength; not to make us proud, but to stir us up to thankfulness, and to a holy life. It is a point not much thought on by the best of us. It is necessary ofttimes to think what a great position God has raised us to in Jesus Christ and that we have this glorious attendance about us wherever we are. Oh, it would move us to comfort and a reverent life!

*The Fountain Opened, Works,* vol. 5, pp. 503-04

# Preaching: Dispensing Truth to Be Received (1)

*Through whom we have received grace and apostleship to bring about the obedience of faith for the sake of his name among all the nations.*—Rom. 1:5

Faith is the issue and fruit of preaching. Christ is first 'preached to the Gentiles' and then 'believed on in the world' (1 Tim. 3:16). All preaching is for 'the obedience of faith' (Rom. 1:5). So, there must be a dispensing and receiving of Christ. We see the sense of this, even in the things among men. It is not sufficient that medicine be provided; but there must be an application of it. It is not sufficient that there is a treasure; but there must be a digging up of it. It was not sufficient that there was a 'brazen serpent,' but the brazen serpent had to be 'lifted up,' that the people might see it (Num. 21:6-9). It is not sufficient that there be a garment, but there must be a putting on of it. It is not sufficient that there be a box of ointment, but the box must be opened, to fill the house with its smell. Therefore, there must be a dispensing and receiving of the mysteries of Christ; for, though Christ is medicine, he must be applied. Though, in truth, he is a treasure, yet he must be dug up through the ministry. Though he is the light, he must be held forth. Of necessity there must be a dispensing and receiving of the gospel, the redemption purchased by Christ.

To preach is to open the mystery of Christ; to break open the box that the savour may be perceived by all. But it is not sufficient to preach Christ, to lay open all this in the view of others; but there must also be an applying of them to the use of God's people, that they may see their interest in them. There must be an alluring of them, for to preach is to woo. Preachers are the friends of the bridegroom, they are to procure the marriage between Christ and his church; they are not only to lay open the riches of the husband, Christ, but likewise to entreat for a marriage, and to use all the gifts and abilities that God has given them, to bring Christ and his church together.

*The Fountain Opened, Works,* vol. 5, pp. 504-06

# Preaching: Dispensing Truth to Be Received (2)

*For this is he who was spoken of by the prophet Isaiah when he said, 'The voice of one crying in the wilderness: "Prepare the way of the Lord; make his paths straight."'* —Matt. 3:3

Because people are in a contrary state to Christ, to preach Christ we must first begin with the law, to show to people their state by nature. Who will marry with Christ, but those that know their own beggary and misery outside of Christ? This must take place or else they will die in their debts eternally. When people are convinced of this, they turn away from themselves and turn to Christ. This therefore must be done first, for 'the full stomach despises a honeycomb' (Prov. 27:7). Who cares for balm who is not sick? Who cares for Christ who sees not the necessity of Christ? We see that John the Baptist came before Christ to make the way for Christ, to level the mountains, to cast down whatever exalts itself in man. He who is to preach must discern what mountains there be between men's hearts and Christ. He must labour to reveal the truth about fallen people and lay flat all the pride of men in the dust, for 'the word of God is forcible to pull down strongholds and imaginations and to bring all into subjection to Christ' (2 Cor. 10:4). Who needs a Saviour except those who are lost? Who needs Christ to be wisdom to us if we were not fools in ourselves? Who needs Christ to be sanctification to us if we were not defiled in ourselves? Who needs him to be redemption if we were not lost and sold in ourselves to Satan, and under his bondage? Therefore, all preaching is to make way for Christ, not only to open the mysteries of Christ, but in the opening and application to let us see our necessity of Christ. To bring Christ and the church together, our aim must be, to persuade people to come out of the state they are in, and to come and take Christ. Whatever makes for this, that course we must use.

*The Fountain Opened, Works,* vol. 5, p. 506

# Preaching: Dispensing Truth to Be Received (3)

*Therefore, we are ambassadors for Christ, God making his appeal through us. We implore you on behalf of Christ, be reconciled to God.*—2 Cor. 5:20

The gospel is declared in a sweet manner. 'I beseech you, brethren, by the mercies of God' (Rom. 12:1). The law comes with curses, but now in the gospel Christ is preached with sweet alluring. 'We as ambassadors beseech you, as if Christ by us did beseech you, be reconciled to God' (2 Cor. 5:20). This is the manner of the spreading of the gospel, even to beg people to be good to their own souls. The great God of heaven and earth begs our love, that we would care for our own souls and be reconciled to him. It is more fit that we should beg of him, but God stoops in the ministry of the gospel, and he becomes the beggar and suitor to us to be good to our souls. He himself becomes a beseecher of reconciliation, as if he were the party that had offended. This is the manner of the publication of the gospel, showing us what it is to preach Christ.

Further, it is more helpful to people's weakness to have men who preach the gospel to speak out of their own experience, to speak of the comfort they have felt for themselves. Those who first preached the gospel, they were such as had felt the sweetness of it themselves. Paul, a great sinner outside of the church, and Peter inside the church. Peter fell after he was in the state of grace, that these great apostles might show to all people that there is no ground for despair. Paul was 'a blasphemer' and 'a persecutor' (1 Tim. 1:13), yet he found mercy. He found mercy for this end, that he 'might teach the mercy of God to others, that he might be an example of the mercy of God' (1 Tim. 1:16). If we relapse and fall, let no one despair. For Peter, a great teacher in the church, an apostle, see how foully he fell! Now, when men subject to the same infirmities, proclaim the mercy of God out of the book of God, their preaching will work more effectively upon their listeners.

*The Fountain Opened, Works*, vol. 5, pp. 506-07

# Preaching: Dispensing Truth to Be Received (4)

*And he gave the apostles, the prophets, the evangelists, the shepherds, and teachers, to equip the saints for the work of ministry, for building up the body of Christ.*—Eph. 4:11, 12

Some may object that preaching is only for the laying of the foundation of the church; it is not for the church when it is built. Then other disciplines like prayer help and we can do without preaching. Those that have such thoughts make themselves wiser than the Spirit of God. For Christ, 'when he ascended on high, he led captivity captive, he gave gifts to men, some apostles, some prophets, some evangelists, for the edifying and building up of the church' (Eph 4:9-12). The ordinance of preaching is still necessary for building up and knitting together the members of Christ. Further, those who are acquainted with their own infirmities know they are naturally dull, forgetful, and unmindful. Though we know, we do not remember; and though we remember, yet we do not apply things. We are naturally weak and need all spiritual supports and helps to keep the vessel of our souls in perpetual good standing. The more we hear and know, the fitter we are for doing and suffering; and for communion with God for all passages, both of life and death. Let us choose Mary's part, 'the better part' (Luke 10:42), that will never depart from us.

The word of God preached is not just to teach us, but the Spirit going with it, to work the grace necessary to 'strengthen us in the inward man' (2 Cor. 4:16). And those that say they know it enough, deceive themselves. Religion is a mystery, and can it be learned all at once? There is no mystery that doesn't require many years to learn. If it be but a handicraft, men are six or seven years learning it. And is religion, and the mysteries and depths of it, learned so soon? There is a mystery in every grace, in repentance, in faith, in patience, that no man knows, but those that have those graces. Let us therefore set a high price upon God's ordinance of preaching. Preaching is the chariot that carries Christ up and down the world. The ordinance of preaching is a great gift. God esteems it so, Christ esteems it so, and so should we esteem it.

*The Fountain Opened, Works,* vol. 5, pp. 508-09

# Preaching: Dispensing Truth to Be Received (5)

*For I decided to know nothing among you except Jesus Christ and him crucified.*—1 Cor. 2:2

Preaching must be of Christ. Some may question, 'But must nothing be preached but Christ?' Yes, nothing but Christ, or that which tends to Christ. Whatever is done in preaching to humble men, it is to raise them up again in Christ. When men are dejected by the law, we must raise them up again in Christ. Whatever we preach, it must lead to Christ. Once men have been taught Christ then they must also be taught to 'walk worthy of Christ, and of their calling' (Col. 1:10), that they may carry themselves fruitfully, constantly, and every way suitable to so glorious a profession. The foundation and graces for these duties must be in Christ; and the reasons and motives of a Christian's lifestyle must be from Christ. This made Paul, when he was among the Corinthians, to profess no knowledge of anything but of 'Christ, and him crucified' (1 Cor. 2:2). He had arts and tongues and abilities. He was a man who was excellently qualified, but he made show of none of these in his preaching. Only Christ, and the good things we have by Christ.

Now Christ must be preached wholly and only. We must not take anything from Christ, nor join anything to Christ. The Galatians believed that the old ceremonies were as necessary as Christ; and the apostle tells them, 'You are fallen from Christ' (Gal. 5:4). It is a destructive addition, to add anything to Christ. Away with other means of satisfaction. The satisfaction of Christ is enough. Away with the merit of works in matter of salvation. Christ's righteousness is that which we must labour to be found in, and 'not in our own' (Phil. 3:9). All is but 'dung and dross' (Phil. 3:8), in comparison to the excellent righteousness we have in Jesus Christ. Paul said, he was 'jealous with a holy jealousy' over those he taught. Why? 'Lest Satan should beguile them and draw them from Christ' to any other thing (2 Cor. 11:2, 3). Those who are true preachers, ambassadors, and messengers, must be 'jealous with a holy jealousy' over the people of God, that they look to nothing but Christ.

*The Fountain Opened, Works,* vol. 5, pp. 509-10

# The Treasure of the Gospel

*Repentance and remission of sins should be preached in his name unto all the nations, beginning from Jerusalem.*—Luke 24:47

There are several degrees of the dispensation of salvation. There is first the ordaining of salvation. That took place before the creation of the worlds. Then the promise of salvation. That was when Adam fell. Then the procuring of the salvation promised. That was by Christ when he came in the flesh. Then the enlarging of salvation to all people. This was after Christ had come in the flesh. Then there is the perfect consummation of salvation in heaven. Now the execution of the promise and the performance of all good concerning salvation was reserved to Christ's coming in the flesh; and the actual enlargement of the promise to all nations was not until then. I do but touch on these things to show that God has had a special care for this latter age of the world. Some account the first age of the world to be the golden age, the next silver, and then an iron age. But indeed, we may invert the order. We live in the golden age when Christ was made manifest in the flesh. What is the glory of times and places? The manifestation of Christ. The more Christ is laid open with his unsearchable riches, the more God glorifies those times and places; and that is this golden age where the gospel is preached.

We have a confidence in the spread of the gospel to all people because the Gentiles now have an interest in Christ. Those merchants and those that give themselves to navigation may with good success carry the gospel to all people. There are none shut out in this last age of the world. Yet, remember, Christ will not abide long where he is not esteemed, where the gospel is undervalued and blended with that which is detrimental to the purity of it. The state of the gospel and truth is such, that if it be mingled with anything false, it overthrows it; and Christ will not endure this indignity. Let us take heed that we keep Christ and his truth with us purely and only; if we would have it stay with us.

*The Fountain Opened, Works*, vol. 5, p. 512

# The Mysteries of the Gospel (1)

*God chose what is low and despised in the world, even things that are*
*not, to bring to nothing things that are.*—1 Cor. 1:28

(1) Consider what the world was, an enemy to Christ; being slaves to Satan, being idolaters in love with their own inventions. Here was the wonder of God's love, mercy, and condescension that he should entrust it to such wretches. We may see from Paul's epistles what kind of people they were before they embraced the gospel; like those who 'sat in darkness, and in the shadow of death' (Luke 1:79). That the world, from the highest to the lowest, should at length stoop to the cross of Christ; that many of the emperors should lay their crowns at Christ's feet, as Constantine and others; that many of the philosophers of the world, who were clever and learned, should at length come to embrace the gospel—for many of the church fathers were philosophers before becoming believers in Christ; that men of status, learning, education, and breeding, should cast all at the feet of Christ; for these to be overcome by plain preaching; for weakness to overcome mightiness; for ignorance to overcome knowledge; these are all great mysteries.

(2) Consider the people who carried the gospel, by which the world was subdued—a company of weak and unlearned men, none of the deepest for knowledge, only they had the Holy Spirit to teach and instruct, to strengthen and fortify them—which the world took no notice of—men of low condition, of low esteem, and few in number. These men came not with weapons, but merely with the word, and with sufferings. Their weapons were nothing but patience, and preaching, offering the word of God to them, and suffering indignities; as Augustine said, 'The world was not overcome by fighting, but by suffering.' Christ said, 'I send you as sheep among wolves' (Matt. 10:16); and how? With nothing but carrying a message and suffering constantly and undauntedly for that message. They had cruel bloody laws made against them which were executed to the utmost; yet by these means they overcame by preaching and by sealing the truth by suffering—a strange kind of conquest.

*The Fountain Opened, Works*, vol. 5, pp. 517-18

# The Mysteries of the Gospel (2)

*Making known to us the mystery of his will, according to his purpose,*
*which he set forth in Christ.*—Eph. 1:9

(3) Consider the truth that they taught which was contrary to the nature and affections of man. To enforce self-denial to men who are naturally full of self-love, who make an idol of their wisdom and will; for them to come to be taught to be fools in respect of their wisdom and to resign their wills to the will of another—for these men to 'believe things that are above belief to carnal men,' as Augustine observed, was a great mystery.

(4) Consider the suddenness of the conquest. In a short time after Christ, one man, Paul, spread the gospel over almost all the world. He spread the savour of the gospel like lightning; suddenly and strongly, because there was the almighty power of the Spirit accompanying the glorious gospel.

(5) Consider Christ; who was he? Indeed, he was the Son of God, but he appeared in abased flesh, in the form of a servant, and he was crucified. For the proud world to believe in a crucified Saviour was a mystery.

(6) Lastly, in respect of faith itself. Faith being so contrary to the nature of man. For the heart of man, where faith is wrought, to go out of itself, to embrace a rising to life from another, to seek justification and salvation by the righteousness and obedience of another; for the proud heart of man to stoop to this, to acknowledge no righteousness of its own, to have all derived from Jesus Christ, to fetch forgiveness of sins out of the death of another, these are all mysterious. The heart of man, without a supernatural work of the Spirit to subdue it, would never yield to this, because proud flesh and blood will always have something in itself to set up before God. Especially for a guilty soul, that has its eyes opened to discern its own state. For these two to meet together; God, and a doubting and galled conscience; by an act of faith, casting itself upon Christ, this is more than can be done by any power of nature.

*The Fountain Opened, Works*, vol. 5, pp. 518-19

# Knowing That Christ Is at the Father's Right Hand (1)

*The LORD says to my Lord: 'Sit at my right hand, until I make your enemies your footstool.'* —Psa. 110:1

It is a great comfort knowing that Christ ascended for us.

It is a singular comfort that Christ ascended as a public person, on our behalf, in our nature, for our good. When we think of Christ in heaven think of ourselves in heaven also. 'We are seated together with Christ in the heavenly places' (Eph. 1:20). We have a glorious life, but it is hidden with Christ in heaven. When Christ himself will be revealed, our life will be revealed with him. Though we creep upon the earth as worms, yet we have communion and fellowship with Christ, who is joined with us in the same mystical body, who is now at the right hand of God in heaven. He took on flesh and blood that he might bring his church to glory. Therefore, we ought to as confidently believe that he will take his mystical body, and every particular member of it, to heaven, as we believe he has already taken his natural body and set it in glory.

It is a comfort, in the hour of death, that we yield up our souls to Christ, who has gone before to provide a place for us (John 14:2). Therefore, when we die, we do not have to seek a place. Our house has already been provided. Even as paradise was provided for Adam before he was made, so we have a heavenly paradise provided for us. We had a place in heaven before we were born. What a comfort this is at the hour of death, and at the death of our friends, who have gone to Christ and glory! We were shut out of the first paradise by the first Adam. But now our comfort is the heavenly paradise that has been opened to us in Christ. There was an angel to guard paradise when Adam was shut out; but there is none to keep us out of heaven. No, the angels are ready to convey our souls to heaven, as they did Lazarus (Luke 16:22), and as they accompanied Christ in his ascension to heaven, so will they attend the souls of his children.

*The Fountain Opened, Works*, Vol. 5, pp. 529-30

# Knowing That Christ Is at the Father's Right Hand (2)

*Who is to condemn? Christ Jesus is the one who died—more than that, who was raised—who is at the right hand of God, who indeed is interceding for us.—Rom. 8:34*

Christ's ascension is a comfort in our sins and infirmities. When we have to deal with God the Father, whom we have offended with our sins, let us receive comfort from this: Christ is ascended into heaven, to appear before his Father as a mediator for us; and, therefore, God turns away his wrath from us. We have a friend, a favourite in the court of heaven, the Son of God himself, at his Father's right hand and he makes intercession for us. As Jonathan appeared in Saul's court to speak a good word and to plead for David (1 Sam. 19:4), so does Jesus Christ appear in the court of heaven for us, but with far better success. He makes intercession for us and continues our peace with God despite our daily breaches. It is as if he should say; 'These are the people that I was born for; that I obeyed for; that I died for; that I was sent into the world to work the great work of redemption for.' He wrought our redemption in his humbled state; but he applies it in his exalted state. Even as there is speech attributed to Abel's blood (Gen. 4:10)—it cried, 'Vengeance, vengeance!'—so Christ appearing now in heaven for us, his blood cries, 'Mercy, mercy! These are those I shed my blood for; mercy, Lord!'

In the law, the high priest, after he had offered a sacrifice of blood, was to go into the holy of holies; so Christ, after he had offered himself for a sacrifice went into the holy of holies, into heaven, to appear before God. As the high priest went into the holy of holies, he had the names of the twelve tribes on his breast, to show that he appeared before God for them all. So Christ, having gone to heaven, has all our names upon his breast; that is, in his heart the name of every particular believer; to present them before God. Therefore, when we have to deal with God, think of Christ, now glorious in heaven, appearing for us.

*The Fountain Opened, Works*, Vol. 5, p. 530

# Knowing That Christ Is at the Father's Right Hand (3)

*Now I rejoice in my sufferings for your sake, and in my flesh, I am filling up what is lacking in Christ's afflictions for the sake of his body, that is, the church.*—Col. 1:24

Christ's ascension is a ground of contentment in all conditions. What if we lack comfort, houses, or anything on earth, when we have heaven provided for us, and glory provided for us in our Head? Will not any condition content a man in this world, who has such a glorious condition in the eye of faith to enter into? We should look up to heaven with comfort: Yonder is my Saviour, yonder is a house provided for me. Here we may lack comforts, we may be thrust out of house and home, out of our country and all; but all the world, and all the devils in hell, cannot thrust us out of heaven, nor dissolve or break the communion that is between Christ and us. Therefore, we should be content with any condition in this world. Christ is ascended into heaven, to keep a blessed condition for us.

Likewise, when we think of the troubles of this world, of the enemies we have here, we must often only think of Christ taken up to glory. But he first suffered, and then he entered into glory. We must be content to suffer first, and then be glorified. We were predestined to be conformed to Christ's image. Where stands our conformity? It is first in being humbled, and then being glorified. Christ entered into glory in this order, and will we think to come to heaven in another order than Christ did? If we are in Christ, all that we suffer in this world, are sufferings of conformity that make us like our Head and fit us for glory. Our greatest humiliations, what are they in comparison to the humiliation of Christ? None was ever so low, and there is none so high. As he was the lowest in humiliation, so he is the highest in glory. When he was at the lowest, in the grave, not only dead, but under the kingdom and command of death, then he rose gloriously and ascended. Our lowest humiliations are forerunners of our advancement and glory.

*The Fountain Opened, Works,* Vol. 5, pp. 530-31

## Knowing That Christ Is at the Father's Right Hand (4)

*For we do not have a high priest who is unable to sympathize with our weaknesses, but one who in every respect has been tempted as we are, yet without sin.*—Heb. 4:15

In all the disconsolations of this life there is a world of comfort from Christ's ascension. We must not think of Christ, as if his honours had changed his manners, as it is among men; that now that he has been glorified, he does not regard his poor church. No, he regards his poor church from heaven as much as he ever did. The members here cannot suffer anything but the Head in heaven is sensible of it; as it is in Acts 9:4, 'Saul, Saul, why are you persecuting me?' Our blessed Saviour is not like Pharaoh's unkind butler, who forgot Joseph when he was out of prison. No; he is as good Joseph, who was sent into Egypt to provide for all his family beforehand. Our Joseph has gone to provide for us all, until we come to heaven. He forgets us not. He disdains not to look on things below (Psa. 33:14; Isa. 49:13-16). He is as merciful now as he was when he was upon the earth. 'He was a man for this end, that he might be a merciful high priest' (Heb. 4:15). It is not, out of sight, out of mind, with him. For he was taken up to heaven in the body, but his Spirit is here with us to the end of the world. 'I will send you the Comforter, and he will abide with you' (John 14:16, 17). It is better for us to have the Comforter here, without his bodily presence, than to have his bodily presence without the abundance of his Spirit, just as it was better with the disciples when he was taken up to heaven and was given his Spirit. We lose nothing by the ascension of Christ. He was given for us, born for us. He lived for us, he died for us, he rose and ascended to heaven for our good. 'It is good for you that I go' (John 16:7). It was to provide a place for us, and to send the Comforter. All was for our good.

*The Fountain Opened, Works*, vol. 5, p. 531

# Knowing That Christ is at the Father's Right Hand (5)

*And I tell you, you are Peter, and on this rock I will build my church,*
*and the gates of hell shall not prevail against it.*—Matt. 16:18

Christ's ascension gives comfort when the church is experiencing affliction. When the church is afflicted, does the church have a glorious Head in heaven who sits and does nothing? No. He sits at the right hand of God and rules his church, even when the church is in the midst of his enemies. If he gives chains to them, it is for special ends. Nothing can befall his church without his control. He lets loose the enemies only so far, and then he restrains them, subdues and conquers them. The enemies seem to domineer now, but before long they will become the church's footstool. He is fitting his church by these afflictions, for greater grace in this world, and for eternal glory in the world to come.

Let us not be offended at the present state of things. For our comfort let us consider that Christ has been taken up to glory, and he sits in heaven and rules his church, and will guide all wars to a good and gracious end. The ship may be tossed where Christ sleeps, but it cannot be drowned (Luke 8:23). The house that is built upon a rock, it may be blown upon, it will never be overthrown (Matt. 7:25). The church may be tossed, but it will never be overcome and subdued (Matt. 16:18). No, in all the things the church suffers, Christ rules, and exercises his church's graces, and mortifies his church's corruptions. As standing waters breed frogs and other low creatures; so it is with Christians. If there isn't some exercise by afflictions, what kind of vices grow? As we see in times of peace, God is so merciful to continue his truth in a proud company who lead lives, under the gospel, no better than if they were in paganism. If troubles come, many of us would be the better for it; afflictions are far from doing us harm; they refine us. In all trouble we lose nothing, but that which hurts us, that which we may easily do without, and that which hinders our joy and comfort.

*The Fountain Opened, Works*, vol. 5, pp. 531-32

# Heavenly-Mindedness

*Therefore, since you have been raised with Christ, strive for the things above, where Christ is seated at the right hand of God.*—Col. 3:1

The mystery of Christ's glory leads us to godliness (1 Tim. 3:16) by stirring us up to being heavenly-minded. The apostle divinely exhorts the Colossians, 'If you are risen with Christ, seek the things that are above' (Col. 3:1). From our communion with Christ, being raised and ascended into heaven, and seated in glory, he calls them to be heavenly-minded. That our thoughts should be where his glory is, where our Head is. Certainly, there is nothing in the world stronger to enforce a heavenly mind than this, to consider where we are, in our Head. There is our inheritance; there are a great many of our fellow-brethren; there is our country; there is our happiness. We are for heaven, and not for this world. This life is but a passage to that glory that Christ has taken up for us. Why should we have our minds grovelling here upon the earth? If we have interest in Christ, who is at the right hand of God, it is necessary that our souls be raised to heaven in our affections before we are there in our bodies. All who are Christians are in heaven in their spirit and lifestyle beforehand. Our heavy, dull, earthly souls, being touched by his Spirit, will ascend. When iron is touched by a magnet, though it is a heavy body, it ascends to the magnet, it follows it. Christ as the magnet of heaven, has an attracting force which draws us up. If we have communion with Christ and have our hearts touched by his Spirit, he will draw us up even though of ourselves we are heavy and lumpish. This meditation, that Christ our Head is in glory, and that we are in heaven in him, and that our happiness is there, it will purge and refine us from our earthliness, and draw up our iron, heavy, cold hearts.

*The Fountain Opened, Works*, vol. 5, pp. 536-37

# Be Mindful of Your Soul (1)

*And do not fear those who kill the body but cannot kill the soul. Rather fear him who can destroy both soul and body in hell.*—Matt. 10:28

Our chief care must be over our souls. We must desire God to preserve our souls. Whatever becomes of the soul; our principal care must be that the soul be not blemished in the least kind. This body of ours, or whatsoever is dear in the world, will be stripped from us, and laid in the dust before long. But here is our comfort, though our body be dead, yet our soul will still be alive. Our body is but the case or tabernacle wherein our soul dwells. A man's self is his soul; keep that and you keep all. You get many compliments and questions in the world concerning your body, but how few will inquire about your soul? The body perhaps is well looked after, that it is clothed, and taken care that nothing be wanting to it, but the poor soul is ragged and wounded, and naked. Oh, that men were sensible of the miserable condition their poor souls are in.

Beloved, the soul is the better part of a man, and if that miscarries, all miscarries. If the soul be not well, the body will not continue long in a good state. Bernard of Clairvaux said sweetly, 'Oh, body, you have a noble guest dwelling in you, a soul of such inestimable worth that it makes you truly noble.' Whatever goodness and excellency are in the body is communicated from the soul; when the soul once departs, the body is an unlovely thing, without life or sense. What an incredible baseness it is therefore that so precious a thing as the soul should serve these vile bodies of ours! Let the body be done with its leisure; the time of the resurrection is the time of the body. In this life the body should be serviceable to our souls by suffering and doing whatever God calls us to. Let our bodies serve our souls now, and then body and soul will be happy forever after. However, if we, to gratify our bodies, do betray our souls, both are undone.

*The Saint's Hiding-Place in the Day of Evil, Works,* vol. 1, p. 408

# Be Mindful of Your Soul (2)

*For God alone my soul waits in silence; from him comes my salvation.*—Psa. 62:1

Beloved, the devil and devilish-minded men have a special spite to the soul. What do they aim at in all their wrongs and injuries to God's children? Do they care to hurt the body? They will do this rather than nothing at all; they will rather play at small game than sit out. The devil will enter the swine rather than stand out altogether. However, his main spite is at the soul, to vex and disquiet the soul, and taint it with sin all he can. Considering that it is Satan's aim to unloose our hold from God by defiling our souls with sin, so to put a separation between his blessed majesty and us, let it be our chief care to see to that which Satan strikes at most! He did not so much care, in Job's trouble, for his goods, or for his house, or children, etc. Alas, he aimed at a further mischief than these! His plot was how to make him blaspheme and wound his soul, that so there might be a division between God and him. He first tempts us to commit sin, and afterwards to despair for sin.

Commit the keeping of your souls to God. Indeed, he only can keep our souls. We cannot keep them ourselves; neither can anything else in the world. Some when they are sick will commit themselves to a physician and put all their trust in him. When they are in trouble, they will commit themselves to a great friend; when they have any bad or disobedient cause to manage, they will commit themselves to their purse, and think it will bear them out in anything. One thinks his cleverness and abilities will secure him, another that his ingenuity may shelter him. Indeed the heart of man is so full of atheism, that it can never light upon the right object, to trust God alone, until it sees everything else fail, as being insufficient to support the soul, or to yield any solid comfort in times of extremity and distress.

*The Saint's Hiding-Place in the Day of Evil, Works,* vol. 1, pp. 408-09

# Man's Happiness Is Found in God Alone

*But for me it is good to be near God; I have made the Lord God my refuge, that I may tell of all your works.*—Psa. 73:28

A wicked man may be convinced that heaven and grace are good things; but his corrupted affections persuade him that it would be better to live in pleasure and lust now; and when death comes then he may repent, for God is merciful. But a good man prefers drawing near to God above anything else. This made Moses in his sober evaluating of things to choose to draw near to God and join with his afflicted brethren, than to live with honour in Pharaoh's court and enjoy worldly pleasures. 'He had respect to the reward' (Heb. 11:25). He was convinced that there was more to be gotten with his brethren than with the Egyptians.

Man's happiness is in communion with God. Before the fall of man, there was familiar conversation with God; but by the sin of our first parents, we lost this great happiness, and now we are strangers, and as contrary to God as light is contrary to darkness, and hell to heaven. He is holy, we are impure; he is full of knowledge, we are stark fools. Instead of delighting in him we tremble at his presence and are even afraid of those who draw near to him. 'What have I to do with you, man of God? Have you come to call my sins to remembrance?' (1 Kings 17:18). We flee from the company of good men, because their behaviour and course of life rebukes us. But God, in his infinite mercy and goodness, did not leave us in that state. He purposed to choose some to draw near to him; and to this end he found a way for man and him to meet. The foundation of this union is in Christ, in whom God reconciled the world to himself. Jesus, being God, became man, so to draw man back to God. He has made a means to make the seeming opposite attributes of justice and mercy to kiss each other. We by his grace are saved, yet at the same time his infinite justice has been fully met.

*The Saint's Happiness, Works*, Vol. 7, pp. 70-72

# Growing Nearer to God (1)

*They said to each other, 'Did not our hearts burn within us while he talked to us on the road, while he opened to us the Scriptures?'*—Luke 24:32

Seek to be nearer to God by submitting to his Spirit. The more we grow in spiritual things, the closer access we have to the secrets of God. In our first state, we are altogether flesh and have no spirit; in our present state of grace, we are partly flesh and partly spirit; in our third state in heaven, we will be all spirit; yea, our bodies will be spiritual (1 Cor. 15:44). Then our bodies will be obedient to our souls in all things. Until that day, grow in spiritual things:

(1) Labour to be conversant in spiritual means, as in hearing the word and receiving the ordinances. God connects his Spirit to his own means of grace. But take heed how we come; think what we have to do, and the one we are approaching. Come with a humble heart, as Elizabeth. 'Who am I, that God himself from heaven should come to me!' (Luke 1:43).

(2) Converse with others who draw near to God. He is present where two or three are assembled in his name, warming their hearts with love and affection, as it is said by the two disciples going to Emmaus, 'Did not our hearts burn within us while we walked in the way, and conferred of the sayings?' (Luke 24:32). It is a noteworthy sign of a spiritual heart to seek spiritual company; for when their hearts are joined together, they warm one another, and by this they are guarded from temptations.

(3) Be much in prayer; for this is not only a main part of the duty of drawing near to God, but it is the most powerful help in drawing near to him. For they are most near to God when their understandings, affections, desires, trust, hope, faith, are occupied about God. Every day's necessities and dangers from the devil, the flesh, and the world; from ill company, and strong corruptions, should invite us to cast ourselves under the protection of an almighty Saviour through prayer. There is not a minute of time in all our lives, but we must either be near God or we are undone.

*The Saint's Happiness, Works, vol. 7, p. 73*

# Growing Nearer to God (2)

*So flee youthful passions and pursue righteousness, faith, love, and peace, along with those who call on the Lord from a pure heart.*—2 Tim. 2:22

(4) Observe and check the first motions of sin in our hearts. 'You, O man of God, fly from the lusts of youth' (2 Tim. 2:22). Rebuke the first motions, before they come to delight or action. God abhors the one who gives liberty and license to his thoughts, more than the one who falls into a grievous sin through a strong temptation. The latter will find comfort sooner of the pardon of their sins, for they realize their offences to be heinous, and so have grounds to abase themselves. But the former, thinking their sins to be small, or at least that God is not much offended with thoughts, fill themselves with contemplative wickedness, and chase away the Spirit of God, who cannot endure an unclean mind and heart. The least sin in thought, if it be entertained, eats out the strength of the soul, so much so that it can receive nothing good from God, nor be close to him, 'If I regard iniquity in my heart, the Lord will not hear my prayer' (Psa. 66:18). This is why there is so little good from the ordinances of God. Men bring their lusts along with them. They neither know nor desire the sweetness of the presence of God's Spirit. It is a true rule that every sin has intrinsically in it some punishment; but it is not the punishment that is the proper venom of sin; but this, that it hinders the Spirit of God from us, and keeps us from him, and unfits us for life or for death. Let men profess what they will, but when they go to lewd company and filthy places, where corruptions are shot into them by all their senses, they can neither take delight in drawing near to God, nor can God take any delight in drawing near to them. By their actions they proclaim to the whole world that they say to God, 'Depart from us, for we will have none of your ways' (Job 21:14). So as God draws away from them, they draw away from him.

*The Saint's Happiness, Works*, vol. 7, pp. 73-74

# Growing Nearer to God (3)

*Humble yourselves, therefore, under the mighty hand of God so that at*
*the proper time he may exalt you.*—1 Pet. 5:6

(5) Be in God's ways and ordinances in all the good you do. Whether in our Christian or civil calling, all must be sanctified by prayer and a holy dependence upon God for strength, wisdom, and success. Whatever we do, labour to do it with perfection, as our Father in heaven is perfect.

(6) Observe God's dealings with the church, both in former days and now in these days; how he deals and has dealt with his people. From the experience of his faithfulness to us in the past we may gather confidence to approach near to him on any occasion. God's works and words do answer one another: 'Has he said, and will he not do it?' (Num. 23:19). Observe how all things work together to help you draw near to him. For if all things do work together for your good (Rom. 8:28), then all must be to draw you nearer to God, and away from this present world. Observe how your affections are bent, and so how all comes out for your benefit at last. See how God in afflictions embitters ill courses in you; how in your successes he encourages you. But evermore think of him as of a Father in covenant with you who wants you to walk with him.

(7) Labour to maintain humility, having a sense of your unworthiness, your needs, and your continual dependence on God. Humble yourself to walk with him. God is 'a consuming fire' (Heb. 12:29) and he will be worshipped and sanctified by all who come near to him. 'He will regard the humble but beholds the proud afar off' (Psa. 138:6). 'Draw near to the Lord, and he will draw near to you' (James 4:8). 'Humble yourselves under the mighty hand of God, and he will lift you up' (1 Pet. 5:6). He that lifts himself up, makes himself a god; and God will endure no rivals. Contrarily, 'he dwells in the heart of the humble' (Isa. 57:15); and 'a humble and a contrite heart, O God, you will not despise' (Psa. 51:17).

*The Saint's Happiness, Works*, vol. 7, pp. 74-75

# Growing Nearer to God (4)

*Behold, I stand at the door and knock. If anyone hears my voice and opens the door, I will come in to him and eat with him, and he with me.*—Rev. 3:20

(8) Labour for sincerity in all our actions. Whatever we do for God or man, do it with a single eye, resolved to please God. Let men say what they will, 'a double-minded man is unstable in all his ways' (James 1:8); and what is a double-minded man, but one that has one eye on God, and the other on those he is trying to please? If God fails him, he will at least have the favour of men, or wealth. Such are gross pretenders; and in time, they will be seen as having a religion that served as a cloak for their vile hypocrisy. These God loathes and will 'spit them out' (Rev. 3:16).

(9) Observe the first motions of God's Spirit; and give diligent heed to them, for by these God knocks for entrance into the heart. 'Behold, I stand at the door and knock' (Rev. 3:20). God is near when he knocks, when he puts inclinations into the heart, and sharpens them with afflictions. If we stop our ears, we may say God was near to us, but if he once ceases knocking, our mouths will forever be stopped. It is for this reason that so many live daily under the means of grace and yet live in vile courses. They resisted the first motions of God's Spirit and follow instead their lusts, and so God pronounces a curse: 'Make this people's heart dull' (Isa. 6:10). On the contrary, those who will open to God while he continues knocking, God will come in and make an everlasting tabernacle in them, and sup with them (Rev. 3:20).

(10) Take up against the daily controversies that arise in us through the inconstancy of our deceivable hearts. Repentance must be every day's work, renewing our covenant, especially every morning and evening. Repair breaches by confession and considering the fickleness of our hearts. Commit your heart to God by prayer; 'Knit my heart to you, that I may fear your name' (Psa. 86:11).

*The Saint's Happiness, Works,* vol. 7, p. 75

# Find God at All Cost

*If this be so, our God whom we serve is able to deliver us from the burning fiery furnace, and he will deliver us out of your hand, O king. But if not, be it known to you, O king, that we will not serve your gods or worship the golden image that you have set up.*—Dan. 3:17, 18

A Christian who, through Christ, draws near to God is the wisest man. He has God's word, reason, and experience to support his choice. Paul suffered, and was not ashamed. Why? 'I know whom I have believed' (2 Tim 1:12). Let men scorn, I care not for man's censure. They will never scorn me out of my faith. The Scriptures, which are the best judge, call those men fools; for they refuse God, who is the highest good, and seek their contentment where none is to be found. In God is all fullness; in Christ are unsearchable riches; in God everlasting strength, 'and his favour is better than life itself' (Psa. 63:3).

From this we learn how to defend zeal in religion. If being near to God is good, then the nearer to him the better; if religion is good, then the more the better; if holiness is good, then the more the better; it is best to excel in the best things. It should shame us to be spiritually cold and to have little zeal, as if we are ashamed of goodness, as most are.

This also teaches us that a man must not break with God for any creature's sake or reason. It is good to lose all for God. Why? Because we have riches in him, liberty in him, all in him. If we lose anything for God, even if it be our own life, we will save it. The Spirit of God, who 'searches the deep things of God' (1 Cor. 2:10), puts a relish into us of the 'unsearchable riches of Christ' (Eph. 3:8). 'Taste and see how good God is' (Psa. 34:8). 'How excellent is your loving-kindness, which you have laid up for those who fear you' (Psa. 36:7). 'How precious are your thoughts to me, O Lord' (Psa. 139:17). 'You have the words of everlasting life, to whom shall we go?' (John 6:68) said Peter, when he caught just a glimpse of Christ's divine power.

*The Saint's Happiness, Works*, vol. 7, pp. 75-76

# Behold! (1)

*Therefore the Lord himself will give you a sign. Behold, the virgin shall conceive and bear a son.*—Isa. 7:14a

'Behold.' This is the usual harbinger in matters concerning Christ. The word has a threefold force. First as a thing presented to the eye of faith. Second the word gets our attention, for it announces a matter of great concern. Third, not only attention, but also our admiration. For it announces a strange and admirable thing. For what stranger thing is there than that a virgin should conceive, that a virgin should be a mother, and that God should become man. We need strong grace to apprehend these strange things. God has provided the suitable grace. A grace above reason, and above nature, and that grace is faith.

'Behold, a virgin shall conceive.' Why a virgin? When God is to be born, it is fitting for a virgin to be the mother. Christ was not to come by the ordinary means of propagation. He was to come from Adam but not by Adam. He was conceived and sanctified by the Holy Spirit, for he had to be without spot or sin when he offered himself as a sacrifice for the sins of others.

'Behold, a virgin shall conceive, and bear a son.' He was conceived as we are, born as we are born, he was hungry, thirsty, and suffered as we. He was like us in all things, except sin. He was a man like us, but he was an extraordinary man. He was conceived, but of a virgin. He was born as we are, but his star appeared, and the wise men came to worship him. He was poor as we are, but he could command a fish to furnish him (Matt. 17:27). He died as we die, but he made the 'earth to quake, the veil of the temple to rend' when he triumphed on the cross (Matt. 27:51). All which declared he was more than an ordinary person. Our response must be to conceive Christ by faith and bear Christ in our words and actions. Our whole outward life must be nothing but a revealing that Christ lives in us. As Paul said, 'I live, yet not I, but Christ lives in me' (Gal. 2:20).

*Miracle of Miracles, Works*, vol. 7, pp. 109-11

# Behold! (2)

*And shall call his name Emmanuel.*—Isa. 7:14b

Emmanuel is a name both of nature and office. It is a name of his nature, God and man; and of his office, which is to reconcile God and man. The pure nature of God, and the fallen nature of man, which were strangers since the fall, are knit together in Christ. What can be in a greater degree of strangeness, except the devil's, than man's unholiness and God's pure nature? Yet the nature of man and of God are met together in one Christ; so that in this one word, Emmanuel, there is heaven and earth, God and man, infinite and finite; therefore, we may well prefix the word, behold! (Isa. 7:14a). A true Saviour of the world must be God with man, whether we consider the good we are to have by a Saviour, or the evil we are to be freed from by a Saviour, both enforce that he must be Emmanuel, God with us. To satisfy the wrath of God, to undergo a punishment due to sin as our surety, to give us title to heaven, and to bring us there, to know our hearts, our wants, our griefs, our infirmities; who can do these things but God?

As he was God, so there was a necessity of his becoming man. For man had sinned, man must suffer for sin, and 'without the shedding of blood there was no remission' (Heb. 9:22). Also, that he might be 'a merciful and faithful Saviour' (Heb. 2:17), he must take the nature on him of those he means to save.

This God and man must be one person; for if there were two persons, there would be two Christs, and the actions of the one could not be attributed to the other. If only as a man he died and shed his blood, it could not have been said that God died; but because there was but one person, God is truly said to die. In all his actions there was concurrence of divinity and humanity; the meaner works being done by the manhood, the greater works by the Godhead, so making him, Emmanuel, God with us.

*Miracle of Miracles, Works,* vol. 7, pp. 111-13

# Behold! (3)

*Behold, the virgin shall conceive and bear a son, and they shall call his name Emmanuel (which means, God with us)*—Matt. 1:23.

Emmanuel, God with us. If God is with us in our nature, then he is with us in his love; 'and if God is with us, who shall be against us?' (Rom. 8:31). For this Emmanuel has taken our nature forever; he has taken it into heaven with him. God and we will forever be in good terms, because God in our nature is forever in heaven, as an intercessor appearing for us. There is no fear of a breach now; for our Brother is in heaven, our Husband is in heaven, to preserve an everlasting union and peace between God and us.

Let us make use of this Emmanuel in all our troubles. He did not take a superior nature, but he took our poverty, our humanity. He is poor with the poor, afflicted with the afflicted, persecuted with the persecuted. He is deserted with those who are deserted, he suffers with those who suffer. He is able to pity and comfort us in our disgrace, in our conflict with God, in our terror of conscience, and in all our temptations and assaults by Satan. Let us not lose the comforts of this sweet name. In the hour of death, think of Emmanuel. Fear not to go to the grave, Emmanuel has been there. He will go into the grave; he will bring us out of the dust again; for Emmanuel is God with us; who is God over death, over sin, over the wrath of God, blessed for evermore, and triumphant over all. We know that nothing can separate us from the love of God in Christ Jesus (Rom. 8:35).

He is not only God with us in our nature, but he is also God for us in heaven. He is God in us by his Spirit. He is God amongst us in our meetings, 'Where two or three are gathered together in my name, I will be in the midst of them' (Matt. 18:20). He is also God for us in heaven; to defend and intercede for us. Therefore, let us enlarge our comforts by this as much as we can.

*Miracle of Miracles, Works,* vol. 7, pp. 113-15

## Determining the Condition of Our Desires (1)

*Teach me your way, O Lord, that I may walk in your truth; unite my heart to fear your name.*—Psa. 86:11

One objective of Christianity is for us to desire to be sound Christians with all our hearts. Religion is more in the affections of the soul than in the effects and operations. It is more in the resolutions and purpose of the soul than in any works we can yield to God. Why are desires such good markers of the truth of grace in our lives? Because they are the immediate issues of the soul. Desires and thoughts are produced immediately from the soul, without any help of the body. They show the temper and frame of the soul. Thereupon God judges a man by his desires.

How can we know the truth and sincerity of our desires?

(1) If they are constant desires and not flashes; for then they come from a new nature. Nature is strong and firm. Fancy is for a moment or to serve a moment. When men impersonate a thing, they do not do it long. Creatures that are forced return to their own natures quickly; but when a man does a thing naturally, he does it constantly. So, constant desires argue a sanctified frame of soul and a new creation. They argue that the image of God has been stamped upon the soul. Thereupon we may know that they are holy desires and that they spring from a holy soul, if they be constant, if they be perpetual desires.

(2) If these desires are hearty, strong desires; and not only strong, but growing desires—desire upon desire, desire fed with desire still, never satisfied till they be satisfied. Strong and growing desires argue the truth of desires; as indeed a child of God has never grace enough, never faith enough, never love enough, or comfort enough, until he comes to heaven. They are growing desires. The Spirit of God, that is the spring in him, who springs up further and further, until it springs to everlasting life, until it ends in heaven, where all desires will be accomplished, and all promises performed, and all imperfections removed.

*At the Throne of Grace, Works*, vol. 6, pp. 98-100

# Determining the Condition of Our Desires (2)

*Behold, you delight in truth in the inward being, and you teach me wisdom in the secret heart.*—Psa. 51:6

(3) True desires are not only for the favour of God, but for the graces that will alter our natures. Now when desire is for these graces, it is a holy desire. To desire grace, which is as opposite to our corrupt nature as fire is from water, this is an argument of a holy principle of grace in us. When a man from the bottom of his heart can desire; 'Oh that I could serve God better! That I had a heart more enlarged, more mortified, more weaned from the world! That I could fear God more!'—it is for certain a true desire.

(4) True desire is carried to grace as well as to glory; the desire of heaven itself. A true spirit that is touched with grace, with the Spirit of God, desires heaven not for the glory, and peace, and abundance of all contentment, as much as it desires it as the place where it will be freed from sin, and where the heart will be enlarged to love God, to serve God, and to cleave to God forever, and as the condition wherein he will have the image and resemblance of Jesus Christ perfectly upon his soul. We pray, 'Your kingdom come,' that is, we desire that you would rule more and more largely in our souls, and subdue all opposite power in us, and bring into captivity all our desires and affections. Let 'Your kingdom come' more and more. 'Let your will be done' in us more and more, 'in earth as it is in heaven' (Matt. 6:10). These desires argue an excellent frame of soul.

(5) Where a man has holy desires of any grace, he will desire the means whereby those graces may most effectually be wrought in his heart. He will hear the word as the word of God. He comes not to hear the word because of the eloquence of the man that delivers it. It is the powerful word of God and with it the efficacy of the Spirit to work the graces he desires.

*At the Throne of Grace, Works,* vol. 6, pp. 99-100

## Praying Christians and God's Sovereignty

*The king's heart is a stream of water in the hand of the Lord; he turns it wherever he will.*—Prov. 21:1

Any good Christian may be a good statesman in one good sense. He who can prevail with God to prevail with the leaders of the earth, surely such a man is a profitable man in the state. We know that God can alter all matters and mould all things. What God can do, prayer can do. Christians can prevail with God for a blessing upon a state. 'The innocent man delivers the land' (Job 22:30). And the 'poor wise man delivers the city' (Eccles. 9:15). A few holy, gracious men, that have grace and credit in heaven may move God to set all things in a blessed frame below. If this holy means were used, things would be better than they are; and until this be used, we can never look for the good that we hope for.

Consider whether God foresees and determines things below based upon his foresight of the way they go; or whether he foreordains how things will go. It is the latter because God is God indeed. He determines how things will be. He determines the series and order of causes, to bring things to pass, and to guide rulers his way. If God has set all men at liberty, in matters of grace especially, to determine this or that for themselves. This is to make every man's will a god, and to divest God of his honour, as if God could only foresee the inclination of the creature and was unable to incline it in any way. This is to make him no God. But in truth, we see that God has everything and particularly the hearts of rulers in his power, and that is our grounds for praying for them. Except we hold this we will never pray heartily or give thanks. But if we do pray and give thanks, he will put thoughts into public servants' minds, strange thoughts and resolutions for the good of all and especially for the church, that we could never have thought of, nor could come otherwise, but from the great God of heaven and earth. We will see a strange providence occur for the good of all.

*At the Throne of Grace, Works*, vol. 6, pp. 106-08

# Martha's Choice

*But the Lord answered her, 'Martha, Martha, you are anxious and troubled about many things.'*—Luke 10:41

Christ does not dislike domestic business and hospitality; but by this Christ shows his pity on Martha's troublesome cares and distractions, which might have been passed over with far less burden to her. Jesus took occasion to heal her error in judgment. She thought Christ came to feast when he had come to feast them.

We must watch over our intentions, even in lawful things. For good intentions do not always justify actions. Peter had good intentions when he tried to persuade Christ not to go to Jerusalem, yet he received no better thanks than 'Get behind me, Satan' (Matt. 16:23). Let us look at all our actions. It is not enough that they be done lawfully, they must be done in a way that is consistent with the word of God.

From this we learn that we often bring upon ourselves more trouble than God places on us. Those that have lived for any length of time realize this is so. In truth, without God's Spirit, we are self-tormentors. Our error in this is doubled; for either we put burdens on ourselves that are too great, or once they are on us, we make them heavier by our careless and faithless straining under them. Let us also not be over-troubled at troubles. Many poor souls are much troubled this way. If they find but a little dullness of spirit, they conclude they have no grace and that they are not one of God's children. Do not censure or vex yourself or others in this way. The children of God are not always alike, nor always in tune. We must take notice of these things and take heed of troubling ourselves and others with the things and burdens of this life. For it divides and weakens the soul; like the dividing of a river weakens the force of the stream. And the soul, when intent upon one thing, though it be strong, yet being turned to many things, will be much weakened. Therefore, we should meddle only with things that concern us, and only so far as is fitting.

*Mary's Choice, Works, vol 7, pp. 290-92*

# Watching

*Watch therefore, for you know neither the day nor the hour.*—Matt.
25:13

The bearing of a Christian in this world is to be a state of watching
until Christ returns, because we are in danger of sin, and danger by sin.
Particularly the sins of drowsiness, deadness, and heaviness of spirit.
Often by drowsiness we fall into other sins whereby we offend God,
give Satan advantage, grieve the good Spirit of God, and put a sting
into all other troubles. We must consider our situation in this world and
what the life of a Christian is compared to. We are travellers through
our enemy's country. This is Satan's place where he reigns, being the 'god
of this world' (2 Cor. 4:4); therefore, we must have our wits and senses
about us. Further, the worst enemy is within us, our own heart, which
joins with Satan to betray us to the world. We also carry a precious jewel,
our soul, in a brittle glass. If once the vessel breaks, all is lost. We are
running in a race. Now those that run must have the goal in their eye,
the prize of their high calling. Of all men runners need to be watchful.
Further, our whole life is not only a race but a warfare. We have enemies
to fight against that never sleep. Satan our enemy never sleeps, 'but goes
about like a roaring lion seeking whom he may devour' (1 Pet. 5:8). We
sleep, but Satan sleeps not, nor those that are his instruments. The disciples slept, but Judas slept not. The traitors of the church sleep not. The
disciples slept, and left Christ to manage his own cause (Matt. 26:40).
We must strive and watch because we are soldiers in a war. We are also
stewards and we all have 'talents' (Matt. 25:15). Because we are all subject
to give an exact account of what we have done in the flesh, we ought to
be watchful. Men who are under observation need to be watchful.

Beloved, since our life is a vigil, a warring time, a race, and a watched
time, we must be waiting and looking for the return of Christ.

*The Christian's Watch, Works*, vol. 7, pp. 300-01

# Each Day

*I therefore, a prisoner for the Lord, urge you to walk in a manner worthy of the calling to which you have been called.*—Eph. 4:1

We must divide the day and keep a daily watch.

In the morning awake with God before the world or the flesh thrust in. Think of all that may happen that day, of all the dangers and troubles; and think about what armour we will need. Then recognize that whatever happens, all will be for our good. Before anything else, let God have the first fruits of our time and our hearts; let him have the first of the day by prayer.

Then set upon the day with this resolution, to do nothing that may offend God or a good conscience, and to regard no iniquity in our hearts, but to pass the day under the shadow of the wings of the Almighty. Be sure to carry a heavenly mind in earthly business to serve God better and fear him more; for nothing happens in life but a gracious heart may draw out something from it to make their heart more Christlike. Daily think, 'God has put me in this place and so I will do this work.' Be watchful, especially in prosperity. The Lord commanded his people, 'take heed when you are in the good land that flows with milk and honey, that you forget not the Lord your God' (Deut. 4:9; 31:20). Be watchful when alone, for every person does not use privacy well. In solitude be watchful because the devil is still busy. Be watchful over who we choose as companions, choosing those who we may either do good to or receive good from; for one is to strengthen the other, as stones in an arch. 'Stir up one another and exhort one another' (Heb. 3:13; 10:24).

At the end of each day, go over all that was done that day. As God did when he created the world, at the end of each day he viewed all that he had done. Let us not allow our bodies to rest until our consciences are peaceful in our salvation.

Let us be sure to watch and renew our resolutions each day.

*The Christian's Watch, Works,* vol. 7, pp. 303-04

# Bibliography

Sibbes, Richard—

*The Bruised Reed*, Edinburgh: Banner of Truth Trust, 2016 [retypeset 2021].

*Christ is Best*, Edinburgh: Banner of Truth Trust, 2012.

*Glorious Freedom*, Edinburgh: Banner of Truth Trust, 2000 [retypeset 2022].

*A Heavenly Conference*, Edinburgh: Banner of Truth Trust, 2015.

*Josiah's Reformation*, Edinburgh: Banner of Truth Trust, 2011 [retypeset 2020].

*The Love of Christ*, Edinburgh: Banner of Truth Trust, 2011 [retypeset 2022].

*Works of Richard Sibbes*, 7 vols., Edinburgh: Banner of Truth Trust, 2001.

# Subject Index

# Scripture Index

The Bruised Reed

Richard Sibbes

PURITAN PAPERBACKS

# A Heavenly Conference

**Between Christ and Mary**

Richard Sibbes

Foreword by Michael Reeves

PURITAN PAPERBACKS

# Josiah's Reformation

### Cultivating and Maintaining a Tender Heart

Richard Sibbes

PURITAN PAPERBACKS

# The Love of Christ

Richard Sibbes

Foreword by Michael Reeves

PURITAN PAPERBACKS

**Glorious Freedom**

Richard Sibbes

PURITAN PAPERBACKS

*The Works of Richard Sibbes*
(7-volume clothbound set)

# BANNER of TRUTH

The Banner of Truth Trust originated in 1957 in London. The founders believed that much of the best literature of historic Christianity had been allowed to fall into oblivion and that, under God, its recovery could well lead not only to a strengthening of the church, but to true revival.

Interdenominational in vision, this publishing work is now international, and our lists include a number of contemporary authors, together with classics from the past. The translation of these books into many languages is encouraged.

A monthly magazine, *The Banner of Truth*, is also published, and further information about this, and all our other publications, may be found on our website, banneroftruth.org, or by contacting the offices below:

*Head Office:*
3 Murrayfield Road
Edinburgh
EH12 6EL
United Kingdom
Email: info@banneroftruth.co.uk

*North America Office:*
PO Box 621
Carlisle, PA 17013
United States of America
Email: info@banneroftruth.org